BLACK LABOR, WHITE SUGAR

BLACK LABOR, WHITE SUGAR

CARIBBEAN BRACEROS AND
THEIR STRUGGLE FOR POWER IN THE
CUBAN SUGAR INDUSTRY

PHILIP A. HOWARD

Louisiana State University Press
Baton Rouge

Published by Louisiana State University Press
Copyright © 2015 by Louisiana State University Press
All rights reserved
Manufactured in the United States of America
First printing

Designer: Barbara Neely Bourgoyne
Typeface: Quadraat
Printer and binder: Maple Press

Portions of chapters 1–3 appeared in somewhat different form in the author's article
"Treated like Slaves: Black Caribbean Workers in the Modern Sugar Industry, 1910–1930,"
Journal of Caribbean History, nos. 1–2, 2014, and are reprinted by permission.

LIBRARY OF CONGRESS CATALOGING-IN-PUBLICATION DATA

Howard, Philip A., 1957–
  Black labor, white sugar : Caribbean braceros and their struggle for power in the Cuban sugar industry / Philip A. Howard.
    pages cm
  Includes bibliographical references and index.
  ISBN 978-0-8071-5952-1 (cloth : alkaline paper) — ISBN 978-0-8071-5953-8 (pdf) — ISBN 978-0-8071-5954-5 (epub) — ISBN 978-0-8071-5955-2 (mobi) 1. Sugar workers—Cuba—History. 2. Foreign workers, Haitian—Cuba—History. 3. Foreign workers, Jamaican—Cuba—History. 4. Sugarcane industry—Social aspects—Cuba—History. 5. Haitians—Cuba—Politics and government. 6. Jamaicans—Cuba—Politics and government. 7. Labor movement—Cuba—History. 8. Protest movements—Cuba—History. 9. Cuba—Economic conditions. 10. Cuba—Emigration and immigration—Social aspects. I. Title.
  HD8039.S86C853 2015
  331.5'440899607291—dc23

2014036417

To my wife,
Kelly Y. Hopkins,

and our children,
Kathleen and Thomas

CONTENTS

TABLES

ACKNOWLEDGMENTS

I would like to thank the officials of the Instituto de Historia de Cuba for sponsoring my research. Amparo Hernández Denis and Belkis Quesada Guerra ensured that I received my researcher's visa, letters of introduction, and assistance from a number of Cuban scholars. Oscar Zanetti's comments on a paper about Haitians and Jamaicans in the Cuban labor movement that I presented at the Fifth International Conference to commemorate May Day in 2003 were insightful. They became foundational for the fourth chapter. Professor Zanetti also guided me to the newspaper collection housed in the Instituto de Literatura y Lingüística. There, Alina Cuadrado Castellón's assistance made my research productive. The director of the Biblioteca Nacional de José Martí, Marta Terry, provided me with services of a number of librarians. The care of Eugenio Suárez Castro and Zenayda Porrúa allowed me to continue my research at the Archivo Histórico Provincial de Camagüey during the daily scheduled blackouts that were common in 1999 and 2000. The research for this book could not have been completed without Olga Portuondo Zúñiga, Rebecca Calderón Berroa, and Reynaldo Cruz Ruíz. Their kindness and generosity made my research trips to Santiago de Cuba wonderful experiences. The same can be said about the caring and knowledgeable archivists and librarians of the Sir Arthur Lewis Institute for Social and Economic Research at the University of the West Indies, Mona, Jamaica; the National Archive of Jamaica in Spanish Town; and the U.S. National Archives at College Park, Maryland. The staff at the Smathers Library's Manuscripts Division at the University of Florida, Gainesville, especially Carl Van Ness, helped me mine the Rionda-Braga Papers.

I would like to thank Leon Fink, Walter Hixson, Tom O'Brien, and Louis A. Pérez Jr. for reading multiple drafts of the manuscript. I have tried to address all of their concerns. Tony Martin helped with my analysis of Marcus Garvey in Cuba. Samuel Martínez's constructive observations resulted in revising my approach and arguments. He discerned the multiple historiographies to which this study hopes to contribute. I am also grateful for the support and generosity that John M. Hart has shown since I arrived at the University of Houston. His kindness and understanding were responsible for my research trip to Jamaica. The funding for my research also came from the University of Florida's Summer Research Grant. As the John Moore Distinguished Chair in African American History, Richard J. Blackett also provided me with a substantial grant that allowed me to travel to Cuba several times. I am extremely indebted to him for his unending support and advice since I was his graduate student at Indiana University. Training me as a social historian, he continues to remind me to be critical toward my sources while never dismissing arrogantly the research of other scholars.

I would like to thank the editorial and production staff of LSU Press, especially Rand Dotson, and my editor, Alisa Plant. Their honesty and commitment to direct a fair and unbiased assessment of my manuscript were exemplary. I would also like to thank freelance editor Margaret Dalrymple. Her keen eye and valuable comments during the book's copy editing have helped me to convey the significance and excitement of the daily lives of the Caribbean braceros in Cuba. Finally, I would like to thank members of my family, which now only consists of my brothers, Albert and Paul. We are the sons of Albert and Harriet Howard of Gary, Indiana. I am forever grateful to my wife, Kelly Y. Hopkins. She not only read sections of the book, but her technical knowledge was critical in putting it together. She is a terrific mother. I am blessed with her presence and love.

BLACK LABOR, WHITE SUGAR

Cartography by Cassandra Seabourn

Legend:
▼ Sugar Mill
★ Capital
• City

0 25 50 100 150 Miles

SUGAR MILLS IN CUBA

Matanzas
1. Soledad

Las Villas
2. Caracas
3. Hormiguero
4. Soledad "C"
5. Trinidad
6. Tuinicú
7. Vitoria

Camagüey
8. Adelaida
9. Algodones
10. Baraguá
11. Camagüey
12. Cespedes

13. Cunagua
14. Elia
15. Florida
16. Francisco
17. Jaronu
18. Jatibonico
19. Lugareno
20. Morón
21. Senado
22. Stewart
23. Vertientes

Oriente
24. Algodonal
25. America
26. Boston

27. Chaparra
28. Delicias
29. Dos Amigos
30. Ermita
31. Esperanza
32. Jobabo
33. Manatí
34. Miranda
35. Niquero
36. Palma
37. Preston
38. Romelie
39. San German
40. Soledad (G.S. Co.)
41. Tacajó
42. Tanamo

INTRODUCTION

From its beginnings in the colonial era, the cultivation of sugarcane in Cuba engendered immeasurable misery for the predominantly black labor force that cut, loaded, and hauled this tropical commodity. Performing manual field work for a small class of wealthy plantation owners, African cane cutters and haulers, or *macheteros* and *carreteros*, suffered under the institution of slavery. By 1910, nearly twenty-five years after their emancipation in 1886, the harsh existence and low social status of the majority of black Cuban sugarcane workers remained unchanged in many ways. After the abolition of slavery, the former slaves and their descendants began to work for wages. During the harvest season, which usually started in late December and lasted through the end of June, they labored daily from sunup to sundown cutting and hauling one to two tons of cane per worker for the sugar mills. Their living quarters continued to consist of poorly constructed, filthy, and overcrowded barracks or *barracones*. The macheteros and carreteros subsisted on a poor diet and received hardly any medical attention when they became ill. Although the majority of workers agreed to exchange their labor for wages, it was very common for the sugar mills to pay them with coupons or *vales*, as they were called in Cuba, redeemable only at a company store usually owned and operated by the sugar mills. If the workers spent all of their wages or vales before the next payday, they received credit from the companies, which put them in debt. Then the black field workers were forced to labor until they repaid their loans. If they refused or were unable to pay their debts and tried to flee the sugar enclaves of the mills, they were hunted and caught either by the companies' guards or by the rural police, known as the *rurales*.

During the U.S. military occupation (1898–1902), white European immigrants joined black and white Cuban field workers in the sugarcane fields. The majority of these laborers came from Spain and the Canary Islands and were brought to Cuba for several reasons. At this time, the Cuban sugar industry lay in a state of ruin, destroyed by the War of Independence (1895–98). Not only were most of the plantations burned, but thousands of black Cubans had been killed as well. In order to revive the industry, many Cuban mill owners operating in the traditional sugar-producing provinces of Havana and Matanzas demanded more field workers than the island's labor market could supply. Under the U.S. military occupation, a host of American sugar producers, refiners, and bankers arrived either to invest in the older mills or to purchase vast tracts of land in the central and eastern areas of the island where large-scale agricultural cultivation had never been done. There, they began to build the most technologically advanced sugar mills in the world. Then, in order to take advantage of recent innovations in sugarcane processing, Cuban and American sugar companies in the provinces of Camagüey and Oriente demanded European workers in order to solve a chronic shortage of laborers, thereby helping to resuscitate the industry as well as expand sugar cultivation. They also hoped that these immigrant workers would "whiten" the island's population.

This racialist policy of "whitening" the Republic of Cuba with Spaniards and Canary Islanders was rooted in the enduring notion of African or black inferiority. The belief that Africans and their descendants were intellectually infantile and culturally backward, as well as preordained by God to labor, had been the basis for their enslavement and the genesis of the institution of African slavery in the Atlantic World. During the nineteenth century and later at the turn of the twentieth century, French and German biologists and British and American social Darwinists such as Arthur de Gobineau, Ernst Haeckel, James Bryce, and Josiah Nott advanced this racist concept with pseudoscientific theories and writings. Informed by these scientists and physicians, Cuban anthropologists like Luis Montane and Fernando Ortiz ultimately convinced the Cuban political and commercial elites that black Cubans were an impediment to the Republic of Cuba's joining the ranks of other modern Western nations. The Cuban government had to promote European immigration while banning the entry of all people of African descent.

Employing European workers in the sugarcane fields and mills along with white and black Cubans created an ethnically diverse transnational labor force that the sugar companies could subjugate and exploit. Classifying their workers according to race, color, and nationality allowed the companies to employ these categories to determine which tasks the workers would perform. These criteria also helped the companies designate the laborers for certain skilled and unskilled occupations. The sugar mill owners believed that by dividing their workers along these lines, they could keep wages low by fostering competition among the workers for the best-paying positions and jobs, setting white European workers against both black and white Cubans. Antagonism between the latter groups was ensured because they had been historically at odds with one another throughout the nineteenth century. Under these racial and ethnic hierarchies, the majority of black Cubans were restricted to performing only field work. Although initially many white Cubans and Europeans joined blacks in the fields, because of their race and ethnicity a large proportion of them gained the opportunity to work in other skilled or unskilled positions around the cane farms and mills. The sugar companies now had an ideology that would help them thwart any type of labor mobilization and organization.

Employing a multiethnic work force was nothing new for sugar producers in Cuba. During the nineteenth century, plantation slaveowners tended to purchase men, women, and children of different African ethnic groups or nations, including individuals of Congo, Ibo, Ibibío, Carabalí, and Yoruba or Lucumí ancestry. Most owners defined the ethnic traits of their slaves and used them to privilege one group over another. For example, they believed that Congo slaves were happy and submissive, while the Lucumí proved to be tireless field workers. Nonetheless, the owners mixed them together to labor in the fields and in the mills.[1] In addition, between 1840 and 1880, Cuban sugar producers recruited thousands of Chinese "coolies" to work alongside their African slaves. Although these Chinese workers were legally considered indentured servants, with contracts lasting as long as eight years, a few historians have discovered that they were treated just as inhumanely as the African slaves.[2] The sugar-producing slavocracy's objectives resembled those of the sugar companies that appeared after 1902. They hoped that traditional African tribal or ethnic animosities and competition would prevent the formation of racial solidarity among the slaves and thereby reduce the possibility of rebellion. The importation of Chinese laborers was based not only upon the planters' fear, induced by the abolition of the slave trade and of slavery itself, but also upon their desire to foster racial hatred toward the indentured workers. Yet the slavocracy did not have to rely on a racially and ethnically segmented labor system as the foundation of their control. Their hegemony remained rooted in the racialist ideology that condemned all black Africans to labor under the coercive institution of slavery.

However, the slavocracy's power never went unchallenged. On numerous occasions during the era of slavery, slaves joined with freed blacks to conspire to overthrow Spanish colonialism and the institution of slavery. Their actions showed how the racial hierarchy that was fundamental to the degrading and exploitative nature of sugar cultivation produced a culture of resistance. Their plans included burning all the plantations and killing the white Cuban and Spanish elites who subjugated and exploited them.[3] The conspiracies articulated a "consciousness of kind," or a psychology and identity based upon the shared experiences of the plotters as blacks that diminished their ethnic differences and fostered racial solidarity.[4] During the Ten Years' War (1868–78) and the Guerra Chiquita (Little War) (1878–80), slaves and freed blacks also helped white Cuban nationalists fight for Cuban independence and the abolition of slavery.

Immediately after the U.S. occupation ended, the sugar companies discovered that many laborers from Spain and the Canary Islands would not accept the degradation and exploitation that accompanied field work. Moreover, some European immigrants began to introduce black and white Cubans to the principles of anarcho-syndicalism. The anarcho-syndicalist ideology of "internationalism" brought about the solidarity among black and white Cubans as well as among European field and mill workers that was necessary for them to contest their living and working conditions. They did so in a series of strikes during the first decade of the Republic. When the call for racial equality announced by the Independent Party of Color reached black macheteros and carreteros after 1908, both Cuban and foreign sugar producers deemed their black native laborers unsuitable for the increasing level of subjugation and exploitation required to expand an increasingly profitable industry into the central and eastern parts of the island.

In 1913, President José Miguel Gómez agreed to allow a number of Cuban and North American sugar companies to import thousands of black workers from the British, Dutch, and French Caribbean colonies. The majority of these black immigrants came from the nearby islands of Haiti and Jamaica. Black Caribbean immigration, Gómez and his supporters believed, would solve the chronic labor problem in the sugar industry. However, Cuban political and com-

4

mercial elites saw the arrival and presence of these black workers as subverting their attempts to "whiten" the Republic and transform Cuba into a modern nation-state. The immigration of black Haitian and Jamaican *braceros*, as they were called by government officials and the sugar companies, also meant the beginning of a new chapter in the subjugation and exploitation of black sugar-cane workers, as well as in their resistance to the ideologies and structures that engendered their marginalization and misery. This study is intended to reveal their socioeconomic and cultural experiences as they labored and lived in the sugarcane enclaves of Cuba.

James C. Scott and other writers have developed concepts to explain public and private forms of domination, and to theorize how a society's powerful elites employ certain ideologies and institutions to control and appropriate the labor of marginal and powerless groups. Their work has influenced the interpretation of my research. These writers have also shown how the most vulnerable members of a society often concoct hidden and overt practices and strategies to contest their subordination. In short, these writers have studied the experiences of the peasantry of medieval Europe, African slaves in the Atlantic world, and pre-industrial and industrial workers in Europe, as well as the castes of India and the Southeastern Pacific islands, to demonstrate how elites have often used public displays of power and violence to convince workers that their conditions are natural and unalterable. Some elites have also employed language and symbols to underline their workers' inferiority and powerlessness. In time, these and other strategies and structures became ideologies that certain ruling classes found efficacious to foster the subjugation and exploitation of their workers.

At the same time, poor and often marginalized laborers created a number of public and private schemes, autonomous sites, identities, and worldviews to defy the elites. While this study uses many of the same theories and postulations, it unequivocally argues that the sugar companies, particularly those owned by U.S. interests, and in some instances their dependent cane farmers, made use of race and ethnicity to construct a host of socioeconomic and cultural structures, arrangements, and measures in geographically isolated Cuban sugar enclaves or communities to marginalize black Caribbean workers and to gain complete control over their labor.[5]

Although hundreds of black workers from Barbados, Curaçao, Trinidad and Tobago, St. Lucia, and Grenada descended upon Cuba to cut, load, and haul cane as well as to labor in the mill factories, Cuban censuses indicate that Haitian and Jamaican workers composed the majority of all black Caribbean immigrants in Cuba. Because of their numerical prominence, this study will focus on them and on the relentless assaults on their dignity, humanity, and physical and psychological well-being. These workers were confronted by ideologies and structures that sought to degrade, humiliate, and exploit them. The subordination of Haitians and Jamaicans was conspicuously apparent, expressed with symbols, tropes, and violence, from the moment they disembarked and were transported into the interior of the sugar-producing areas of Camagüey and Oriente provinces and put to work in the cane fields as macheteros and carreteros. The material conditions that they endured after their long, arduous workdays also reinforced their inferior status. The housing and quality of food that they received were inadequate and dangerous to their health. More important, the braceros' race, ethnicity, and nationality only exacerbated their powerlessness, because the ideology of domination that the sugar companies had constructed underlined their "otherness" and caused these black foreign-born workers to be segregated from black and white native laborers.[6] Their racial and ethnic differences, which transformed them into "undesirable" immigrants, made them more vulnerable to physical abuse and violence. Anti-immigrant acts of intimidation commonly were engendered by their very presence on Cuban soil, and not only when they sought justice by challenging the power of the sugar mills and farmers. In order to convince the black Caribbean workers to submit to their inferior status, the sugar companies employed the assistance of native workers (black and white), Cuban politicians, newspaper editors, and journalists. Collectively, they helped to incite anti-bracero sentiments and violence.

This study will show that as the collapse of the price of sugar and the financial crisis that ensued after 1920 made the material conditions and exploitation of the braceros worse, black Caribbean workers developed a conscious identity that encouraged many of them to conclude that the ideas and doctrines of anarcho-syndicalism introduced by some Cuban labor leaders could help them expose their dire circumstances and resist their subjugation. Because the sugar companies had adopted a segmented labor system that divided their work force according to race, ethnicity, and nationality, the most important doctrine that resonated among the braceros became "internationalism." To foster worker solidarity, "internationalism" explained how capitalism and imperialism alienated and degraded *all* workers, regardless of their racial and ethnic identities. Cuban and Spanish anarcho-syndicalists had employed "internationalism" during the first years of the Republic to mobilize black and white Cuban and Spanish workers in the tobacco and sugar industries. The sense of "internationalism" reemerged when some labor leaders, influenced by the Russian Revolution of 1917 and Vladimir Lenin's critique of imperialism, made the organization of sugar workers, including the black Caribbean workers, an imperative for the liberation of all workers in Cuba. By 1924 and 1925, the Jamaicans and Haitians articulated this consciousness by participating in a number of protests and strikes.

The development of a black Caribbean workers' consciousness occurred after the Pan-African nationalist Marcus M. Garvey introduced and disseminated his ideology within the sugar communities. When Garvey arrived in Cuba in the spring of 1921, he hoped to gain the moral and financial support of black and white Cubans. Their approval of his dogma and programs would have helped him and his disciples transform Garveyism into a transnational movement. His doctrine of self-help and the redemption of Africa was rejected by the black Cuban leadership, however. As a result, Garvey had to focus his campaign on the black Caribbean communities. There, he emphasized that the braceros' subordination and exploitation were expressions of white American and European racism. He also insisted that the workers ought not to submit to Europocentrism, ethnocentrism, and U.S. imperialism because blacks were equal racially with whites. If they joined the Universal Negro Improvement Association (UNIA), the workers could acquire the sense of identity and the ideology and strategies required to struggle for their rights.

Although some writers have concluded that Garveyism either competed with or was incompatible with other ideologies of resistance and liberation, such as Marxism and anarcho-syndicalism, their contention is not supported by the black Caribbean experience in Cuba. Although Garvey explained the subordination of the braceros in racial and ethnic terms, many workers interpreted his dogma in class terms. The convergence of anarcho-syndicalism and Garveyism encouraged many black Caribbean workers to challenge their material conditions and degradation. They pursued fair wages and refused to be exploited as strikebreakers. Black Caribbean workers also participated in the Cuban labor movement's attempt to organize all sugarcane workers. In doing so, they demonstrated a militant working-class identity.

Before developing a radical working-class ideology, the black Caribbean braceros also determined the responses to their subordination in specific ways. Although they had left dire circumstances on their home islands in order to obtain better jobs and wages seasonally, many soon realized that they had to reassemble their households in Cuba within the segregated barrios of the sugar enclaves as well as on the peripheries of the cane fields and *bateyes*—the central plazas attached to the sugar mills. To mitigate their alienation and marginalization, thousands of black immigrants decamped with their families to make Cuba their permanent home, and in so doing they recreated Haiti and Jamaica both physically and psychologically.

They also sacralized their new homes and communities, practicing their traditional religions. Millenarian in nature, their worldviews allowed both the Haitians and the Jamaicans to interpret their experiences in the sugar enclaves, and to either accommodate or challenge their subordination and exploitation. Both groups shared the belief that their deities and spiritual ancestors would not only protect them but also assist them in defeating the malevolence of the companies and farmers.

In addition, the Jamaican braceros established benevolent societies to openly resist attacks on their dignity and humanity. Some of these socioeconomic and political structures helped to familiarize the braceros with the principles of racial and interethnic solidarity and collectivism. In so doing, they prepared many immigrant workers to consider joining the larger multiethnic or transnational organizations that appeared in the 1920s to contest the power of the sugar companies.

With these public and private strategies, schemes, and institutions, the Haitian and Jamaican braceros comprised what Arthur Stinchcombe and others have called a "community of fate." Enduring extreme levels of repression and exploitation, the black Caribbean workers resembled other workers, such as miners, merchant mariners, loggers, and dockworkers, who faced similarly degrading, impoverished, and dangerous working and living conditions and who developed unified responses to their circumstances. Worker solidarity, based upon shared occupations and socioreligious values and beliefs, along with fellowship and cooperation, allowed them to unite and resist their subjugation.[7]

When the activism of black Caribbean workers failed to improve their conditions by the late 1920s, many Haitians and Jamaicans either returned home or moved on to other Caribbean destinations, such as the Dominican Republic,

8

or to the United States, in search of better jobs and wages. But many had no choice in this matter. After the braceros refused to accept their marginalization, the Cuban government's dominant ideology mandated their repatriation, in spite of the antithetical ideology and objections of the North American sugar companies. In order to obtain what profits they could still earn after 1925, the majority of North American sugar producers continued to import Haitian and Jamaican laborers. The braceros' subordination, exploitation, and subsequent repatriation revealed the multiple ideologies of the elites that were engendered by the neocolonial relationship between Cuba and the United States.

Understanding how Haitian and Jamaican macheteros and carreteros became expendable commodities; how the companies, farmers, and government functionaries treated them; and how they rejected the dominant society's ideologies associated with their recruitment, employment, work, and living conditions on the farm–sugar mill complexes will help us recognize the public and private forms of resistance that they employed to survive as immigrant workers in Cuba. This study will reveal the voices and activities of a segment of the black diaspora that encountered both Cuban and North American forms of subjugation. It will also reveal that the resuscitation and expansion of the Cuban sugar industry and the island's overall growth and prosperity were carried on the backs of these black Caribbean people. I will also consider how Haitian and Jamaican workers informed Cuban society at large.

The first chapter examines the factors and processes that led to the revival and expansion of sugar cultivation in the central and eastern provinces of Camagüey and Oriente. An examination of how the sugar companies' deceptive lament of a so-called chronic shortage of labor compelled Cuban officials to reform immigration laws during the first decade of the twentieth century will follow. Then I analyze and discuss the reasons black foreign workers replaced black Cubans. This chapter examines how the socioeconomic, political, and cultural lives of both Haitians and Jamaicans shaped their values and beliefs and encouraged them to emigrate to Cuba. The first chapter also reveals the role the sugar companies played in recruiting the braceros.

Chapter 2 illuminates how the sugar companies subjugated and exploited black Caribbean workers after the government permitted sugar producers to import them in 1913. It will show that as soon as they arrived, they were confronted by ideologies and structures designed to reinforce their "otherness," transforming them into "undesirable" laborers outside of the sugar enclaves of Camagüey and Oriente. Examining how race and ethnicity as ideologies informed the segmented labor system, producing what Philippe Bourgois calls "conjugated oppression," helps us realize the basis for the hegemonic relationship the companies had with their workers in the plantation production process.

Chapter 3 begins the exploration and analysis of how the black Caribbean braceros resisted the sugar companies' attempts to subjugate and exploit them. It discusses the role that Haitian and Jamaican cultural identity played in creating autonomous private and public institutions that mitigated the level of degradation, subjugation, and exploitation that characterized their lives during the 1910s. Their spiritual worldviews and practices became critical in this endeavor, and I will consider the hidden and public strategies that they collectively and individually created to accommodate and resist the power of the sugar companies.

The first part of Chapter 4 reveals the hidden strategies of resistance that Haitian and Jamaican macheteros and carreteros adopted during and after World War I (1914–19). It will show that when those plans and activities proved unsuccessful in improving their lives after the price of sugar dramatically declined in the early 1920s, some braceros became involved in the Cuban labor movement's efforts to organize all sugarcane workers. I then discuss how anarcho-syndicalists came to dominate the labor movement, as well as why their principles resonated among the field workers. I also show how some braceros interpreted the Cuban labor ideology of anarcho-syndicalism, and how that ideology contested the race- and ethnicity-based segmented labor system, engendering worker solidarity by the mid-1920s.

Chapter 5 discusses the impact that Marcus Garvey and his philosophy of Pan-African nationalism had within both the black Cuban and the black Caribbean communities. It examines why some black Cubans rejected Garveyism while Haitians and Jamaicans adopted it after Garvey's brief visit in the spring of 1921. It will show that Garveyism was never the competing counter-ideology that some scholars suggest. Instead, in Cuba the braceros used his philosophy and joined his organizations while simultaneously being organized by anarcho-syndicalist labor leaders. Many braceros used both ideologies to interpret their marginalization and exploitation in racial and class terms. The convergence of anarcho-syndicalism and Garveyism ultimately helped to establish among black and white Cubans and Spanish and black immigrants a transnational militant working-class ideology. This ideology promoted ethnic, racial, and class solidarity, bringing together all sugarcane workers to challenge the power of the sugar companies, as well as of the state that supported their hegemony.

Chapter 6 explores how black Caribbean immigration produced competing hegemonic ideologies among Cuban government officials and the owners and administrators of the North American sugar companies. This chapter shows that the evolution and articulation of Cuban nationalism and identity were embedded in nativism, an ideology that inspired intense anti-black immigrant rhetoric and violence. The convergence of Cuban nationalism and nativism that emerged before and during the dictatorial government of Gerardo Machado (1924–33) divided Cuban and North American elites. Publicly weakening the stature and power of the U.S. sugar companies, which saw black immigrant labor as a necessary evil, Cuban nationalists campaigned for the repatriation of all braceros by the 1930s. How the Machado and the Ramón Grau San Martín governments reformed the immigration laws and removed Haitians and Jamaicans from the island during the early 1930s concludes the chapter. The epilogue briefly looks at the braceros' lives once they returned home.

My study is important in a number of ways. It seeks to engage in and to contribute to the literature that has focused on the Cuban sugar industry after its collapse during the War of 1895. Historians, economic historians, and economists have primarily discussed how North American investors and companies took advantage of a broken country and industry as well as of the Republic of Cuba's evolving neocolonial relationship with the United States to resuscitate the sugar industry. Producing a consensus regarding this era, the recent scholarship of Alan Dye and César Ayala reveals that between 1902 and 1930 North American, European, and Cuban-American sugar companies, funded and supported by a number of New England refineries and East Coast financial institutions, were responsible for not only reviving the industry but also expanding it into regions that never experienced the large-scale production of sugar during the nineteenth century. These companies built the largest and most technologically advanced modern sugar mills on large tracts of land in the central and eastern provinces of Camagüey and Oriente.[8]

The structural studies of Ayala and Dye, however, have either glossed over or completely ignored how the renewal and expansion of the Cuban sugar industry affected the daily lives of the workers who cut, loaded, and hauled the sugarcane and assisted in the manufacture of raw sugar within the walls of the *centrales*, or mill-factories. Undoubtedly the dearth of archival documents produced by these workers, as well as the scarcity of other public and private records, has made any in-depth examination of the lives and experiences of cane cutters and haulers problematic. Nonetheless, I seek with this book-length study to accomplish what only a dozen articles and a few books and dissertations have addressed, and that is to reposition the field workers within the center of an examination of the Cuban sugar industry and reveal not only how the sugar companies treated them, but also how the workers influenced their socioeconomic relations with the sugar mills. Such a study is important because, in spite of the critical role played by North American and foreign capital and credit as well as by the introduction and adoption of new processing technologies, the amount of sugar that the North American, Cuban, and some European companies produced continued to be based upon the appropriation of manual labor. In other words, "the volume of production and the yield was measured in arrobas per Negro. The growth of sugar manufacturing was determined by the ability to employ labor on a grand scale."9 More important, in order to increase their grinding capacities as they attempted to keep labor costs at a minimum, the sugar companies imported tens of thousands of black Caribbean workers, particularly from Jamaica and Haiti. As a result, this study is also about the socioeconomic and cultural experiences of these black immigrants in Cuba.

This study also hopes to illuminate the socioeconomic arrangements associated with the production of sugar. In order to solve the labor shortage that accompanied the abolition of slavery, as well as to mitigate the effects derived from the scarcity of capital and credit which stifled the expansion of a sugar mill's grinding capacity, sugar producers in Cuba handed the responsibility of growing and harvesting cane to two types of sugarcane farmers, or *colonos*, according to Ramiro Guerra. The first were called *labradores*, who often rented their land from the mill owners or later from the sugar companies. Some of these colonos had been estate owners themselves. Guerra also referred to this type of colono as *sitios de labor*, because they not only grew sugarcane but also food for the nearby towns and villages. These sitios de labor usually depended upon their families' labor power to assist them.10 The second type of colono Guerra called "agricultural entrepreneurs." These farmers usually owned their lands and employed a good-size waged labor force to help them grow, cut, and carry the sugarcane to the sugar mill or *central* for grinding. Examining colonos across the island between the 1880s and the 1920s, Guerra found that the majority of labradores cultivated sugarcane in the western provinces of Havana and Matanzas, while the agricultural entrepreneurs cultivated sugarcane in the central and eastern provinces of Las Villas, Camagüey, and Oriente, where U.S. capital and credit transformed and expanded the sugar industry between the 1890s and the 1920s. The size of their farms also distinguished the two classes of colonos. In the western part of Cuba, where the older sugar regions were located, the labradores usually produced 30,000 arrobas (one arroba equaled twenty-five pounds) of cane or less during each harvest. On the other hand, agricultural entrepreneurs produced 50,000 arrobas of cane or more in Camagüey and Oriente after 1902. In fact, by the 1930s the majority of colonos of Camagüey and Oriente annually produced over 500,000 arrobas of sugarcane.[11] Guerra and other scholars believed that the agricultural entrepreneurial class was responsible for the recruitment of their field workers. But as we shall see, the majority of the sugar companies, particularly the U.S.-owned mills, invested substantial amounts of time, energy, and resources to recruit and hire thousands of foreign-born workers from Haiti, Jamaica, and elsewhere in the Caribbean for their sugar mills.

The work of Jorge Ibarra and the recent study by Gillian McGillivray support many of Guerra's findings, including how the colonos' occupation and relationship with the sugar mills established something of a class consciousness among them.[12] McGillivray also claims that the most important workers involved in the production of sugarcane for the Cuban-American mills owned by Manuel Rionda and others were their colonos. My study of the black braceros, however, departs somewhat from the paradigms of Guerra and McGillivray in one fundamental way. Using the records of the Cuban Cane Company and the Rionda-Braga Papers to reconstruct the daily lives of the braceros, I have concluded that the colonos ought not be viewed nor historically treated as sugarcane workers. Their trichotomous role and position within the capitalist social structure rooted in the sugar complex made their status as workers very ambiguous. In Das Kapital, Karl Marx would have described the colono in the following way:

When an independent laborer—let us take a small farmer, since all three forms of revenue may here be applied—works for himself and sells his own product, he is first considered as his own employer (capitalist) who makes use of

13

himself as a laborer, and second as his own landlord, who makes use of himself as his own tenant. To himself as a wageworker, he pays wages, to himself as a capitalist he gives the profit, and to himself as landlord he pays rent. Assuming the capitalist mode of production and the relations corresponding to it to be the general basis of society, this subsumption is correct, in so far as it is not thanks to his labor, but to his ownership of the means of production . . . that he is in position to appropriate his own surplus labor.[13]

In this light, the colonos were not real "workers in the cane" since they controlled, like the planters before 1895 and the sugar companies after 1902, the means of production.[14] Their socioeconomic arrangements and relations with the black immigrants usually resembled those between the cane farmers and the former slaves described by Esteban Montejo. Interviewed in 1963 when he was 103 years old, Montejo, who lived as a fugitive slave before the Ten Years' War and returned to plantation life as a wage laborer after the abolition of slavery, noted that the field workers' relations with the farmers had not changed after the abolition of slavery in 1886, nor after the advent of the Republic. He remembered that the colonos' interests were significantly at odds with those of the macheteros and carreteros whom they hired and supervised.

> Sometimes they were pushy, and planted cane right up to the edges of the batey twenty-five to thirty feet away [from the barracks]. The tenant farmers were a bunch of sourpusses . . . They didn't have enough land to become rich, that came later. They sure were mean sons of bitches, meaner and stingier than the plantation owners themselves. The tenant farmers overworked the soil. They nagged the workers everyday, and they were more watchful than the sugar mill owners. If there was a piece of land that cost forty pesos to work, they paid twenty, half, that is, and at times you had to put up with it because they had their cohorts.[15]

How the sugarcane farmer treated Montejo, conduct that Montejo and undoubtedly other field workers resented, was based upon the colonos' socioeconomic arrangement with the sugar mills. Contracted to produce and deliver a specified amount of sugarcane to the mills, and paid in kind or with a percentage of the cane in exchange, the colonos had no incentive to treat their field workers equitably or to offer them fair wages. In other words, since the sugar mills tied the colonos' profits and privileged social position to the production level of their field workers, the farmers acted in the same fashion as the sugar companies, appropriating as much labor as they could from the workers with discipline that reinforced the workers' inferior status.[16] Because of the convergence of interests between the colonos, sugar mills, and companies, I will only draw attention to the braceros' relationships with the colonos when my archival materials dictate. And because my study is not limited to those companies that relied upon a group of dependent farmers for their sugarcane, but instead includes a host of sugar mills that grew and harvested their own sugarcane, known as institutional cane, I will be able to illuminate not only how the predominantly modern North American sugar firms, operating on foreign soil, adopted and controlled a foreign-born work force, but also how the workers' color and cultural identity helped support their own exploitation. I shall also show how the immigrant laborers employed their race and ethnicity to challenge the power of the sugar companies and their supporters.

How race and ethnicity informed the braceros' relationships with the companies occurred within the isolated "social territories" that the North American–owned sugar mills carved out of Camagüey and Oriente provinces. The sugar enclaves were designed to reproduce what Barry Carr describes as a "quasi-colonial ruling-class culture."[17] This culture consisted of North American beliefs regarding race, ethnicity, and color that determined the braceros' treatment, housing, dict, and occupation. The rigid class-color stratification that resulted, however, was softened by a "paternalistic management style" used as a "powerful mechanism of control," states Carr.[18] Although I agree with Carr's assessment of the nature of the "social territories" and what they sought to foster, my study will show that the "dramaturgy of power" or the hegemonic actions and policies that the owners, managers, and in some instances the farmers staged publicly for the braceros' consumption sought not only to exaggerate the privileged status and power of white North Americans and Cubans but also to regulate and magnify the subordination of all black immigrant workers. Moreover, when public displays of power failed to achieve these goals, violence against black immigrants helped to produce that reality.

This study hopes to add to our understanding of the development of a labor movement among sugarcane workers. The introduction of North American capital and its surging dominance in the sugar industry immediately led to tensions between sugar companies and the macheteros and carreteros. Their antagonism, engendered by a racialized social and labor hierarchy in the sugar enclaves, not only degraded the workers but also limited their material well-being. John Dumoulin and Rebecca Scott were the first to examine how race and ethnicity contributed to the first important labor strikes in Cuba after independence. Between 1902 and 1905, several mills located around the town of Cruces in Santa Clara Province experienced work stoppages after black and white Cubans and Spanish immigrant workers forged a cross-ethnic or transnational alliance to protest their work conditions and poor wages.[19] The solidarity and actions of the workers were based upon the principles of anarcho-syndicalism. For the most part, scholars who study the history of the Cuban labor movement and the role that sugarcane workers played in it have either glossed over the ways in which the dynamics of race and ethnicity stifled the organization of the majority of sugarcane workers, or have ignored the participation of the black immigrant braceros. As a result, they have failed to see how black Caribbean workers participated in contesting the power of the sugar companies.[20] My study reveals how the black braceros were incorporated into the movement to organize all sugarcane workers. It also traces the evolution and construction of a militant worker consciousness and identity, and shows how some workers articulated that consciousness. Because labor leaders organized the black Caribbean workers in nonpublic spaces, archival evidence surrounding this process is limited. As a result, I have had to rely on the memories of a few field workers as well as on the writings of a former Jamaican bracero who was radicalized by his Cuban experiences to illuminate the principles and processes that led to the mobilization of black Caribbean field workers. I hope to add to the literature on the Cuban labor movement as well as to the history of black Caribbean labor influenced by the research and methodology of Philippe Bourgois, Aviva Chomsky, and Ken Post.[21]

Finally, I plan to engage and contribute to the historiography on black Caribbean workers not only in Cuba but in other Caribbean sites where North American businesses and capital recruited them. The scholarship of Franklin Knight, Barry Carr, Elizabeth McLean Petras, Marc McLeod, and Jorge L. Giovannetti is foundational to this book. Knight's and Petras's studies on the immigration of British West Indians to Cuba examined the push-pull factors leading to the exodus of thousands of Jamaicans as well as other subjects from the colonies of England. Among other factors, they argue that not only was the nature of the peasant-based economy of Jamaica a variable that led to widespread dissatisfaction among rural workers, but a series of natural disasters, such as hurricanes and earthquakes that took place during the first decade of the twentieth century, when taken together were responsible for sending Jamaicans first to Panama and then to Cuba in search of better lives. They also point out that these workers commonly made multiple trips to Cuba to participate in the annual *zafras*, or sugar harvests, during the 1910s and 1920s.[22] Although I consider the nature of the peasant economy to explain why Jamaican workers left home, as well as other aspects of their lives, I also use the oral testimonies and memories of a host of former braceros and their family members to reveal that a more pervasive motive for the exodus of thousands of Jamaicans was the desire to be reunited with a loved one or relative already working in Cuba. It appears that Jamaican workers who either sent for or retrieved their wives or families had decided to remain in Cuba after the zafras, and in so doing, they sought to reassemble their homes in Camagüey or Oriente for periods that ranged from two years to seven or more. Others would stay on indefinitely, well beyond the scope of this study. As a result, for thousands of Jamaican braceros, their objectives and experiences resembled those of their compatriots who decided to make Colón, Panama, and Limón, Costa Rica, their permanent residence.[23]

The sociocultural experiences of black Caribbean workers in Cuba have been the primary focus of Marc McLeod and Jorge L. Giovannetti. Contrasting the status and experiences of both Haitians and Jamaicans and how the categories of race, ethnicity, and nationality influenced their daily lives, McLeod determined that Jamaicans were held in high esteem by both North American and Cuban sugar producers, while Haitians became the most degraded and exploited workers in the sugar industry. Using the methodologies of both the social and cultural historian, McLeod clarified how, as English-speakers who also shared other cultural attributes with North Americans, the Jamaicans and other British West Indians became a privileged segment of workers not only in front of the representatives of the sugar companies but also before the government officials and native workers. At the same time, the color and ethnicity of the majority of Haitians usually disqualified them from obtaining better jobs on the farms and sugar mills. They also lived on the margins of society, completely segregated racially. To their credit, the Haitians took advantage of these circumstances to establish their own communities where they were able to retain their identity.

Giovannetti, on the other hand, believes that the presence of black workers from the other islands of the British West Indies—Barbados, Trinidad and Tobago, Grenada, and St. Lucia, just to name a few—who arrived with their own distinct island identities makes any exploration and analysis of the experiences of black Caribbean workers in Cuba complex and difficult. This complexity is created not only by the distinct insular identities that they articulated, but by another one, which he calls a British colonial identity. Their colonial relationship with Great Britain informed this orientation, according to Giovannetti. These multiple identities made it difficult for the sugar companies to implement their segmented labor system. The expression of multiple black-English Caribbean identities also stifled racial solidarity, as Barbadians disliked the Jamaicans, while Jamaicans expressed contempt for Trinidadians and Grenadians.

My study hopes to advance both McLeod's and Giovannetti's research regarding these themes and processes by employing new archival evidence as well as a paradigm to explain the nuances associated with the subordination of black braceros. I will argue that because of the "demographic thickness" of both Haitians and Jamaicans, their experiences were generally more similar than different. In brief, the sugar companies subjected the majority of black Caribbean workers, whatever their origin, to the same indignities, humiliation, contrived deference, and punishments as members of a class of surplus black immigrant labor. In so doing, they sought to persuade the braceros that their status and circumstances were natural and unassailable. I am not suggesting that there were no exceptions to the rule, because there were. However, their position as black immigrants stigmatized all braceros regardless of their ethnicity or insular identity. In addition, I will address why some elements of the Haitians' culture were more pronounced than those of other ethnic groups. However, Jamaicans and Haitians shared a similar worldview, allowing them possibly to forge a multiethnic alliance in the cane fields that deflected attacks on their dignity, humanity, and labor.

McLeod's study of Garveyism in Cuba inspired me to revisit this important ideology among members of the black diaspora living in the Americas. McLeod discovered that Garvey's ideology resonated with some black Cubans, even though it was largely rejected by the urban-centered black Cuban middle class. He lists several important obstacles that confronted Garvey's movement in Cuba,[24] the most important of which was their sense of patriotism, a sentiment rooted in the vision of a raceless "patria" first articulated by José Martí. Nonetheless, by the end of the 1920s many black Cubans saw Garveyism both as a paradigm to interpret their condition and as an ideology to solve their socioeconomic marginalization. Using Cuban archival evidence produced by leaders of the black Cuban middle class as well as the memories and voices of former black braceros, I have elaborated on McLeod's research and have reached an entirely new understanding of Garvey's significance and impact. In brief, his solicitation fell on the deaf ears of black Cubans because they, at least publicly, refused to contest their marginalization in racial terms. In addition, they also concluded that they had redeemed themselves personally, becoming modern Cuban men and women. On the other hand, Giovannetti believes that after Garvey focused his attention on the black Caribbean workers, his movement became a religious one. This characteristic explains why Garveyism resonated among the braceros. I believe, however, that, as the most degraded and exploited class of workers in Cuba, the braceros found Garveyism essential to deconstruct their subordination in both racial and class terms. As a result, Garvey and his movement assisted in the evolution of a militant worker consciousness. They helped to expose the nature and qualities of the socioeconomic and political structures and arrangements that the sugar companies and the Cuban government sought to hide and obfuscate in order to prevent the workers from challenging their power. I hope to reveal the levels of resiliency, imagination, and inner strength that this segment of the modern black diaspora displayed as they produced specific socioeconomic, political, and cultural structures, as well as arrangements and identities to foil the prescriptions required for their marginalization and exploitation.

Although my study seeks to reveal the hidden and public ideologies, strategies, and activities that both Haitians and Jamaicans constructed to resist their subjugation and exploitation, which culminated in the development of a militant working-class identity, the sociopolitical status of the Haitian immigrant workers after they returned home in the 1930s has limited the scope of my investigations. The antidemocratic character and the hostility to social science research of the dictatorial regimes of the Duvalier family of Haiti help to explain a lack of Haitian bracero materials. After the braceros were repatriated from Cuba during the early 1930s, many of them emigrated to the Dominican Republic to work in the sugar industry there. During the 1960s and 1970s, human rights activists discovered that these workers were confronting the same levels of subjugation and exploitation that their predecessors had experienced in Cuba forty and fifty years earlier. Their plight became an issue to discredit the Duvalier Regime. Unfortunately, the friends and activists of the workers decided to speak for them instead of helping these migrants construct their own historical narrative. The Haitian braceros also continued to confront the prejudices of the light-skinned Haitian elites upon their return from Cuba. Because Haiti's black peasantry is considered inferior and is treated with contempt by light-skinned political and commercial elites, unlike the Jamaican immigrants who were interviewed in the 1960s, their experiences were considered not worth recording. As a result, they remained voiceless and without a history.

Nonetheless, I have sincerely tried to reconstruct their lives by contextualizing their experience with North American and Cuban documents. In some instances, I have used the testimony of their friends and co-workers. In other places, I have relied on the records of Cuban officials and of the owners and administrators of the sugar companies to reveal the attitudes and actions of the Haitians, and in some cases of the Jamaicans as well. I have used secondary sources to critically interpret these materials and to make inferences about and corroborate my assumptions and conclusions.

1

ADOPTING BLACK CARIBBEAN WORKERS

> Any thinking person will realize the cause for hundreds leaving Jamaica weekly
> for Cuba and other republics. It is not for the beauty of Cuba, and the other
> republics, or for their glorious entertainment(s) . . . The civilized Jamaican has
> to think of schooling for his children, for a suitable home, church fees, and
> putting by a little for the doctor and old age. Would I not rather work at home,
> having my family by me, than be hundreds of miles from home? I and ninety
> percent of Jamaicans in Cuba would prefer to work in Jamaica could we obtain
> fifty percent of the wages paid to us here.[1]

The tone of frustration so evident in this bracero's comments accents some
of the more important feelings that thousands of Jamaicans and other black
Caribbean emigrants undoubtedly shared after departing for Cuba as early as
1912. His statements also reflect the hope for a better future that motivated these
workers to go to Cuba. Once they returned from working the sugar harvest, all
they sought was to assist their families. Nonetheless, his testament does not
completely answer why Jamaicans and Haitians saw Cuba as a site where they
could improve, at least materially, their daily lives in the immediate future. Why
black Antilleans left their respective villages, towns, and families is illuminated
in the following pages. Besides the economic motives so eloquently described by
the bracero quoted above, what other factors influenced the emigrant workers'
decision to leave Haiti and Jamaica? How did the Cuban government's repeal of
the ban that had prohibited black immigration foster their arrival? Announced a
year after the Independent Party of Color led an islandwide protest to obtain civil
rights for all black Cubans, to what extent did this civil rights movement and the
subsequent Race War of 1912 that their demonstration engendered affect the
sugar companies, encouraging them to petition the Cuban government to open

its borders to black immigrant workers? How did government functionaries convince proponents of the national project to "whiten" the island to abandon their scheme? What role did U.S. sugar companies play in corrupting the national project by enticing thousands of Haitians and Jamaicans to come to their isolated and self-contained Cuban enclaves? Finally, what socioeconomic and cultural institutions, symbols, and motifs did government functionaries, sugar officials, and native elites develop to achieve the marginalization and powerlessness of black Antilleans within the sugar enclaves of Camagüey and Oriente?

This chapter will argue that black Caribbean immigration was an act of protest against the structures, policies, and social arrangements that reduced these workers' socioeconomic opportunities and mobility at home. In Haiti, the U.S. military government's repressive measures and structures destroyed any hope for black Haitians to improve their well-being, while the British colonial officials' indifference and benign neglect made the lives of Jamaican rural and urban workers difficult. Both societies denied their workers the fundamental sources of social advancement, such as good wages, educational opportunities, and access to property. As a result, Haitians and Jamaicans decided to go to Cuba to secure those resources. Many also left to reestablish familial ties abroad. In doing so, they sought to articulate their own notions of home in Cuba. At the same time, the Cuban government's decision to alter its immigration policies was inspired by its failure to recruit enough European workers to establish a modern white European nation in the Caribbean. The financial power and wealth of North American sugar companies, whose profits depended upon expanding their mills' grinding capacities while keeping the cost of labor at a minimum, proved incompatible with the objective of "whitening" the island, a standard held dear among native political and commercial elites. It is obvious that proponents of the national project to "whiten" Cuban society had to accept immigration reform and the intrusion of North American capital when they realized that black Cubans were no longer exploitable after having participated in an armed movement to claim their civil rights led by the Independent Party of Color. Cuban elites also accepted immigration reform when they understood that they would retain control and power over the structures, labor regimes, and sites that relegated black Caribbean immigrants to a realm where their powerlessness, marginalization, and exploitation were institutionalized. These hegemonic systems and symbols became reserved for the black immigrant workers. The elites would add to these nodes of domination an ideology that remade the black braceros into an "undesirable" yet compliant and impotent work force that the sugar companies could seize and control to enhance their profits and therefore generate Cuban prosperity. Before discussing in detail why both Haitians and Jamaicans left for Cuba, it is important to look briefly at the characteristics and developments of the Cuban sugar industry that made the shortage of labor both a political and an economic issue.

Around the turn of the twentieth century, the sugar producers adopted a series of technological advances that created a shortage of field workers. One development that helped some sugar mills cut costs and remain competitive was the construction of private railway lines. The utilization of these lines was the first step in the reorganization of the sugar industry after the abolition of slavery, according to Alan Dye. These railway networks lowered the cost of transporting sugarcane from the fields to the mills for processing, and of transporting the raw sugar to nearby seaports for export. The expansion of private railway construction took off between the 1880s and 1895 and influenced the sugar industry in several ways. It afforded the owners the opportunity to plant sugarcane or situate a number of *colonias*, or farms, further away from the mill. This development allowed the mill owners to expand their land holdings. To save costs to export their commodity, they then linked their railroad networks to the mills' private docks on the northern coast. Mill owners in Matanzas and Las Villas, for instance, would no longer have to trans-ship their sugar to Havana before exporting it to the United States or Europe. Finally, the steel rails that they imported from the United States helped to establish stronger ties between the Cuban sugar industry's leaders and a number of North American financial institutions. One can argue that financing the expansion of these private railroad networks was where North American capital first began to play an important role in the Cuban sugar industry by 1895. These networks of rail lines reduced the cost of transporting cane to market so much that sugar producers used their savings to construct, by 1895, three hundred and fifty miles of private rail lines, compared to the eight hundred miles of railroads built by Spain during the entire nineteenth century.[2] More important, during and after the U.S. military occupation (1898–1902), foreign-owned companies continued this trend, constructing additional rail lines. The only sugar mills that could construct enough rail lines and thus keep their cost of production low, however, had to have access to an unlimited supply of capital and credit.[3]

Although the construction and expansion of the private railways reduced one fixed cost associated with the production of sugar, other technological advances continued to improve a sugar mill's economies of scale. In brief, the advent of "multiple milling" added more than eighteen rollers in the grinding of cane, and the use of better filtering devices and up-to-date hydraulic technologies designed to squeeze more juice from the canes further increased production.[4] Prior to the adoption of these innovations, the standard sugar mill employed centrifugal machines that consisted of three rollers.[5] With multiple milling technologies, a mill was able to greatly increase its capacity to crush more cane and extract more juice. Better-designed rollers meant fewer breakdowns due to stress. Advances in hydraulic machinery that regulated pressure to force juice from the cane meant that these essential machines seldom broke down. And improvements in cane-juice filtering and vacuum evaporation all led to a more efficient sugar-producing enterprise. Taken together, these innovations revolutionized the continuous-processing technique of grinding cane and evaporating the juice into raw sugar.[6] The fact that the sucrose content of sugarcane rapidly declines after it is cut created the need for such innovations. In the end, if a sugar mill was unable to afford these technologies, the owner usually had to sell or close his mill. Others who sought to remain in the industry did so by becoming colonos. Nonetheless, the technological advances that transformed the cultivation of sugarcane into an agricultural industry opened the door for foreigners, particularly North Americans, to enter. Such was the case in the burgeoning province of Las Villas, east of Matanzas. In time, North Americans would also come to dominate the industry in Camagüey and Oriente provinces after the 1895 War of Independence and the U.S. military occupation of the island.

In spite of the adoption of these technologies, the sugar companies could not obtain larger economies of scale without first improving the coordination of delivering sugarcane from the fields to the mills at the precise time they were scheduled to grind the cane. The connection between the fields and the mill was the most critical juncture in the flow of materials through the factory.[7] In order to prevent bottlenecks from forming and suspending or slowing the manufacturing process, the mills had to match their scale of production with a sufficient and compliant field work force. The search for an abundant supply of field workers began as early as the 1880s.[8] When they could not recruit a surplus of native and Spanish immigrant workers, particularly after 1910, the sugar mills sought other sources of labor, and Haitians and Jamaicans helped to solve the labor shortage. But the pressure to obtain additional workers increased because of competition between the Cuban-based sugar companies and European and North American beet producers, as well as with other sugarcane-producing areas, such as Hawaii and Java. World War I created a huge demand for Cuban sugar, so in order to profitably supply the Allied nations, the sugar companies dramatically increased the grinding capacities of their mills. The only way to compete and supply the North Atlantic markets was to recruit a surplus of Haitian and Jamaican workers, and to appropriate their labor power.

A number of North American sugar companies and their investors in the United States took advantage of the advances in milling technologies to reduce their costs and to solve the unreliability of labor in the cane fields of Cuba. By solving the labor problem of the Cuban industry, they hoped that they could meet the North American demand for sugar, something that beet producers were unable to do alone. According to both Cleona Lewis and Mira Wilkins, the need for sugar in the United States explains why U.S. commercial agents like the Edwin Atkins family and Minor C. Keith "backed into" the sugar industry, having gone from being brokers and merchants of Caribbean tropical goods, to investing in Caribbean-based agricultural enterprises, and finally to owning "extra-national" and multinational companies that operated, in this context, in Cuba.[9]

This process started as early as 1883 when E. Atkins and Company of Boston decided to foreclose on five sugar properties owned by Juan Sarria and his family in Las Villas (later called Santa Clara). The company's most important acquisition was the Soledad sugar mill. Atkins and Company then proceeded to modernize the Soledad's 4,500 acres of cane fields, and within less than a decade they had transformed the Soledad into one of the most productive sugar properties not only in Cuba, but also in the world. By the end of the 1880s, the Soledad had produced over 4,000 tons of sugar.[10] Eventually occupying some 12,000 acres, 5,000 of which consisted of cane fields, and using twenty-three miles of private rail lines, the Soledad employed 1,200 workers during the zafra alone. Its size made it the largest U.S. investment in the sugar industry.[11]

Atkins and Company not only developed the Soledad but also purchased other plantations surrounding it from owners who went bankrupt due to the drop in sugar prices and the cost associated with the introduction of new sugar technologies. Other North American and European enterprises adopted Atkins's strategy and established themselves in Cuba as well. For example, many of the plantations surrounding the Soledad became the properties of the U.S. bankers of Eaton Stafford and Company, Guillermo Schmidt of Denmark, the German firm of Fritze and Company, and its scion, Meyers and Thode. By the end of the century, all of these financial and commercial institutions had merged with the companies owned by Atkins and by Henry O. Havemeyer, president of the American Sugar Refining Company. During the 1890s, Havemeyer became the wealthiest sugar refiner on the East Coast of the United States. Their merger created the Trinidad Sugar Company.[12] By 1900, H. O. Havemeyer would bring together most of the smaller and larger North American sugar refiners, including his archrival, Claus Spreckels, owner of the California Sugar Refining Company, which controlled the raw sugar trade with Hawaii, in order to create the "Sugar Trust," a monopoly that dictated both the quantity and the price of refined sugar in the United States. The policies and practices of the Sugar Trust encouraged plantation owners to acquire additional mill-factories and employ the cheapest labor possible to provide the North American market with inexpensive raw sugar that the Trust could manufacture profitably.

As a result, Atkins and Company and its partners also acquired properties located in between the southern rim of the Escambray Mountains and the southern coast of Las Villas. There, the Trinidad sugar mill, located a few miles from the south-central coast of the island, had been developed out of ten nonoperational mills on estates left vacant between 1868 and 1890. In the early 1890s, Atkins purchased additional lands surrounding the Trinidad, and in so doing caused the closing of several smaller and inefficient mills.[13] Representing the interests of a number of sugar refiners located on the U.S. East Coast, the Atkins properties surrounding the town of Trinidad reflected the refiners' attempt to determine the volume of raw sugar the Cuban-based mills produced, and to control the amount of sugar exported to their refineries in North America. In brief, they sought to "establish vertically integrated structures" that exclusively tied U.S.-owned and -operated Cuban sugar mills to North American refineries in order to manipulate the price of sugar in the United States, according to César Ayala.[14] Undoubtedly other North Americans who arrived in Cuba shared this objective and assisted in transforming the sugar industry of not only Las Villas, but also of Camagüey and Oriente.

Before the 1895 War of Independence, the Pouvét Brothers of New York City arrived in Cienfuegos to purchase the Hormiguero mill located near the towns of Cruces and Palmira.[15] Another New York City firm, Perkins and Welsh, bought the Constancia *central* (factory) located outside Sagua la Grande on the north-central coast.[16] Further east, the Manuel Rionda family, along with a number of New York City merchants, established itself in the province of Puerto Príncipe (or Camagüey) when in 1893 the Tuinicú Cane Sugar Company appeared to cultivate and grind sugarcane. Manuel Rionda had earlier gained the commercial connections and business experience necessary to operate not only in the Cuban sugar industry but also in the European beet industry while he was employed as a managing partner of the international sugar firm Czarnikow Limited of London, which had become a very prominent merchant house trading in beet sugar in Great Britain and Europe.[17] As we shall see below, after the turn of the century, Rionda acquired other plantations and mills, the most important of which was the Francisco *central*.[18]

The United Fruit Company of Boston participated in developing the sugar industry in the eastern provinces of Cuba. In the late 1880s, operating primarily in Central America under the name of the Tropical Trading Company and owned by Minor C. Keith, United Fruit merged with Lorenzo Dew Baker's and Andrew Preston's Boston Fruit Company to buy the banana plantations of the Banes Fruit Company. In 1887, this company held an estimated 3,000 *caballerias* (one caballeria is approximately equal to thirty-three acres) or 99,000 acres, located on the coastal plain of Nipe Bay, a region along the northern coast of Cuba's easternmost province, Santiago de Cuba or Oriente. Keith had become wealthy building railway lines throughout Central America, particularly in Costa Rica, in order to facilitate the export of another tropical commodity, bananas, while Baker has been credited with introducing this fruit to the American diet as early as 1870.[19] By 1895, the Banes Fruit Company began to grow sugarcane on its plantations alongside its banana trees. Now called the Division Banes, the company dedicated 8 percent of its Cuban holdings, or 1,650 acres, to the cultivation of sugar. Although sugar involved only an insignificant percentage of its land, the value of its first zafra was substantial, amounting to one million dollars. This figure was $300,000 less than the total value of its banana crop.[20] The War of Independence of 1895 destroyed the Cuban banana industry, and within a year of the war's conclusion the Division Banes had changed its name to the United Fruit Company and proceeded to construct its first sugar *central*.

In fact, during the U.S. military occupation of Cuba United Fruit acquired an additional 73,333 acres of land near the coastal inlets of Banes and Nipe. There it constructed two *centrales*, one called the Preston and another named the Boston.[21] The properties of the United Fruit Company eventually extended through the three *terminos municipales*, or townships, of Banes, Antilla, and Mayarí. By the mid-1890s, the infusion of new technology and capital from U.S. investors, along with a new mode of production, had increased the production of sugarcane while making the island dependent upon the North American market. Table 1 indicates the total amount of sugar that Cuban mills produced and exported with the help of North American investment capital during the 1890s.

TABLE 1. Production and Distribution of Cuban Sugar in Tons, 1893–1897

	U.S.	Canada	Spain	England	Cuba	Total
1893	680,642	25,069	9,448	3,045	50,000	768,204
1894	965,524	24,372	23,295	10,528	50,000	1,073,719
1895	769,958	28,324	28,428	5,674	50,000	882,384
1896	235,659		9,969		40,000	285,628
1897	202,659		1,337		38,000	241,996

Source: J. P. Sanger, *Informe sobre el censo de Cuba, 1899* (Washington, D.C., 1900), 539. Cuba also exported 83 tons in 1897 to Nassau, Bahamas.

The Hawley Group became one of the first foreign companies to involve itself in the sugar industry of Matanzas. Presided over by the Texan Robert B. Hawley, this New Jersey–based holding company became the Cuban American Sugar Company in 1899 while it constructed the Tinguaro *central* on a 7,000-acre site. Unlike other U.S. companies at the time, the Cuban American Sugar Company extended its operation beyond the production of raw sugar, purchasing the only refinery in Cuba, which was located on the northern coast at Cardenas.[22] After the turn of the century, the company also acquired some 63,333 acres on the eastern end of the island in the northern region of Oriente Province in order to construct a number of *centrales*, including the Chaparra.

The emergence of North American–based companies in the Cuban sugar industry had several consequences. First, their appearance increased the overall miles of privately owned rail lines, and the amount of land dedicated to sugar cultivation increased dramatically. As early as 1905, there were twenty-nine North American–owned mills, which processed 21 percent of the island's sugar crop.[23] Second, the concentration of capital, technology, and the organizational model of production that the North Americans assisted in making standard in the form of the *central* transformed the landscape of the provinces of Camagüey and Oriente into enclaves consisting of colonias, bateyes, and their respective mills, connected by rail to the seaports. Finally, this process intensified after 1902, gained momentum during World War I, and lasted well into the 1920s.

The historiography on the experiences of the black Caribbean immigrants in Cuba has emphasized that their official arrival in large and noticeable numbers began between 1911 and 1913.[24] However, in 1900 the United Fruit Company received special permission from the U.S. military government of General Leonard Wood to import some three hundred black immigrant workers. They came from banana plantations that the company owned and operated in Jamaica. These Jamaicans entered Cuba to work on the construction of the United Fruit Company's private rail lines that connected its cane fields to the Boston Mill, as well as to its port facilities at Banes. Although the United Fruit Company promised the U.S. military government that it would repatriate these black workers after the rail lines had been constructed, it did not.

Instead, the workers supplemented a growing pool of multiethnic laborers, including Chinese and Spanish workers, that the United Fruit Company employed. Undoubtedly paid the same wage rate as in their homeland, the Jamaicans increased the company's supply of workers and allowed the Boston to reduce generally its cost of labor. This small contingent of Jamaican braceros lived in a racially segregated housing district that the company created in the town of Banes. Located near the docks, the "barrio Jamaiquino," as it was called, allowed the United Fruit Company to use its own steamship line to clandestinely deliver a small number of immigrants annually from Jamaica.[25]

As United Fruit expanded its holdings by constructing the Preston, its other mill, it probably used its private line of steamships to pick up a small number of Haitian braceros in a similar fashion during the first decade of the Cuban Republic. It is also very likely that other sugar companies imitated its actions. They did so secretly and at a time when Cuban law prohibited the immigration of people of African descent to the island. Nevertheless, these workers started to arrive in visible numbers as early as 1903 to work not only on the cane farms but also on the construction of the central railway line that connected Havana with Santiago de Cuba, and on its branches that joined the interior of the island to some of the most important ports and harbors on both the northern and southern coasts.[26] Because Cuban immigration policy banned the admission of black workers, it is impossible to know the total number of black Caribbean workers who arrived covertly before the end of the decade, but the census of 1907 may have underestimated their numbers, counting 4,280 immigrants from the West Indies.[27] The government's unofficial and illegal practice of allowing North American sugar companies to import black Antillean workers, as they were called at this time, during the first decade of the twentieth century, coincided with the policy empowering the municipal governments in the central and eastern provinces to round up poor and unemployed native workers who had been arrested for violating a series of vagrancy laws in general, and deliver them to the cane farms and sugar mills that needed their labor power. This practice, however, failed to satisfy the growing demand for labor in the sugar industry.

In the summer of 1908, Charles E. Magoon, the provisional governor of the island during the second U.S. military occupation (1906–1909), amended the immigration law, hoping to enhance the government's power to carry out Military Order Number 155 of 1902, which prohibited black immigration, as well as the law of immigration and colonization of 1906. In 1908, Magoon's first amendment required the Cuban government to cover the total cost of transporting all European immigrants to and from the island. His second decree ordered the government to remit one peso to the steamship lines for every foreigner that they disembarked in Cuba.[28] Magoon soon abolished this payment as it became too expensive for the government. His revisions of both the 1902 and 1906 immigration laws never succeeded in attracting and transporting enough European immigrants to work on the plantations of the sugar companies, even though Cuba received some 134,000 immigrants from Spain, 7,000 from England, and 500 from Germany between 1907 and 1911.[29]

Nonetheless, the chronic labor shortage of which the owners and managers of the sugar companies began incessantly to complain encouraged them to continue to violate the ban on black immigration. By 1910, even the provincial government of Oriente had realized that a surplus of black Antillean workers meant lower costs of labor and hence the accumulation of greater wealth for the companies, and it refused to enforce the immigration law, which required municipal and provincial government officials to arrest and deport as soon as possible all undocumented immigrants and foreigners who had arrived illegally.

Between 1905 and 1911, the provincial government of Oriente only repatriated 190 illegal aliens, all of them from Haiti.[30] In June 1911, an officer of the Santiago de Cuba Department of Immigration working inside of the Cuban Consulate in Port-au-Prince, Haiti, informed the Secretary of Agriculture of the provincial government of Oriente that between 10,000 and 12,000 Haitians were living in the region of Guantánamo.[31] In January 1912, this information prompted the governor of Oriente, Rafael Manduley de Rio, disingenuously to show concern over the presence of these black illegal aliens, reporting to his superiors in Havana that "Haitians and Jamaicans have been secretly entering the province of Oriente in large numbers for a year past, thereby breaking the immigration laws . . . They [are] being brought by small sailing vessels and disembarked at convenient landing places."[32] Although there is no doubt that the provincial government sanctioned the clandestine traffic of black Antillean braceros, Manduley's report persuaded the sugar mills that had been involved to stop this practice.

Manduley's revelation scared some companies into reconsidering their involvement in the illegal trafficking of braceros. It also convinced representatives of the sugar industry to wage a propaganda campaign to show how the scarcity of workers affected sugar production. For example, representing the industry's interests in Oriente Province, the Santiago de Cuba newspaper La Independencia reported how the Preston Mill, constructed in 1904 by the United Fruit Company on Nipe Bay, began its harvest under "disadvantageous labor conditions." Stressing the importance that the cane cutters had not only to the industry but also on the local and municipal economies, the paper stated that the situation was so serious that the inhabitants of the neighboring town of Mayarí never knew when the mill started its harvest and the grinding of its cane because when one walked "through the Preston's cane fields [you] find them like a cemetery for their silence."[33] It is noteworthy that by 1912 the Preston consisted of 4,970 caballerias—164,010 acres of cultivable cane land—none of which was cultivated by any colonos. With an adequate work force, the mill was said to have the capacity to grind daily between 600,000 and 1 million arrobas of sugarcane.[34] La Independencia also reported that the mill's lack of macheteros and carreteros forced its administrator to postpone the beginning of its harvest for four days.

The delay of the start of the 1912 harvest by the Preston and other sugar mills prompted the Cuban Agricultural Department to investigate the labor problems that the companies lamented. The department's agents quickly learned that the scarcity of labor that the sugar mill owners fussed over stemmed from the refusal of a large number of Spanish immigrants to work under slavelike conditions. In addition, many Spaniards and Canary Islanders expressed their distaste for such labor by simply leaving the countryside for the nearby towns and cities of both Camagüey and Oriente to find employment in other sectors of the economy. The agents discovered that at least 17,000 immigrants had either enlisted in the regular army, become members of the rural guard, or joined the local police forces. Another 20,000 Spanish immigrants had applied for civil service positions in the provincial governments of Camagüey and Oriente. The report also stated that 6,000 more immigrants from Spain and other parts of Europe had abandoned their farms as colonos as well as the centrales in order to move into nearby towns to work in government positions and in the offices of the national lottery selling tickets. The report that the commissioners handed to the government concluded that the sugar industry lacked at least 30,000 workers to harvest the crop of 1912. But this number of European laborers could not be recruited nor hired. The 43,000 immigrants who found alternative employment elsewhere could have made a difference, according to the industry's experts, but they had decided that macheteros or carreteros were unattractive occupations.[35] This state of affairs prompted a writer of the daily pro-business periodical, Avisador Comercial, to declare that "a great scarcity of labor was felt everywhere," although there was "a superabundance of café loafers in every town."[36]

Finally, the agents of the Agricultural Department also examined the reasons the sugar companies were unable to attract black Cubans to work on their colonias and inside the mill factories. They concluded that after the abolition of slavery and the introduction of wage labor that accompanied the adoption of the modern central factory, black Cubans had "shunned with abhorrence the labor in the fields, which they considered as a sequel to slavery."[37] This conclusion was, however, disingenuous, given the fact that black Cubans had composed the majority of field workers after the War of 1895 and before the strike that they staged with white Cuban and Spanish workers in Las Villas between 1902 and 1905. Nonetheless, black Cubans' dissatisfaction with the work and social conditions created by the cane farm and mill factory system became the official explanation of the sugar companies. The black Cubans' reluctance to work in the cane fields explained why the companies had become dependent upon either white Cuban males or European immigrants for their principal workers since independence. It is noteworthy that the functionaries of the Agricultural Department drew their conclusions during the Race War of 1912. As I shall show in greater detail below, this war was the culmination of an attempt by both urban and rural blacks to end their socioeconomic and political marginalization and to obtain their civil rights. In this light, perhaps officials of the Agricultural Department made such a claim hoping to convince the Gómez government that black native workers, after being radicalized by the events of 1912, would never accept being the largest proportion of a surplus of poorly paid and generally exploited workers just to keep the labor costs of the sugar companies at a minimum. Therefore, lifting the ban on black immigration was the only solution available, according to the officials of the Agricultural Department and the sugar companies.

The earlier experiences that some North American sugar mills had with black Cuban workers may have influenced the Agricultural Department's assessment of the role that black Cuban workers could play in solving the labor crisis. As mentioned above, they had participated in a series of strikes a decade earlier. Their actions at that time may have led Cuban officials and representatives of the sugar industry to conclude that these workers were no longer exploitable. The strikes of 1902 took place at several mills located around the town of Cruces in Santa Clara Province. These work stoppages occurred after black and white Cubans and Spanish immigrant workers forged a cross-ethnic or transnational alliance to protest their work conditions and poor wages, according to both John Dumoulin and Rebecca Scott.[38] The solidarity and actions of the workers were based upon the principles of anarcho-syndicalism, which among other things emphasized the establishment of workers' cooperatives and the use of such direct actions as the strike to improve working conditions and wages, as well as the antihegemonic theory that all laborers, regardless of ethnicity and nationality, had the right to self-determination and self-reliance to contest colonialism and capitalism. Although the strike centered on the Hormiguero central, the workers' protest alarmed all the sugar companies located not only in Santa Clara but also in Matanzas and Camagüey, and for a number of reasons. First, the strikers met in the Centro Africano, the site of the black mutual-aid society, or cabildo de nación de Congo. Here they established a number of multiethnic and provincewide unions. Second, the Gremio Braceros de Cruces and the Gremio General de Braceros de Lejas became the syndicates that extended the strike to the mills surrounding Cienfuegos. Third, the strike leaders—Evaristo

Landa, a mulatto and veteran of the War of 1895, and the Spaniards Manuel Machado and Facundo Alonso—insisted that the syndicates or unions that directed the strikes were critical communities, guaranteeing a brighter future for all workers. Nonetheless, given the multiethnic composition of the striking workers, the leaders recognized that their challenge to the sugar mills rested on adopting the anarcho-syndicalist principle of worker solidarity. Landa's call for "internationalism" emphasized that a worker's nationality did not matter in the struggle against capitalism. The strikers' major concern was fostering "the unity of everyone whose soiled and sweat-drenched clothes demonstrated an attempt to reduce the daily misery of being unable to acquire the necessities of life."[39]

In response to the strikes in Santa Clara Province, which had become Cuba's second largest producer of sugar and where 22 percent of the industry's work force was composed of Spanish and Canary Islanders, the mill owners set a precedent of assisting North American companies that had to deal with labor disturbances in the future. In 1902, the owners called for a reorganization of the rural guard to suppress strikes with violence. The labor leaders were arrested and murdered. The owners also employed their own newspapers to demonize black Cubans and Spanish immigrants. When their attempts failed to persuade public opinion, they incited ethnic prejudices within the ranks of the workers to destroy their solidarity. The effectiveness of this last strategy was enhanced by the introduction of North American conceptions of whiteness, racial separation, and the degenerative effects of miscegenation.[40] The strikes in Santa Clara and Cienfuegos were the first in a long line of labor conflicts that the sugar industry experienced, particularly during the 1910s.

To further disparage black Cubans, some sugar functionaries produced an ideology that denigrated the quality of their labor. Although the majority of mill owners praised the qualities of native workers, especially black Cubans, they still found them unsuitable. While discussing this issue with Santiago Dod, a Cuban journalist covering the labor shortage for the U.S. trade paper of sugar producers, the unidentified North American owner of a sugar mill mentioned that he paid his cane cutters ten cents per 100 arrobas or 2,500 pounds of cane cut. If they worked hard, they could earn $1.40 per day. He also indicated that his best cutters were usually "those of the colored race . . . [and] generally women." Although black Cubans worked hard, he complained that they were capable of working even harder, and could cut "twice or thrice that amount in

34

the best fields, and earn very high wages, but seldom have ambition enough to do so."[41] His current workers lacked ambition, he claimed, as well as physical stamina: they "are not strong enough to endure the heavy strain for a whole week, and when no rest is given Sundays they are forced to recuperate from six to eight days every month or succumb." In the mind of this owner, "the average Cuban toiler certainly leaves much to be desired."[42] Given the circumstances that all the sugar companies confronted, this owner offered a strategy to his competitors that if adopted would encourage a higher degree of labor efficiency and production in their sugar mills. He suggested that "anyone who in Cuba will pay day laborers the highest rate, feed them decently, permit no insulting language to be used to them, and adopt the plan of always noting the poorest lot and discharging him as soon as a more promising substitute offers, will in short time get together a set of men who will, despite a broiling tropical sun, do as much work if well directed as can be obtained anywhere."[43] Such expressions reflected the same patronizing ideology that members of the old nineteenth-century sugar oligarchy and former slaveowners had shared during the immediate post-emancipation period throughout the plantation economies of the Caribbean. This philosophy also outlined the level of power that mill owners sought to wield not only over issues of industrial labor relations but also over all social arrangements.[44] Yet some owners argued that this doctrine alone would not guarantee the retention and use of productive cane workers. Cuban and American businessmen commonly believed that the racial and ethnic characteristics of the average black Cuban toilers made them defective workers. They described them as "happy-go-lucky shirkers of work" with a "careless inaptitude," who "perform half the work that they should do because they are rendered useless by a pernicious ignorance." Some managers of sugar companies even encouraged each other not to extol or applaud their black workers because no matter how faithful and obedient a worker may be, "you cannot give him one word of praise without being compelled to discharge him soon after. Commendation affects him very much as good wine does those who are unaccustomed to its use . . . it is an exhilarant so entirely new to the laborer's experience that it goes to his head at once, intoxicating him with the conviction that his place is thenceforth secure against any eventuality."[45] The images that these racist remarks drew ultimately degraded the black Cuban workers in a way that their labor power was no longer coveted by North American sugar producers as it had been by Cubans during the nineteenth century.

How U.S. sugar producers assessed black Cuban workers had to be considered by the investigators of the Cuban Agricultural Department because of their financial domination of the industry. The introduction of North American as well as European finance capital, new technology, and superior machinery allowed Cuban-, European-, and North American–owned sugar companies to plant high-quality cane on land that had never before been cultivated. Between 1909 and 1913, the amount of investment was substantial. Capital invested in Cuba by British banks and businesses amounted to $60,419,190. French financiers and companies had invested $12,500,000, while German capitalists spent another $4,500,000 during this time.[46] The amount of European investment in Cuba, however, paled in comparison to the amount invested by U.S. banks and businesses. Investments and holdings by American citizens and companies totaled $205 million in 1911, according to U.S. Consul General J. L. Rodgers. Of that total, almost half went into industries and sectors of the Cuban economy that were related to the production of sugar. Specifically, North Americans had spent $50 million on sugar mills, $25 million on railroad construction, $5 million on shipping, another $5 million on banking, and $20 million more on mortgages and credits.[47] A year later, in 1912, U.S. Deputy Consul General H. P. Starrett reported that the amount of investments and stocks held by American and non-American citizens in U.S. companies exclusively associated with the sugar industry totaled $3 million in Havana, $5,750,000 in Matanzas, $14,500,000 in Santa Clara, $4,700,000 in Camagüey, and $25,300,000 in Oriente. Starrett emphasized that "sugar in western Cuba has about reached the law of diminishing returns in agriculture, but the prediction is that eastern Cuba—Santa Clara, Camagüey and Oriente provinces—will continue to develop and expand."[48]

In order to take advantage of this economic situation, the Association for the Development of Immigration recommended to the government that it allow the recruitment and immigration of thousands of black Antillean braceros to cut and haul sugarcane. Representing the sugar industry, the association was dominated by officials of the Cuban American Sugar Company, which between 1908 and 1910 had come to own the controlling interests of the only sugar refinery in Cuba as well as of a number of mills, including the San Manuel Sugar Company and the Chaparra Sugar Company. Located next to each other, these two companies merged their sugar farms and mills in order to "establish the largest sugar plantation in the world."[49] A future president of Cuba, General

Mario García Menocal (1913–20), became the senior administrator of both mills. The association concluded that Cuba had to take advantage of the large capital investments that North Americans had made and would continue to make in order to construct new mills or refurbish and modernize the older ones. Of the 171 mills that produced raw sugar between 1911 and 1915, 161 had been modernized with North American capital.[50] The majority of these factories were located in the provinces of Camagüey and Oriente. The powerful influence of North American capital could not be ignored. The association's proposal was not only an acknowledgment of the presence and role of North American capital, but also of the danger that black Cubans presented to the commercial power of the United States.

Established in 1907, the Partido Independiente de Color (PIC), or Independent Party of Color, sought to reverse the social, economic, and political marginalization of black Cubans. Led by Evaristo Estenoz, the PIC drew its leadership from a handful of black Liberal Party leaders of the 1906 rebellion, who along with white liberals tried to topple the government of Tomás Estrada Palma. In their view, Estrada Palma had been fraudulently reelected to a second four-year term as president. Upset over the reelection of the person responsible for their status as second-class citizens, black Cubans fled the ranks of both the liberal and conservative parties. Joining the PIC, they hoped to express their grievances. Estenoz charged that although blacks had composed 85 percent of the rank-and-file of the rebel army during the War of 1895, they "had been robbed . . . of all the fruits of victory."[51] The Cuban censuses of 1899 and 1907 supported Estenoz's claim. They showed that blacks were dramatically excluded from the economic spheres of commerce, transportation, manufacturing, and industrial mechanics. They were also severely underrepresented in the professional service sector of the economy.[52] The Liberal Party candidate for president, José Miguel Gómez, considered the merits of Estenoz's argument in 1908 and promised that in exchange for black support he would address the concerns of the PIC when he won office.

Gómez never fulfilled his pledge. As a result, Estenoz and his closest associate, Pedro Ivonet, established a grass-roots political organization that scored electoral victories against both liberal and conservative candidates, winning a host of municipal and provincial offices between 1908 and 1910. Afraid of the potential political power that black Cubans could exert if they were mobilized to vote as a collective block at the national level, in April 1910 the Cuban government arrested Estenoz and Ivonet on concocted charges of illicit association and conspiring to overthrow the government. Cuban officials also arrested 220 of their followers.[53]

Understanding that the black population represented 33 percent, or 520,400, of the island's total population of 1,500,000, Gómez asked the provincial authorities for evidence the government could use against the PIC. Between March 1910 and April 1912, the governor of Oriente, Rafael Manduley, sent numerous reports to the Gómez government that portrayed the speeches that Estenoz and others were making as racist and as a crime against whites. In March 1910, before the authorities arrested Estenoz and his cohort, Manduley reported to the secretary of state in Havana, Francisco López Levia, that "because Evaristo Estenoz and the Partido Independiente de la Raza de Color had appeared in the province in order to actively disseminate their dangerous propaganda," he was "taking steps to stop and put an end to these regrettable racist speeches since the majority of blacks in the towns and cities like Guantánamo, Baracoa, Santiago, Manzanillo, La Maya, Songo . . . have been organized. They have also behaved shamelessly and been insolent toward whites directing threats, insults, and gross provocations at them."[54] Manduley concluded that something had to be done, since respectable white people had come to him for protection, "at the moment when the blacks announce that it is time to finish off the whites with fire and blood."[55] The governors of Santa Clara, Camagüey, and other provinces sent similar reports to the authorities in Havana. Undoubtedly their reports, as well as the one sent by Manduley, justified the arrest of Estenoz and Ivonet the following month.

In late April, the ideas of the PIC began to reach and resonate among blacks living in the countryside, including in the sugar enclaves. Manduley received a report dated 27 April 1910 from the office of the mayor of Guantánamo that stated that the leaders of the "racist movement" had made their way onto some of the sugar plantations and mills, like Romelie, Isabel, and others. Functionaries from the mayor's office discussed how "almost all of the black workers in those mills stopped attending to their own respective tasks, and have shown a lot of impatience. In the town of Jamaica, where their propaganda has been promoted, the element of color has purchased nearly all of the machetes that the only store sold."[56] According to the authorities, a lack of vigilance encouraged the PIC's "propaganda to continue to become more seditious and perverse. In the town of Jamaica, there are people like [Emilio] Wilson, Hechavarria, and others who instead of discouraging the [black] masses excite them to direct their political insults at the white element."[57] The philosophy of racial equality and the right to participate in civil society articulated by the PIC's leaders had to have resonated in the black rural communities, including those on the colonias and plantations. During the U.S. occupation, many rural blacks suffered the government appropriation of their communal holdings, which were then sold to North American businesses.[58] Displaced and now segregated on plantations, farms, or other agricultural sites, blacks were confined to spaces where their activities were prescribed, while white North Americans and Cubans controlled and appropriated their labor. The PIC sought to empower these disenfranchised and displaced people.

The Gómez government convinced Martín Morúa Delgado, a former leader of the black civil rights movement of the 1880s and 1890s, to introduce legislation that made any political party established along color or racial lines unconstitutional. Morúa Delgado believed that the Constitution of 1902 had made "racial privileges disappear from Cuba, therefore political parties founded on race could not be constitutional."[59] In spite of Morúa Delgado's amendment, PIC officials continued to travel throughout the island, particularly in the regions with the greatest concentration of blacks, in order to disseminate their message.

Their efforts to gain supporters obtained success in Santa Clara and Oriente. Local party newspapers helped to increase PIC membership in Sagua La Grande, Guantánamo, and Santiago de Cuba. Then in the fall of 1911, Estenoz and Ivonet decided to stage an armed public demonstration, hoping that it would result in civil disorder. They adopted this strategy from the multiracial National Council for Veterans of Independence, which had successfully employed it earlier to convince Gómez to employ its members in the municipal and national government bureaucracies. The government had acquiesced, fearing that any threat to civil society and private property would force the United States to re-impose its military occupation, as it had done after the August Revolution of 1906. In fact, the PIC leadership hoped that its scheduled public demonstration would cause the United States to intervene again. Estenoz believed that an American provisional government would not only be approachable, but once it understood the grievances of blacks, would do the right thing and extend as well as enforce the civil rights of blacks.

During the first months of 1912, Estenoz and Ivonet sought additional allies for their cause. Publicly supporting immigration reform and the rights of all foreign-born workers, they began to court the first wave of black Caribbean immigrants. In February, their party's newspaper, Libertad, published an article that promoted racial solidarity. It also expressed the PIC's desire to establish a multiethnic alliance with sympathetic whites. It stated: "Presently it is inhumane to criminally persecute and mercilessly prohibit the aspiring black immigrants from disembarking in Cuba. They will promote liberty and independence in a colonized and controlled Cuba."[60] To unite all blacks and even whites who supported the idea of democracy, the paper said, "We have to speak clearly, very loudly and precisely, and to say once and for all to every black Cuban, to all of the nonwhites in Cuba, and to all of the whites who love and desire democracy, the time has come for the Cuban government to open all of the ports of the island to [individuals] of every foreign race who wish to help us share in our native land the rewards and hazards of life without privileges of any kind. We insist that the government allow them inside of Cuba. And once inside, permit them to comply and respect the laws and customs of the Republic."[61] In addition to expressing their support for black Caribbean workers, leaders of the PIC began to nurture a close relationship with socialist and anarchist labor leaders, particularly in Oriente.[62]

Learning that Gómez would not repeal the Morúa Law, on 20 May 1912 the PIC staged its armed protest to reclaim the honor and dignity of blacks. By the end of May, the government had labeled the protesters as rebels. They had been defeated in Pinar del Río and Havana. In Camagüey, where whites outnumbered blacks, four hundred men of color rejected the PIC's call for civil disobedience. Not only did they sign a manifesto condemning Estenoz and Ivonet, but they also called the "race war" in neighboring Oriente an astonishing act of genocide.[63]

The protesters, however, remained a threat to the government. As a result, Gómez ordered most of the country's troops to the eastern provinces. At the same time, the U.S. government landed marines at Guantánamo, in addition to transporting three hundred soldiers to Nipe Bay and Banes in order to protect the properties of the United Fruit Company and to ensure the completion of its zafra.[64] The Boston central had become a critical asset of the sugar industry. It consisted of stores, shops, and houses valued at $8 million, and it was where 2,000 braceros worked out of a municipal population of 7,155.[65] The government also made sure that every sugar company in Santa Clara, Camagüey, and Oriente received rifles and ammunition to defend its properties.

A small number of Haitian and Jamaican braceros participated in the armed protest. Oriente's chief of police, Enrique Tomás, reported that two blacks from the Jamaiquino barrio—the segregated neighborhood exclusively for workers from the British Caribbean that was attached to the United Fruit Company sugar mill's batey—had shot a police officer in Banes. They had been identified as belonging to a group of rebels who had disturbed the peace in the Bijaru barrio.[66] Meanwhile, in the Guantánamo Valley, where Estenoz and Ivonet camped between the jungles and cane fields, their supporters attempted to burn as many mills as possible. At one mill owned by the Guantánamo Sugar Company, some Haitian braceros residing on the colonia of San Carlos joined the protest led by Ivonet because "they were very badly treated for being black." They asked Ivonet "to burn the colono's office, to requisition horses, and to give death to Sir Ramsden y Baradat and . . . to a young white very despotic with all people of color."[67] Ivonet refused the urgings of the Haitians. Nonetheless, their appeal for justice showed how the race and ethnicity of both black Cubans and Haitians engendered similar episodes in the sugar enclaves. This became quite clear as the government increased the level of repression.

On 27 May, the Haitian consul informed Manduley that a disgraceful act had occurred on the property of the San Antonio central, located near Guantánamo. Based upon the testimony of a seventy-year-old Haitian named Septema Septembre, who worked nearby at the Romelie mill, at around 5 o'clock Sunday morning, 26 May, his nephew Duperon Fils and his friend Dinnor, both Haitian macheteros at the San Antonio, started to walk to the Romelie to spend the day. While leaving the batey of the San Antonio, they encountered members of the rural guard. The guardsmen asked Fils and Dinnor for identification. "They answered we are Haitians. A guard shouted back, black Haitians and black Cubans, they are all the same, and shot the two defenseless and unfortunate unarmed men."[68] Fils died from a shot in the chest. Dinnor survived, sustaining only minor wounds. He was able to walk to the Romelie for help. Septembre also reported that a number of braceros at the San Antonio had witnessed the murder and told him that they were willing to testify because, after Septembre's nephew was shot, the guardsmen left "completely unconcerned about the two victims whom they treated like dogs."[69] The attitude and actions of the rural guard that Fils and Dinnor encountered demonstrate that repression had assumed an ethnic dimension; black Haitians had become black Cubans in the eyes of the guardsmen. The assault on the two braceros also shows how "repression has historically been directed most severely against foreigners whose employment status was tenuous."[70] Caught within the hyper-racialized context that generated the Race War of 1912, the ethnic differences between black Caribbean workers and Cubans dissolved. The former now shared in the reality and identity of the latter. As a result, Haitians and Jamaicans fled the cane fields to escape the government-sponsored violence and to join the PIC.

The Race War of 1912 ended on 12 July, when Ivonet was shot and killed near El Caney. Estenoz had died earlier, on 27 June 1912, near the town of La Maya. Thousands of blacks had been placed in concentration camps in order to discover the identity of the so-called rebels. The Race War resulted in the deaths of an estimated 5,000 to 6,000 black Cubans.[71] The government's repression also led to the displacement of thousands of blacks. Many were forcibly removed from the countryside and relocated in the nearby towns and cities. According to the chief of police of Oriente, each provincial city faced the daunting task of caring for approximately 3,000 persons of color. It is unknown how many had been supporters of the PIC, but we do know that most of the displaced blacks had been employed as field workers and in other occupations for the sugar companies.[72] Although the majority of the sugar mills sustained little damage, Cuban and North American and other foreign sugar companies began to replace black Cubans with black Caribbean workers. Undoubtedly they believed that the insolence and violence that black Cubans had displayed ultimately disqualified them from being the industry's main workers. Field workers who had been introduced to the ideas of the PIC had become too militant to tolerate the levels of subjugation and exploitation that the companies wanted to impose in order to improve the grinding capacities of their mills and increase their revenue. Although the decision among the companies to employ more black Caribbean immigrants than black Cubans remains hidden due to the lack of documentation, the history of a North American multinational company in Latin America and the Caribbean suggests that when "the relative exploitability of [an] ethnic group has changed" because of "changing forces (economic and ideological) among the various groups . . . distinct patterns of ethnic succession in the occupational hierarchy [has obtained] since the turn of the century."[73] Studying how race and ethnicity informed the labor system and policies of the United Fruit Company in Costa Rica, Philippe Bourgois, Aviva Chomsky, and Ronald N. Harpelle discovered that when West Indian workers, particularly Jamaicans, tried to unionize on the company's banana plantations during the 1920s, the company decided to replace them with local and indigenous workers.[74] It is clear that in Cuba, when the PIC articulated its ideology of racial equality with acts of violence, the relationship between black Cubans and the sugar companies dramatically changed. The latter sought a more submissive pool of workers.

It was against this backdrop that José Miguel Gómez endorsed the plan of the Nipe Bay Company, a subsidiary of the United Fruit Company and owner of the Preston *central*, to import one thousand West Indians to work on its estate in Oriente Province in 1913. Government Decree Number 23 stated, "Considering that the Nipe Bay Company has assisted in illuminating the reasons why there evidently exists a scarcity of workers and braceros in the Republic, this deficiency of the general interest must be remedied, [by] using the powers confirmed by Article Sixteen of the Immigration Law of 11 June 1906, and proposed by the Secretary of Agriculture, Commerce, and Labor: [the president] resolves to authorize the Nipe Bay Company to transport one thousand West Indian workers who will have to be employed as workers on the Preston *central*."[75] Granting the Nipe Bay Company the right to import black Caribbean workers for its mill proved to be a watershed event that altered the lives of thousands of Haitians, Jamaicans, and other black immigrants, as well as black and white Cubans. Their presence would influence not only the island's economy but also aspects of its society and culture, particularly in the central and eastern provinces.

The initial motives that prompted workers to leave Jamaica for Cuba were the same as those of other British West Indians who had migrated to Panama and Costa Rica during the last half of the nineteenth century. Comparing how much they could earn abroad with how much they needed at home, the majority left to locate better wages. Others also understood that only "through emigration could the former British West Indian slaves attain the sense of freedom for which they yearned."[76] Seeking financial independence, the majority of Jamaicans decided to go to Cuba simply to get a job.

One such emigrant was Benjamin T. Unable to find work that would provide him with the means toward independence, he felt he had no other choice but to leave his village. He and other Jamaicans went to Cuba in 1918 because, "Well, we couldn't get any more work. We had worked in the cane fields, [and] we worked in a factory too."[77] Poor economic conditions in Jamaica also caused

Enos McKenzie of Airy Mountain, in Westmoreland Parish, initially to travel to Panama in 1912 and then to Cuba in 1919. McKenzie stated, "Life was just poor, and dull. At least we were alive and could help ourselves . . . I mean feed our selves, and all like that. And in many cases we weren't so unusually bad like many other districts, but it wasn't nice at all . . . It wasn't so great."[78] The definition of financial well-being, according to another Jamaican bracero, was the ability to take care of his family: "If your children are hungry then you'll cut the canes. You've got to feed dem pickney."[79]

The news that Cuba offered better jobs and wages encouraged Jamaicans to emigrate to Cuba. Some workers who left the village of Heywood Hall, in St. Mary Parish, heard that "Cuba was the place where money was being given away . . . you know most of the people always liked to travel to Cuba to earn a livelihood, for at that time sugar cane . . . the cutting of cane and sugar . . . even my husband . . . he traveled to Cuba. At that time Cuba was very bright. And they went to Cuba to see what Cuba was like."[80] John Barry was encouraged to try his luck in Cuba after hearing about the experience of other emigrants: "People were going to Cuba . . . and there was a boom there. The cane crop was there you know, and people were leaving Jamaica for Cuba. So I went along."[81] Finally, the entire family of Hilda Durrant embarked for Cuba in 1914 because "Jamaicans could earn only one shilling a day, and we went to Cuba [to] get a £1 pound a day . . . So that now means $5.00—$5.00 was £1 pound in those days."[82]

The Jamaicans living in Panama also heard that sugar companies in Cuba were offering wages that would provide them with financial independence. In fact, once they discovered that they were preferred over other ethnic workers, particularly black Cubans and Haitians, to fill the most skilled craft jobs in the mills and on the farms, they flocked to Camagüey and Oriente. Writing from the Violeta *central* located near the port town of Morón, Camagüey, Nathaniel Vaughn informed the West Indians living in the Panama Canal Zone and the city of Colón that "there is plenty of work in Cuba, the least a man can make is $2.70 a day. I have not been here three months, yet I can balance the difference between a canal worker, and a man working in Cuba as 3 to 6 . . . There is room for carpenters, painters, masons, plumbers, firemen, timber-fallers, and in fact all kinds of skilled workmen. The door of opportunity is open. Oh ye sturdy West Indians enter in!"[83] It is important to note that, for the most part, light-skinned blacks of mixed African and European ancestry had traditionally monopolized these trades on Jamaica and other British West Indian islands since the middle of the nineteenth century. They were also employed as overseers or foremen and accountants on Jamaican sugar estates, and as office and business clerks.[84] Their physical appearance privileged them within the ethnically segmented work force in the Cuban sugar mills, and thus provided them with the opportunity to enter these industrial trades under the auspices of the North Americans. Concurrently, their favored position shows how the sugar companies employed ethnicity to foster competition and antagonism among their workers, while limiting the chances of labor solidarity.

That thousands of Jamaicans entered Cuba from Panama cannot be disputed. The opportunity to work in occupations other than cutting and hauling cane persuaded Jamaicans and other West Indians to leave for Cuba. This wave of Jamaican braceros swelled the ranks of artisans and craftsmen employed by the sugar mills. Some black leaders in Panama noticed this phenomenon immediately following the sugar harvest of 1920. In an editorial, one community official wrote that "the Panama Canal is . . . losing its best [workers] and most efficient men. During the past three months over 2,000 able-bodied, and hard-working men have sailed away from these shores to Cuba . . . our most experienced carpenters, masons, and blacksmiths are going or have gone, and we can't call them back loud enough for them to hear."[85] The appeal for skilled Jamaican workers was prompted by the alleged cultural superiority they held compared to the Haitian braceros. The fact that they spoke English and had already displayed their work ethic during the construction of the Panama Canal made them attractive to North American and Cuban sugar companies seeking to expand their capacities and production.

Most blacks from the British islands also recognized the importance that their income had not just on their families but also on the people of their predominantly rural communities back home. As the unidentified and frustrated bracero quoted at the beginning of this chapter reminded everyone back home, not only would their wages feed, clothe, and house the immediate members of their families, but they also caused those small local economies to thrive once they returned with their savings. Understanding that their wages represented "the mouse's share for doing the lion's part of the work and the crumbs that fall from the tables of the first powers of earth," they migrated to Cuba with the hope of returning to Jamaica to demand "the real bread of life, like the rest of men, for our families and [for] our selves."[86] This ambitious spirit undoubtedly became the most salient impulse that drew thousands of Jamaicans to the sugarcane farms and mills. Having worked at the Preston since 1917, S. O. Gayle reported encountering "some fellows here who are not disposed to come home with less than $500 dollars," a figure that put a "smile on one side of my face, and [a] look of serious[ness] with the other; but I am sure the ambition is there. Whether it will be realized is another matter. But I know that after living in Cuba for two years, a man's ambition simply grows, and he gets a determination simply miraculous."[87] Sam Burt from Brighton, in Westmoreland Parish, came to rely so much on the salary that he earned from cutting cane that he ventured to work in Cuba on three separate occasions between 1919 and 1927. His first zafra took place in 1919. He stayed until the end of the harvest of 1920. Burt then returned for the harvest of 1922. His last trip to cut cane occurred in 1926.[88] Hibbert Morris, of St. Thomas Parish, also remembered that "people were going to Cuba backward and forward." Although he found the work of cutting cane challenging, Morris, like Sam Burt, traveled to Cuba three times, beginning in 1919. In 1921, Morris worked his second harvest not by cutting cane but by working inside the sugar mill "curing sugar, sewing sacks, and painting." Now employed as a skilled worker, Morris decided to stay until 1927, when he returned to Jamaica briefly. His last journey occurred before the end of that year. Resuming his work inside the mill during the next two zafras, in 1929 he returned to Jamaica for good.[89] Although the possibility of transferring the wages accumulated from cutting and hauling cane proved decisive in compelling these men to go and work in Cuba, their savings when they returned to Jamaica were ultimately inadequate to alter dramatically their material standard of living or that of their families.[90]

That thousands of Jamaicans decided to leave their families and homes to work in Cuba was in response to the absence of good-paying jobs at home. Unlike other colonies of the British West Indies, parts of the interior of Jamaica were left underdeveloped by the sugar industry, and many blacks subsisted there by growing small quantities of coffee and other cash crops. Others squatted on what was called "Crown land," located around many of the densely populated areas of the island, where the sugar plantations were centered. To recruit and retain black workers for their plantations, the colonial legislature, which was made up largely of members of the sugar industry, discouraged blacks from owning land by passing laws that prohibited them from squatting on Crown land. Moreover, plantation owners denied blacks the opportunity to own land by rejecting their attempts to buy even the worst lands attached to their planta-

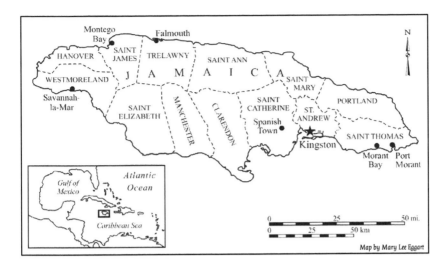

Map by Mary Lee Eggart

tions. Imposing prohibitive taxes on small property owners and licensing fees on those who grew and sold relatively small amounts of sugarcane and coffee also became effective strategies of the Jamaican plantocracy to retain black workers for their estates. In spite of these obstacles, many blacks purchased land from some plantation owners who hoped to gain their favor as well as to attract them with wages. As a result, many found themselves splitting half of their time working on their small plots and the other half working on the nearby sugar estates or coffee farms for less than adequate wages as the only way to survive. These processes led to the appearance of a "reconstituted peasantry." Rural blacks survived by attending to their own small plots while becoming "semi-proletarians" working for the plantocracy.[91]

The emergence of a peasantry in Jamaica resulted in the number of black rural property holders owning 5–50 acres to grow from 13,189 in 1880 to 24,226 by 1902, according to Gisela Eisner.[92] After the turn of the twentieth century, these peasants began to produce items such as sugar, coffee, pimento, ginger, and bananas for export. They soon realized, however, that they could no longer make ends meet by subsisting and growing small amounts of these tropical staples. One Jamaican worker who left the village of Watson's Gate, in Manchester Parish, for Cuba in 1919 remembered that although his father cultivated coffee, yams, bananas, oranges, and other fruit, he could not earn enough money to care for his family. As a result, he left Watson's Gate for Kingston, before he made his way to Cuba. Meanwhile, before Sam Burt traveled to Cuba, he had

47

rented some land "up in the mountain to break pimento, and plant, cultivate ground [with] cane," to no avail. In Kingston Parish, a Mr. Burke recalled that when he was a boy near August Town, "people made a living by going in the fields to plant cane, gungo peas, yam, red peas, turnip and carrot." Nonetheless, he and others decided to migrate to Cuba in 1919.[93]

The increasing population of Jamaica made these attempts to survive and care for their families—values that informed their identity—futile. Opportunities to own a piece of land declined. In 1881, the population of Jamaica totaled 580,804, of which 444,186 were black, comprising 76.5 percent of the population. By 1911, the island's population had witnessed an increase of 250,579, a figure that brought the total to 831,383. Much of that increase occurred among the black sector of the population, as that segment now totaled 630,181.[94] The segment of the population between the ages of fifteen years and fifty years increased from approximately 321,500 in 1891 to 333,500 by 1911. The sector of the work force that grew most was between the ages of twenty and twenty-nine. That portion of Jamaican society rose by 37,000, going from 116,400 in 1891 to 153,500 in 1911.[95]

The growth of the population affected society in two ways, engendering massive emigration to Cuba. First, the increase of the population in Jamaica, particularly the black population, reduced the availability of land in the countryside. This hampered attempts by individual blacks to retain their independence as peasants. More important, though, the growth of the laboring classes created a surplus of workers who were paid very low wages. These systemic characteristics of Jamaican society prompted the landless and the poorly paid and unemployed semi-proletarians to reject these wages and seek a better life abroad. Others abandoned Jamaica after realizing that any kind of socioeconomic mobility was tied to the acquisition of an education. Because Jamaica's educational system had always been poorly funded, a quality education proved to be out of reach for many unless the parents obtained higher wages to spend for their children.

The poor quality of the island's public educational system in the 1910s stemmed from the Legislative Council's 1844 Act to Promote Education of the Industrial Classes in This Island, which usually allocated only £2,000 sterling annually through the end of the nineteenth century. This amount was inadequate to pay the monthly salary of teachers as well as to keep schools open. By the 1910s, not much had changed. Fearon, a teacher to first- and second-year students in the town of Wilbury, in Clarendon Parish, left Jamaica first for Panama, and later for Cuba, because "in those days they pay a teacher one shilling and six pence per day . . . So that was nothing at all."[96] Not providing rural teachers with adequate wages became a disincentive that some members of the Assembly employed to maintain the subordination of blacks. Restricting the number of teachers denied adequate educational opportunities for black children, making their marginalization generational in scope.

As a result, most rural black folks had to send their children to elementary schools managed by the Baptist and Wesleyan churches. Others, who were more fortunate, could have their young ones attend private schools if they sought to continue their education beyond the sixth year. Many students pursued their studies if they could pass a series of stringent exams before graduating to the next level of instruction, or if their parents had the money "to keep you going until you got into college . . . But if not, they send you out with the boys to learn carpentry, any trade at all," according to Ms. Dove of Orange Field, in St. Catherine Parish, whose entire family emigrated to Cuba.[97] The desire to see their children educated stemmed from the belief among members of the peasantry that an education or at least an elementary level of literacy were required for their sons and daughters to "get a good job" and "to get ahead," according to Judith Blake.[98] Thus excluded from the socioeconomic and political institutions of the island, many Jamaicans abandoned the British colony for a better life elsewhere not only for themselves but in some instances also for their families. This became another incentive to emigrate to Cuba.

Born in Old Harbour, in Kingston Parish, Mrs. Bennett remembered that her fiancé went to Cuba to gain employment, as many Jamaicans had, as a machetero "working in the cane fields, because most of their work there [was] in cane sugar." After the zafra, he returned home for her and her sister. Now together in Cuba, Mrs. Bennett married her fiancé, and they had two children.[99] Meanwhile, Miss Lyn from Belle Castle, in Portland Parish, revealed how her father left for Cuba alone. Then after completing the zafra, he sent for Lyn's brothers, and "they all were there with him . . . spending some years there." The stories of Mrs. Bennett and Lyn show not only how extra-residential unions and common-law relationships among the peasantry of Jamaica fostered their migratory experiences, but also the value they placed on the institutions of marriage and family. Discovering that extra-residential unions and common-law relationships were not substitutes for marriage among the Caribbean peasantry, particularly in Jamaica, Judith Blake, Edith Clarke, and Michael Horowitz believe that they were progressive processes that ultimately led men and women to enter into legal unions.[100] The decision to do so rested upon a number of economic and cultural variables. First of all, males were viewed as the primary breadwinners. This obligation encouraged them to believe that before they could marry their common-law partners, they had to acquire either a piece of land or an adequate-paying job. These were prerequisites not only for building a home but for doing things "in the right way . . . because pride and fear of ridicule extends throughout many aspects of lower-class Jamaican life."[101] In addition, both men and women valued marriage because they sought the respectability that the institution afforded. It convinced each partner that they were emotionally and financially committed to the union. And they hoped that their marriage served as a model for their children, showing them that marriage was the foundation of a stable family.

To that end, Hilda Durrant of Hanover Parish, who went to Cuba in 1914 to be reunited with her family, vividly remembered that her friends could not believe that an eighteen-year-old girl was leaving home and traveling alone to Cuba. But this was very common, she said: "In those days . . . I went to my brother and sister. And I went to my [other] brother. I went to my [other] sister. I went to my aunt. All of my family was over there. They went there from 1914, so I went to their weddings, and everything." Durrant stayed with her family for three years in Cuba, returning briefly to Hanover in 1917. The following year, she returned to Cuba and married a Jamaican who worked as a carpenter at the Miranda. They had fourteen children while living in Cuba. During the 1920s, she worked as a domestic servant and as a cook at the Miranda sugar mill, often training other girls in the same duties, until the family all returned to Jamaica in 1932.[102]

The transcripts of these three Jamaican female emigrants reveal how they and their families and possibly thousands more sought to reconstitute a semblance of home in Camagüey and Oriente. Besides being a place in which collective practices and rituals are reproduced, the conception of home also became the site where domestic life is controlled in order to foster an individual's memory and aspirations, as well as the division and consumption of resources.[103] As transients, moving to and from Cuba sporadically or after longer durations, Jamaican braceros sought to "achieve a sense of belonging." In other words, the emigration of Jamaicans, particularly those who left their families and loved ones behind only to retrieve or send for them while they worked in the sugar enclaves of Cuba, consisted of a movement of workers between homes. As a result, Jamaicans re-imagined home not only as "a safe place to leave and return to, but also a mobile site that can be taken along whenever one decamps."[104] Such was the case when Laura McKenzie's father, who did not have enough land to farm in Kellits, in Clarendon Parish, sold his property "and went away foreign. Yes, he went and took up his children and his wife too. That time . . . Cuba was doing [a] good job and it was calling Jamaicans, just like how America is calling Jamaica when farm working starts . . . so that time it was Cuba, and lots of Jamaicans went away to Cuba lots of them yes."[105] The experiences of an unidentified black woman from Heywood Hall, in St. Mary Parish, also reveal how Cuba became another home for her and her family. Hearing that "Cuba was the place where money giving away," she and her husband as well as her brother and sister went there: "you know most of the people always like to travel to Cuba to earn a livelihood, for at that time sugar cane . . . the cutting of cane [made] Cuba very bright."[106] A bracero known only as Uncle B. from Chandewey, St. Thomas Parish, traveled with his brother to Cuba as early as 1911. "Getting on nicely" before he became ill, he and his brother worked together as macheteros near Antilla and later Naranjal. After they returned to Antilla, the brothers decided to pool their resources to rent a piece of land from the Cuban American Sugar Company for fifty dollars. They then went into business burning coal on their plot and selling it for eighty cents a bag at the local market.[107] By privileging the institutions of marriage, family, and home in Cuba, the experiences of hundreds of Jamaicans may be used to challenge the interpretations of George Beckford, Sidney Mintz, and Charles Wagley. They claim that the plantation system of the Caribbean engendered weak and disorganized community organizations and structures, and unstable family and kinship systems.[108] It will become apparent that the experiences of black Caribbean braceros reveal the opposite.

The historical literature on the causes of black Haitian immigration to Cuba has emphasized a number of factors that contributed to their decision to leave home. Because of a lack of historical evidence produced by Haitian braceros regarding their motives for leaving their country, writers have stressed the socioeconomic status of black rural workers as well as their material condition. As a result, some believe that by the turn of the twentieth century, Haiti had evolved into a color-based segmented society of approximately two million people where at least 95 percent could not read or write. Concurrently, the light-skinned "people of color" held sway over the dark-skinned former slaves. Differences of skin color reinforced class antagonisms as the colored elites, representing only 3 percent of the total population, exploited the black peasantry. The former British consul general in Haiti succinctly described what the differences of color had produced there. Sir Spenser St. John wrote that "the black hates the mulatto, the mulatto despises the black; proscriptions, judicial murders, massacres have arisen, and will continue to arise as long as this deplorable feeling prevails. There is no sign of its abatement."[109] In order to mitigate their exploitation and repression, black Haitians went to Cuba.[110]

The effects of the Haitian caste system were articulated throughout the economy. At the top and middle rungs of the socioeconomic ladder were mulattoes and some blacks. They dominated the government bureaucracy, the financial and commercial institutions, and businesses, in addition to the officer corps of the military. Most blacks composed the urban working class. They were found in occupations such as dockworkers, street vendors, and the rank-and-file soldiers of the army.[111] The rest of society lived and worked in the countryside. This segment accounted for 85 percent of the population and included both mulatto and black owners of large landed estates, who sought to exploit the majority of rural workers. The rural elites held most of their property in the northern plains, but also in the western and southern regions as well as near the mountains. They employed managers to take care of these plantations and farms, and even leased some or all of their land to tenant farmers and peasants.[112] Below the class of large estate owners and their managerial class was the large and impoverished black peasantry.

Living the most precarious existence of all, the peasants— landless rural workers—simply did not possess any resources to improve their lives. Without either land or money, "they were at the mercy of the landlords, commercial speculators, money lenders, and government agents."[113] Alex Dupuy discovered that a number of prohibitively expensive taxes on the peasantry resulted in their flight to Cuba. The government taxed the coffee they produced for the export economy. They also were required to pay local sales and retail taxes, in addition to a fee that permitted them to sell and market their agricultural goods. A property tax and a tax on livestock owned by the peasants became another source of revenue for the government.[114]

Mats Lundahl also believes that Haitians ventured to Cuba in response to the intensification of the exploitation and growing misery of the peasantry fostered by a dramatic growth of the population, which increased from 500,000 in 1818 to one million by 1860. The census of 1920 counted another million, making a total population of two million at the end of World War I.[115] Haiti's demographic change has been attributed to the desire of the peasantry to increase its productivity by increasing the size of its families. Unfortunately, the outcome placed additional pressure on the land-tenure and cooperative-labor systems. As peasant families grew from the addition of biological and assumed kin, the division of land among multiple claimants became more and more extreme. The growing population meant limiting access to land held in common. It also reduced the size of subsistence plots and of land dedicated to coffee cultivation. Population growth in Haiti also prohibited the younger generation of rural people from gaining access to land suitable for subsistence farming.

The analysis of these historians and others who have contended that Haiti's socioeconomic traditions and institutions led to the miserable condition and exploitation of thousands of black rural workers, resulting in their immigration to Cuba, is convincing and valid.[116] Yet they ignore the role and value that the Haitian peasantry placed on family, religion, and marriage, which became significant factors in their decision to emigrate to Cuba. The majority of Haitians left their country for many of the same reasons as their Jamaican counterparts. They arrived hoping to obtain a better life. Elia Miguel Dorse, who was born in Guantánamo in 1926 to Haitian parents who arrived in 1915, was told by her mother and father that they came to Cuba "with the objectives of improving their economic condition and to assume a life a little more humane."[117] Other Haitians decided to emigrate after becoming uprooted, unemployed, or vagrants with no place to go, understanding that their government could no longer protect them. The Haitian nationalist Jacques Roumain addressed the alienation that these migrants experienced in his acclaimed novel, *Masters of the Dew*, about the Haitian peasantry. Unable to subsist and thus maintain his dignity, his fictional character, Manuel, tells his mother why he went to Cuba to cut sugarcane. Like thousands of desperate Haitians faced with hopelessness, he decided to be "uprooted like a tree in the current of a river. I drifted to foreign lands."[118]

Landless Haitian peasants were not alone in sharing these sentiments of hope. The same aspirations could have been held by braceros who owned a little property in Haiti and sought to either develop or add to it. Citing field research conducted by Maurice Dartigue on the condition of 884 rural Haitian peasant families in 1938, Samuel Martínez argues that because landowning Haitians had

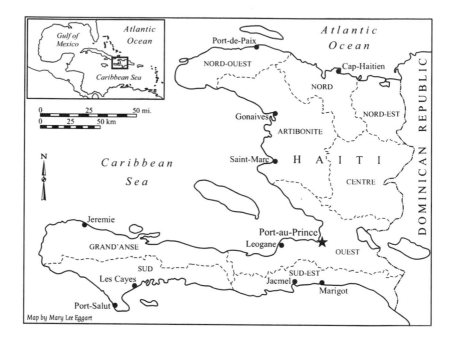

Map by Mary Lee Eggart

migrated to the Dominican Republic to cut and haul cane in the 1930s, it is very likely that a good number of Haitian peasants who worked in Cuba during the 1910s and 1920s also held property.[119] As a result, one immediate cause for the migration of Haitians to Cuba was the desire to use their savings to improve their holdings at home in a number of ways. They could grow different crops that could "withstand droughts, flooding, the attack of pests . . . [in order] to diminish their risk of crop loss."[120] Other braceros who returned from Cuba hoped to become renters or sharecroppers of small plots either to grow their own crops or to divide their property among kindred and friends. In doing so, they would assist in enhancing the general well-being of their immediate and extended families, both biological and assumed, since landlords and tenants usually were "sisters, brothers, or uncles and nephews."[121] This was not the only example where braceros' familial obligations encouraged them to leave for Cuba.

Similar to the duties and expectations that Jamaican parents had for their children, Haitians deliberately returned from Cuba with their savings in order to take care of their families and elderly parents. As we shall see in a later chapter, while in Cuba many Haitian macheteros and carreteros also spent their wages on elaborate wakes and funerals to ensure that the soul of a deceased loved one would return home to spend eternity with his or her ancestors.[122] They also went to Cuba to earn enough money to get married after being involved in common-law unions. Similar to the sociocultural pattern among the Jamaican peasantry, consensual unions had become the most common form of relationship between rural Haitian men and women. Ira Lowenthal discovered that Haitian males waited to marry for the same socioeconomic and cultural reasons as their Jamaican counterparts.[123] In addition, their inability to do it "the right way" resulted in the same community ridicule that Jamaican peasants experienced.

Doing it "the right way," however, also meant fulfilling familial responsibilities while moving between Haiti and Cuba. In short, paralleling their Jamaican counterparts, many Haitians returned home to retrieve their spouses and children. Interviewing a number of Cubans of Haitian ancestry living in Guantánamo at the turn of the twenty-first century, Bernarda Sevillano Andrés discovered that the majority of their relatives initially arrived during the 1910s and 1920s to work only one harvest. After their first zafra, however, they went home, returning to Cuba with a loved one or a friend the following year. In so doing, "many Haitians . . . formed families increasing the number of descendants among the first generation or 'los pichones,'" as they were called.[124] Meanwhile, others traveled to Cuba on their own to join a spouse, relative, or friend. For example, Verónica Maslén's mother told her that she refused to accompany a labor broker to a mill that paid well "because I wanted to be reunited with my father."[125]

The desire of Haitian peasants to improve their own lives as well as those of their families cannot be fully appreciated, however, if one does not illuminate in detail the more immediate and salient context that undermined their socioeconomic and religious obligations. The inability to satisfy those expectations encouraged thousands to go and work in Cuba, as well as to view it as a land of opportunity, a place that they called home after 1912. Their reality and experiences were exposed when a U.S. Senate Committee, convened in 1922 to assess the role and impact that the U.S. Marines' occupation had on the people of Haiti, invited a number of expert witnesses to convey the nuances of Haitian society during the first seven years of the occupation. The testimonies of several observers living in the country are insightful and break the silence created by a lack of historical evidence produced by Haitians who emigrated to Cuba. As impassioned opponents of the occupation of the country, the testimony of these observers must be weighed critically. Their friendship and care for the people of Haiti, particularly the poor peasantry, undoubtedly encouraged them to make an emotional appeal for justice by emphasizing the wretched conditions engendered by the military occupation. Nonetheless, the memories of the individuals brought before the committee illuminate the context that many workers tried to flee.

Speaking on behalf of the black peasantry before members of the U.S. Congressional Select Committee on Haiti and Santo Domingo, L. Ton Evans, a white Baptist missionary who lived in Haiti before and during the U.S. military occupation, blamed the *corvée* labor system for the attack on the peasantry's dignity, an assault that created a mood of dissatisfaction and angst among black rural workers. His testimony emphasized how North American intervention had dramatically altered this traditional labor system. Having never been codified by law before the occupation, the corvée was "an old custom where farmers or those who have their . . . small holdings in Haiti, once or twice a year devote two or three days or so to help repair roads opposite their own farms." But "the occupation in Haiti . . . intentionally or ignorantly put a new and altogether an erroneous meaning to it . . . turning it into an instrument for oppressing and torturing the Haitian people, and exciting their passions . . . and sometimes for no other purpose than to provide them [the gendarmes employed by U.S. Marines] with an excuse to beat, if not shoot them down." Evans, as a Baptist minister, was morally repulsed when told that many "have met their deaths through the corvée thus illegally practiced, willfully or ignorantly, by the marines and the gendarmerie, and acquiesced by those in the U.S. Supreme Command [in Port-au-Prince] and at Washington."[126]

Not only had Evans relied upon Haitian informants to publicly expose how the U.S. Marines reimagined and reassembled this traditional labor system, he also described how members of the gendarmerie, a militia force composed of Haitians and created by the marines, subjugated their own people. Traveling from Gros Morne to Jacmel in the southeastern region, where the majority of emigrant Haitians lived before going to Cuba, Evans was told by a group of gendarmerie officers that corvée workers were paid "one gourde or in American money, twenty cents a week, without any food." Humiliated, many Haitians decided to resist this mistreatment. "It is easy to imagine how such ill-paid, ill-fed natives driven to work like these, many miles away from homes and families as there [sic] were, become uneasy, irritated, and even revolt, which invariably means death."[127]

Evans also reported painful scenes staged to legitimatize the mastery of the North Americans and their Haitian cohort, as well as to demean the workers on a daily basis: "Men, working under the corvée, lined up . . . [and were] driven out about 6:00 in the morning, often without nothing but a little coffee, marched under armed guard to work miles away, and then brought back . . . carefully searched and compelled to wait from about 4:00 until 6:00 without being fed." He continued: "At St. Marc, I have seen these men here struck with such force by the gendarme officer and for the merest trifle, until they would fall like logs. Many for want of food fainting . . . on the hard floor."[128] Undoubtedly the public use of corporal punishment became a component of North American domination designed to physically abuse the workers and to humiliate them.

Evans concluded his testimony by summarizing what he had been told by dozens of Haitians working under the corvée system, thereby revealing why thousands of Haitians desired to leave for Cuba: "Is it not sad, indeed, to have to state that after nearly five years of the American occupation in Haiti, people of the little black Republic sincerely and firmly believe that the real mission of the U.S. government and the American people there is to reestablish slavery in their midst once more; [and] to abrogate and annul the work of Toussaint L'Overture."[129] Imagining that they were to be re-enslaved, many workers fled to Cuba, and in so doing, adopted the most popular form of resistance employed by bonded men and women under slavery—flight.

Comparing the corvée to slavery was not an exaggeration for most Haitians. Lieutenant Colonel Alexander S. Williams, who may have come to realize that the administration of the occupation was difficult to carry out, testified how the U.S.-trained gendarmerie collected workers for road construction and other projects. Commonly, they apprehended the entire work force from small and large businesses as well as from farms. As a result, businesses were forced to close and farms went unattended. He also discussed how the gendarmerie controlled Haitian laborers for extended periods of time. The corvée workers were issued identification cards to show that they had completed their "tour of duty" and were ineligible for future work, and they confidently showed their cards when pressed by the gendarmerie. The latter, however, took the cards and "tore them up and sent them on to work."[130] This practice, according to Williams, was repeated daily.

The corvée labor system proved so disruptive to the economic activities and initiatives of the Haitians that poverty remained rampant. This feature of Haitian society caused Carl Kelsey, a professor of the University of Pennsylvania and a member of the American Academy of Political and Social Science, to remark in front of the Senate committee: "From what has been said it must be evident that the Haitians are poor. This is perhaps the first strong impression the visitor gets. Only a poor people will work for twenty cents a day, the prevailing wage today. Only a hungry people will pick and deliver coffee for three cents a pound, which is all the peasants got in 1921."[131] The conditions created by the occupation forced thousands of Haitians to decide that a better home awaited them in Cuba.

A host of unscrupulous emigrant brokers, as U.S. military officials called them, took advantage of Haitian workers who confronted this dire poverty and repression. Supervising the trade in braceros, these individuals often lied to the workers to convince them that Cuba was a land of great opportunity. Haitian women proved the most gullible to the narratives of the brokers. In 1920, a woman named Chati traveled to Camagüey under the assumption that she and other women would earn one peso per day working as domestics, custodians, or cleaning women. They primarily would be put to work to "limpiar botellas" (clean bottles), according to the brokers. Once they arrived in Cuba, however, many realized that they had been recruited to work as prostitutes. Such was the case for Verónica Maslén's mother, who was deceived by a labor broker who took her to Guantánamo because "she was young and beautiful."[132] If the immigrants sought to return to Haiti, the agents and the guards of the mills used force to prevent them from leaving, said Chati.[133] Some agents became very rich by providing this service to the predominantly male immigrant work force of the sugar companies. The emergence of female prostitution accompanied the development and expansion of the plantation model of production throughout the Caribbean during the first quarter of the twentieth century.[134] In Cuba, the managers of the sugar mills made prostitutes readily available in order to attract and retain large numbers of field workers. The companies' top priority, however, was to get the men to Cuba and to transform them into a cheap, compliant, and docile work force.

———～———

The sugar companies operating in the provinces of Santa Clara, Camagüey, and Oriente became successful importing Haitians and British West Indians, particularly Jamaicans, because they had already established the infrastructure on these Caribbean islands. By the start of the second decade of the twentieth century, North American companies, such as the United Fruit Company and later the Atlantic Fruit Company, had developed the shipping routes that carried out the Isthmian and Caribbean fruit trade. In Jamaica, these U.S. companies invested heavily in the banana industry. The seaports that handled the export of this commodity also became centers where laborers encountered the sugar companies' recruiters. In fact, dockyards throughout the Caribbean "became hives of information exchanges among individuals from many different places," and thus promoted, by word of mouth, news that better jobs and wages could be had in Cuba.[135] After Portland Parish experienced the growth of its banana industry at the end of the nineteenth century, its main harbor and commercial center, Port Antonio, became the site of embarkation for many of the Jamaican emigrants to Cuba and elsewhere.[136] The labor recruiters around Port Antonio probably hoped to use the good will that Jamaicans felt toward North Americans in general to encourage them to travel to Cuba. Their empathy for North Americans may have stemmed from the fact that 65 percent of the island's exports went to the United States. In fact, the nature of race relations between North Americans and Jamaicans in Port Antonio likely contributed to successful recruiting activities. While visiting Port Antonio in 1910, H. G. de Lisser observed that "the American . . . is pleased to find a Negro population altogether unlike the American Negro, and it is sometimes amusing to hear a party of Americans extolling the virtues of a little black boy or brown girl with whom they have been talking."[137] For the American sugar mill owners, and possibly for the Cuban colonos, those virtues, defined as singularly Jamaican, would include a degree of deference toward one's superiors, proper manners, proficiency in the English language, and ambition. Nonetheless, in Cuba, as the companies' administrators along with government officials deliberately exploited the race and ethnicity of Jamaicans to marginalize them, the term *Jamaiquino* or *Jamaicano* became a pejorative, often used synonymously with "undesirable."[138]

Haitian peasants and unemployed workers embarked from the port towns and cities developed with the assistance of the German and French companies that controlled the country's coffee industry. By 1914, American, Cuban, and Haitian emigrant brokers had discovered a large surplus of poor and unemployed laborers around the dockyards in or near Port-au-Prince and Port de Paix, located on the northern coast, as well as Les Cayes on the southwestern coast. There, they often established hiring centers to recruit and contract laborers. Some sugar companies also encouraged their representatives to smuggle large numbers of emigrants across the Haitian–Dominican Republic border in order to subvert the Haitian government's laws, which required emigrants to purchase passports, identification cards, and other official travel documents. When this strategy failed to obtain a good supply of workers for the sugar companies, some of the emigrant brokers who had signed contracts with specific mills to deliver a cargo of workers tried a couple of different steps to circumvent Haiti's emigration laws. For example, some would simply petition the Haitian authorities to permit them to direct the embarkation of three hundred or more undocumented workers. The Haitian government, with U.S. military approval, consented after the brokers swore that they would submit the necessary forms to customs and immigration officials, but only after they had delivered the workers to Cuba. When they failed to comply, neither the Americans nor the Haitians seemed to care. Another scheme used by the brokers included the attempt to smuggle a contingent of undocumented braceros among a shipment of two to three hundred documented migrants departing from Les Cayes.[139] Such subterfuge prompted Carl Kelsey to describe the immigration of Haitian workers to Cuba under the U.S. military occupation as "a disguised slave trade," carried out with the blessing of the Haitian government.[140] Between 1912 and 1925, Les Cayes became the port town where this trade was centered and which saw the majority of braceros exit the island for Cuba, according to U.S. officials. This is contrary to the findings of some writers who claimed that the majority of Haitians came from the northern plains, particularly from the region between Cap-Haïtien on the northern coast and Mirebalais in the central valley.[141]

Some Haitian emigrant brokers made a good living by infamously extracting additional earnings from this commercial activity while taking advantage of the braceros.[142] According to Arsenio Luis, a Haitian bracero who worked on the Jatibonico central in Camagüey Province during the early 1920s, Haitian-born labor contractors generally traveled to either the ports of Les Cayes or Jeremie every fifteen days in order to hire groups of macheteros after the zafras started. Luis also remembered that this type of business "permitted the agents who permanently resided in Haiti to return there very rich."[143] Some Haitian brokers, such as A. Pierre Paul, the Bonnefil brothers, and Solgnac Esperance, often signed contracts with the United Fruit Company and the Francisco Sugar Company to deliver three hundred braceros or more, sometimes weekly or as needed during the harvest. That they lobbied Haitian and U.S. authorities to provide them with exclusive rights to handle this commercial enterprise speaks volumes to the lucrative nature of the trade in braceros. In exchange for the revenue that some of the brokers generated for the Haitian government, which sold and processed the workers' passports and the visas, the brokers received kickbacks from the authorities. In addition, much of brokers' profits was obtained from having each bracero sign, before departing the island, a promissory note "bearing high rates of interest to pay [the broker] as much as $500 at times before they are out of debt."[144] This became a prerequisite for nearly all the migrant workers who sought to leave the country, who agreed to sign away their future wages after being convinced by the brokers that they would never leave Haiti or find a job once they landed in Cuba without their aid.

Meanwhile in Jamaica, the agents or brokers of the sister companies of the sugar mills also received compensation for delivering cargos of braceros. This was discussed between Eduardo Díaz Ulzurrun, the manager of the Francisco, and the owner, Manuel Rionda. In order to import gangs of workers, especially after 1915 when most mills stopped offering contracts to individual workers and decided to obtain a number of cuadrillas, or work teams, through the enganche labor system, the manager proposed that "we could pay some type of small commission to those who pack these ships and sell the laborers directly to us and at our [private] ports."[145] It appears that the Cuban Cane Sugar Company hired C. E. Burton for this purpose. Operating out of an office located at 62 Port Royal Street in Kingston, Burton informed potential recruits that the Manatí Sugar Company required laborers to perform field work in exchange for "good pay, good treatment and no contracts." According to Burton, the emigrants needed ten dollars for their passage, as well as their passports and police permits to travel to Cuba. The enlisted workers then boarded the S.S. Manatí and sailed directly to the mill's port at Manatí, Cuba.[146]

The sugar companies' labor agents who traveled throughout the Caribbean also descended upon Cuban towns and ports in search of macheteros and carreteros. They made their presence known at the train stations that dotted the railway lines constructed in response to the expansion of the sugar industry into the central and eastern provinces. Most of the companies followed the lead of the United Fruit Company and sent their brokers to the large bracero markets in Guantánamo and Baracoa to contract hundreds of workers.[147] Usually these agents were employees of the sugar mills themselves. Some worked as porters and company store operators, while others were cane farmers. In order to make the recruitment process seem more personable and generate a sense of trust between the braceros and the brokers, many of the labor recruiters that the sugar companies employed inside and outside of Cuba shared the phenotype of the workers. Many were Cuban males of color, either mestizo or mulatto, single, and between the ages of thirty and forty. Other sugar mills also employed nationals from Haiti and Jamaica. Robert Palmer from Roehampton, in St. James Parish, Jamaica, remembered how two agents were waiting to recruit him after he disembarked at the port of Santiago de Cuba. One recruiter was Cuban and the other Jamaican. Both agents represented the same mill. Arriving in 1916 at the age of seventeen and unable to speak Spanish, Palmer credited the Jamaican recruiter with helping him, along with fifty other emigrants, to obtain work because, "[Y]ou see, the Jamaican knows the languages . . . The Cuban wanted me to go and do such a work . . . [in Spanish] he says I will pay your fare if you all will come . . . The Jamaican says alright come I will pay you[r] fare. We said yes."[148] In addition, it appears that representatives of the Haitian consulate as well as their Jamaican counterparts participated in the business of the labor trade.[149] As we shall see below, the fact that officials representing the governments of Haiti and Great Britain in Cuba were involved in assisting the sugar companies in recruiting and retaining manual agricultural laborers resulted in a conflict of interest for these officials. Charged with protecting the rights of their nationals in Cuba but paid by the companies for delivering a cuadrilla of contracted workers to the mills, many simply turned a blind eye to the abuses that workers confronted in the sugar enclaves.

But before the sugar companies could take advantage of an elastic supply of labor, they had to solve a couple of problems.[150] One problem that some mill owners dealt with after the Cuban government reformed its immigration law in 1913 was the lack of passenger ships to accommodate the large and incessant bracero traffic. Many companies did not own or operate enough steam-powered schooners large enough to ship 250–300 men every week to their multiple mill factories and cane farms. For the sugar companies, a surplus of workers had to be already on site in order to prevent a bottleneck from forming during the initial stage of production, a situation that often resulted in having to suspend grinding the cane. To take advantage of the continuous-process technology responsible for their economies of scale, a superabundance of black Caribbean macheteros and carreteros proved indispensable. For example, by 1919, not only would the Cuban Cane Sugar Company need to supply the largest mill in Cuba, the Manatí, with macheteros and carreteros to harvest the 208,000 acres of sugarcane grown by its farmers so that the mill could grind 10,000 tons of sugar daily; it also needed to supply the expansive Francisco Mill, which was built in 1901 near Guayabal, as well as the Céspedes and Elia mills in Camagüey and the Tuinicú in Las Villas.[151] Meanwhile, between 1911 and 1930 the United Fruit Company's Division Banes required 3,000 braceros delivered annually for its own cane fields attached to the Boston Mill. Between 1915 and 1919, its predominantly Haitian work force helped to produce approximately 2,269,000 sacks of sugar.[152] Further east, the Guantánamo Sugar Company was compelled to acquire more than a few ships to supply hundreds of black foreign workers for its mills—the Isabel, Los Canos, and Soledad—in order to take advantage of its properties, which totaled over 100,000 acres of sugarcane. The common wisdom was that if a company had its own fleet of passenger ships, the cost of competing with other companies for labor would be dramatically reduced.

Because the majority of black immigrants were eager to go to Cuba, they contributed to solving the sugar companies' problem of transporting and acquiring an oversupply of emigrants. Labor recruiters such as C. E. Burton did not have to encourage John Barry from the village of Lloyds in St. Thomas Parish, Jamaica, to venture to Cuba. Leaving under his own volition, he described his trip to Havana in 1916 as a simple affair. Barry recalled how at twenty-two years of age, "the [cost for] passage was about £3 pounds, a small amount of money . . . Get a passport . . . then after you got your passport, then you went to the shipping office, book your ticket, and sail on the boat."[153] Barry described the ship that took him to Havana as a very small vessel named the Frankenny. Three years later, the experience of some black workers emigrating from Jamaica to Cuba had not changed. Although there were several vessels that sailed to Cuba, in 1919 it cost only 50 shillings to travel by sailboat rather than steamship, according to a Mr. Burke of August Town in Kingston Parish. If you departed from Kingston harbor you went directly to Santiago de Cuba, he recalled. Before one could leave the island, "you had to get your passport. In those days [it cost] five shillings for a passport, and the Governor signed it at King's House, and then you went and had your photograph [taken], and you paid so much for your photograph, and you went and booked your passage, you were ready." It took Mr. Burke three days to sail to Cuba on a vessel that "held about over 50 [passengers]."[154] The experiences of John Barry and Mr. Burke suggest that, unlike the emigrants who embarked for Cuba as members of a work gang that the sugar companies recruited systematically and often illegally, individual laborers who departed alone and under their own volition usually paid for their transportation.

However, it appears that this was never the case for the majority of Haitian emigrants who entered Cuba during World War I, when the expansion of the sugar industry was critical to meeting the demands of the Allied nations. According to Felipe García, Pablo Pérez, and Francisco Hernández, Haitian macheteros employed at the Jatibonico *central* before 1920, the sugar companies always financed "the traffic in Haitians to Camagüey. . . They paid $100 for each worker."[155] The poor perception of the Haitian braceros held by many company administrators encouraged them to finance "the disguised slave trade." They believed that when compared to other black Caribbean field workers, the Haitians were superior macheteros but nothing more. The Haitians' ethnicity was the reason for this assessment of the sugar managers, as well as of some Cuban journalists. That the Haitian braceros were perceived as savages who lacked the skills that "the races of a superior civilization" possessed not only made them ideal macheteros, but natural-born ones.[156] As a result, in order to obtain a surplus of black Caribbean workers to cut, load, and haul cane among other materials, after 1912 the North American–owned sugar mills had to spend approximately $50,000 to $150,000 annually. Not only did they hire agents and sent them throughout the Caribbean, but they also placed advertisements in newspapers and nailed fliers to buildings and telegraph poles in every port city. One such notice read: "1000 workers are wanted by the Central 'Manatí'-Oriente to cut sugarcane, to plant and clean. Free round trip travel. We also need cart loaders."[157] Table 2 indicates that thousands of black Caribbean immigrants were interested in traveling and working in Cuba.

Once the black Caribbean braceros arrived in Cuba, their experiences hauntingly resembled those of their ancestors who had been enslaved more than a century earlier. And similar to that era, the historical record produced by the officials of the Cuban government and the sugar mills consisted of metaphorical and idiomatic expressions of the workers' inferiority. How these functionaries welcomed and treated the emigrants underscored the beginning of their degradation in Cuba. Landing in Havana, Nuevitas, Morón, Banes, Baracoa, and Santiago de Cuba, the black immigrants arrived carrying their few possessions in suitcases or bundles wrapped with string or rope. They also carried between five and ten dollars, which was more than enough to enter the island, according to the immigration laws. If they disembarked in Santiago de Cuba, Cuban officials directed them to the quarantine ground, where they stayed for two or three days in order to receive medical examinations to check "if you have any

TABLE 2. Selected Immigration Figures for 1912–1919

	1912	1913	1914	1915	1916	1917	1918	1919	Total
South America	89	83	54	38	0	93	160	60	577
British Antilles	21	27	7	0	0	0	0	0	55
Barbados	0	0	5	0	0	0	0	0	5
Costa Rica	0	1,010	0	0	520	629	251	0	2,410
United States	2,884	2,763	2,901	1,988	2,468	2,237	1,705	2,654	19,600
Haiti	172	1,422	120	2,416	4,829	9,730	10,860	10,136	39,685
Jamaica	1,269	2,716	1,792	1,649	6,005	5,866	7,317	23,754	50,368
Panama	213	147	100	0	666	1,609	1,100	136	3,971
Puerto Rico	523	943	738	1,091	1,576	975	629	1,031	7,506
Spain	30,660	32,140	17,764	23,183	36,286	33,757	13,378	32,157	219,325
China	0	0	0	0	0	0	7	1,100	1,107
Total	35,831	41,251	23,481	30,365	52,350	54,896	35,407	71,028	344,609

Source: *Census of the Republic of Cuba, 1919* (Havana, 1919), 183–84.

fever or any plague," according to the Jamaican named Fearon, who traveled to Cuba in 1915 at the age of nineteen.[158] Undoubtedly the government's concern with the health of the braceros had more to do with a potential health threat to Cuban society than an interest in the welfare of the braceros. The medical checkups also reinforced their alien status. Once the doctors had verified that the immigrants were healthy and without some kind of contagion, the workers were given a round of vaccinations. Then Cuban officials asked them a series of questions. After they had responded satisfactorily to the inquiries posed by customs and immigration agents, the braceros were admitted into the country. Some immigration officials in Havana noticed that "the labor agents have selected perfect specimens physically in order to ensure that their workers were permitted to enter the island."[159] This preoccupation with the physical attributes of the immigrants harks back to the buyers who attended the slave markets in the Caribbean during the eighteenth and nineteenth centuries. Beyond the vigilance of the port authorities, the brokers either began to recruit the recently arrived immigrants who had traveled alone and without a contract, or they reassembled the contingent of workers that they had accompanied from Barbados,

Curaçao, Jamaica, Haiti, Puerto Rico, Costa Rica, and Colón and Bocas del Toro, Panama. Separated into their respective cuadrillas by their agents, they were marched to the train station and ordered to enter the cars reserved for hauling sugarcane. Transporting the braceros in these dirty, musty rattletraps helped the mills reduce their expenses, while making clear to the workers, in no uncertain terms, that they had become commodities like the sugarcane they were assigned to cut, load, and haul. As they traveled into the sugar-growing regions of Camagüey and Oriente, they probably observed thousands of fallen trees that were once part of the vast forests of the countryside. If some had been contracted to cut cane on the Victoria colonia—a farm that supplied the Manatí central—they would have entered an area that consisted of 1,833 acres. In order to establish this farm, more than half of the region's trees had been felled and burned. By May 1913, 1,666 acres of the total 1,833 had been planted with sugarcane.[160]

Workers like John Barry, who arrived alone, boarded a train operated by the Cuban Central Railroad "that the cane cutters used to embark from Santiago de Cuba to the town of Banes."[161] A former Banes Division foreman of the Boston central vividly remembered the scene of the black Caribbean braceros entering the batey of that mill: "They came heaped inside of cane cars until reaching the final stop. Like many of them, they were collected and picked out on the side of the Calle Tráfico that was located in front of the [mill's] office. There they were organized and told to wear a number that each one received. Then the mayoral or administrator and the emigrant brokers forcefully divided them up, pushing and shoving the braceros causing some of them to fall. When order had been restored they were referred to as number so and so or nothing more than John Doe."[162] The dramatic chaos experienced by the workers suggests that it could have been staged, since what the foreman witnessed resembled the activities of a slave market. Then and during the 1910s, the braceros were treated in this fashion in order to distract and disorient them so the officials of the sugar mill could complete the transformative process associated with the recruitment of the workers as soon as they landed in Cuba. In a matter of moments, the newcomers had become things, not people, identified only by a number without a name. Lured to Cuba by the opportunity to earn better wages in exchange for cutting sugarcane, Haitian, Jamaican, and other British West Indian immigrants confronted living and working conditions that reinforced their marginalization and powerlessness.

2

THE SUBJUGATION OF THE BRACEROS

Life and Work on the Sugar Estates

In order to go cut cane they [Jamaicans] passed in groups in front of my bohío and even at a great distance one could still hear them yelling at one another in a language that we could not understand. They wore their filthy and sweaty clothes, their hemp-made sandals, and carried their knapsacks in their hands. Frightened, my mother closed and locked the doors until they had completely walked away and out of sight.[1]

This is how Ursinio Rojas, a Cuban labor activist, recalled the physical appearance of the black Caribbean braceros he had seen as a child, and his family's reaction to them. A sugarcane farmer added that they were "odd": They wore "any old tattered garment as an outside protection to their clothing; on their arms are tied all sorts of old cloth, odd halves of pants, and old stockings, which they laughingly call 'finger stockings,' the old name given to gloves by the long-ago Africans."[2]

What is clear from these accounts is that some Cuban denizens of the sugar enclaves had appropriated the ideology of domination that white Cubans and North Americans from the farms and the sugar mills had constructed. It appears that Cubans and North Americans alike had demonized the workers to a degree where their clothes, language, and skin color had transformed them into gangs of disfigured and terrifying monsters, the brood of enslaved Africans from a century earlier. The Caribbean workers' metamorphosis into the "other" was accelerated by the labor they performed. The institutions, traditions, and policies that constituted the sugar enclaves of the central and eastern provinces reinforced and articulated this perception of inferiority. What were the institutions and customs on the colonias and *centrales* of the enclaves that reinforced the braceros' subordinate status? How these structures and doctrines affected their daily lives will be explored in this chapter. Were they timeworn schemes used in the past to control and appropriate the labor of semi-industrial and agricultural workers, or were they fragments reconstituted after the sugar companies standardized the production and sites of their manufacturing? How did the large numbers of black immigrants affect the nature of the enclaves? What socioeconomic and cultural narratives did white Cubans and North Americans conceptualize to express black Caribbean inferiority? How important were they in institutionalizing the marginalization and exploitation of braceros in the sugar enclaves as well as in Cuban society in general? Finally, what role did violence play in substantiating the braceros' powerlessness?

I shall show that sugarcane farmers as well as the managers of the sugar companies employed cultural artifacts from the slave era and refurbished them to foster and reinforce the inferior position of the braceros. They also deliberately emphasized the black immigrants' race, ethnicity, and color to determine the type and nature of their housing, their occupations, and the level of their wages in an attempt to convince the workers that their circumstances were unalterable. More important, as tens of thousands of braceros were put to work by the farmers and mills as macheteros and carreteros, the native and North American elites crafted an ideology of domination that portrayed black Caribbean workers as threats to Cuban society, culture, and nationhood. Articulated by members of the middle and working classes, xenophobia and Cuban nationalism also became ideologies that established a hostile atmosphere for the braceros that only worsened their circumscribed status as immigrant workers.

———≈———

The practice of domination that the braceros confronted within what Barry Carr described as the "social territory" of the colonia-*central* complex, the site where "the colono, mill owners, factory supervisors, and field workers struggled to control space . . . and production," was intrinsic to the work regime of the macheteros and carreteros.[3] A typical workday for these braceros usually began between three and four in the morning. Depending upon the manager's wishes, some macheteros and other field workers were gathered and led to the mill's eating house or "fonda" to enjoy a breakfast of rice and beans or bread. For others less fortunate, before they left the barracks, a cup of sugar water or coffee was their daily morning meal. In addition, some colonos who operated a mill's company store provided their braceros with food taken from the store for free. But this gesture appeared to have been an exception rather than the rule.[4] When the workers had finished their breakfast, they gathered their machetes and hoes as they exited the batey and marched into the fields like soldiers ready to wage war against the cane under a hot, glaring sun.[5] In order to make sure that their gangs of macheteros were prepared to engage the thousands of acres of sugarcane, the colonos and foremen who looked after them checked the workers' tools. After making sure that all the machetes had been sharpened for the day's toil, the foremen separated the braceros into teams of four men. Walking into fields of sugarcane that stood ten feet high, the gangs of Jamaican and Haitian cutters and loaders who worked for the Cunagua *central*, near the town of Morón on the northern coast of Camagüey, confronted 925 caballerias, or 30,525 acres, of cane to cut. Meanwhile, the macheteros who left the barracks of the Chaparra *central* in Oriente, which was once managed by the president of Cuba, Mario Menocal (1913–20), looked in awe at 75,900 acres of uncut sugarcane.[6] Often planted up to the very edges of the batey, sugarcane appeared everywhere, "on the roads, its smell filled the air, the hair from its surface penetrated the skin of the workers . . . men who work in the cane fields speak of doing battle with it."[7] And like soldiers, the braceros' every gesture was scripted by either the farmers or the overseers.

Once in the fields, the strongest Haitian and Jamaican men formed the gangs of macheteros. The less-capable workers helped to clear the paths and roads that the oxen-drawn carts utilized to haul the cane. Each machetero proceeded to cut the cane stalks as close to the topsoil as possible. The workers' contracts required that the macheteros pull off the leaves from the stalks, then cut the stalks at the joints into three pieces, each no less than three feet long. The Jamaican John Barry vividly remembered fifty years later how, as a novice machetero, he was instructed in how to cut the cane: "You cut the joint in the center here and you cut the joint of the center there, and . . . save the joint." Then the tops of the stalks were rounded off so they could be gathered and bundled safely.[8] Because the workers were paid by the weight of the cane they cut, and because the managers feared that bottlenecks would form between the fields and the factories, the tempo of work was regimented and incessant. After becoming skilled in their craft, the braceros accepted the intensity of field work, knowing that they had only approximately one hundred and fifty days to make as much money as possible.

In order to maximize the efficiency of the black Caribbean laborers, the cane farmers and the companies demanded that the field workers also load their cuttings onto wagons so they could be picked up by the carreteros.[9] This task seemed insurmountable, given the size of the fields. Yet this job had to be completed before the workers could receive their pay. Knowing that none of them would be paid without delivering the cane to the mill, each gang member assisted other field workers charged with the specific chore of loading the cane. Loading the wagons was considered painstaking and skilled work. Some sugar industry experts acknowledged that even this job in the cane fields required trained men. If a crew of cutters included expert loaders, they could load ten to twelve tons of cane per man per day. If they were inexperienced, a company's manager expected only eight to ten tons of cane from a gang of cutters. The wagon driver hauled the cane back to the batey of the mill, where it was weighed on an elaborate set of scales. It was then that the cane cutters sensed how much cane they had produced for that day, and the wages that they would receive.[10]

Cutting, loading, and hauling cane made for an exhaustingly long day for all of the field workers because the farmers and sugar companies squeezed as much labor from them as possible. One Jamaican carretero named Fearon, who worked for the Ermita central near Guantánamo, remembered that it was not unusual for ten to twelve macheteros to load his oxen-drawn cart three to four times a day during the harvest. He delivered the first load at 2:00 p.m. and the last one after 8:00 p.m. Everyone "worked like an animal . . . The men know that you will load them up here and will come back, so they wait out in the fields, and stay there with their lanterns lit and cut cane until you came back and loaded your cart again," recalled Fearon.[11] The majority of mill owners calculated that a good industrial cane worker could cut between three and one-half to four and one-half tons per day of mature, healthy sugarcane.

In addition to cutting cane, Jamaican and Haitian braceros performed other faenas, or chores, keeping the roads, paths, and bridges clear and in good shape so that the carts used to retrieve the cane from the fields could move smoothly in sequence according to the grinding schedule of the factories. Such work became very dangerous for the workers. Mr. Burke from August Town, Jamaica, stated that "you had to work in plenty of rain, and water. In some places the water was bad, a lot of swamp. Fever, malarial fever, the whole country was susceptible to malaria fever because it was a swampy place. Plenty of men lost their lives there."[12] Other workers were responsible for overhauling and maintaining the wagons to ensure that they were kept in working order.

As the grinding season came to an end in June and July, the braceros were assigned to work as ditchers and seeders, particularly when the sugar mills were expanding their hinterlands by establishing new farms. Having to create new *formentos*, or fields, required time as well as a large number of men. The forest had to be cleared and the trees burned before any new planting began. This entailed sending several teams of macheteros out to strip the trees of their vines and reeds so that the trunks were exposed. Afterwards, the great and ancient trees such as mahogany, cedar, and ebony were felled. A month later, all the cut trees were burned along with the undergrowth.[13] The labor power involved in expanding a mill's hinterland was never ethnically differentiated. The process was a dangerous one for the braceros. Teresa Casuso remembers helping her father attend to numerous workers hurt while creating new formentos. Casting the immigrant workers in the role of soldiers, Casuso recounted how when she was a child in the forests of Oriente, "Haitians and Jamaicans would come to us with terrible machete wounds inflicted as they fought to open breaches in the forests. Father would dress the wounds while I handed him the materials . . . the mountains burned to make way for sugarcane, and the beat of the bongos came to us from the immigrants' shacks."[14] Using the same planting methods that African slaves had employed in Cuba since the 1860s, field workers from Jamaica and Haiti used a hoe to create a hole in the dirt. They pushed the hoe down several times while making a circular motion to widen it. They then dropped two to four seedlings into the hole. They cut the tops off the ratoons with their machetes, then covered them with topsoil. Different individuals performed these specific tasks. Work gangs were made up of hole-makers, planters, choppers, and coverers. This planting system, described as "back-breaking work," had become popular as early as 1864 with the publication of Alvaro Reynoso's *Ensayo sobre el cultivo de la caña de azúcar*. Hoe men and seeders received comparatively better wages than cane cutters. In Oriente Province, some earned as much as four and five dollars per day.[15] Undoubtedly, the war in Europe as well as the demand for Cuban sugar contributed to increasing the wages of these braceros.

Nonetheless, the drudgery that became the braceros' lot during and at the end of the zafras has caused some writers to conclude that the status of the black

Caribbean workers resembled that of the former black slaves during the late nineteenth century. "For the miserable salaries, the machetero continued working ten, twelve, and fourteen hours daily, the same amount of time during the colonial era. That is to say, the conditions and life of the machetero had not fundamentally changed since the abolition of slavery . . . The only advantage, however, which this sector of the working class enjoyed because of the resumption of their relationship with the capitalist class, was the fact that they could sell their labor on the open market."[16]

Between 1912 and 1917, agricultural field laborers earned from seventy-five cents to five dollars per one hundred arrobas, or one and one-quarter tons, of cane cut.[17] The geographical expansion of the industry, the increase in subsequent production levels, and the relatively high price of sugar, which is detailed in table 3, that the war in Europe prompted after 1914, help to explain the increase in wages for cane cutters. Competition for agricultural workers among the sugar companies also caused wages to grow slightly. In short, despite offering what the industry described as "reasonable" wages to field workers, the companies could never resolve the problem that sugarcane increasingly grew at a much faster pace than did the supply of native workers or the desirable surplus of Haitians and Jamaicans. As a result, the companies tended to complain annually of a chronic labor shortage. Their dependence on an oversupply of cheap workers also explains why the braceros performed multiple jobs for the companies during and after the harvest season. In addition, in order to recruit enough workers, the majority of mills had to react to the slight wage increases given to field workers by their competitors.[18]

The immigrant workers also benefited from internecine strife among Cuban political elites when, in February 1917, members of the Liberal Party led by former president José Miguel Gómez rebelled against the government of Mario Menocal. The Liberals claimed that Menocal and his Conservative Party had used fraud and corruption to steal the election of 1916. Much of the Liberals' protest occurred in Camagüey and Oriente. The Chambelona Rebellion's impact on the sugar industry resembled that of the Race War of 1912, disrupting the flow of labor into the sugar enclaves. In doing so, it exacerbated the chronic shortage of migrant laborers and encouraged a number of mills to suspend operations. This state of affairs in turn discouraged Jamaican workers from traveling to Cuba. Writing to Walter H. Long, Secretary of State for the British Colonies, the governor of Jamaica, W. H. Manning, reported that although there had been

TABLE 3. Average Annual Price per Pound of Centrifugal Cuban Sugar
Sold in New York, 1912–1921

1912	2.5 cents
1913	4.2 cents
1914	3.7 cents
1915	4.2 cents
1916	4.3 cents
1917	4.8 cents
1918	4.3 cents
1919	9.0 cents
1920	15.0 cents*
1921	4.5 cents

Source: Louisiana Planter and Sugar Manufacturer 48, no. 3 (20 January 1912): 41, through 66, no. 6 (5 February 1921): 90.

*In October 1920, sugar sold for 22.5 cents per pound. See Louisiana Planter and Sugar Manufacturer 65, no. 16 (16 October 1920): 1.

"considerable emigration to Cuba [it] has only recently diminished owing to the revolution in that island."[19] Some black immigrant workers, however, reacted to the political violence of 1917 by moving from one mill to another in search of factories unaffected by the rebellion. The Liberal uprising allowed the braceros to negotiate for better wages. The manager of the Florida central located outside Camagüey told reporters that the political situation made it "impossible to keep the crew of workmen on a job for a few days at a time; just long enough for the men to earn a few dollars so they can live for the next few days with nothing to do but join in the animated discussions that Cubans are noted for, about the revolution." He continued: "The cane cutters are being paid as high as seven dollars a day to cut cane, and some women are now working in the fields."[20] After the revolution fizzled out in the fall of 1917, mill owners believed that they faced a severe shortage of laborers. Because the industry's experts believed that 50,000 black Caribbean workers were required for the harvest of 1918, most companies paid their imported work force wages at double the 1916 rate. The cane cutters were offered anywhere from $1.20 to $1.40 per hundred arrobas. Some sugar mills, such as the Senado central owned by Bernabe Sánchez Aballi, still could

73

not obtain enough macheteros before the start of the 1918 zafra.[21] The owners of the Manatí allocated $50,000 to recruit and contract alien workers for their colonias, while petitioning the Menocal government to grant them the right to import one thousand Jamaicans and Haitians. They hoped that the arrival of these workers would create a larger surplus of laborers and thus reduce their labor costs. The government approved their request in March 1918.[22]

By 1918, the laws governing the recruitment and employment of Haitian and Jamaican braceros had been revised by the Menocal government. In August 1917, President Menocal authorized his Secretary of Agriculture, Commerce, and Labor, Leopoldo Cancio, to change the immigration laws of 1902 and 1910. The new law, which became effective on 7 August 1917, gave the sugar companies the right to supervise the immigration of braceros for up to two years following the end of World War I, or until 1921, as long as the "braceros do not become public charges of the state, and threaten the hygiene of the nation."[23] Composed of five articles, the law of 1917 stipulated the terms that both the immigrants and the mill owners had to obey. To control the supply of braceros, it required that all black immigrants be identified and registered by the Department of Immigration before entering the country. In addition, to gain entry into the country the foreign workers had to show proof of being contracted to perform either agricultural or industrial work. During their sojourn in Cuba, all immigrant workers had to abide by the laws of the island. Any immigrant who committed a crime faced expulsion and repatriation to his home country or prosecution and sentencing by a Cuban court of law.[24] In a requirement reminiscent of the Código Negro—the Spanish American slave code of the colonial era—which compelled the plantocracy to care for their bondsmen and women, sugar companies were required to pay the entire cost of transporting the braceros to and from Cuba. They were also required to provide medical assistance and to ensure that conditions in the workplace and inside the workers' housing were sanitary. Any worker who suffered an injury and became incapacitated had to be immediately repatriated by the sugar company, since the unemployed worker would ultimately become a charge of the state.[25] Article 5 of the law allowed the braceros' wives and children to join them if they decided to reside permanently in Cuba. However, these wives and daughters had to immediately find work in a number of traditional "occupations reserved for women," such as hairdressers, librarians, and secretaries, or as sales clerks in a store—occupations usually readily available on the bateyes. Others, however, had to locate work in the towns and villages surrounding the sugar mills. Any infraction of these terms would result in a fine of one to as much as thirty pesos, whether the infraction was committed by an immigrant worker, a mill owner, or an administrator.[26]

The Immigration Law of 1917 had dire consequences for the braceros because it gave the labor recruiters even greater power than before. Enlisting gangs or detachments of workers under the *enganchamiento* labor system, these men were referred to as modern "slave traffickers." All the sugar companies hired these middlemen. The Cuban, Haitian, and Jamaican governments acknowledged their role in providing the sugar companies with much-needed labor, and they accepted the abusive and exploitative relationship that the "traffickers" established with the workers. It is not surprising, then, that the majority of labor agents enriched themselves, receiving a commission from a colono or company for every worker they delivered. As I discussed in the last chapter, Haitian labor brokers also charged contracted workers as much as $500 under the pretext that only they could find work for the immigrants in Cuba.[27]

The macheteros who entered into such an arrangement were unmercifully exploited. For example, workers who earned $1.20 for each 100 arrobas, and who were expected to cut between three and one-half to four and one-half tons of cane per day and thereby earn between $3.36 and $4.32 daily, would have to labor over 125 days out of the approximately 150 that the zafra entailed simply to repay the broker. This was just one form of abuse that black Caribbean workers faced after their arrival. The isolated agrarian landscapes around the sugar enclaves where the workers resided fostered their subjugation and exploitation as well. Becoming what James Kunstler has called "nowhere spaces," these enclaves were "designed and regulated to fit the needs of capitalist accumulation and . . . to optimize control over labor, goods or consumers."[28] Central to fulfilling these objectives were two artifacts of the slave era that were modernized at the turn of the twentieth century—the batey and the barracón.

Barry Carr has described the bateyes in Camagüey and Oriente as "the central yard[s]" where the sugar factories were located. These sites "incorporated the buildings involved in the processing of sugarcane, administrative offices, sugar laboratories, foundries, carpentry and machine shops," as well as other ancillary offices and shops. He believes the bateyes acted like small cities that offered their inhabitants the goods and services typical of an urban center.[29] But the bateyes were also where the colonos, mill owners, and their cohorts exercised their domination over the black Caribbean workers. In order to understand how these spatial settings were manufactured for this purpose, a more detailed portrait is required.

Batey, in the language of Cuba's indigenous people, referred to a simple, clean place, a commons where people met to hold social, political, and cultural activities. The Spanish conquistadors incorporated the term into their vocabulary and employed it in reference to the center of a town or the middle point of a hacienda.[30] During the period of African slavery, the batey became the central plaza of the sugar plantation and was surrounded by casas viviendas (the owner's, managers', and staff's homes), bohíos (thatch-roofed peasant homes), and barracones (slave barracks or quarters). Other structures housed free laborers, such as the mayoral, or overseer, and the slave drivers. Finally, the machine shop, the infirmary, and the mill itself surrounded and enclosed the batey. The batey was where the slaves were collected in the morning and commanded into the fields. The plantation owners also employed this space to demonstrate their total power, using it for the public punishment of slaves.[31] At the same time, the slaves were permitted to employ the batey for social functions. They used it to celebrate the births of their children, mourn the death of loved ones, and meet with each other to sing and dance.[32]

The organization of the plantations and bateyes changed after the abolition of slavery and the advent of wage labor. A degree of uniformity was established among plantations in Cuba as well as on other Caribbean islands.[33] They became part of more regimented enclaves where the owners, managers, and later company officials could closely supervise and thereby control the spaces and behavior of their work force. An "international style" of plantation enclave emerged at the turn of the twentieth century when a host of multinational corporations became the primary producers of sugar worldwide, according to Samuel Martínez.[34] For example, the majority of sugar companies used the batey as the principal site where they recruited and hired seasonal and day laborers. The tenure of their workers encouraged owners of the central factories to establish commercial businesses that catered to the needs of their employees. La tienda mixta, or the company store, became one of the most important means to control and retain sugarcane workers. The store often sold such necessities as food, clothes, soap, and medicines at prices often well beyond what they cost outside the plantations. Luxury items like rum, beer, and jewelry, as well as playing cards and dominoes, were also available at prohibitive prices. For example, the company store situated on the Victoria colonia, which was part of the Manatí central's properties, sold tasajo (jerked beef), Jamaican rum, shoes, hats, and clothing. During the zafra, the store reportedly sold between $200 and $400 worth of merchandise per day. Many workers also went to the company store (sometimes referred to as the bodega) to supplement their daily food rations or whenever they simply wanted to eat "a little more rice and beans that cost them a few centavos . . . [But] they often did this only during the zafra when they could pay their bills in full."[35] If their wages were inadequate, or when they were completely without funds, many workers purchased what they needed on credit. It is interesting to note that on a noticeable number of bateyes, it was common for the labor brokers to operate the mills' company stores. In addition, the braceros had to deal with numerous loan sharks who worked with the shopkeepers to cheat the workers out of their savings and wages. These moneylenders positioned themselves in front of the stores and waited for their victims—workers who were unable to pay for food and other items they needed from the stores. Presenting themselves as sympathetic patrons, the moneylenders made cash readily available to workers. They also issued scrip printed by the companies that was redeemable only at their stores. But the mechanism that forced many workers to roll over their debt every month was the usurious interest rates imposed by the stores as well as by their duplicitous moneylenders. For example, in order to loan small sums of money, the loan sharks charged 20–30 percent interest.[36]

Orestes Ferrera, the Cuban ambassador to the United States, defended the operations of these usurious company stores. Because cane cutting and cane cultivation were precarious endeavors, he insisted, the stores allowed workers and farmers the opportunity to buy the necessities of life without using cash. When this happened, the establishments extended them credit and advanced them the barest essentials for their existence against the workers' wages or, if they were colonos, against their next crop. Ferrera claimed that "no store owner outside of the bateyes or in the nearest towns would ever agree to do such a thing. In fact, the company stores are not run at a profit but try to sell their customers goods at cost. They generally succeed and usually are operated at a loss."[37] If Ferrera's observations about the role that the company stores played in the lives of the sugar workers were accurate, then the managers of the mill factories would not have had to use their own security guards or the rural guards to "closely follow peddlers, who against the orders of the administrator, boldly trespassed on to the property of the batey in order to sell their trinkets, novelties, and foods and meats, a business here on the central that was a monopoly of the company store."[38] Administrators would not have banned these traveling salesmen if their bodegas had not been profitable, as well as having become institutions that helped the companies fleece their workers of the little income they earned. Once the wage workers fell into debt, they were compelled to labor in the cane fields to settle their accounts. If this strategy did not work in controlling the work forces, then the company store simply cheated workers. One carretero remembered how in 1912 the clerk of the company store on the Cuban-owned Mercedita *central* altered the entries of the notebook in which the name of every worker who carried a debt was written. Understanding that some braceros could not read or write, most clerks simply altered and increased the amount owed to the store.[39] As a result, indebtedness supplemented coercion as a form of control.

Clerks in the company stores also exploited the inability of some Caribbean workers to speak Spanish. As a thirty-eight-year-old immigrant from St. Elizabeth Parish, Jamaica, Benjamin T. arrived in Cuba in 1918 to cut cane, knowing only enough Spanish "to buy me bread."[40] The Jamaican Robert Palmer initially had to use sign language in order to communicate with a Cuban shopkeeper if he wanted to buy something: "You see something in the Cuban's hand that you want, he makes a sign and if say it costs $2.00 he will show you a $2.00 [bill], and you hand it to him, and he gives you change."[41] In addition, the mills had the opportunity to take advantage of their braceros whenever the administrators lacked Cuban pesos or U.S. dollars to pay them. In this instance, they often minted their own currency, or vales, which were in essence IOUs, tokens, or coupons. The vales were only redeemable at the company stores. They became another instrument to enhance the general powers of the mill owners as they sought to control and appropriate the labor of their workers. The vales became so popular among mill owners that after Cuban workers and Spanish immigrants complained about being paid with this counterfeit money, the government in 1902 passed the Ley Arteaga, which banned owners from using them. Introduced by Emilio Arteaga Quesada, a Liberal senator from Camagüey Province, the law was primarily directed at North American and European mill owners.[42] Nevertheless, most mill owners ignored the prohibition and continued to pay their workers with vales, particularly after the collapse of the price of sugar in the autumn of 1920. Before and after the period known as the Vacas Gordas, or "Fat Cows" (1916–20), the existence of the company store reflected the decision among the sugar companies to retain their field laborers with more than just piece-rate wages. Supplementing or substituting their low wages with scrip or credit allowed the mills to use a degree of compulsion whenever a bracero went into debt. In brief, the worker was required to repay the loan with his labor before being allowed to leave and return home. In addition, paying workers with scrip or coupons kept them in the fields until the mills had enough capital to pay them with real money wages.[43]

The company stores were not the only edifices that shaped the landscape of the bateyes and reinforced the subordinate status of the braceros. Designed in the nineteenth century to house plantation slaves, barracones were constructed along the lines of a jail or prison. As pointed out by the former slave Esteban Montejo, the purpose of the barracón, during and after the slave era, was to collect the manual work force under one roof in order to scrutinize and control it. The front of the barracón became the site where the overseer counted the members of the work gang as they went to work in the morning and returned at night. These barracks were often constructed as close to the mill factory and as far from the owner's mansion as possible. Unlike the senzalas or slave quarters of Brazil, access to a Cuban barracón was through a single outside door. The barracón had no windows, and the sole entrance ensured that the slaves would not escape unnoticed. In the middle of this four-walled structure was an open-air patio. A series of doors that ran along the walls of the patio marked a collection of rooms where the workers lived and slept.[44] The barracón also contained a common kitchen area and a bathroom, a room designated simply by a pit latrine dug into the dirt floor.[45] By 1910, the mill owners in Cuba and elsewhere had slightly altered the architectural style of the barracón. Now a large rectangular building, the size of which was determined by the number of workers set aside for a particular colonia, these common dormitories often consisted of fifteen rooms, each of which was shared by five or more braceros. In order to provide the workers with a sense of freedom, the doors of all of the rooms were now positioned on the outside of the building.[46] The conditions inside the barracones were critical for the physical and psychological well-being of the workers. Leaving their homes and families to work in Cuba, these workers were promised that their living quarters would be clean and hospitable, in order to reduce the physical and mental stress of cutting cane for as long as sixteen hours a day. Nonetheless, the challenge of providing adequate housing for the workers became a controversial issue for managers of some of the mills.

As long as the sugar industry required black immigrant laborers, the issue of providing adequate housing for the cane cutters and all the other mill workers remained a priority. In order to compete with other companies for black workers, one mill operator insisted that his employer help him solve his farmers' housing problem. Asking for funds to construct more living quarters for the company's field workers at the height of the industry's prosperity created by World War I, the manager of the Manatí made it clear to the directors of Cuba Cane in New York that "[W]e already have . . . a number of employees and laborers who are living under very bad conditions on account of our not having buildings where to lodge them."[47] Understanding that the physical well-being of the field workers was essential for a successful harvest, he proposed increasing the mill's housing budget in order to construct better lodgings to accommodate the growing field work force, as well as the wives and children of the mill workers and administrative staff. At the start of the harvest of 1919, Gerard Smith, manager of the Francisco central in Camagüey, complained to Manuel Rionda, who was then residing at the Tuinicú central in Las Villas, that the company's colonos were providing poor housing for the cane cutters. The condition of the barracones was so awful, he concluded, even the Chinese government officials in charge of recruiting Chinese emigrants for the company would never agree to bring and lodge them in such dreadful barracks.[48] Estimating that it would cost only thirty dollars per man "to build the required number of buildings, and to provide proper barracks," Smith advised Rionda "that the company needs to make sacrifices in order to better the labor conditions which now are becoming almost unbearable."[49] Because of the internationalization of the sugar enclave, a process that encouraged multinational sugar producers to adopt similar architectural designs for all buildings located on their bateyes, the intolerable living conditions that black macheteros and carreteros endured on the Francisco likely resembled those experienced by some Haitian braceros working at the Esperanza central in the province of Guantánamo. According to Bernarda Sevillano Andrés's Cuban-Haitian informants, of the two barracks located in the batey's exclusively Haitian barrio of Pueblo Nuevo, only one "had three latrines for all of the blacks." The workers who lived in the other barracks had to use the nearby Río La Bomba as a latrine and place to bathe. In addition, they described the rooms in both barracks as being very small but in each "there lived four or five Haitians."[50]

The conditions in these North American–built barracks explain why so many braceros returned home in poor health at the end of the zafra. While working for the Preston *central*, a Jamaican bracero, S. O. Gayle, revealed that the workers' living quarters were intolerable. He believed that the mill's barracones caused "diseases among the laborers, sometimes consumption, sometimes fevers, and [as a result] deaths take place regularly."[51] A former manual laborer at the Algodones *central* remembered "the poor, the workers, those who produced everything lived in humble homes or in the inhumane barracks."[52] Even a foreman of the Boston *central* noted the miserable housing for Haitian macheteros: "[T]his was no life, having only a few barracones for thousands of Haitians, heaped together like pigs in a corral. Many became very sick and later died."[53] A former machetero from the Brasil also recounted the overcrowded conditions of the workers who lived in the barracks on its batey and the effects on their health. Agricultural laborers were housed in the usual barracks that consisted of one door, a living room, a dining room, a bathroom, and one kitchen. Their sleeping quarters had just enough space for either two beds or two hammocks. These barracks never had electricity. "It did not matter how many workers shared these rooms," he recalled. "The sanitation was dreadful . . . they were always neglected by the administrator of the central, and for this reason, the shining hygiene of the batey was absent there."[54]

By failing to make the construction of salubrious domiciles a priority, the companies placed the lives of the braceros in jeopardy. The unsanitary conditions inside the barracks on the Jaguelles colonia, attached to the Santa Lucia *central* in Gibara, Oriente, led to an outbreak of influenza in 1918, according to Juan Martín Nieves, a bracero from Puerto Rico. As the epidemic spread from one barracón to another, it killed a lot of people not only on the batey but also in Santiago de Cuba and elsewhere. By the time the company realized that it had a lethal virus on its property and began to evacuate workers from the barracones so they could be attended to at the mill's hospital, Nieves reported that he had lost sixty pounds. In addition, between 1915 and 1917, hundreds of workers living in the barracks on the batey of the Teresa *central* in Cruces, Santa Clara, suffered from a series of outbreaks of dengue fever. The unavailability of medical attention caused many to die.[55]

Meanwhile, "as the batey grew and as more workers were recruited by the central, more workers' housing went up and [was] usually made flimsily of wood, zinc, and guano," according to the same field worker who lived on the batey of the Brasil *central*.[56] *Guano* here referred to the palm tree leaves used to construct the thatched roofs of the braceros' homes. Some companies took the recommendations of their managers seriously and began to build better housing. The directors of Cuba Cane, for example, eventually consented to build improved living quarters for its black work force, but they had ulterior motives. Although thousands of Haitians and Jamaican braceros had contracted malaria during the mid-1910s while cutting cane and clearing the forests of Camagüey and Oriente to expand the sugar hinterland, the officials of Cuba Cane believed that by improving the quality of the barracones they would discourage their workers from organizing some type of labor protest. If they did not solve this problem, they envisioned that "the men [will] have nothing to do and no other topic [except this] to discuss. They [will] naturally talk about their imaginary grievances and create discontent."[57] That the directors of Cuba Cane linked the possibility of worker activism and protest to the poor quality of the workers' housing shows how management knew that the degradation that accompanied the process to "standardize not only the product [of sugar] but also the space of production itself," would lead inevitably to the workers' defiance.[58] Yet they chose not to improve conditions; manual laborers were considered as no more than assets to be exploited to the maximum. Although black Antillian braceros were viewed as cheap labor and "undesirable immigrants," the Cuba Cane Company as well as other companies nonetheless knew that since 1912 the industry as a whole had enjoyed a steady stream of these workers. Between 1912 and 1919, 39,685 Haitians and 50,368 Jamaicans officially entered Cuba to help the sugar companies meet the demand for Cuban sugar abroad as well as increase their production capacities.[59]

The socioracial and ethnic hierarchy rooted in the colonia-*central* complex that marginalized these workers was reinforced by the privileged treatment and status accorded to white Cubans and North Americans on the bateyes. With large investments of capital, North American, Cuban, and European sugar companies modernized the bateyes by transforming them into isolated and self-contained villages or towns.[60] Surrounded by parks and gardens, and consisting of contemporary homes and bungalows for the managerial staff and their assistants, these enclaves sought to create a quasi-colonial ruling-class culture.[61] For example, the batey of the Victoria colonia attached to the estate of the Manatí *central* reinforced the impression of white privilege and power through amenities reserved only for them, including comfortable homes for the owners and their staff, a number of reserved wells from which they retrieved potable water, pump tanks, and forty-two separate family dwellings for white workers predominantly from Spain and the Canary Islands. The batey also contained a company store that held $40,000 worth of general merchandise, a cafeteria with intermediate and first-class dining rooms, and a railroad station where the sugarcane arrived from the fields to be weighed on cane scales.[62] Whiteness was also privileged in the neatly built homes and living quarters that surrounded the batey at the Concepción central. "There is a well-organized hospital for taking care of the sick. [But] there is only a 'crèche' or nursery where old women take care of the piccannanies of such mothers as work in the fields. A lovely garden is also laid out in a tasteful manner with orange groves and fragrant walks," observed Robert T. Hill.[63] In 1921, the Compania Azucarera Cubana, a subsidiary of the American Sugar Refinery Company, broke up the Brasil, allowing it to be absorbed by the Jaronú and Cunagua centrales, both located on the northern coast of Camagüey near the municipality of Esmeralda in the barrio of Jaronú. During World War I, the company ensured that the top administrators of the mill lived in single-family homes made of wood. Its middle- and lower-ranking white officials meanwhile inhabited multifamily accommodations with living rooms, two bedrooms, dining rooms, kitchens, and single bathrooms. The manager's abode had all the modern amenities, such as electricity and running potable water. The dwellings for the rest of the workers, particularly the field hands, lacked any of these conveniences.[64] The Brasil was not the only mill that provided its top-ranking administrators with living quarters superior to those of other workers on the batey. For their counterparts who managed the Algodones central, the top administrators "and their families lived in houses in whatever style they so desired with servants, luxuries, and anything else they wanted."[65] Even the garbage was collected for those who ran and operated the sugar factories.[66]

U.S. imperialism assisted in demonstrating white superiority with structures of modernity. Some bateyes consisted of more than a hundred structures. The majority of the North American–owned mills had their own independent electrical power plants that illuminated the streets and homes of the administrators of the mills, as well as the cane fields. The United Fruit Company noted that it spent over $1 million on constructing and maintaining its parks and streets as well as on supplying clean water to all its farms and centers of population. In fact, it proudly revealed that "all dwellings in the populated areas have running water and sanitary installations."[67] Reporting for the Cuban journal El Imparcial, J. H. Dodd, an industry expert, concluded that "today [the bateyes] of the Cuban sugar factories are real towns but with one advantage that most of the towns in the most civilized countries do not possess. They are all by necessity railroad stations that generally have their own [private] tracks, locomotives, and cars."[68] By concluding that the majority of bateyes or towns located on the same grounds as the sugar mills had become more advanced sites of modernity than the majority of towns in Cuba as well as in the most civilized countries of the world, Dodd was exalting not only the sugar mill complex's economic contribution to the island's development but its white cultural endowment. The sugar factory towns that emerged out of the virgin forests of the central and eastern provinces and that were connected to the North Atlantic community of nations by an elaborate and extensive system of rail networks and seaports had placed the island's population, primarily white Cubans and North Americans, among the most superior and modern of the world.

It is important to note that because of the important role played by railroads in the sugar industry, railroad workers displayed a great deal of agency, becoming the vanguard that sought to empower all sugarcane workers, including the Caribbean agricultural workers from Jamaica, Haiti, and elsewhere. In the meantime, race and ethnicity also became dynamic factors that informed both social and labor-management relations in the bateyes, producing a system that Philippe Bourgois calls "conjugated oppression."[69] From the turn of the twentieth century, multinational companies operating in the "plantation region" of the Caribbean constructed ideologies that either defined or manipulated race and ethnicity, states Bourgois. They did so hoping to control and exploit the ethnically diverse work force that was a result of a steady stream of immigration. The companies manufactured an unequal power relationship in the plantation production process with "dual hierarchies, one occupational and the other ethnic." Although the companies effectively could have used the class system that would have positioned immigrant workers at the bottom of society to control and exploit them, the multiethnic composition of the labor supply encouraged the companies to converge both systems of strata along with class, making them reinforce one another, according to Bourgois. In Cuba, black Caribbean workers experienced this "conjugated oppression" when the companies reserved some occupations and jobs for members of a specific ethnicity. The workers' own immigrant status or class buttressed this sort of "occupational apartheid" or ethnic discrimination.[70] Of course there were exceptions, but together they undergirded the companies' division-of-labor paradigm while allowing the sugar mills to dictate and prescribe the workers' social lives. The social arrangements on the bateyes illustrate how the companies' "conjugated oppression" created black Caribbean subordination.

A former black Cuban cane cutter who lived on the batey of the Brasil central during the era of prosperity stimulated by World War I recounted how "the families of the batey were divided into various racial and ethnic groups and classes. First, there existed the division between whites and blacks. There was a social club for whites, and another club for blacks. Whites held the best jobs and enjoyed special rights than the blacks."[71] The sugar companies also reserved certain occupations for white employees. Whites from the United States, Spain, and Cuba itself dominated all the office jobs. For example, the head of the Commerce Department of the Brasil—the Jaronú central as it was later renamed in the 1920s—was always white. Undoubtedly, the ethnic division of labor that was common on the sugar estates reflected popular notions surrounding the level of black intelligence and learning. The same psychological value system also determined which ethnic groups would occupy the skilled and unskilled positions at the centrales.

The racial attitudes that supported occupational segregation also informed social arrangements in the enclaves. In order to naturalize the degradation of the black foreign work force, the social institutions of the bateyes were designed to underline the racial, ethnic, and class hierarchies constructed by whites. In 1917, the Cuban Sugar Company, which owned the Algodones central, built a private school for the children of its white North American, Cuban, and Spanish workers. But the children of black Antillean and Cuban laborers had to attend very small public schools called escuelitas publicas. Although it was uncommon for a government to assist in remedying the plight of plantation workers in the Caribbean, these schools, located just off the property of the mill, were never funded by the company but financed with "the embezzled funds stolen by the local political bosses who openly stuffed their pockets with thousands of dollars critical for the education of the Cuban people," according to the former black Cuban machetero of the Brasil.[72]

The fact that local politicians misused public funds reserved for the education of black and white Cuban children shows how some municipal government officials sought to ingratiate themselves with the companies. They knew that they would be rewarded for their illicit cooperation with the mills by subsidizing the cost of building schools for their workers' children. The economic and political power that these mills wielded within their geographical spheres of influence meant that the local political elites could share in the revenue that the companies generated after they had incorporated a municipality. For example, the town of Banes, located on the northern coast of Oriente Province, emerged from the batey on which the United Fruit Company had constructed the Boston central. By 1915, Banes, now positioned some fifteen miles from the Boston, consisted of a number of distinct commercial as well as residential districts. A worker's ethnicity determined which neighborhood he lived in. On one side of town, U.S.-born workers occupied the barrio americano. It resembled an American borough with not only the offices of the United Fruit Company located there but also a host of North American–styled bungalows, paved streets, and recreational green space, such as parks, gardens, and even a golf course that its white North American and Cuban administrators and office workers enjoyed. The existence of a North American town in Cuba was striking to traveler Erna Fergusson. About Banes, she wrote: the "Company town is like any garden village at home with flower and vegetable beds, a lawn, clotheslines, and a driveway. In Banes there is a palm in every lawn, hibiscus and butterfly bushes, and rampant bougainvillea, royal purple or candent red, hanging heavily on fences. Young people were coming home from tennis or swimming, older people from golf, pianos sounded from the houses and chatting from the screened porches. This is the way salaried folk live."[73] The United Fruit Company even separated the members of its white work force along ethnic lines; the Banes River physically cut off the white Cubans from the North Americans. The Cuban residential district of Banes remained distinctly Cuban, according to Fergusson:

> Cuban town is still pleasantly colonial except where the company influence has led to a few separate houses with lawns. The company has invested $47,000 in a sewer, put up a slaughterhouse, provided a playground, and given material aid to the Friends School. But Cuban Banes is still Cuban. In the evening people were sitting in their long windows with iron grilles. Beyond were lighted rooms with tiled floors, tidies on pianos and tables, artificial flowers in tall vases, and painted or plaster saints on the walls. Children ran and shouted, girls giggled in groups, pairs strolled and spoke low.[74]

Meanwhile, on the other side of Banes—literally across the railroad tracks that the company's foremen used to direct the deliveries of sugarcane to the mill—were situated the ethnic barrios: *jamaiquino, haitiano, chino,* and *europeo.* These neighborhoods, which were reminiscent of the ethnic and immigrant slums that appeared in most of the major cities of industrialized countries, contained hundreds of foreign contracted workers and their families.[75] The value that the company's North American administrators placed on the labor and culture of their Jamaican and British West Indian immigrant workers prompted the United Fruit Company to offer the denizens of the *barrio jamaiquino* better material conditions than those of the Haitian and Chinese braceros. A large group of British West Indians returning to Colón, Panama, appreciated this preferential treatment when they spoke favorably about their experiences in Cuba. Arriving on a steamer that the United Fruit Company operated so they could visit their relatives, the migrants stated that they had received good wages after finding plenty of work. They all agreed that "Cuba is the field for them; that they don't know of any country offering better working and living conditions than the Pearl of the Antilles at present, and so back to Cuba they go for the opening up of the crop season."[76] Nevertheless, compared to the amenities enjoyed by the North Americans and the Cubans, the living conditions of the Jamaicans remained undeniably inferior. Their race, class, and ethnicity placed them low in the socioracial hierarchy that privileged whiteness.

The black Caribbean workers of the United Fruit Company were not the only immigrants to experience racial segregation. It was normal for other sugar companies in Camagüey and other regions of Oriente to separate the races. And like the experience of the braceros who lived in Banes, race and ethnicity determined the material quality of the housing and neighborhoods. For example, the batey of the Cunagua *central* had an excellent sewer system that was cleaned daily and serviced the living quarters of the administrators and office workers of the mill, "but one cannot say the same thing about the barrios that were created as the laboring population increased," according to a field laborer.[77] The Cunagua created exclusively white and black barrios. The housing for the whites, particularly the office staff, clerks, and foremen, was made of wood and accommodated between ten and twelve workers. The manager of the mill and his assistants, however, lived in single-family homes that had all the modern amenities. Their accommodations were better than the housing for the blacks,

87

according to the same machetero who commented on the poor quality of life for those who lived in the barracks.

Finally, social gatherings that occurred outside the workplace symbolically amplified the low social status of black Caribbeans in these rural outposts. Racial segregation meant that the whites and the blacks had their own exclusive soccer clubs that seldom played one another. The white workers had their own movie houses. Inside, they sat in front and on the right side, while the blacks were forced to sit on the left side and completely in the back. Even the seating arrangements inside the Catholic church on the batey of the Brasil central segregated blacks from whites. Meanwhile, public spaces such as parks and beaches were reserved exclusively for white workers.[78]

This segregation was a common aspect of Cuban society as well. On the bateyes of the sugar properties of the United Fruit Company, the white office workers, mechanics, timekeepers, sugar boilers, and storekeepers founded social confraternities or employees' clubs. Using a number of company-owned buildings as their headquarters, these workers enjoyed a host of diversions such as dances, card parties, and games of chance. These buildings also contained libraries and reading rooms, as well as bars and restaurants where the more skilled workers could meet and socialize. Ironically, to add a semblance of sophistication and civility to this Cuban social world, "a Jamaican, speaking English with the British accent of the Caribbean always attended the workers" during their socials.[79]

The social meaning associated with the material disparity of the quality and location of the housing of white administrators and office workers on the one hand, and black Caribbean field workers on the other, as well as the social structures that privileged whiteness, were never lost on the black immigrants. Some were able to strip away the false consciousness that naturalized their inferiority and which the companies sought to engender. By the early 1920s, their degradation and humiliation inspired anger and resentment, and made many immigrant field workers receptive to the ideas of anarcho-syndicalism and the Pan-African philosophy of Marcus M. Garvey. The convergence of these ideologies resulted in a militant workers' consciousness that altered the unequal power relations in the sugar enclaves. In his classic novel on Haitian peasant life during this period, *Masters of the Dew*, the Communist writer and Haitian nationalist Jacques Roumain, who had visited Cuba more than once to obtain a better understanding of the life of poor peasant emigrants, vividly articulated the feelings of resentment of several Haitian braceros who had returned home after cutting cane for fifteen years in Antilla, located between Banes and Nipe Bay in Oriente. The first told his family and friends that the workers who cut cane "got nothing but the strength of their arms, not a handful of soil, not a drop of water—except their own sweat. They all work for Mr. Wilson, and this Mr. Wilson sits in the garden of his fine house all the time under a parasol, or else he's playing with the other whites knocking a white ball back and forth with a kind of washerwoman's paddle." Another Haitian machetero who spent time in Oriente continued the conversation: "I left thousands and thousands of Haitians over there in Antilla. They live and die like dogs." His statement was joined by the observations of yet another Haitian emigrant to Cuba: "that's how it is . . . and it's wrong! The poor work in the sun, the rich play in the shade. Some plant, others reap."[80] A cane cutter at the Algodones central echoed the feelings of Roumain's characters when he remembered: "On one side [of the batey] were the workers starving and living in misery, on the other side the luxury of a minority, exploiting and living the life off of the sweat and blood of the workers."[81]

The social system constructed along racial and ethnic lines that separated the races exacerbated the degradation of black Caribbean workers in Cuba. They were not alone. Other black Caribbean workers faced identical systems of strata based on race, ethnicity, and class that white North American officials of the United Fruit Company had constructed on the banana plantations surrounding Limón, Costa Rica. Attending to the spiritual concerns of West Indian workers there, Bishop Herbert Bury of the Anglican Church commented on how serious North American racism and the issue of color had become. Because definitions of race and color in the United States were different than those in the British colonial Caribbean, Bury believed that black immigrant workers found them unintelligible. He claimed that in the Caribbean those hierarchies were not as exclusionary: "We all worship together, receive communion together and meet together socially without restraint, black and white and coloured . . . where the Americans are the great employers of labour and have their own countrymen in all their offices and superintending departments, a very different state of things obtains. They will not come into the same church with black or coloured people, nor even dream of accepting the ministrations of coloured clergy, nor allow them as guests in their hotels."[82] During the construction of the Panama Canal, the authorities had imposed a racial and ethnic caste system that divided whites from black workers from North America and the Caribbean in Colón and Panama City.[83] The subordination of black Caribbean workers in Cuba made it possible for the sugar companies to unconditionally seize their labor.

Together with the agricultural workers, skilled migrant workers assisted in increasing the average production of the mills located in the central and eastern provinces by over 400 percent between 1904 and 1919. For example, in the province of Camagüey, the amount of cane cut grew from 969,089 tons between 1910 and 1911, to 4,960,354 tons between 1917 and 1918. The amount of sugar processed increased from 111,453 tons for the period of 1910–11, to 545,639 during 1917 and 1918.[84] In Oriente, 19,575,938 arrobas of cut cane allowed mill owners to produce 2,270,904 tons of sugar in 1907. That amount grew to 8,479,847 tons after Haitians and Jamaicans contributed to cutting 88,275,000 arrobas of cane during 1917–18.[85] In spite of this amazing growth in production capacity, the mill owners desired to increase their volume even further and so demanded more workers from abroad. They knew exactly how many macheteros and carreteros they would need to import to make a zafra successful. In 1917, the Association for the Promotion of Immigration, directed by Higinio Fanjul, the uncle of Manuel Rionda, owner of a number of mills including the Francisco, Tuinicú, and Manatí, announced that in order for the zafra of 1918 to be a success, the seventy-two mills operating in Santa Clara Province would need 28,419 men as cane cutters, 9,477 to haul the cane to the mill, and another 30,767 to bag the raw sugar. Together, this work force would help process an estimated 852,332,240 arrobas of cane. Meanwhile, as the second leading sugar-producing region, Oriente Province with its forty-one mills would require 24,090 macheteros, 8,018 carreteros, and 32,211 baggers. These braceros would likely process 720,226,546 arrobas of sugarcane during the 1918 zafra, according to Fanjul's calculations.[86] Although the black Caribbean workers produced considerably less than what Fanjul had predicted, his calculations nonetheless demonstrated the amount of labor that the sugar companies hoped to extract from their imported black work force. However, their prospects were dashed when the political violence instigated by José Miguel Gómez and the Liberals in 1917 made it unsafe for braceros to travel to Cuba.

In spite of their economic contributions to the expansion and modernization of the Cuban sugar industry, black Caribbean braceros became "undesirable" aliens. This negative image, constructed by the Cuban press, government functionaries, and individuals of the upper and middle class, inspired xenophobia, Cuban nationalism, and anti-immigrant violence. More important, it revealed how the government and its "ideological state apparatuses" employed the "rhetoric of differences" to foil the class interests shared by native and black Caribbean workers in the sugar enclaves. It was not until the mid-1920s that an alliance developed to help ameliorate the marginalization of Haitians and Jamaicans.

One of the earliest examples of how government officials used the "rhetoric of differences" to support their claim that the ethnicity and race of the black braceros were dangerous to Cuban society occurred at the end of the zafra of 1911. Before the Cuban government permitted the sugar companies to officially import black workers from Jamaica and Haiti, the governor of Oriente Province received a report highly critical of the presence of Haitian immigrants. In May 1911, an official in the mayor's office in Guantánamo informed the governor that the Haitians were a danger to the local population in a number of ways. They threatened public health because they brought the bubonic plague virus to Cuba. If they were allowed to move from one region of the province to another, they could spread this contagion as well as other sicknesses. The Guantánamo official's assumption that Haitian workers were carriers of infectious diseases was based upon the belief that people of African descent belonged to a filthy and disease-ridden race, and it was part of the larger notion that they were "a lower grade of human, or even sub-human . . . brutish, animal-like, insensitive to pain, and certainly biologically different from whites."[87] This racialist concept had emerged more than a half century earlier in the U.S. South during the antebellum period. Southern medical doctors such as Samuel Cartwright, Josiah C. Nott, and Henry Ramsay studied the somatic traits of blacks and their cranial sizes in order to measure their mental state and capacity to justify African slavery with science that "proved" the biological inferiority of blacks. They also explained the etiologies of "negro diseases" and in so doing, popularized the "medical-cum-political argument of the blacks' physiological distinctiveness or 'niggerology' as Nott termed it, among southerners of all classes."[88] This ideology also became the basis for the adoption of the socioeconomic arrangements and structures of Jim Crow in the United States and as a result may have informed the racial beliefs of the North Americans who established and managed the sugar mills. These notions became commonplace in Cuba at the turn of the twentieth century.

The writings and theories of a number of European biologists and eugenicists, such as Arthur de Gobineau, Gustave Le Bon, and Georges Vacher de Lapouge, further advanced the body of pseudoscientific racialist literature. It was read by influential members of the Cuban social sciences community like the anthropologists Luis Montane and Fernando Ortiz, as well as by public policymakers concerned with the issue of immigration. The latter continued to emphasize the blacks' supposed resistance to certain forms of diseases. This "fact" made blacks the ideal carriers of harmful infections that could wipe out the white European populations in the multiracial or multiethnic societies of the Americas.[89] As a result, four years after President Gómez opened Cuban ports to large numbers of black Antillean workers, in 1916 Cuban officials blamed "Jamaican immigrants for the frequent cases of malaria which have occurred in parts of Oriente province."[90]

As early as the spring of 1916, white Cubans questioned the immigration policies that allowed so many black Caribbean braceros to work in the sugar industry. A concerned citizen using the pseudonym "Billiken" submitted an editorial entitled "El peligro Negro" (The Black Threat) to the Havana daily La Prensa. The unidentified writer attempted to persuade his fellow countrymen that the Jamaican braceros had already disrupted the peace and tranquility of the Republic. He explicitly warned that their presence endangered cordial relations between white and black Cubans. Moreover, these thousands of Jamaicans would cause the historical enmity between the two races to resurface. Cuban blacks did not need this additional animosity because they were already victims of an intense level of prejudice. The magnitude of racial prejudice and discrimination would increase, "Billiken" claimed, if whites realized that members of the black and colored middle classes supported this type of immigration with hopes of changing the island's political system.

In order to reduce tensions between the races and to persuade both blacks and whites to oppose further black immigration, "Billiken" argued that Jamaicans were the wrong type of immigrants for Cuban society. To support his contention, he praised the personal qualities of black Cubans while denigrating the Jamaicans. He employed racist stereotypes in his assessment: "It is a general rule that the black Cubans are better than all the other blacks of the world. They are intelligent workers. They are almost never drunk. Rarely do they show any criminal instincts. They are the children of uneducated and [God-] fearing parents and grandparents who lived in a desperate state of oppression with brutish passions." By 1916, the majority of black Cubans were perceived as a jovial and humble people. Yet the writer also had encountered some people of

92

color who believed that racial equality with whites had been achieved, and as a result conducted themselves poorly. Nevertheless, most black Cubans were no longer a menace to society since "they understood that in order to be someone they must always return to their place." Society would continue to extend the rights of citizenship to only those blacks who accommodated the privileges of whites, according to "Billiken."

Having lived with Jamaicans sometime in the past, "Billiken" claimed that these blacks were a worthless people who refused to accept and stay in their place. The majority tended to be quarrelsome drunkards and thieves. According to "Billiken," "[T]hey will stab and kill a saintly soul, and short-change you as well. Not everyone knows this but they are a dangerous, pernicious and noxious people to everyone who lives near them." Because of their wretched excesses, he warned black Cubans not to become their allies. Black Cubans would face dire consequences if they ignored him: "Let me now tell black Cubans that if they reach an understanding with these people, who after arriving to Cuba mix their families together, they will contribute further to the profound divisions between whites and blacks." He recommended that Cuban blacks and whites close ranks and together reject this type of immigration, which was "injecting a bad virus into the veins of the race of color."[91]

It is impossible to discern how many other citizens shared the attitude of "Billiken." But the xenophobia expressed in one of the country's most important newspapers sought to define the Jamaicans as "other," to the point where any type of alliance with them was ultimately unacceptable to members of the dominant society. Appearing just four years after the Race War of 1912, "Billiken"'s threatening editorial made his interpretation permissible and reasonable among whites. His message probably resonated in the black Cuban communities as well, because their position in Cuban society could be harmed by white perceptions of a possible transnational coalition composed of thousands of Haitians, Jamaicans, and black Cubans. Such an image raised the specter of another race war. In addition, the tenor and content of the above editorial meant that it could not be ignored. La Prensa's editors recognized that they were "in a position to influence attitudes and lend authority and legitimacy to stated positions. Principally through editorials and 'comment' columns, they encourage[d] their readers to adopt certain attitudes and interpret events in particular ways."[92] In multiethnic societies like Cuba, white newspaper editors commonly portrayed blacks, particularly black immigrants, as a threat to their societies. Primarily owned and controlled by whites, the newspapers of Cuba consciously and subconsciously offered a "white" perspective that usually characterized black immigrants as a group that could endanger the social and political culture of the island. Typical of that time, Cuban newspapers used "dramatic presentations of stories . . . provocative or damning quotations and statements as well as popular stereotypes . . . to create and manipulate popular fears."[93]

In addition to "Billiken," there were other individuals who called attention to the black Caribbean threat to the island. A black Cuban and cook by trade named Tristán also used the pages of La Prensa to argue for an end to black immigration. Writing in the column "Palpitaciones de la Raza de Color" (Pulse of the Colored Race), Tristán admitted that he had become annoyed and embarrassed by all the racist letters that La Prensa had published on the impact of Haitian immigration. The hatred and anger expressed in the newspaper alone caused him to demand that the government prohibit black migrants from entering Cuba. Injecting Cuban nationalism into the debate, Tristán believed that the presence of black immigrants compromised the country's sovereignty. He did not blame the immigrants for coming to Cuba, but he chastised the American sugar companies for sponsoring the arrival of "2000, 3000, 4000 or more blacks."[94] The recruitment of large numbers of transients, as he labeled them, reflected the power and influence that the sugar mills wielded inside the government. Employing these workers to solve the industry's labor shortages was unimaginable only a few years ago, Tristán wrote. Evidently, as a black Cuban himself, Tristán had assimilated the dominant culture's ideology, becoming a proponent of white European immigration.

He also opposed black immigration on social and cultural grounds. Challenging "Billiken"'s thesis, Tristán believed that the black foreigners would never integrate themselves into Cuban society. He pointed out that the seasonal work that the migrants performed discouraged them from making Cuba their home. Not understanding the source of black subordination, the immigrants had decided to segregate themselves, he said: "Although they assist in the general evolution of the country, so many foreigners such as the Jamaicans and Haitians create national problems . . . by always maintaining their distance sociologically speaking from the natives."[95] As a result, their cultural diversity exacerbated the numerous domestic antagonisms existing in Cuba. Nevertheless, Tristán believed that Cubans had nothing to fear from the black immigrants. Describing them as cheap manual laborers and "resilient peons who had suffered a lot and whose only fault was being the source of the vanity and racism of whites," he asked how such people could challenge the existing political system by increasing the electoral power of black Cubans.

As the sugar industries expanded their hinterlands to increase their grinding capacities, the increasing number of Jamaican and Haitian braceros who entered Cuba fueled white racism and violence. During the zafra of 1917, an unidentified white army officer ordered the massacre of seventeen Jamaican braceros in Camagüey. Defenseless, the workmen had been rounded up so that the officer could take their photographs in accord with the Department of Immigration's policy of identifying workers.[96] Cuban nativism assisted in the subordination of the braceros when it exploded later that year; four Jamaicans were killed on the property of the Jobabo *central* in Las Tunas, Oriente.

On 5 March 1919, the manager of the *central* at the Palma Soriano Sugar Company, Rafael Aguirre, informed the governor of Oriente Province that the steady stream of recently imported braceros suffered frequent assaults and fustigations at the hands of white citizens. The attacks often occurred inside the train station in Santiago de Cuba while the workers waited to be transported to the mill. White citizens not only attacked the black workers but also the labor agents who accompanied the contracted work gangs to the *central*. The reason for the beatings was clear to Aguirre. He wrote: "The workers and the agents are constantly harassed and assaulted by groups of Cubans who converge on the station. These people are inflamed by cruel and malicious propaganda. As a result, some of the workers of the mill have been severely injured after being struck with machetes. However, rarely are the police present to notice such behavior and never do they come to stop and arrest these individuals."[97] That the rite of passage for many black Caribbean immigrants consisted of violent beatings upon their entry proves how ethnicity as an ideology helped "to structure power relations."[98] The violence that developed from that power was caused by "the local population 'essentializing' the 'objective' characteristics of various cohorts of workers in a racial idiom."[99] Many Cubans had come to believe that the "undesirable" black Caribbean workers were a threat that needed to be eradicated. In response to Aguirre's appeal, the governor ordered the municipal police chief to resolve the matter. He also promised Aguirre that his workers would never be bothered again.

The use of violence was intended to not only produce a docile work force but also to dissuade black workers from entering Cuba. At the same time, the fact that fewer Spanish laborers arrived probably also helps to explain white anger toward the braceros.[100] Whites accused black Caribbean workers of making Cuba an unattractive destination for most Spanish migrants. Disingenuously, they complained that the braceros took away jobs from white immigrants and accepted lower wages as well. These critics refused to accept the real reasons for the lack of European workers. The Cuban Department of Immigration blamed the effects of German submarine attacks on Atlantic shipping during the world war, a lack of Spanish ships to transport European emigrants, the high cost of transatlantic passage to Cuba, and the higher wages being offered to workers in Spain and the Canary Islands. Fe Iglesias García discovered that the total number of Spanish immigrants entering Cuba dropped from 34,795 in 1917 to 14,293 in 1918. The level of Spanish immigration, however, rebounded after the war, increasing from 39,573 in 1919 to 94,294 in 1920. This situation caused government officials and sugar producers to reach a consensus on what to do with the "undesirables": "If Cuba can replace the [black Caribbean] class of labor with Spaniards and other whites, then the country would decidedly be the better [when] the entire Haitian and Jamaican colonies leave."[101] That the sugar companies would support this contention shows that they understood fully how the race and ethnicity of their workers had infuriated many sectors of society. In order to appear just as repulsed as most Cubans, they conveniently allowed the anti-immigrant forces to express their racism with the "rhetoric of differences" and violence. The state of the economy and its impact on European immigration helped the companies control their immigrant work force.

The collapse of the price of sugar and its effects on the island's economy destroyed the aspirations of the government to encourage European immigration. Unlike the black braceros, in 1921 Europeans decided not to risk their lives in a country faced with an economic crisis. Spanish immigration dropped dramatically from 94,294 in 1920 to 26,340 in 1921. It continued to decline; only 16,397 arrived in 1922.[102] As a result, white Cubans were forced to accept more black immigrants from the Caribbean. Even Jamaica felt the effects of black emigration to Cuba. In December 1919, the colonial government of Jamaica informed David Marchalleck, a sugar planter in Morant Bay, to expect a shortage of laborers for his estate because 20,000 Jamaicans had left for Cuba in order to "take advantage of the opportunity to earn very much higher wages than they can get on the banana or sugar estates." This figure was nearly three times the number of emigrants who had left to work in Cuba for the zafra of 1919. According to the Jamaican government's Blue Book, only 7,351 emigrants went to Cuba that year. Jamaican officials also estimated that by September 1920 there would be more than 100,000 Jamaicans in Oriente Province waiting for the harvest of 1921 to start.[103]

Unable to stop the influx of black workers destined for the sugar industry, some white Cubans once again expressed their displeasure by questioning the island's immigration laws. In late December 1922, the Diario de la Marina, a conservative daily published in Havana, editorialized about the Immigration Law. The paper reported that the problems associated with Haitian and Jamaican immigration were under investigation, and that the study was very important to the progress and future of the nation. According to statistics obtained from the Treasury Department, Cuba had received 44,855 Haitians and Jamaicans for the fiscal year of 1919–20. Alarmed by these numbers, the editors of the paper then reached a conclusion based purely on speculation. They argued: "The immigration of undesirable elements reached the high number of 72,855 persons a year. This number is bigger than the population of Santiago de Cuba which alone counts 63,000 inhabitants."[104] The presence of these immigrants, the editors believed, would progressively harm the Cuban peoples' cultural identity. If the number of Haitians and Jamaicans continued to increase, "Cuba will lose its national character and civilization and become a very different nation with other customs and habits not in keeping with our traditions and education."[105] Indicting the hacendados (estate owners) and colonos for the corrupt role they played in this matter, the Diario de la Marina stated that the loss of the country's cultural attributes was not worth the revenue that the sugar industry generated for the island's economy.

The editors of the Diario de la Marina called for the immediate and complete end to black immigration. They argued that the Immigration Law of 1906 had been designed to protect Cuba from the alleged undesirables. Since it was only amended in 1912 and again in 1917, theoretically the Law of 1906 was still in effect. The paper therefore demanded that Secretary of Agriculture, Commerce, and Labor Pedro Betancourt first rescind the amendments and then strictly apply the 1906 law in order to end this immigration. The so-called chronic labor shortage that mills such as the Manatí continued to report and use to justify suspending its operations until it obtained additional workers discouraged Betancourt from acceding to the demands and wishes of the conservative newspaper. It was in this context that the frequency of anti-black-immigrant violence increased.

In April 1922, while sitting on the sidewalk, a bracero named Charles Sadler was shot and killed by a police officer in the town of Nuevitas in Camagüey. In March 1923, on the batey of the Miranda central in Oriente, three rural guards who sought to question a field worker, Oscar Taylor, instead fired several shots through the door of his barracón and killed him. In both instances, the employers of the two men showed indifference to the murder of their workers; the policeman and the guards were never arrested. In fact, the citizens of Nuevitas strongly demonstrated their approval of the constable's actions, and he continued to serve his community as a policeman. After a perfunctory trial ended in his acquittal, a mob of townspeople publicly rejoiced at the news of the verdict. Meanwhile, two months passed before the authorities arrested one of the guards involved in the Taylor shooting.[106]

Such anti-immigrant violence had taken place before. A year earlier, a group of Spanish immigrants attacked and shot a Jamaican named Patric Brown, a twenty-eight-year-old bracero living in Bayate, Oriente. The assault occurred on the Suárez colonia near Bayate. His brother, Lorenzo Brown, witnessed the incident and told the authorities that at 9:00 p.m., "the men appeared very drunk when they approached Patric while he was tying a palm leaf to the thatched roof of his home. After one of the Spaniards ordered my brother to stop what he was doing, he pulled out a gun and shot him twice, gravely wounding him in the stomach." Lorenzo Brown then rushed his brother to the hospital, where he told the police that they did not recognize the assailants.[107]

In April 1923, while detained at the quarantine station in Santiago de Cuba, Locksley Roye refused to take a cup of medicine from one of the station's marine guards. Upset at Roye's resistance and perhaps by his insolence, the marine officer started to beat the migrant with his rifle, then shot and killed him. The testimony of several braceros also detained inside of the station, who witnessed the assault, stated that before the shooting Roye seemed to be in good health. Nor was he armed. In May 1923, another defenseless black Caribbean worker was killed. Although Moses Buchanan had been accused of stealing from another bracero, the guard who shot and killed him at the Tacajó central never proved that he was armed and dangerous at the time.[108] As members of a racialized state, white Cubans resorted to violence against people whom they defined as "other" whenever they imagined or actually perceived that their "normalized racial governance through the order of law" was either threatened or had collapsed.[109] In addition, anti-immigration violence often reflected the endeavors of members of the dominant society to deny foreigners the privileges and rights that they had defined as their own. As a result, attacks committed by whites against black braceros were in a way a display of their power to exclude the immigrants because of their class, race, ethnicity, and color—ideologies articulated by the sugar companies' "conjugated oppression."

Not only were braceros senselessly assaulted and killed, they were also harassed. Sometime in 1922, the police of Ciego de Avila, Camagüey, without justification or provocation raided and ransacked the headquarters of a Jamaican benevolent society. They arrested the members of the association but soon released them. During the raid, the police confiscated the Jamaicans' personal possessions. Finally, the sugar companies used rural guards to intimidate the macheteros and carreteros. When two hundred black Caribbean field workers at the Candelaria central demanded their pay after cutting cane, the manager ordered guards to immediately expel them from the batey.

As early as January 1920, the Haitian consul in Guantánamo informed the governor of Oriente that one of his nationals had been "leveled to the ground with a machete by a rural guard who continued to stand over the worker cruelly punishing him as the victim uncontrollably moaned like an animal."[110] A crowd of Cuban citizens witnessed the beating. This fact, along with the vicious nature of the assault, caused the Haitian consul to declare: "There hasn't been a citizen or a migrant who has suffered so many indignities nor more misery than a Haitian . . . The constant struggles of my people, who are treated like kaffirs, in this country that I have come to love, [continue] in spite of the great service provided by Haitian emigration. I now see the disgusted and ugly hatred Cuba has for my race, that is like the others, worthy of respect."[111] The consul's observation regarding the frequency of violence against Haitians underscores how that reality was engendered by the Haitians' race and ethnicity. It also illustrates how the very presence of these workers on Cuban soil evoked the wrath and resentment of so many Cubans. But because of the Haitian government's relationship with numerous labor brokers, one has to take the consul's emotional statement with a degree of cynicism. His objection to the ferocious barbarity that some workers experienced undoubtedly stemmed from the revenue that the bracero trade generated for the Haitian government. Because anti-immigrant violence sought to dissuade black Caribbean workers from traveling to Cuba, out of Haitian national interest the consul had to inform Cuban functionaries that his people should not be treated like "kaffirs."

In March 1921, a twenty-eight-year-old Haitian, Dionisio Liso of Cabonico, Oriente, was beaten so badly by a group of citizens that he had to be taken to the provincial hospital. However, Liso no longer worked as a field laborer. Making Cuba his home, he had bought a small plot of land to grow a little food in order to become a seller of "quality staples" that were purchased by local bars and restaurants.[112] A year later, another Haitian named Eduardo Fis died after being thrown under a train carrying sugarcane on the America central near Palma Soriano in Oriente. After the Haitian consul, Laporte, requested an investigation to determine whether Fis's death was murder, the governor informed Laporte that the municipal authorities of Baire would maintain constant vigilance "so something like this never happens again."[113] Then in January 1924, Felipe Blanco, a drunk thirty-two-year-old Cuban, threatened and later beat José García, a bracero from Haiti, about the face.[114] Because of the severity of such violence, the Haitian government decided to place a consul on nearly all of the bateyes of the mills with the hope of improving the treatment of its nationals.

The use of violence to undergird the labor system and the social arrangements in the enclaves, which together sought to ensure the marginalization and exploitation of the black Caribbean braceros, reflected the effectiveness of the "rhetoric of differences" that became a central element of the Cuban and North American elites' ideology of domination. They constructed an image of the braceros as being utterly different and without any redeeming qualities, an image that spread outward from the "places of nowhere" and encouraged other sectors of Cuban society to degrade as well as control the immigrant workers inside and outside of the sugar enclaves. The members of the dominant society isolated the braceros as "undesirables" who could threaten the political, social, racial, and cultural structures and customs of the island, thereby discouraging black and white Cuban workers from forging an alliance with the black immigrants. The subordination of the black Caribbean workers had become part of the social and institutional fabric of the Republic of Cuba and its relationship with the U.S.-owned sugar mills. How Haitian and Jamaican workers responded to their marginalization and challenged those accountable for their dire condition is explored in the next chapter.

3

SOCIAL STRATEGIES OF RESISTANCE

The Disclosed and Undisclosed Lives of Black Caribbean Braceros

The Haitians who lived on the batey of the *central* Jaronú specifically employed their *conucos* [small plots of land or gardens] to grow sweet potatoes that they attended to patiently . . . In order to eat a little meat during the *tiempo muerto*, they raised some small pigs in a sugar rattan or in the wild with great difficulty, and which they kept outside of the *central*'s batey . . . They grew their own food even though the administrator prohibited independent farming and the raising of livestock outside of the field workers' barracks.[1]

In May 1913, in Paso Estancia, Oriente, a group of Jamaicans "bought a large tract of land from the Illinois-Cuban Land Company. When black Cuban squatters failed to leave the property, the Jamaicans solicited the help of the British consul in Santiago de Cuba, telling him that they had purchased the disputed acres to build a few homes and to grow a little food."[2] That Haitian and Jamaican workers were able to create autonomous spaces on the bateyes to organize their own homes and support themselves by growing food and raising livestock illustrates that their lives in the sugar enclaves consisted of more than just working twelve to fifteen hours a day in the cane fields during the harvest season. What they did to mitigate the effects of those long, arduous days in which the cane farmers and sugar mills appropriated their labor while attacking their dignity is the subject of this chapter. The measures that they adopted became critical for them to survive in the enclaves and in Cuban society in general. Black Caribbean agency was also important in limiting the power of those who dominated them. Were their strategies individually or collectively constructed? Did their formulas include social and cultural productions that helped them challenge the racialized and hegemonic ideologies that were integrated into the fabric of the enclaves? Were their plans surreptitious in nature? And if so, how did they create a black Caribbean consciousness and identity that allowed them to stave off incessant attacks on their dignity and humanity? Finally, did their experiences as emigrant workers elsewhere in the Caribbean prepare them to develop responses to the power of the Cuban and North American sugar companies that sought to control their lives?

As we address these questions, it will become clear that outside of work the Haitian and Jamaican braceros attempted to reassemble their homes in Camagüey and Oriente. This included reconstituting a peasant lifestyle similar to what they knew at home. They also met with other braceros as well as with Cubans for social purposes. The social arrangements and activities that they pursued on paydays and on weekends, especially on Sundays, became critical to their physical and mental well-being. Their wages also helped them to establish a number of formal benevolent and social associations. Pooling their resources allowed the workers to establish "autonomous assemblies" where they shared their common experiences and helped one another deal with the uncertainties and stress of working and living in Cuba.[3] This too may be viewed as part of their effort to make Cuba into their home. By socially and culturally redefining the days on which they were paid, along with organizing their own "autonomous assemblies" into "privileged social sites," the braceros were able to contest their subordination beyond the supervision of the white cane farmers or the sugar mill administrators. In other words, the social spaces that the farmers and the sugar mills set aside for their workers gave many braceros the options of either expressing certain elements of their culture, particularly the beliefs and rituals of their mental world, or of assimilating Cuban materials. Both options may be viewed as projects to limit the power of the individuals and companies that tried to control them. To these methods was added a narrative, produced by some Jamaicans and other British West Indians, which was based upon their experiences in Panama and elsewhere. This paradigm helped them to develop responses to their racially and ethnically based marginalization and exploitation. The result was a survival tactic that saw many try to ingratiate themselves with their superiors by becoming submissive and deferential; others adopted Cuban cultural traits. Either way, the first response that they developed focused on negating the harmful effects of the "artifacts of the exercise of power," which included the structures and social arrangements of the bateyes.

As the opening passage of this chapter reveals, some Haitians and Jamaicans confronted the "sites of domination" by growing their own food and establishing their own independent housing in which to live. Besides the Haitians who raised livestock and established small-scale gardens without permission of the manager of the Jaronú, other Haitian braceros who cut cane for the United Fruit Company and lived in the company's segregated barrio and barracks frequently built their own huts made completely of palm leaves on the outer edges of the cane farms. There, twenty to forty of them raised a little food, including some pigs and chickens.[4] That these Haitians carved out a small piece of land to squat, build a hut, and raise crops and livestock within the mill's hinterland reflected a long tradition and their desire for property. More important, it represented their effort to establish a sense of community along the lines of the traditional African compound, called a lakou in Haiti. The lakou was a courtyard that included a half-dozen or more separate homes inhabited by a similar number of related families.[5] One hut was often used as a temple, while another belonged to the patriarch of the related families. The patriarch's role was to resolve social, political, and economic problems in order to ensure that all the families survived, according to Leslie Desmangles.[6] Although the Haitian workers were in Cuba to earn a seasonal income from cutting cane, the lakou helped them to combine elements of their peasant society and culture that esteemed both an agrarian lifestyle and the family. The sugar mill administrators and their foremen probably ignored the braceros' squatting, aware that their raising livestock and truck gardening served several purposes. They saw how the workers took pleasure in gardening, and as a result realized that this could be used as a "carrot" to promote the workers' loyalty. Second, although some sugar mills like the Francisco directly "import[ed] large quantities of rice and beans, flour, coffee, codfish and other similar foods of the working class, the workers' agricultural pursuits could supplement the company's provisions and thereby saved us money."[7] Finally, the ability to squat in order to grow a little food and raise a few animals would have enabled the workers to reside permanently in Cuba and survive the tiempo muerto as unemployed seasonal workers. This put the sugar companies in a more advantageous position to appropriate labor from a surplus of workers during the dead period. The Haitians who were able to make ends meet during the tiempo muerto benefited too, since they potentially could be part of the first gangs of workers hired by the companies in December before the start of the next zafra.

Haitian braceros relied on their conjugal partners and wives to help establish an agrarian lifestyle and family during and after the zafra. Although Lara Putnam argues that the immigration of Caribbean females was often lower when multinational companies recruited a predominantly male work force, it appears that there were enough Haitian women present in the enclaves to reproduce the traditional lakou. Haitian women usually arrived in large numbers when the sugar companies were unsuccessful in obtaining sufficient male workers to perform field work. This was the case as early as 1917, during the Liberal Revolt against the Menocal government.[8] By the mid-1920s, the entry of more women had become so common that the American consul in Port-au-Prince, Maurice P. Dunlop, indicated that the nature and composition of Haitian emigration had completely changed. He reported: "Formerly it was customary for single men to go to Cuba to work, returning each year to visit their families. Now it is more usual for entire families to emigrate, many of them remaining permanently."[9] That Haitian men and women decided to emigrate as family units even after the price of sugar dropped, making employment in the sugar industry tenuous, suggests that this development probably started when jobs were plentiful during World War I. In Cuba, Haitian women performed the same tasks they had performed at home and later in the Dominican Republic. The majority took care of the homes their conjugal partners built in the hinterlands of the enclaves. They cooked and cleaned. According to the Haitian parents of Justina Masino Leollesy, learning these two skills would prepare her for paid work outside the home.[10] Performing these tasks for a partner, however, culturally indicated the woman's agreement to form an independent Haitian household with her mate. The same sociocultural significance obtained if they performed these tasks for partners who were housed in the companies' squalid barracones.

Since field work was rare for women, except during times of crisis, some females had no choice but to participate in the informal economy that developed in the enclaves. As they had in Haiti, they made and sold confections such as jams, chocolate candies, and sweet cakes, as well as breads. On the bateyes of a couple of mills located around Guantánamo, they sewed linens, sheets, bandanas, work shirts, and clothes for women involved in prostitution. They also butchered livestock that they raised and sold the meat to Cuban, North American, and immigrant workers. Many also sold charcoal to the field workers.

Haitian women often walked into the cane fields to market their various goods daily. However, the money that they earned as petty merchants was never enough to establish their own independent businesses or lives. Their incomes usually supplemented the piece-rate wages of their husbands and partners. As a result, they helped Haitian men avoid becoming indebted to the company stores. By earning a little money, they also helped their families survive the dead season, when there was little or no employment for their spouses.[11]

Many Haitian females were also involved in the sex trade. As discussed earlier, Haitian brokers often tricked them with promises of work as laundresses and domestic servants. Those who spoke English indeed often found work in these occupations, but many more became prostitutes. For this reason, their arrival and presence were viewed by Cuban officials as unlawful.[12] As a result, the archival records of Cuban government officials stereotypically described Haitian women as harlots and whores. However, they never questioned the sugar companies' involvement in the sex trade. That the brokers had to lie and trick Haitian girls and women into accompanying them to Cuba is proof enough that the administrators of the sugar companies were complicit in the sex trade. Most believed that sex could be used to control and retain their male work force. For example, when an administrator of a North American sugar company in the Dominican Republic stated that "a batey without women will not take long in becoming a batey without men," he revealed how these sex workers had become important to the production of sugarcane.[13]

It is impossible to know how many Haitian women or immigrant women in general were involved in prostitution, but Cuban archival sources reveal not only the biases of the authorities as they possibly overestimated the numbers to incriminate black Caribbean immigration, but also how important the issue had become. Whether this problem was real or imagined, the authorities' preoccupation with this subject warranted the production of nearly fifteen years of reports from municipal and provincial functionaries. A brief examination of one document is sufficient, because its contents are typical of the majority. It charges that Haitian women solely were responsible for the illicit sex trade, as well as for the impact of prostitution on Cuban society. Municipal and provincial officials of Oriente thought that Haitian women constituted not only a moral threat to the braceros but also a danger to public health. Some even believed that Haitian prostitutes would wreck the economy. According to the governor of Oriente, "in all of the provincial towns and cities our police and rural guard have witnessed a great number of braceros being accompanied by Haitian women to the homes where they have been hired to work as domestic servants. They also commonly lead the workers inside of other buildings that are used to carry out their licentious lives. Because these Haitian women no longer represent a small number, they now have become harmful not only to the morals of the Republic, but also a danger to our economy and public health."[14] The governor therefore advised his superiors in Havana to expel the Haitian females immediately. The executives of the sugar companies would never let this happen, however. To compete with the other mills, they understood that women were required to keep their male workers content.

It is important to note that some Haitian females realized that prostitution was their only way to make a living in Cuba. As long as they did not work in a brothel or were managed and exploited by a pimp, their families and relatives understood that the local conditions of the bateyes caused their predicament and never ostracized them. Their families sensed that this way of life was possibly the only way for their daughters and wives to ameliorate their misery and dependency in a foreign country.[15]

Producing their own food became another method that Haitian men and women employed to foster a sense of independence and power. When given the opportunity, many Haitians preferred to grow their own food. A former worker at the Algodones central, Orlando González, remembered how some Haitian cane cutters ate only food that they had grown themselves. Owned by a Cuban company and located near the town of Majagua in Camagüey, the Algodones was one of four new sugar mills that began to grind cane in the province in January 1917. It received much of its cane from the San Miguel colonia, where Haitians made up the majority of macheteros and carreteros.

González recalled how on the cane farm the Haitians "practically lived from one starchy meal to the next preferring the yams that they had grown within the boundaries of the cane fields . . . [Along] with them, they cooked codfish tails that they ate more or less with every meal."[16] During the 1910s, the Haitian braceros living on the Caidije batey near the town of Minas in the northern region of Camagüey, which was attached to the Senado central, also cultivated a string of gardens on the fringes of the batey. Farming helped them to "preserve the custom of cultivating such crops as plantains, yucca, yams, rice, corn, malanga, calabash, and other starchy tubers in small open areas on the side of the mountains or in extremely rugged places."[17] Since these gardens usually lay some three to four miles from the center of the batey, the only way the Haitians could work their plots was in the early hours of the morning before they went off to cut and haul cane. Some men traveled by horse, while others walked to their small gardens before the sun came up. The Haitians of Caidije and of the colonia of Saturnino, near the Esperanza central in Guantánamo, also attended to their conucos on the weekends, cultivating, weeding, and picking their crops.[18] This adaptive strategy of using small plots of land to supplement or fulfill their nutritional needs was reminiscent of how African slaves had employed similar provisional grounds throughout the Caribbean. These conucos were a testament to how the Haitian braceros sought to reassemble their homes in Cuba, as well as to how they maximized, economically, the limited space or land that the cane farmers and the mills left fallow. "This was not a consequence of the problem of coming from a country where there was not much land available for agriculture, but one of routine, and having tended to small plots back home . . . they came to a country where the braceros had to farm an area practically the size of a house's patio."[19] Employing agricultural knowledge learned at home, many Haitians grew crops between the rows of sugarcane or along the periphery of the sugar enclaves.

It is important to note that the only farm implement they used while working their small plots was the same instrument they used to cut sugarcane, the machete. This large, heavy knife was commonly used to perform agricultural work in the roughest and most inhospitable landscapes. While studying Haitian society and culture, Carl Kelsey observed the Haitians' proficient use of this tool. In March 1922, he informed members of the U.S. Senate that "a plow is rarely seen even in the plains and would be valueless . . . The one universal tool of the Haitian peasant is the machete (almost identical with our corn knife). With this he clears the ground, piling and burning the brush. Then with his machete he digs up the soil a little in just the place where he is to put his seed or plant. He cultivates with his machete by cutting the weeds or stirring the soil about the plants. Axes, hoes . . . are known but seldom seen."[20] Farming with the same implement that they used in the cane fields also allowed the braceros to avoid becoming indebted to the sugar mills' company stores for farming tools. In so doing, they reduced the amount of control the sugar companies wielded over their labor. Their agricultural pursuits also helped them to accomplish what many of them had set out to do by going to work in Cuba—they were able to save some of their wages and return home to take care of their families and communities.

Through the years, "I got to know some of the Haitians and Jamaicans who made up the cheap work force. Most of the time they fed themselves with codfish tails and the food they grew so that they would not be dependent on the company store like everyone else," Oscar Arbesón Estévez of the Algodones central remembered.[21] Their desire to avoid the corrupt and fraudulent bodegas prompted other immigrant workers to attempt to feed themselves in imaginative ways. Some survived by picking through food thrown out as garbage. On the Tacajó central, Ursinio Rojas recounted how "there existed a slaughter house close to our bohío. Nearby the Haitians and Jamaicans waited to pick through the vital parts of the sacrificed livestock including the heads, ears, and the discarded intestines of the animals with which they fed themselves."[22] This activity indicated that some sugar mills failed to provide adequate food for their work force. The workers' practice of sifting through the garbage bins on the bateyes also demonstrates how conscious they were about not spending all of their meager wages on food. Since they were required to leave Cuba after the completion of the zafra, they had only six or seven months to earn money until the following January, when commonly they would return for the next harvest. They wanted to limit the amount of debt, "the same debts that our brothers from the cane colonias expected to [incur] for two or three months during the zafra in order to live."[23] A foreman who worked on the Boston central noticed that not all the black Caribbean workers were practical at saving what little wages they earned. He considered the Jamaicans more prudent in this endeavor than the Haitians. The foreman believed that the Jamaicans often saved their wages, while workers from Haiti spent their income enjoying parties and cockfights.[24] This observation, however, misrepresented the facts.

Maurice Dunlop, the American consul in Port-au-Prince, reported how the majority of Haitian men and women successfully returned home, particularly to Aux Cayes, with most of their wages. Although his statements were intended to persuade his superiors that Haiti and its workers had benefited greatly from the bracero trade—a conclusion that Carl Kelsey and other observers would have found disingenuous only a few years earlier—the country's customs receipts and the amount of imports consumed by people living around Aux Cayes convinced Dunlop that the return of the workers made a significant impact on the local economy. He told State Department officials that "the stream of labor going and returning to Aux Cayes with money earned in Cuba creates an economic condition different to any other in this district." Dunlop described Haiti's southern peninsula, where the majority of braceros originated and which included Aux Cayes, "with only a population of 12,000 as the most prosperous part of the country."[25] The savings that the migrant workers brought back had transformed Aux Cayes into the second leading town in the country, improving the region's roads and communications, reported Dunlop. He remarked how the workers' good fortune "is marked by a steady influx of capital. Many of the laborers who left with nothing return with enough to buy small farms and the entire district around Cayes enjoys the benefit of this prosperity."[26]

However, it appears that the braceros' desire to save their paltry wages ran counter to the plans of the sugar mills. Ursinio Rojas recalled how the majority of braceros on the Tacajó, not just the Haitians, were tempted by the sugar companies to spend nearly all of their wages on payday and on items that brought them immediate satisfaction. Payday at the mill transformed the usual features of the batey. All the workers lined up to collect their wages. Even the colonos were in attendance to receive payment for the bundles of sugarcane they had delivered to the mill. After being paid, a good number of workers gathered at the company store, the bakery, and the bar—places where all of the braceros carried a running debt, particularly during the tiempo muerto. A roving band of hucksters who waited for the workers on the streets of the batey also tried to persuade them to spend wantonly. These itinerants sold cheaply made perfumes, razor blades, soap, cosmetics for women, fake jewelry, and work clothes. The workers purchased coffee, candy, cigars, cigarettes, and wallets from these salesmen. A host of prostitutes, gamblers, and cockfights also diverted the attention of the workers. The manager of the Tacajó permitted organ-grinders and other musicians to walk into the batey "in order to turn Saturdays into weekly festivals," according to Rojas.[27] In spite of these weekly saturnalias, the majority of braceros exercised some self-discipline in order to make their journey worthwhile. Their self-restraint was in response to the general condition of the Cuban economy. Growing inflation encouraged them to squirrel away some of their wages.

Although the insatiable demand for sugar among the Allied nations allowed the sugar companies to enjoy huge profits during World War I, the island's neocolonial relationship with the United States caused most foodstuffs and consumer goods to be imported. As a result, the cost of living considerably increased, particularly in the sugar enclaves and among the workers who earned the poor piece-rate wages of one to three dollars per day. The amount they earned proved inadequate, given the inflated prices not only of food but also of clothing and the tools that the sugar companies required the workers to possess to perform their jobs. A pair of shoes that had cost $3.50 in 1917 and 1918 cost more than double, $7 or $8, by 1919. The machetes that the braceros purchased from the company store, which cost $12 per dozen or one dollar a piece in 1915 and 1916, had increased to $50 a dozen or a little more than $4 each by 1919.[28] In order to reduce the cost of such items to a sugar company, and to increase its profit margin as well, mill owners and their administrators in Cuba passed the cost of producing sugar on to the workers themselves, including the colonos and macheteros. They tried to keep the piece-rate wages as low as possible while at the same time insisting that the workers buy their own tools. The mills even required their carreteros to own or rent the team of oxen that pulled the wagons loaded with cane to the *pesadores* to be weighed.[29]

———————

The Haitian braceros attempted to reassemble their homes in other ways. They often "met one another on Sunday afternoons in order to attend their religious activities, which included drinking their nasty grog, and singing songs to the accompaniment of tin cans and boxes. They drank a lot of alcohol . . . as they danced to their rhythmic music," observed Ursinio Rojas at the Tacajó *central*.[30] The scenes of Haitians performing their liturgies, which stuck out in Rojas's memory, were religious and recreational expressions that had undergone a lengthy transcultural fusion. These beliefs, ceremonies, and musical forms came from the Aja-Fon and Dahomean peoples of West Africa, and during the slave era they had provided black Haitians with their spirituality, called Vodun (also spelled *voodoo* or *vodou*). In Cuba, the Haitian worldview became intertwined with Kongo elements. This spiritual hybridization started at the end of the eighteenth century, when the first wave of black Haitians arrived with their French masters during the slave rebellion on Saint Domingue. After 1912, the Haitians arrived with similar but modified beliefs, rituals, and musical forms. Their liturgies were a product of the "fragile and tractable nature of these sects [that] allow[ed] any of their numerous followers to introduce into them their own individual forms and features. This process of give-and-take means that some elements were lost and not replaced. Transculturation had the effect of transforming the original expressive form," according to Miguel Barnet.[31] In addition, Michel Laguerre believed that in order to understand the origins of

Vodun liturgies such as songs, one had to examine "the migration of individuals from one place to another. Migrants carry with them their own traditions and will eventually teach it to their new congregations to form a niche for their own spirits. The migration of songs may occur also by way of borrowing. A devotee visiting relatives . . . may learn a few new songs sung there in honor of his spirit protector."[32] Unlike the private or secret dances that were designed to venerate and propitiate the pantheon of deities or *loa* of Vodun, and which were led by a *houngan* or priest as well as a number of assistants called *hounsi*, the ceremonies that Rojas attended were public and social events witnessed by as many as 100 to 150 workers and their families, including other black Caribbean braceros. In fact, the more people who attended them and the higher the level of excitement expressed by the workers determined how "hot" the celebrations were judged. Although they too were displays of Vodun, characterized by multiple spirit possessions, the dances were performed in recognition of a momentous experience.

The Haitian braceros staged these dances to commemorate a host of special occasions, including the planting and harvesting of their garden plots, the marriage of loved ones, and the death of family members and friends. The participants in one type of dance formed a chorus line and moved "generally in Indian file . . . [they] may link arms or place their hands on each other's shoulders, but the two parties that dance a duo generally do so more in the style of the old minuet."[33] The Haitians usually cooked elaborate meals for the celebratory dances. On the Caidije batey they lunched on "either roasted or fried pork, or chicken, rice with fat-back, fried plantains, and malanga, a fish called boniato as well as a lot of rum," to celebrate the birth and baptism of a child.[34] Such a meal reflected the value that Haitians placed on childbirth and christening. Both events began the process whereby the infant became a member of the family and of the community.[35] Christening with the rites of baptism also empowered the infant, because the powers of a deity were believed to reside in the names given at baptism. As a result, Haitians had to defend and judiciously honor their names since "to pronounce his name is to call . . . the person [and] the divine essence with which he or she is indissolubly linked."[36]

Meanwhile, during the funeral of a loved one, those in attendance performed a variety of plays. The most common play for the Haitians on the Caidije was called the *jeu bak*. In this variant of the ring shout, a number of performers "made a circle by holding a piece of rope or cord with their hands until they completed a ring. Each dancer then took turns running or pretending to run into the ring to see who entered the circle." In order to strengthen the bonds between members of the grieving family and other braceros, a banquet was usually given before the jeu bak.[37] Performances such as the jeu bak were undoubtedly part of the elaborate "lingua sacra" that all Africans brought to the Americas to articulate their socioreligious and political ideologies.[38] The community performed mortuary rituals to ensure that the soul of the deceased would join the ancestral spirits not in Africa but in a mythical place under the sea, a river, or someplace deep inside the earth or in the sky.[39] "When the appropriate ritual sequences are performed by the community, the [soul] can be reclaimed from [the community of ancestors] and become an important influence in the lives of the community," according to Leslie Desmangles.[40]

Not only were these dances social sites and arrangements where Haitians were assisted by other black Caribbean workers to commemorate an important date or event, they were also venues where people could release their frustrations and emotions while reinforcing their cultural identity and solidarity in Cuba. Speaking with his family about what the Legba ceremonies meant to him, Jacques Roumain's fictional character, Manuel, the machetero who spent fifteen years working in Antilla, stated: "I danced and sang to my heart's content. I'm black, no? And I enjoyed myself like a real black. When the drums beat, I feel it in the pit of my stomach. I feel an itch in my loins and an electric current in my legs, and I've got to join the dance."[41] How song, dance, and the incessant drumming helped workers like Manuel to reaffirm their Haitianness at home and abroad was reflected in the nature of Vodun. As a "dance religion," the essence of Vodun is "the very varied drumbeats, named after the African tribes which introduced them to Haiti, [the rhythm] governs the steps and movements of the diviners. They also invoke numerous families of gods since dancing is a ritualistic act releasing mystical forces, which work on the invisibles. Music and dancing please the gods, because, they too are dancers carried away by the magic of the rhythm."[42] Although the dances usually took place on Saturday nights in Haiti, the braceros retained this aspect of their culture by moving them to Sundays, because the sugar mills' work regimes forced many to work at the start of the weekend.

The Haitians expressed their cultural solidarity on other holidays as well, when "they dressed up to [perform] their dances and rituals. The 'banda rara' became the most cherished holiday among the Haitian sugarcane workers." Involving hundreds of braceros who gathered around a sacral campfire, dancing before parading from one batey to the next, it started during the first weekend of the Lenten season and culminated on the Saturday night before Easter. Among Central Africans such as the Kongo, fire not only was the physical location where rituals occurred but also symbolized life-giving energy. Fire "carried a mystical force and was used to make sacred certain moments or events and to demark certain acts from the normal flow of routine," like a birth or baptism, but in this case, the death and resurrection of Christ.[43]

During these ceremonies, the braceros played rhythms that they brought from their homeland until they became tired. "I do not remember if they called it 'Bacongo,' [but] it was something that they played with cowbells, boxes, bongos and other drums," Orlando González remembered from his days working on the Algodones central.[44] Referring to the style of music that he heard, González employed the name of the enslaved ancestors of the Kongo who had been brought to Cuba. The Bakongo had "exchanged religious knowledge with Dahomey ethnic groups in Africa and later in eastern Cuba."[45] González's observation suggests that the liturgies of the Haitian workers were borrowed from their Kongo ancestors in both Haiti and Cuba and later fused with Catholicism.[46] Their cosmographies included belief in a supreme being and a pantheon of deities that controlled all the good and evil forces of the universe. They used similar rituals and ceremonies to venerate and propitiate their ancestors and to invoke spirit possession.[47] González's inability to recognize the name of the dance with certainty meant that he did not realize that the Haitians commonly used dance and music in multiple ways. If they used these activities to communicate with the loa, then the rituals were intended to empower them. Having their honor constantly attacked on the cane farms and the bateyes, as well as suffering bodily harm due to the sugar companies' labor regimen, according to one peasant woman, Haitians contacted their deities because "the loa love us, protect and watch over us. They show us what is happening to our relatives living far away and they tell us what medicines will do us good when we are sick. If we are hungry they appear to us in dreams and say don't despair, you will soon earn some money, and money comes." She added, "[T]he loa inform us of the plots being hatched by our enemies."[48] Calling upon the loa to protect and watch over them gave the Haitians the confidence and strength to establish dynamic communities on the peripheries of the Tacajó, Algodones, and Jaronú enclaves. It would be the workers of these small colonies whom certain anarcho-syndicalist Cuban labor leaders as well as the agents of Marcus M.

Garvey's Universal Negro Improvement League would try to organize in order to challenge the hegemony of the sugar companies and the state.

The retention of the Haitian braceros' cultural identity, which provided them with the strength and resilience to withstand the racial and ethnic ideologies of the companies and of Cuban society in general, was fostered by a number of social processes. First, the Haitians composed the majority of black Caribbean immigrants who arrived in Camagüey and Oriente provinces between 1917 and 1931, so their numbers were always greater than their British West Indian counterparts, especially the Jamaicans. For example, while 75,461 Haitians officially arrived between 1921 and 1926, and another 38,130 landed from 1927 to 1930, the number of Jamaicans who came to Cuba during that first period totaled 31,816, and only 3,603 for the years 1927–1930.[49] As a result, Haitians composed almost 44 percent of all immigrants in Camagüey and approximately 55 percent of all black foreigners in Oriente.[50] More important, by going to Cuba they were joining and establishing contact with black Cubans whose ancestors had arrived in the previous century from the same geographical and cultural areas of West-Central Africa as the Haitians. As slaves, the Kongo were able to retain their cultural identity inside their *cabildos de naciones de afro-cubanos*.[51] The Haitians' success at resisting the forces of assimilation was engendered by the same factors that allowed their enslaved relatives to articulate their identity. The culture and institutions of diasporas "require a demographic thickness—a sufficient number of diasporans to constitute a critical mass in urban settings."[52] This critical mass developed as the demand for surplus labor increased with the expansion of the mills' grinding capacity. The surplus laborers were placed in the black barrios or in the barracones to live. However, many Haitians decided to live in isolation, squatting in the marginal hinterlands in order to build huts and grow a little food. These spaces became transnational lakous or compounds for the Haitian families, and their cultural activities permitted the workers to re-create the villages or towns surrounding Les Cayes and Jeremie in Cuba.

Second, the North American and Cuban administrators of the sugar companies decided that the Haitians' race and ethnicity made them suitable only for field work. Usually excluded from working inside the sugar mills, the majority of Haitians were denied occupational mobility. This made them the most exploited and discriminated workers in the sugar industry.[53] However, their marginal status, even among other black Caribbean braceros, produced a "community of fate" of which they were members and which tended to strengthen their solidarity. Their occupations and geographical isolation, along with high levels of racial discrimination, repression, and exploitation, collectively engendered their identity. In short, "Haitianness" extended from the processes that "in part [were caused] by the level of exploitation and repression due to their race, ethnicity, class and color." As poor, black, and Haitian, "all of these successive and concurrent discriminations . . . required them to defend themselves by saving their identity as they moved to express their culture aggressively."[54] In fact, their deprivation was reflected not only by the generic term *Haitian*, which referred to cane cutters, but also by the name that the majority of white administrators, foremen, and colonos used to refer to the Haitian bracero: *cadaso*, or a "piece." *Cadaso* had multiple meanings. It referred to someone who could hardly speak or understand Spanish or English in order to buy food and other items at the company store, and also to a bracero unfamiliar with Cuban customs. The word itself is a Haitian Creole derivative of *coddace*, or foreigner. It became very popular in Camagüey and often carried the same connotations that the Spanish word *bozal* had for black African slaves born in Africa.[55] The use of this term demonstrates the intimate knowledge that the colonos, administrators, and foremen obtained from the Haitian-born emigrant brokers who delivered thousands of workers. Its cross-cultural usage symbolized the workers' marginalization and powerlessness. Table 4 even demonstrates the contempt that Cubans had for the Haitian workers. Not only did the Cuban census of 1919 fail to count and recognize their presence, it also classified them as "other" West Indians.

Despite their marginalized status, the Haitian immigrants who met on Sundays and Christian holidays for social and religious reasons imposed "a cultural stamp with their presence and defined the original personality of the bateyes. The Haitian immigrants and their descendants, called 'pichones,' preserved their songs, dances, and beliefs no matter how many years they stayed facing the attempts of assimilation. In spite of learning Spanish, they continued to transmit to their descendants the language of their Creole origins."[56] At the same time, they modified their rites and ceremonies to make them more effective in the material reality of Cuba while giving them new meanings. Yet the lure of at least seasonal employment as field workers prompted many Haitians to develop a transnational identity.

While some Haitian immigrants kept their original names after they arrived in Cuba, others were quick to take Spanish first names. Several Haitians who worked at the Uruguay and Jaronú *centrales* in Camagüey remembered that when

TABLE 4. Total Number of Foreign-Born by Sex and Ethnicity in the Principal Sugar-Producing Provinces of Santa Clara, Camagüey, and Oriente in 1919

	Santa Clara		Camagüey		Oriente		Total
	Male	Female	Male	Female	Male	Female	
Spain	48,652	11,543	23,170	4,269	22,289	6,774	116,697
Jamaica	1,021*	85*	2,429*	760*	10,226*	2,888*	17,409
Puerto Rico	6*	1*	—	—	536*	373*	916
Central America, South America	30*	9*	200*	96*	2,091*	343*	2,769
United States	316	228	324	250	466	190	1,774
China	2,907	30	1,305	4	1,676	16	5,938
Other West Indian	340*	126*	4,673*	419*	13,574*	1,556*	20,688

Source: Angel C. Betancourt y Miranda, *Census of the Republic of Cuba*, 1919 (Havana, 1919), 436–37. The asterisks indicate the inclusion of black, mixed, and "yellow" people, according to the census. The figures for China were found in both the white and "colored" columns. Figures for Spain and the United States only refer to whites. There is no column for Haiti in the census. One can assume that Haitians were counted as part of the category designated as "other West Indians."

they arrived at the bateyes, the foremen of the work gangs, unable to pronounce their Haitian names, began to call the immigrants Felix, Hilario, and Camilo. This practice appears to have been common. The way in which the names were given to the Haitian braceros on the batey of the San Miguel colonia reminded Orlando González of the Algodones *central* of how the children of African slaves were forced to take the surnames of their owners.[57] It was not unusual, however, for some immigrants to adopt the names of important Cuban patriots from the War of 1895, such as Antonio Maceo, Máximo Gómez, and Calixto García, according to González. They also took the names of the places where they worked, like Camagüey and Cunagua. Meanwhile, José Manolo, José Pepe, Panchuco, and Francisco became popular first names among the braceros on the Jaronú and Uruguay *centrales*. Many hoped that by adopting Spanish names and those from the Cuban pantheon of heroes, they could legitimize their presence in Cuba.[58] In other words, by appropriating the names of important individuals in Cuban history as well as of the sites of their existence in Cuba, some Haitian immigrants were selecting powerful symbols "of freedom, personhood, empowerment, and recreation of identity." This often occurred in the oppositional societies of the Caribbean where members of the black diaspora found themselves as slaves and later as peasants.[59] In so doing, they hoped that their new names, laden with historical value and power, would engender a degree of respect and cause some Cubans to embrace them more than if they kept their own Haitian Creole names. Other writers have interpreted this adaptive strategy among black diasporans as a decision on their part to manufacture a transnational identity through a process of creolization or assimilation, to conceal their cultural identity and ethnicity, and to resist their inferior status by reestablishing their self-esteem through the reinvention of their identity.[60] However, the Haitian Creole appellations Pol, Fis, and Pie remained the most common surnames for the immigrants who worked in Camagüey and reflected their desire to retain their personal heritage and identity.[61] Nonetheless, as contracted immigrant laborers they also sought to express, for practical reasons, an alteration of their identity with the hope of giving the impression of becoming Cuban.

The Haitians who decided to stay in Cuba during the *tiempo muerto* or beyond the period of their contracts had a better chance of evading the authorities if they changed their name. In February 1918, the mayor's office of the town of Baracoa wrote to the governor of Oriente to inform him that the police of the barrio of Sabanillo had detained a black Haitian by the name of Antonio Salomon. The police had arrested him because he was an undocumented worker who had lost his identification papers, which included his work permit. Before the local authorities of Baracoa could deport Salomon, he escaped from jail. Although he was spotted traveling through the town of Marcane near Guantánamo, his acquaintances were unable to tell the authorities where he was going next.[62] By concealing his ethnicity and assuming a transnational identity with a Spanish name and the ability to speak Spanish, Salomon was able to evade the police and move through Cuban society until he found work at another mill in a different region. The use of Spanish appellations by some Haitian immigrants proved to be powerful instruments to challenge their marginalization and exploitation. Archival records reveal that the immigrants' use of aliases became problematic for the government.

It also appears that the sugar companies assisted workers in evading the police while they attempted to stay in Cuba. The Immigration Law of 1917 required representatives of the mills to identify and register all their contracted workers with the Secretary of the Department of Agriculture, Commerce, and Labor.[63] In order to expedite the paperwork, and using Spanish, the company managers invented both first and family names for their braceros. When the workers' contracts expired at the end of the zafra but the men never arrived at Santiago de Cuba or Nuevitas to be repatriated, the authorities went looking for them. In order to identify and locate the illegal aliens, the government unsuccessfully tried to use the passenger manifests of the steamships that had brought them to Cuba.[64] Now carrying fraudulent identification documents, the Haitians moved from one mill to another, depending upon the labor market. Concurrently, the managers of the sugar companies used this illegal status to their advantage. Some threatened the braceros and forced them to remain in the cane fields to cut cane for nothing. If they refused, they were jailed and subsequently turned over to the authorities for deportation.

The experiences of the Jamaicans and other British West Indians were similar to those of their Haitian counterparts, although in some ways their lives were quite different. Although the majority of Jamaicans arrived to perform field work as macheteros and carreteros, others came to provide the factory mills with skilled artisan labor. The latter were held in higher esteem, reflecting how whites defined and evaluated their race and ethnicity. Some administrators manipulated race and ethnicity, concluding that, unlike the Haitian braceros, the Jamaican immigrants did not demonstrate the tendency to purposely isolate themselves in order to retain their linguistic and cultural differences.[65] This generalization may have been the case for some Jamaicans, but when the opportunity to re-create their own homes and communities presented itself, their desire to own some land and to establish homesteads similar to those of the Haitians was very strong.

As mentioned at the beginning of this chapter, a large number of Jamaicans attempted to reassemble their homes in Paso Estancia, Oriente. Their effort to buy a large tract of land to build a few homes and to farm was initially thwarted by a community of black Cuban squatters who refused to leave. After officials of the Illinois-Cuban Land Company failed to oust the black Cubans, the Jamaicans informed the British consul in Santiago de Cuba of their problems. The British minister proceeded to take their case to the provincial governor, arguing that the sale of the land was legal and that the black Cubans no longer had the legal right to squat on the Jamaicans' newly acquired property. The British consul hoped that "the Governor will quickly solve the problems faced by these British subjects."[66] It took four weeks before the problem was resolved. In September 1913, the mayor of Palma Soriano informed the governor that the municipal judge, Gregorio de Llano y Raimet, had ruled against the Jamaicans and in favor of the black Cuban squatters. In short, he discovered that the Illinois-Cuban Land Company had swindled the Jamaicans. The land that they bought had not originally belonged to the company; instead, the black Cubans had secured the right to settle on the piece of property the year before, in July 1912, after the Race War of 1912 had ended. Thus, the sale was illegal. Undoubtedly the black Cubans who had moved onto the disputed property had been among the large number of blacks uprooted by the violence accompanying the government's repression of the Independent Party of Color. Judge Llano y Raimet ruled that if the Jamaicans still desired to live on the land, they would have to buy it again, but this time from the black Cuban squatters.[67] The judicial ruling against the Jamaican braceros demonstrated that even when supported by the diplomatic pressure of the British consul, their rights would never supersede those of black Cubans.

The British West Indians of the Baraguá *central* in Camagüey, outside Ciego de Avila, sought to improve their lives by transforming two segregated barrios of the batey reserved for them into a place resembling their own islands, where they could retain their cultural identity. Our understanding of the historical transformation of Baraguá into an exclusively British West Indian town is based in part on the interviews of Stanley Whitaker and William Preston Stone, two black Caribbean immigrants who arrived in Cuba in 1917, a year after an Edwin Atkins company built the mill in 1916. Whitaker came to the Baraguá *central* when he was seventeen years old; he worked in the factory mill as a carpenter. Preston Stone came from Panama in the same year and remembered that British West Indians from Trinidad and Tobago, Grenada, and St. Lucia filled a number of occupations at the mill.[68] Besides cutting cane, the West Indians worked on the batey as cooks and gardeners. Enjoying the opportunity to grow a little food on the grounds of the plantation, both these men insisted that the daily diet for most immigrants from the British West Indies consisted of bacalao (salt cod) with akee or breadfruit. Their most popular dish, which they often ate on Sundays, was rice and peas with coconut.

Sending for his wife and family at the end of World War I stood out in Preston Stone's memory. He never forgot the indifference that the administrators displayed when they failed to provide basic necessities, such as housing and schools, for the workers' families. Instead, the West Indians had to build their own homes and a private schoolhouse for their children on the batey. They recruited teachers in the same way that Ernest Johnston Bennett, of the Lomo del Chivo barrio in Guantánamo, described. Using the traditional fictive kinship system of godparentage, or *compadrazgo*, in Cuba, all the children acquired a second set of parents and relatives who became responsible for providing them with an education.[69] When time permitted, the elders took turns serving as teachers for the children of their friends and coworkers. In addition, if Jamaican craftsmen or manual laborers living in the eastern part of Cuba during the 1920s saved enough money, they could send their children to a private school established exclusively for black immigrants located in La Guira, just west of Banes in Oriente. This practice reflected their belief in the educational and occupational rights of both sons and daughters.[70]

For the most part, Cuban government officials and the administrators of the sugar mills responsible for producing archival records on the daily lives of the Jamaican braceros overlooked their educational needs and aspirations, as well as those of other British West Indians. As a result, one has to search through the Jamaicans' experiences as both colonial subjects in Jamaica and as emigrants in places such as Costa Rica and Panama in order to surmise that the schools they established in Cuba were modeled along the lines of those established at home and abroad in other Jamaican emigrant communities. If the educational experience of their children in Cuba resembled that of British West Indians in Panama, then the schools would have been seriously overcrowded and the teachers probably poorly trained and recruited in Kingston. Some teachers, however, who had taught in Jamaica before leaving, would have carried the title of "pupil-teacher" and been "ordinary" or "college" trained.[71] Adopting the forms of the British colonial school, the children in Cuba would have been expected to complete the curricula of years one through six before turning fifteen years of age. Based on their experiences in Panama as English speakers in the sugar enclaves, they would have obtained most of their textbooks and other school supplies from children of the white North American mill workers who had discarded them. The black instructors' pedagogy included the use of rote memorization, discipline, oration, and manners in order to teach the basics of reading and writing English, history, and arithmetic with an emphasis on long division. Attending small, superior, and segregated schools, the sons and daughters of white employees, besides receiving the basics, also gained vocational training in office work such as stenography, composition, and accounting.[72] Black students, unlike the white children, had to attend school throughout the year so their parents could work during and after the zafra. Finally, in order to move on to the next year of instruction, black Caribbean students had to pass a set of exams, "some [the] first year, preliminary, second year, third year and so on," according to a Mrs. Dove.[73] Because of the inferior quality of the schools that black immigrant children attended, Stanley Whitaker decided that his children must also learn a trade such as carpentry, tailoring, or shoemaking. Two of his daughters became seamstresses on the batey. Such aspirations were also common back home in Jamaica. There, many parents provided their daughters with vocational training, understanding that "not every women gets a husband to help her through life and if she don't get, she will be able to live off her learning."[74]

The sacralization of the Jamaicans' Cuban homes and communities included attending church services every Sunday while wearing their best suits and dresses. According to Stanley Holdip, an immigrant from Montserrat, there were four Protestant denominations present on the batey: the Salvation Army, the Christian Mission, the Anglican Church, and the Church of the Seventh-Day Adventists. Because Holdip never revealed what role these groups played, one must again look to the Jamaicans' religious experiences at home and at other destinations in order to uncover this hidden aspect of their lives in Cuba. The Anglican Church probably served the black immigrants from Panama, while the Baptist Church, a denomination that Holdip never acknowledged, catered to the Jamaican peasants who came directly from the island. Since British officials reported that the Baptist Church of Guantánamo served a large congregation in 1916, as well as the fact that rural Jamaicans represented the majority of British West Indian workers on the sugar enclaves in general, an examination of the characteristics and significance of the Baptist Church may offer some insights.[75]

The Baptist Church had been a central force in the daily lives of Jamaicans since the 1830s, assisting former slaves in acquiring land from the planters as well as from the colonial government. The services that the Jamaican workers attended in Baraguá, Guantánamo, and elsewhere in Cuba may have been informed by the liturgical and theological developments that the church experienced during the middle part of the nineteenth century. In 1860, a dynamic evangelical movement that started in Ireland and was called the "Great Revival" swept throughout the British Empire, including Jamaica. Its effects were immediately felt by members of the Moravian, Wesleyan, and Baptist churches. The Baptist faith became Africanized when it mixed with the Myalist Revival, a series of "outbreaks of an Afro-creole" prophetic and millennial faith movement.

Myalists considered themselves ordained by God himself to stamp out evil in order to prepare the world for Jesus Christ.[76] This cosmography was later infused with the Kongo tenets and rituals that Jamaican practitioners called Kumina. Similar to how Vodun became imbued with Kongo materials, Kumina introduced Myalists to the belief that the deities held spiritual secrets that could "protect them, bring them good fortune, and assist them in performing magic or *obeah*."[77] In addition, the conviction that the spirits or ancestors could be persuaded to perform both benevolent and malevolent acts also parallels the beliefs that empowered the Haitian braceros. For example, in order to eradicate evil (*obeah*) from the world, Myalists as well as Kumina devotees performed a host of public rituals that included drinking a potent libation, with songs and dances as well as drumming that caused the practitioners to experience a trance-like state. This dissociated and altered reality was believed to give devotees the spiritual power to locate wicked persons responsible for using sorcery and to exorcise the evil from them. In Kumina, "it is the immigrant ancestors who return to enjoy themselves in the bodies of the living, and who give advice to the community's descendants."[78]

Given the sacral innovations that became part of the ethnic identity of the Jamaican peasantry, and which had developed sixty years earlier, it is safe to say that the churches of their children established in Baraguá and other bateyes during the 1910s and 1920s became venues for these same beliefs and practices. After all, the same folks who cut sugarcane were given memories of Africa from their parents and understood that "in the matrix of family, clan, and nation, communication with departed family and ancestors was essential in the maintenance of social well-being, order, and peace."[79] This tenet informed ritual performances at memorials, funerals, and burials, as well as during birthdays and baptismal ceremonies in the isolated enclaves. That the enclaves were remote "nowhere spaces" composed of Jamaicans and other British West Indians may have made this Afro-Jamaican spiritual worldview more important than those of the other common churches like the Anglican and the Seventh-Day Adventist. These last two required their followers to congregate at specific sites to observe their liturgies. On the other hand, Myalist-Kumina adherents shared beliefs and rituals with non-Kongo people such as the Yoruba, Hausa, and other

Sahelian Africans, according to Maureen Warner-Lewis.[80] These ethnic groups predominated in the black populations of Trinidad, Guyana, and Guadeloupe. The central spiritual element that tied these groups together was the veneration and propitiation of their ancestors.

This Myalist- and Kumina-influenced Baptist faith offered its devotees an explanation of the socioeconomic and cultural context in which they found themselves in Cuba. Both Myalists and Kumina adherents understood that "malevolent magic or 'obeah' emanated from envy and wickedness"—forces that the African slaves had understood were responsible for their bondage and misery.[81] Some Jamaican braceros might have employed this article of faith as well. More important, the theological doctrine that "good can and should prevail . . . to prevent misfortune and maximize good fortune for the community" could also have informed their attitudes and behavior.[82] In other words, the braceros optimistically believed that with the aid of God and their ancestors they would not only overcome their ordeal, including the attacks on their dignity and humanity, but also reap the fruits of defeating those responsible. In 1841, the freedman Robert Scott had summed up this spiritual and earthly conflict before an audience of other ex-bondsmen and women. In a post-emancipation Jamaican society where racial and ethnic hierarchies reinforced the notion of black inferiority and justified the exploitation of the former slaves, Scott's beliefs may have encouraged many in his audience, as well as their grandchildren, to eventually emigrate to Panama, Costa Rica, and later Cuba. He commanded that they "try to get all you can for [your]self, and for your wife, and for your children, and try to get it that you may serve God . . . Yes, and the time is coming when black people will get rich and ride in their carriages as well as white people."[83]

The power that Myalism gave its devotees through African and Christian-based rituals and tenets mirrored the Haitian workers' cosmography and helped them to challenge their degradation. In spite of the ethnic or national differences between the Jamaicans and Haitians, which the companies used to divide them by privileging the former, the Jamaican immigrants' millenarian faith potentially may have brought both groups together in a "community of fate." Not only were they sharing the same hardships as field workers, but they also held similar spiritual convictions that made sense of their material reality. Establishing a multiethnic "community of fate" may have been the first step for the braceros in mitigating the role that the segmented labor system played in their lives. As macheteros and carreteros, they had the opportunity to individually and collectively resist their condition through acts of sabotage. The class solidarity constructed around their shared cosmographies may have also made the organizational efforts of the anarcho-syndicalists and the Garveyites in Cuba more efficacious. The on-going immigration of Jamaican braceros assisted in the reproduction and retention of a spiritual praxis and identity in Cuba that helped them forge a multiethnic or transnational alliance with the Haitians. For example, John Barry was pulled to Cuba not only because of its "economic boom" but also in order to join his cousin, who lived in Ciego de Avila.[84] Dinna Edna Rowe, a resident of the Lomo del Chivo barrio, remembered: "When my parents left us in Jamaica with my grandparents, and after they settled and established themselves in [Guantánamo], they sent for us to come. We came with our aunt and uncle who also decided to stay."[85]

Another way that black British Caribbean workers helped make Baraguá a place resembling their homeland was by introducing the game of cricket. Both Whitaker and Stone remembered how cricket allowed everyone from the British West Indies—Jamaicans, Barbadians, and Grenadians—to show their insular identities. It brought them together and encouraged everyone to remain proud of their British heritage and customs.[86] Thus the sport of cricket played a special role in fostering racial solidarity while dissolving interisland animosity. It also engendered a British colonial identity, according to Jorge Giovannetti. Central to this identity was the belief that all British subjects were persons of honor and dignity. After confronting the same types of subjugation and exploitation, processes that standardized their experiences as black immigrants, Jamaicans, Barbadians, Grenadians, and others usually articulated this colonial identity to demand that British functionaries in Cuba, England, or at home protect them from abuse and violence.[87] As a sport that expressed "Britishness," cricket was important in British West Indian emigrant communities throughout the Caribbean. Such was the case in the town of San Pedro de Macoris, in the Dominican Republic. Emigrants went there to cut cane on the Consuelo central. According to some macheteros there, cricket "fostered a spirit of self-celebration in which a sense of community and ethnic identity were forged." More important, many cricket teams represented the fraternal lodges and benevolent organizations that black Caribbean workers from St. Martin, Nevis, Tortola, and Montserrat had established.[88] These institutions also sought to promote a sense of fellowship.

In Cuba, Jamaicans and other British West Indians also created mutual-aid societies for similar reasons. Charles Watkins and A. T. Dottin represented a lodge of British Caribbean workers called La Estrella Naciente de Cuba (the Rising Star of Cuba). Composed of both men and women, in 1918 this Freemasons' organization opened its doors to its members on the second Monday of every month in order to preserve the secrets of the six grades of liturgy of the Rite of York. Anyone who revealed these secrets or other information about the lodge faced expulsion. The members were also forbidden to discuss the politics and religions of blacks and whites in Cuba.[89] This clause of its constitution accorded with the Law of Association that governed every type of benevolent society, club, or lodge in Cuba, regardless of ethnicity or nationality. Watkins's decision to write this principle into his association's bylaws demonstrated that he and the members were keenly aware that they must eschew any sentiments or actions that the government could interpret as illegal or as an act of insubordination.[90] Nonetheless, because La Estrella Naciente de Cuba was located off-site, outside the confines of the sugar enclaves, where Jamaicans and other British West Indians could gather beyond the vigilance of the authorities, it would be very surprising if they did not discuss sensitive issues that they were prohibited from addressing elsewhere.[91] For example, a Mr. Azariam from St. Ann Parish remembered that he and his brother landed in Cuba during the 1917 Chambolena Revolt led by the former president of Cuba, José Miguel Gómez. Not only did he and his brother discuss the causes of the rebellion, they and other black Caribbean workers found themselves caught up in this political conflict. Azariam remembered that the dispute between the Liberals and Conservatives occurred when the Cubans "were voting for two men. And when they voting, the people [became] cross man! Because they say, they will come to you, them meet with you [and ask] who you voting for? Sometimes some of the Jamaicans, them link up with the Cubans—them getting in[to] you[r] know[ledge], 'who you voting for, my friend.' If you did not tell them! It was a dangerous thing because perhaps the man who you go tell them say to you who to vote for, and the same one them against [who you like], you see. Them never attacked me, but they attacked my brother. My brother paid, gave them some money and say [to them] "go on man."[92] Mr. Azariam's memory of the Liberal Rebellion of 1917 suggests that some Jamaicans had been in Cuba for a lengthy period of time and were seen by some Cubans as having a vested interest in the country's politics. His comments also reveal that although Jamaican workers lived in geographically isolated communities and were banned from discussing Cuban politics inside their organizations, they were nevertheless cognizant of the country's affairs, sharing that information as well as their experiences within their "hush arbors," or mutual-aid societies. In this case, the political troubles of the country brought the braceros together to discuss the dangers of Cuban politics. That men and women joined such fellowships is interesting, since La Estrella Naciente de Cuba as well as other British Antillean clubs established in Cuba were different from the mutual-aid societies founded by West Indian immigrants who worked on the banana plantations surrounding Limón, Costa Rica, where all the lodges were associated with a particular church and were composed of only men.[93]

La Estrella Naciente de Cuba served its members in another way. It provided mutual aid to its members as well as to their spouses and children when they became ill. The lodge also covered funeral and burial expenses when an associate or a family member died. The money that the lodge employed to aid its members during times of distress came from a membership fee of fifteen pesos and monthly dues of one peso. The lodge also fined its members ten to fifty centavos for missing a meeting or disgracing the group with public misconduct. This revenue allowed the society to give the family of a deceased member forty pesos to cover funeral and burial expenses, twenty pesos for an associate's spouse, and as much as ten pesos for the proper burial for a child.[94]

Jamaicans and other immigrants from the British Caribbean founded another lodge, La Estrella de Belén Central, Numero Uno (The Central Star of Belén), in the small town of Guaro near the municipality of Mayarí. Like La Estrella Naciente de Cuba, this organization sought to "improve the cultural and economic well-being of its members and take care of them when they became ill. It promises to protect a member's family in case of death by covering the cost of their burial."[95] That the majority of Jamaican mutual-aid societies provided their members with proper mortuary rituals shows another aspect of their identity. This trait was undoubtedly rooted in the Kongo-derived Jamaican belief of a dual soul. Persisting to this day, "and probably deriving from multiple sources . . . The dual soul consists of a personal spirit and a duppy or shadow. At death the personal spirit departs this earth, but the duppy or shadow remains with the corpse and, if not properly buried, can wander around, haunting people for various reasons, and perhaps behaving like [a] poltergeist."[96] As a small organization composed of sugarcane workers, La Estrella de Belén Central had a very small budget based upon an initiation fee of two pesos and monthly dues of 1.50 pesos. Meanwhile, the Luz Unida Numero 10,973 in the town of Antilla charged an initiation fee of fifteen pesos and monthly dues of only fifty centavos in 1926.[97] The small budgets of these mutual-aid societies undoubtedly restricted their ability to support their membership and families during times of sickness or death. Nonetheless, the fact that Jamaicans and other immigrants from the British Caribbean created these organizations with limited resources demonstrates their desire to share in the costs of the health risks associated with field work.[98] The poor medical attention they received from the farmers and the companies created their need to do so. Benjamin T. from St. Elizabeth Parish, Jamaica, recounted how after he arrived in 1918, "life was rough. You had to walk in water all the time! When you heard it was cold . . . The cold was the same as in England, you know . . . the natives had a warm fire. When you looked at them they just trembled. I say you were so cold that your teeth, just knocked against you . . . I did not like it at all for it was too cold."[99] Mr. Burke agreed that the dangers of performing field work were real: "It was a very rough country. Plenty [of] hard work . . . You have to work in plenty [of] rain, water and some places the water is bad. A lot of swamp. Fever, malaria fever . . . When I came back here, I come back here sick."[100] It is no wonder that some Jamaican braceros required assistance to cover their medical costs.

At the same time, the attempt to pool resources in order to help fellow immigrants showed a degree of ethnic and national esprit de corps. And when a member failed to live up to the expectations of these organizations, his countrymen and women felt betrayed and disappointed. Such was the case when Ethel Green informed the governor of Santiago de Cuba that a number of abuses had occurred in her lodge, La Brillante Estrella de Cuba, established in November 1919. In order to qualify for membership in this lodge, an individual had to be an honorable person of the immigrant community and in good health. Members were also required to have a full-time job. To join this association, men were required to pay ten pesos and women six pesos. Every member vowed to uphold the lodge's morality code, which included a sobriety requirement. They also promised to attend all the meetings and pay the monthly dues of one peso. When Ethel Green introduced herself by letter to the governor, she indicated that everyone knew her to be a pleasant, passive, and honorable person. Green then wrote that some members of her lodge had begun to publicly defame her character inside and outside of the association. In fact, she had just been expelled without being accused of any imputable offense. She claimed that her expulsion was unwarranted.

Green noted that the personal attacks began when she inquired about the lodge's financial situation and budget. She had asked Mrs. Josephine Gray, the lodge's treasurer, for a report. According to Green, Gray used every excuse to ignore her. Green then discovered that the lodge's coffers were empty and that it was therefore unable to "legally protect its members."[101] It was the possibility that the funds had been embezzled that prompted Green to write to the governor. She requested an immediate investigation into the disappearance of the lodge's funds. The governor's inquest into the matter forced the president of the lodge, Jeremiah Carlyle, to respond and explain the actions of the lodge's treasurer. After reminding the governor that it was the responsibility of the treasurer to keep the financial records and to report the fiscal status of the lodge every three months to its officers and members, Carlyle wrote that when Ethel Green and other members solicited the records from Gray, Gray "refused to do so and used insulting words during the act of noncompliance. Her words caused some members of the lodge to leave, never to return."[102]

Upon learning what had happened to Green, Carlyle informed the governor that he confronted Gray. Presenting his showdown with Gray in gender-sensitive terms, the president told her that he could not believe that a married and respectable woman would act this way toward her friends. He asked Gray, "Where is your husband?" She answered that he was in Jamaica. Carlyle continued: "Are you two still together?" Gray responded: "No, I have left him." Carlyle then proceeded to chastise the treasurer: "It is clear that you did not have any right to treat the decent people of this lodge that way, and because you have left your husband, you will never be a leader of this lodge again. No woman who leaves her husband and who is now living an immoral life will ever lead this society."[103]

Carlyle's statements reveal his definition and expectation of Jamaican womanhood. He believed that married Jamaican women were to conduct themselves morally and remain faithful to their husbands before they could be considered for an honorable leadership position. In the end, he told the governor that Ethel Green had helped him discover that Josephine Gray as well as her brother and sister, who also were members, had stolen the lodge's money and had tried to blame Green for the theft. Gray's prevarication led to her expulsion, and after the lodge had discovered the truth, it decided to expel her family in addition to several other members who had helped them. Gray probably began stealing the funds after she decided to leave her husband, as a way to support herself and remain in Cuba. Nonetheless, that Carlyle banished Gray and her family demonstrated that members of a "community of fate" valued cohesion as they attempted to establish a "unified subculture" within a site that required the members to live up to their own set of "codes and social standards in order to protect their own autonomous reality beyond the scope of the dominant."[104] The penalty imposed upon Gray was also intended to discourage other members of the La Brillante Estrella de Cuba from betraying the community of Jamaican workers in general. Ostracism became the penalty that community leaders imposed to promote conformity and loyalty. And by using the provincial government of Oriente to protect what little money black immigrants pooled in order to establish these types of organizations, the power of leaders like Carlyle was enhanced. Adopting the doctrine of self-help to pool their incomes also helped to prescribe the workers' conduct. In so doing, they collectively protected their honor.

These immigrant benevolent societies played another role. As part of the "alternative society that the West Indians [living in Limón, Costa Rica] maintained in the shadows of the plantations . . . this intricate network of religious, mutual aid, and beneficent societies gave the Jamaicans a strong institutional framework for creating labor unions."[105] As we shall see in the next chapter, between 1920 and 1925 black Caribbean braceros participated in the labor movement that sought to organize workers in the sugar industry. Their involvement came after understanding that some trade unionists were committed to the principles of class solidarity and collective action. These tenets were the cornerstones of their benevolent societies as well.

While many of the organizations established by Jamaicans provided mutual aid to their members, others became venues of entertainment and education. Some British West Indians created organizations dedicated to offering members recreational activities like cricket, boxing, and soccer, and an opportunity to acquire an education. Such was the case for the West Indian Star Society. In order to join this organization, a person had to swear to "help advance the mission of the organization and fulfill its objectives by lending their moral, material, and intellectual support."[106] Unlike La Estrella Naciente de Cuba, the West Indian Star encouraged its members to participate in a range of discussions and activities that explored a host of political and religious themes and principles. Its leaders, S. H. Smith and T. M. Huntley, probably viewed these meetings as central to carrying out the educational mission of the organization, which provided formal elementary and secondary instruction. The West Indian Star offered classes in English not only to its members and their children but also to anyone who was willing to pay for its school. They hoped that the education the children received would prepare them to enter secondary school back home. In this way this group sought to improve the lives of its associates and their families.[107]

Besides creating a social site that provided formal elementary and secondary instruction, the leaders of the West Indian Star may have realized that it was beneficial for its members and their children to combine the traditional curriculum with counter-narratives that interpreted and explained their subordination in Cuba and elsewhere in the Americas. To help in this endeavor, they undoubtedly relied upon the writings and assessments of race relations produced by leaders of the Brotherhood of Canal Workers, such as H. N. Walrond, Nicholas Carter, and William Stoute. From Panama, they published news stories that illuminated the problems that black Caribbean immigrants confronted in Panama, Costa Rica, and Cuba. Their articles also supported the rights of black workers to organize, primarily on plantations owned and operated by North American multinational companies. In so doing, they hoped to create a network of literate and informed black Caribbean immigrant workers.[108] To this end, the leaders of the Brotherhood of Canal Workers wrote extensively about the social and economic relationships that black immigrants had with North American functionaries and workers. Their opinions and observations were published in *The Workman*, founded in 1912 by Walrond, an immigrant from Barbados, and may be seen as a formula to prepare many of the black workers to work and live in Cuba. They advised black workers in Panama, Cuba, and elsewhere that although there were some white North Americans who respected blacks and believed in treating them as human beings, there were others who found it unimaginable to recognize their humanity. Most of the whites had internalized this latter attitude over the generations. Walrond and his cohort blamed the whites' animus toward blacks on the consumption of excessive amounts of alcohol, cultural transmission, and an ingrained preference for the physical features of heredity or whiteness.

Realizing that North Americans dominated the Cuban sugar industry, and that these people may have come from the sugar-producing states of the U.S. South, particularly Louisiana, black Caribbean immigrants were instructed on how to live under the Jim Crow sociocultural ideology of white privilege and power buttressed and articulated by violence and racial segregation. To black immigrants living under Jim Crow customs in Panama, Costa Rica, and Cuba, Walrond advised that they conceal their honor and dignity and be deferential to individuals from "the southern states of the North American Union, where it is almost criminal for a Negro or a mule to step on the sidewalk or enter a public store or any other business place, the difference in treatment being that the mule would be driven off the sidewalk or out of the shop whereas the Negro would have a mighty slim chance of breathing five minutes after."[109] He warned his readers not to be naïve and believe that a North American's social class would allow him to transcend the racism of others who administered the neocolonial multinationals established throughout the Caribbean. Braceros who found themselves working for "educated and more refined white people" could never count on them to put an end to the inhumane attitudes and treatment of their uncultured counterparts, because "men and women born under the most elevating of conditions and transplanted among such rabid haters of our race do not take long to breathe in, and become contaminated with the poisonous atmosphere with which they are now prone."[110] Finally, black immigrants who belonged to the West Indian Star and other associations that offered their members educational opportunities and access to The Workman were provided with the historical context that fostered these racialist attitudes and the rationale behind the treatment that they could expect from whites not only from North America but also in Cuba:

> On the whole, this anti-racial sentiment is responsible for the economic slavery which has been introduced as a super-session of the human slavery that died at the mouth of the gun and the thrust of the sword. Whenever the Negro receives anything from these people it does not come to him as his desert, but as a condescension on the part of the benefactor, and the true claims are denied because those whose duty it is to answer them are naturally skeptical about doling out equal treatment to a race of people whom they regard as physical and mental inferiors.[111]

Anticipating that racial discrimination and violence would inform their experiences in Cuba, black immigrants from Jamaica adapted to the working conditions on the farms and mills, making the most of their circumstances on the bateyes. In addition, their familiarity with North Americans gave them an advantage over the Haitian braceros in several ways. Compared to the Haitians, the Jamaicans' race and ethnicity, particularly those of light-skinned black workers, were privileged and manipulated by the North Americans, who offered those with some qualifications employment as skilled laborers inside the mills. Jamaicans were trusted to work on the docks and railroads as well. Their gracious comportment or urbanity in front of white supervisors also generally caused company administrators to prefer Jamaicans to Haitians. Arriving in Cuba in 1919, Hibbert Morris explained the reason he adopted such an attitude after discovering that cutting cane was too tough: "Once you realize the Americans are in charge, you can take a chance and work hard to learn a trade. This is what they want. If you can't do a job, don't tell them you can't. If they want you to lift a table, you say 'alright boss-man, I'll try it.' [But] when he goes away and returns only to see that you didn't lift it, he will send for someone else. You must try and lift it you know, because if you don't he will say that you are lazy!"[112] It is noteworthy that this public persona had become part of the Jamaican work ethic in Panama as well as in Costa Rica. The Jamaicans displayed "pride, ritual deference to one's supervisor, and cynicism regarding rewards for initiative, individualism, and responsibility," according to some old-timers who still lived in the Canal Zone in the late 1970s and early 1980s.[113] The administrators of the Limón, Costa Rica, division of the United Fruit Company noted similar behavioral patterns among black Jamaicans contracted to work on its banana plantations during World War I, particularly the show of deference to those in authority. In February 1915, one local newspaper in Limón, quoting a United Fruit Company official, wrote: "The Jamaicans are the most tranquil peace-loving people in existence."[114]

Adopting this public persona was an ingenious method that masked the strong desire among Jamaican immigrants to improve their socioeconomic lives in Cuba and elsewhere in the Caribbean under European and North American colonialism. They hid their ethnic pride and the sense of honor and dignity that stemmed from their colonial identity as British subjects. Their self-esteem, which was demonstrated privately in their homes and mutual-aid societies, was based upon their own recognition that they were more ambitious and harder workers than other blacks of the diaspora in the Americas.[115] These sentiments engendered more dignity and greater confidence while dealing with whites. Jamaican society itself may have promoted the emergence of this ethnic pride among its emigrants in Cuba. The braceros living in Cuba had grown up in a society governed by a visible number of mulattoes or coloreds and blacks since the last half of the nineteenth century. Their tenure in government proved that they were equal in intelligence and skill to the whites on the island. And although Jamaica had its own class and racial hierarchies that also privileged whiteness, it was never as racist as Cuba and North America. Race relations in Cuba had become informed by North American imperialism and the racialist principles that accompanied the U.S. influence during the first decade of the twentieth century. The Race War of 1912 also influenced how whites on the island treated blacks.[116] The so-called invasion of the "undesirables"—nonwhites from Haiti and Jamaica—after 1912 further exacerbated racial tensions. Prepared by their Central American experiences with white North Americans, some Jamaicans arrived better suited to cope with the Cuban-constructed Jim Crow culture than the Haitians were.

In order to disarm white fears and suspicions, the Jamaicans took on a public persona that hid their more authentic and confident one. Only they themselves knew how domineering and combative they could become. If they displayed their true identity, they were bound to alienate most whites and blacks in Cuba, and thereby intensify the level of degradation and repression they encountered. Informing Jamaicans who were leaving Panama for Cuba "to escape starvation and death," an anonymous writer reminded them "to not try and run the place. The experiences gained in Panama should help them maintain sensible and discreet attitudes towards the Cubans . . . The West Indians should at once make up their minds to respect the laws of Cuba, inculcate a friendly esteem for Cubans, keep out of politics and try like the deuce to save their monies with which after four or five years they can return to their native homes and live in comfort."[117] This advice fell on the deaf ears of some braceros. When they believed that they were overly exploited or mistreated, they sought social and economic justice.

4

THE EVOLUTION AND EXPRESSION OF
A WORKER CONSCIOUSNESS

Black Caribbean Protest, Resistance, and the Cuban Labor Movement

"Some days ago the master of a plantation would not pay the laborers for days after they had finished their work," recounted a Jamaican bracero who had returned home from Cuba. Asking the mill's manager if he did not realize that the men would desert his cane farms to search for better wages and conditions, the boss simply answered: "For every ten men who leave, fifty more will come. And this is a fact. There are more dogs than bones in Cuba."[1]

Although this bracero's encounter with his employer occurred a couple of years after the Cuban government had lifted the ban on black Caribbean immigration, and during a period of expansion of the sugar industry when the demand for black macheteros and carreteros was great, the manager's response not only conveyed the sugar companies' power over the braceros, but also explicitly revealed the ideology on which the socioeconomic subordination of the black immigrants was based. Their inferior status would intensify as the immigration of black laborers reached its peak between 1917 and 1926. With 154,708 Haitians and 112,633 Jamaicans and other British West Indians arriving primarily to live and work in Camagüey and Oriente provinces, the surplus of cheap black foreign labor as well as the dramatic drop in the price of sugar afforded some sugar companies the opportunity not to pay the macheteros and carreteros the piece-rate wages they were promised before leaving Haiti and Jamaica.[2] Some completely suspended paying their workers, while others compensated field workers with vales redeemable only at the mills' company stores. How the braceros responded to the sugar companies' maximization of

134

their labor without reimbursement, as well as how they challenged the mills' hegemonic ideology that devalued their labor and humanity, are the subjects of this chapter. What strategies did they employ to persuade the owners of the sugar companies and their colonos to remunerate them for the work that they performed? Were these strategies effective? To what extent were the activities of the braceros influenced by their relationships with European and native workers? And were the bonds that they established with white and black workers strong enough to contest successfully the racial, ethnic, and color-segmented labor system that the sugar mills had adopted to divide and control their native and foreign-born work force?

Even before the collapse of the price of sugar in November 1920, the black braceros were employing a host of strategies to compel the owners and colonos to not only pay them their wages but also to improve work conditions. Their actions became more radical during the first half of the 1920s. In brief, between 1915 and 1920, the braceros often responded individually to unfair working conditions and poor wages, fleeing the estates and farms in search of better salaries and conditions. Other immigrant workers sabotaged the plantation complexes by burning the cane fields. But as their status and condition grew worse after 1920, black immigrant workers became involved in a movement to organize the sugar industry's workers. Some labor leaders introduced the ideology of anarcho-syndicalism to mobilize the workers. They denounced and discredited the labor model that fostered the "conjugated oppression" of workers and created divisions among their ranks. As a result, the anarcho-syndicalists were able to recruit and organize the braceros without arousing white worker resentment. These Cuban and Spanish-born labor leaders, influenced by the ideas of Mikhail Bakunin, Karl Marx, and Vladimir Lenin, cultivated a militant worker's consciousness among Jamaicans and Haitians that helped them see capitalism as the cause of their subjugation and immiserization. Between 1923 and 1925, the development of this consciousness, one that de-emphasized the variables of color and ethnicity that had articulated their marginalization, encouraged a noticeable number of braceros to participate in the numerous labor protests that the sugar industry experienced. No longer could the sugar companies use black Antillean immigrants as strikebreakers. Black immigrant workers would become critical to forging an industry-wide labor movement by the middle of the 1920s.

As the sugar companies expanded the capacity of their mills to meet the demand of the Allies during World War I, some braceros demonstrated that they would not allow themselves to be exploited. As part of an increasing reserve army of workers that the mills had established in order to suppress the wages of their work force, particularly of the field workers, the braceros resisted by attempting to walk away from their employers. They did so hoping to locate better wages and living conditions. As early as the spring of 1918, many planters reported that although Jamaicans and Haitians were still being imported into the eastern part of the country, "some trouble is [being] experienced in holding the laborers in any one place, due to the high cost of living. The men work just long enough to get enough money to take them to another place in search of cheaper living conditions."[3] They moved from one mill to the next after learning that white cane cutters could earn between $1.20 and $1.40 per one hundred arrobas. Some mill owners also promised $2.80 a day for skilled laborers.[4] Undoubtedly, both Haitian and Jamaican workers understood the critical role of their labor. John B., a bracero from St. Thomas Parish, Jamaica, recalled how upon landing in Santiago de Cuba, he—unlike the hundreds of other Jamaican macheteros who used the Central Railroad of Cuba to take them to the town of Banes to work for the mills owned and operated by the United Fruit Company—used this same railway to travel to Ciego de Avila to locate employment at the Jaronú *central*. Later, in order to "take the laboring work," he used the Central Railroad of Cuba to go back and forth between Júcaro and Jaronú, which was on the Nuevitas Line in Camagüey.[5] Many of these workers, particularly the Haitians, decided to leave the sugar industry altogether and find work on coffee farms.[6] They tended to leave the sugar enclaves at the end of the zafra. Haitians working in Las Villas, for instance, often moved to Oriente between June and September to harvest coffee throughout the fall. In fact, the continued expansion of the sugar hinterlands in central and eastern Cuba allowed many black Caribbean workers to move from mill to mill and province to province every three to four years to obtain better wages and working conditions.[7] Their mobility made it impossible for the mills and colonos to successfully dominate their workers. Archival evidence illuminates that the most anxious and uncompetitive sugar companies responded to their workers' agency by employing their own security personnel as well as the rural guard to prevent flight.

Claims that braceros were being physically constrained by the companies' guards at the mills as well as by the rural police were reported in Jamaica and other islands of the Caribbean. In Kingston, the Daily Gleaner published a letter from a bracero by the name of Demme. In the spring of 1919, Demme disclosed to his brother that laborers were paid $1.50 for cutting cane and "are treated like slaves."[8] Demme warned his brother and other possible emigrants that once they arrived to cut cane in Cuba, they would not be allowed to leave: "All entrances to the estates are guarded by armed men and the only way to escape is by stealth, a forty mile flight through the woods."[9] The detention and mistreatment of braceros had become so frequent that many Jamaican field workers reported the abuses to the British consul in Santiago de Cuba. Their statements and petitions for assistance were initially ignored by the consulate agent.[10]

When representatives of the Manatí central arrived in Kingston in March 1919 to recruit and contract a "good number of emigrants," they were presented with these allegations, which they vehemently denied. The vice-president and general administrator of the mill, Miguel D'Aguaya, insisted that he "takes a great interest in all of his workers and does all he can do to make them as comfortable as possible on the Manatí."[11] The attempt to refute Demme's exposé on the abuse of braceros did not prevent other stories about their confinement and harassment from being published. On 10 April 1920, the Daily Gleaner reported that Jamaican laborers were suffering and were being worked under armed guards.[12] Such coercion had become ubiquitous. On the Algodones central, a worker recounted how the manager and his foremen threatened the workers daily to establish an atmosphere of fear and insecurity in order to control and intimidate them: "The fear of being fired without any explanation, and if you protested the conditions they imprisoned or killed you. Many times I saw my fellow workers rounded up and handcuffed as their honor and pride were reduced by the glare of the unjust manager."[13] When government officials from Jamaica and Great Britain paid only lip service to reports of the mistreatment of the braceros, the workers decided upon a different course of action to protest their conditions and defy the companies.

The sense of being stranded and without protection from the whims of the sugar companies encouraged the braceros to employ different forms of sabotage to protest the conditions they endured. Setting the cane fields afire became a popular form of resistance, along with flight. In 1916, this deed became so common in Oriente Province that the government's administrator for all sugar mills in the jurisdiction of Manzanillo, Ramón Ros, informed the governor in Santiago de Cuba that he was proceeding to investigate the frequent number of fires that had been started on the Teresa central. Ros asserted that an investigation was warranted because "the succession of fires started in the cane fields of the Teresa central were so extreme that they had paralyzed the grinding and have caused a great deal of anxiety among the different managers of the mills in the area."[14] In order to assist Ros in his investigation, the governor ordered José Inglesia, the military captain of the district, to place the Fourth Squadron at Ros's service. Inglesia eventually selected Pedro Pérez González, commanding officer of the squadron, to handle the inquiry into the causes of the fires. He discovered that there were six fires started in the fields belonging to the Teresa, and that the first fire was set accidentally. "The other five, however, had been intentionally set." Completing his report, Pérez informed Ros that he was unable to discover the identity of the people responsible for the series of fires that had burned 35,000 arrobas of cane.[15]

In February 1918, the managers of a number of mills reported a host of cane fires that had been deliberately set throughout the island. Although arrests had been made, "the number of fires reported seems to be increasing."[16] Functionaries of the Office of the Secretary of Agriculture believed that most of the fires were not hidden acts of protest by the workers. Instead, the Cuban officials believed that the colonos were burning the cane fields "to get [their] cane into the mills immediately. Most factories give burned cane the preference over sound cane, as no sucrose is lost if the cane is ground immediately, and such a practice as that given above is not at all uncommon, particularly when labor is as scarce as it is now."[17] Nonetheless, the majority of company administrators concluded that the cane fires indeed represented a strategy used by field workers to oppose their conditions. The differences of opinion regarding who was responsible for the fires make it problematic for the historian to interpret this form of protest. We may never know which cohort of laborers was involved. Records show that no one was ever apprehended. Nonetheless, administrators who believed that the macheteros caused the fires produced a lengthier body of archival materials supporting their contention than did those who accused the colonos. Undoubtedly, the managers' conclusions could have resulted from pure speculation and were based upon the daily reports they obtained from the mills' foremen. The information that these employees provided also could have stemmed from their biases toward the black Caribbean workers. Since the foremen mostly viewed the black braceros as an immoral lot whose presence was a necessary evil, that the braceros could sabotage operations did not seem out of the question. It was seen as proof of their wretched excesses. In addition, by blaming the braceros the administrators of the mills successfully obtained the assistance of the state to help them protect their properties. The braceros' class, race, and ethnicity permitted the police and rural guard to punish them with impunity. After all, they were immigrant workers without any recourse except from their consulates.

Archival evidence also points to the role that labor organizers possibly played in inciting incendiarism. They could have helped the braceros to interpret their reality and perhaps suggested the use of a traditional form of sabotage that black laborers had used to protest their conditions during and after slavery. If the Haitian and Jamaican field workers had created a "community of fate" based upon their shared occupations and millenarian cosmographies, then it is plausible that they could have cooperated clandestinely to set the fields afire to obtain work.

In 1919, Federico Fernández, manager of the America central near Palma Soriano, sent a telegram to the governor of Oriente informing him that some of his workers had intentionally set fire to his cane fields. Of the three locations affected, one contained four caballerias of cane. He emphasized that the previous day, another five fires had been deliberately started, resulting in over eight thousand tons of sugarcane being burned. Because of these acts of sabotage, he informed the governor that he had placed members of the rural guard in groups of three throughout the cane fields as a precaution and as a way to stop the numerous fires.[18] It appears that every mill in Oriente Province experienced this form of protest. Guillermo F. Mascaró, the governor of Oriente, advised all the administrators who operated mills in the province to increase their vigilance in order to stop cane from being burned as well as to prevent the destruction of their factories' machines and other critical equipment. He believed that their "enemy" had pledged to stop the present harvest in every possible way. Mascaró told them that certain foreign provocateurs had realized that burning the cane fields was not enough to stop the zafra that Cuba had committed to the Allied forces in Europe. The governor never explicitly identified the "enemy," but undoubtedly he was referring to some anarcho-syndicalist leaders of the Cuban labor movement.

Between 1918 and 1919, provincial as well as U.S. officials closely watched individuals whom they identified as provocateurs. For instance, a reliable U.S. military source informed Edward Wise, the American consul at Guantánamo, that José Tallon Reigada, "a dangerous agitator of the I.W.W. type," had disappeared after having "stirred up trouble in several places in Oriente Province where he has worked. He was last discharged at Daiquiri . . . He is said to be at either Los Canos or Soldedad [mills]."[19] Cuban and American authorities tried to follow such persons of interest because they had concluded that an international anarchist conspiracy had developed. In fact, a U.S. State Department telegram to Cuban authorities indicated that a series of strikes the year before had been supervised by a cadre of Spanish agitators tied to the IWW.[20] Their paranoia also was based on the anarcho-syndicalists' opposition to World War I. Anarchists commonly believed that the war was a competition among the Western capitalist countries to obtain additional colonies. The braceros, however, probably acted out of vengeance and to protest their conditions. Nonetheless, Mascaró's "enemy" had aspirations of stopping the harvest by "systematically destroying the centrales' ability to grind the sugarcane in order to cause the owners to abandon their properties that had created such a precious product."[21] The governor explained that it was critical to be vigilant on the estates and to pay close attention to employees and workers charged with operating the equipment inside the mill factories as well.

Responding to Mascaró's mandate, some sugar mill administrators in Oriente realized that it was not the factory workers who needed to be scrutinized, but the field laborers. Federico Fernández, manager of the America central, was the first to point this out. Fernández informed the governor that he and his guards had taken every step imaginable to ascertain the identity of anyone who tried to commit a crime at the America. He also reported that "we have adopted the same strategies in the cane fields in order to stop them from being burned in the future since our colonia Xavier had had three fires started during the present zafra."[22] The manager of the Dos Amigos central shared Fernández's concern about his cane cutters, loaders, and wagon drivers: "Extreme vigilance is not enough for just the bateyes and the factories. There is no way to stop the manual workers, particularly the field workers who are at the mercy of our feared enemy and who share the same disposition of our workers. Their lack of respect has undermined and corrupted the rural population with their ideology." He continued: "It is just impossible to take care of the cane fields with a lot of rural guards stationed on every mill and cane farm. These same classes of workers share the same feelings as the others. There is not one ounce of morality among them."[23] That they were insolent and "lacked morality" defined most black braceros, according to white Cuban national and provincial functionaries and immigration officials. In the end, the administrators of the Río Cauto at Bayamo and the Niquero, as well as others, reported that they had taken steps to prevent criminal activity that would cause them to suspend the zafra. The manager of the Niquero had placed a considerable number of the company's guards inside the mill. He also informed the governor that they had decided to use a detail of twenty undercover agents recruited from among the rural guard, and had positioned them everywhere on the batey.

In spite of the government's efforts to stop this fiery form of subversion, it remained a significant method of resistance and protest for the workers. As we shall see below, the number of fires set by agricultural workers spiked during the presidency of Alfredo Zayas (1920–24), the same period when they were being organized by the anarcho-syndicalists.[24] Before 1920, the rise of incendiarism may therefore be seen as the nascent expression of the workers' consciousness, an awareness that their condition was the source of the mills' privileged position. They showed their dissatisfaction with being humiliated and forcibly detained as well as with being paid unfair wages by compelling the mills to alter their grinding schedules. This was a small victory, but a victory nonetheless.

During the last quarter of the nineteenth century, fire had been used through-out the British and French Caribbean to protest the material condition of the black working class.[25] During the World War I era, the workers who took part in burning the cane farms were probably more upset with the low wages they received as the cost of living dramatically increased. Food, particularly flour, milk, lard, refined sugar, and meat, as well as clothes and charcoal, became costly for the majority of workers. In fact, the city of Santiago de Cuba and its surrounding districts experienced a shortage of lard and, ironically, sugar.[26] The shortages of basic staples led to price speculation and the emergence of a black market for these items. The price of a tin of canned milk climbed from 15 to 25 centavos in 1917, and by 1918 to 35 centavos. The cost of eggs increased to 25 centavos by the fall of 1918 after being 5 centavos in 1917. A pound of beef went for 75 centavos, while clothes became prohibitively expensive. A pair of shoes, pants, and shirt cost five hundred times more in 1918 than these items had before the start of the war.[27]

The U.S. Commission on Cuban Affairs examined the impact that the sugar industry's piece-rate wage system and the seasonal employment pattern had on the lives of black Caribbean field workers. Citing the industry's downturn nearly a decade earlier as an important variable in their lives, and before the U.S. economic depression brought down the Cuban economy further, the commission discovered that the total value of the household articles owned by most migrant laborers during the early 1930s had not drastically changed since the mid-1920s, ranging from as low as $15 to as high as approximately $40. Such was the case for the majority of cane cutters and wagon drivers who earned one dollar a day. Their standard of living was also influenced by their marriage status, whether they had children, and in what province they worked. The seasonal or annual income that many manual laborers received ranged from $204 to $360. The latter figure was typical of a Haitian carretero who worked picking coffee after the sugar harvest ended in June.[28] After the commissioners interviewed the field workers, they made a number of observations regarding their material condition. They discovered that an average Haitian agricultural worker living with his wife in Camagüey had a net household value of $38. In addition, their annual incomes totaled $204. The Haitians' material existence allowed them to "have enough to eat and tobacco to smoke during the zafra."[29] A field worker who was permitted by his employer to cultivate a one-acre conuco, whose household consisted of three persons, and who earned $320 a year had an eight-month income that generally gave him the opportunity to choose his family's diet only during the zafra. However, the small plot allowed a worker and his family to augment their food supply while saving more of his wages. Even a mechanic who worked inside a sugar factory in Camagüey was not immune to the effects of seasonal work. The commission discovered that one father of eight children who possessed household goods valued at $50 and earned an income of $281 had a very limited diet. His circumstances compelled his family to squat on a portion of the sugar company's land, and during the tiempo muerto, they all had to go to the nearest town or village to beg until the next zafra began the following January.[30] Given the economic circumstances that the black braceros continued to confront during the early 1930s, it is not surprising that more than a decade earlier they had adopted a strategy to increase their small piece-rate wages.

For example, as the Preston central began the zafra of January 1918, the mill's manager, Harold Harty, informed Joseph Buck, the U.S. vice-consul in Antilla, that his cane cutters had asked that their wages be increased. If Harty refused, they would stop working. He also told Buck that the United Fruit Company's labor troubles were not serious, and that if a strike did occur he was ready to ask his emigrant broker in Haiti, E. J. Pauley, "to send 200 men every two weeks to this port . . . in one of his own vessels."[31] Somehow, news of Harty's plans to import gangs of strikebreakers reached the workers, and they began to burn the cane fields. Because the Preston owned and grew nearly all of the sugarcane it processed, Harty could not blame any colono for the "unknown causes" of the fires. Between 3 February 1918 and 20 April 1918, Harty's workers burned the company's fields eleven times. The amount of cane the Preston lost to incendiarism totaled 292,762 arrobas.[32] This use of fire against Harty and the United Fruit Company supports James Scott's contention that when the lower orders' prerogatives are denied, they employ "collective insistence through petitioning, for the 'rights' to which subordinate groups feel entitled, [claims that] carry the understood [proposition] 'or else' with the precise consequence of a refusal left to the imagination of the lord."[33] In other words, when Harty failed to negotiate seriously with his macheteros, the workers, as a last option, burned the fields both as an act of retribution toward him and also as a strategy to force the mill to harvest the cane immediately. In doing so, they obtained, in as little time as possible, the wages to which they felt entitled, before being replaced with a new contingent of braceros.

The following year, nothing had changed. As a result, during the last month of the 1919 harvest, the field workers' defiance compelled the managers of the sugar companies to guard against "the intentional burning of the poorest cane fields in order to facilitate the cutting of the cane by some of the most audacious gangs."[34] Even W. B. Houston, the U.S. consular agent in Caimanera, took note of this activity in May 1919 when he told his superior, Harold Clum, stationed in Santiago de Cuba: "Fires [in the valley of Guantánamo] have been frequent but most of the burned cane have been saved by rapid cutting and grinding."[35] Most of the industry's experts concurred that the fires reflected a new reality, that the "cane cutters . . . are becoming contaminated by the all-prevailing greed for money that is really and truly filthy. Not satisfied with the high wages they are now receiving, they seek to increase their gains where they get a stipulated price for the 100 arrobas, by secretly burning all of the fields they commence cutting."[36] Describiing the burning as an "evil" subterfuge, the plantation managers had to stop such activity because it increased the labor costs of production. Besides having to be processed immediately, burnt cane became an obstruction to the wagon drivers, littering the cart paths they used to haul the cane to the mill. This in turn slowed or altogether stopped the production cycle of the mill itself, since the field workers had to be shifted to tasks outside the fields. These braceros had to be paid as well. Finally, the fires that the cane cutters set often engulfed neighboring fields or spread out of control, destroying the entire mill. If not prevented, these acts of rebellion could doom the entire industry:

> The lighting of a cane field . . . is so easily accomplished and it can be done so secretly that, with so many foreign emissaries inciting the laboring classes to commit abuses, this kind of incendiarism may rapidly extend over the whole island . . . Cuba is proving day by day how difficult it is for a people . . . to learn that the basis of all true democracy is morality and not trickery, and that unlimited license must in the end be the ruin of Cuba's main industry, the greatest of its kind in the world.[37]

That the industry's representatives in Cuba and the United States described the black Caribbean incendiaries as insolent, evil, immoral, and avaricious demonstrated their inability to discern the hidden meaning of the use of fire among black workers in the Caribbean in general, and in Cuba specifically. "Fire carries with it a strong connotation, a distinction created by the region's human history of remarkable and persistent social oppression exerted by local planters and other officials, oppression that has in turn been met by the resistance and creativity of the region's working people."[38] One can argue that black immigrant field workers became incendiaries after realizing that they were fundamental to the sugar industry's expansion, yet the sugar mills refused to fairly compensate their labor and sacrifice. The majority of workers had arrived hoping to earn a livable wage that they could save before they returned home. By 1918, many of them had realized, however, that their piece-rate wages were inadequate as the cost of living continued to increase between 1914 and 1920. In addition, they were coping with living conditions that were inhumane. When their grievances went unheard or ignored, they decided to reject their circumstances with a strategy that succeeded at least in increasing their dignity and the opportunity to earn a little more money. As a result, with an evolving worker consciousness as part of their immigrant identity, some black Caribbean workers did not have to be encouraged to become involved in the movement to organize the industry's work force.

Before this occurred, however, they made many attempts to present their grievances to Cuban officials as well as to their own consular agents. When the braceros informed the Cuban authorities and the owners of the mills of their mistreatment, they were threatened and intimidated. Some black migrants were beaten, jailed, deported, or killed. Because many immigrants were inspired by British patriotism, particularly after some had served in the British military during World War I, they believed that British functionaries in Cuba would offer them protection.[39] As a result, between February and April 1919, the British consul in Santiago de Cuba, W. Mason, received numerous complaints from predominantly Jamaican workers who had been physically harassed. Initially, Mason tried to keep their claims secret. In fact, in a letter dated 18 February 1919 to the governor of Jamaica, Leslie Probyn, Mason maintained that the majority of claims were entirely false. Questioning Mason's view, the governor asked if he could publish in the local papers Mason's statements denying the charges that some workers had been mistreated.[40] In March 1919, Mason admitted to his superiors that he had occasionally received complaints from workers who allegedly had been beaten on the sugar estates. But after he looked deeper into the allegations, he reported that the basis for their grievances was chiefly one of a misunderstanding between "the quarrelsome class of laborers and the policemen caused by their lack of knowing the Spanish language and Cuban customs." Mason ended by arguing that the Jamaicans were as safe in Cuba as they were at home. Governor Probyn rejected Mason's explanation. Armed with contradictory evidence submitted by the British minister in Havana, Probyn informed the Colonial Secretary in London that he was going to gather "unbiased testimony" on the mistreatment of workers from inquiries made among Jamaicans returning home from Cuba. In so doing, he hoped "to find out whether there is cause for complaint against Mr. Mason."[41]

The commercial relationship that the two countries had developed during the war helps to explain the disingenuous conclusion offered by Mason. England had become dependent upon Cuban sugar, and its commercial dependence required the British government to assist the sugar companies to acquire a surplus of cheap workers. For example, the proportion of sugar that the industry provided the Allies grew from 14.3 percent in 1913 to 18.4 percent in 1916. The zafra of 1919 allowed the Cuban sugar industry to provide 26.02 percent of the sugar consumed by the Allied nations during that year.[42] Between 1914 and 1918, the amount of sugar that Cuba sold to Great Britain nearly doubled, increasing from 450,000 to 883,000 tons.[43]

In addition to its mercantile relationship with Cuba, British consumption of Cuban sugar had cultural significance as well. Sugar had become "an essential ingredient in the British national diet. Combined with bitter beverages, it was consumed daily by almost every living Briton . . . It could be found in prepared delicacies such as jams, biscuits, and pastries, which were consumed at tea and frequently with meals. Sugar had also become a common feature of festive and ceremonial foods from season to season and from birth to death." As a result, when the government decided to ration this dietary carbohydrate and sweetener during World War I, its policy was seen "as among the most painful and immediate of the petty hardships caused by the war," Sidney Mintz discovered.[44]

Mason was not only protecting an aspect of British mercantile policy when he trivialized the numerous cases of physical abuse suffered by Jamaican braceros. It would soon come to light that he had another, more personal reason to downplay the cases of mistreatment. Sensing that Mason was trying to cover up anti-Jamaican violence and abuse, the British authorities in Jamaica looked further into the matter and sought to learn the real nature of the relationship between the migrant workers and the sugar companies.

When the Legislative Council of Jamaica addressed the mistreatment of the braceros, its members discovered that "circumstances were very bad in Cuba as the laborers . . . were being worked under armed guards." They learned that a Jamaican who had been arrested several months before still sat in jail because no judge would hear his case. Based upon the testimony of an agent of the British consulate in Havana who had returned to Jamaica, the Legislative Council discovered the true motive behind Mason's indifference and deception. Its members were told that Mason and a Mr. Brice, who served as the British consul and vice-consul respectively in Santiago de Cuba, "carried on large businesses of their own and . . . were engaged in the labor trade themselves in Cuba through agents they employed. As soon as Jamaican laborers got there, they were at once held by those agents and were bound to go and work on the estates." This conflict of interest inside the British Legation in Cuba would always prevent Jamaican immigrants from receiving adequate protection, the Council concluded.[45]

The Council's findings dispel important assumptions that some scholars have made about the status and treatment of Jamaican workers. They argue that because the majority of Jamaican braceros arrived alone after having usually paid their way to the island, they were not susceptible to the same coercive and abusive practices that Haitian workers endured at the hands of their government's emigrant brokers. They also maintain that in recognition of the military service

146

that some Jamaican and other West Indian braceros had offered the Union Jack during the war, British authorities would go to great lengths to defend their rights as workers in Panama, Costa Rica, and Cuba.[46] In the end, the majority of councilmen believed that "every man out of the colony should be protected . . . If the laborers were promised so much pay per day, they should be assured that they would get it; if they were promised to be given a certain amount of work in a month, offered housing conditions, and medical attendance, they should be guaranteed."[47] After further debate, the Council agreed to send agents independent of the British Legation not only to Cuba but also to Panama, Colombia, and Costa Rica in order to protect black British West Indians. They based their decision on the grounds that the immigration acts passed by the Council between 1893 and 1905 gave the governor and legislature the power to protect Jamaican citizens abroad and to supervise their repatriation. More important, these decrees gave "supreme control" to the Jamaican government to prohibit or allow emigration to Cuba on the condition that the Cuban government maintained and enforced the work and living conditions stipulated by the workers' contracts.[48] It also created a Department of Immigration to supervise the flow of workers to Cuba and to other Caribbean destinations. Despite these decrees, the level of mistreatment and abuse that Jamaican and Haitian workers experienced did not decline. After all, the Cuban government as well as the sugar companies condoned and benefited from such maltreatment.

During the first half of the 1920s, expressions of xenophobia and Cuban nationalism fueled anti-immigration violence and sentiment. It was in this context that James Ward arrived in Havana from London to investigate the killing of a number of Jamaicans at the Jobabo *central* near Las Tunas in Oriente in 1917. In September 1920, he replaced the British minister to Cuba, who had been declared persona non grata a month earlier by the Cuban government because of his insistence that the government pay an "indemnity for the killing of the Jamaican subjects."[49] This happened when government soldiers massacred more than a dozen workers during the Liberal revolt led by José Miguel Gómez. Those who committed the crime believed that the workers were involved in the Chambolena Rebellion, and as a result the soldiers were never charged. However, it appears that the matter of paying an indemnity had remained unresolved because Cuban congressmen believed that if they continued to postpone the vote on granting compensation to the victims' families, their claims would disappear with time. The grieving families proved them wrong as they tirelessly pressed for some kind of resolution, even though their loved ones had been killed three years earlier. In the end, however, Ward's efforts also proved fruitless.

The continued abuse of braceros caused some of them to pay heed to Cuban labor leaders who spoke about how they could challenge their marginalized status. The ideology of the anarcho-syndicalists adopted by Cuban labor leaders after 1912 appears to have been informed by the thoughts and writings of the Russian anarchist Mikhail Bakunin, who often stressed the collectivist and socialist principle of "from each according to his ability to each according to his work."[50] European anarchists such as Bakunin, however, were not convinced of the efficaciousness of trade unions to challenge and overthrow capitalism. After individual efforts that included the use of violence failed to effect revolutionary change, other anarchists, particularly Peter Kropotkin of Russia and two very important Spanish anarchists, Sebastien Faure and Fernand Pelloutier, supported the use of syndicates or unions to introduce and disseminate anarchist principles among rural and urban workers in Western Europe.[51] In Cuba, anarcho-syndicalists established labor unions initially among tobacco workers in order to gradually destroy capitalism and take control of the means of production. Before the workers' revolution could occur, however, anarcho-syndicates or associations would not only address the bread-and-butter issue of securing a fair wage for their members through direct action, but also provide educational, cultural, and social activities, acting in ways similar to the mutual-aid societies that the Cuban and Jamaican workers had established and relied on before and after 1910. These activities were intended to prepare workers for the struggle against the nation's government, which the anarcho-syndicalists considered inherently corrupt and incapable of establishing institutions that could create virtuous and productive laborers. For those Cuban anarcho-syndicalists influenced by Bakunin, "[S]tates sought to impose a stifling and oppressive unity without roots in the common people. [And] by its very nature, the state was violent and power hungry, a hunger evident in its tendency toward centralization and expansion. It was elitist and so hostile to the common good."[52] Introduced to this historical interpretation of the nature of Western governments, the braceros better understood how the state condoned their subjugation and exploitation in the sugar enclaves of Cuba. The antigovernment position held by anarcho-syndicalists also helped the black Caribbean workers understand the indifference of their consular officials in Cuba to their abuse, subordination, and exploitation. It clarified also the reasons why functionaries like Mason and

Brice had cooperated with the mills and colonos to appropriate their labor. More important, the notion that all Western states were oppressive led the braceros to realize that the Jamaican and Haitian authorities would never ameliorate their circumstances.

Anarcho-syndicalism also helped braceros who had migrated first to Panama and later to Cuba to interpret why race and labor relations were so contentious at home and abroad. For the majority, the British colonial governor and the U.S. military government in Haiti were duplicitous for creating the socioeconomic conditions and institutions that fostered the exploitation, powerlessness, and misery of the workers at home. Unable to survive and take care of their families, the braceros decided to leave and go work in Cuba. Antigovernment theories also led Cuban anarcho-syndicalists to oppose the imperial relationship between the United States and the Republic of Cuba. Carlos Baliño, an influential anarchist leader of the Cuban emigrant tobacco workers in Tampa, Florida, had not only supported the War of 1895 led by Cuban nationalists José Martí and Antonio Maceo, but after the island had claimed its independence in 1902, he argued that the "liberation of Cuba from the U.S. would result in the liberation of the working class."[53] Paradoxically, because the anarcho-syndicalists concluded that a state structure could never truly represent the interests of the laboring classes, they refused to involve themselves in the electoral politics of the island. As a result, they could never help other segments of Cuban society, such as the middle class, to contest American hegemony.[54]

Instead of using the political process to change the socioeconomic and political system, anarcho-syndicalists had their organizers and unions teach the working class that "it did not matter who exploited them and dominated the country . . . their struggle was against capitalism without distinctions." Emphasizing this theme became the basis of developing and nurturing workers' consciousness. The workers themselves would have to discover that foreign and native capitalists were the same. "The native bourgeoisie exploited the workers in the same fashion as the largest American and British companies," they stated.[55]

Although Cuban tobacco and railroad workers were the first segments of the working class to comprehend this role of capitalism before and after 1912, black emigrant workers in Cuba and in the United States had also become aware of this truth. "Out of every nation where the negro, white, or green were, there were classes, and the working class and the capitalist class were at each other's throat at all times, fighting for the control of the nation," claimed Otto Huiswoud, a black emigrant from Suriname.[56] Huiswoud's disclosure reflected the "refracted" consciousness of most black Caribbean laborers, whose experiences as emigrant workers, Ken Post argues, introduced them to new ideas and movements of protest.[57] The evolution of this doctrine among Jamaican and Haitian braceros was engendered by the same factors that had led the Cuban and Spanish-born tobacco and railroad workers to recognize the incessant struggle between labor and capital.

As the railroad industry became critical to the sugar industry's efficiencies, production, and expansion, white and black Cuban workers faced discrimination while employed on the private and public lines owned and operated by North American businessmen. The companies manipulated the nationality and race of their black workers to deny them the best-paying jobs while appointing white Spanish-born workers overwhelmingly to skilled and high-paying occupations. Understanding how foreign and even native companies applied racial and ethnic categories to discourage worker solidarity in a particular industry, Spanish-born anarchists led the effort to organize the railroad industry's work force. Between 1914 and 1920, they used direct action or strikes on several occasions to promote their interests.[58]

Although the sugar companies and their dependent cane farmers used the same labor policy to segregate and control their workers, specific conditions associated with the cultivation of sugarcane and the production of sugar also assisted in the evolution of a consciousness among the braceros. A U.S. official who surprisingly was charged with protecting and enhancing U.S. commercial interests in Cuba, especially the power of the sugar companies, revealed how conditions in the sugarcane industry structured the workers' psychology and identity. As early as 1907, Charles Magoon, U.S. ambassador to Cuba, reported to his superiors in Washington the abysmal living and working conditions of the industry's field workers. He advised both Cuban and American authorities that if the quality of life of the army of macheteros and the carreteros were not improved, they should expect the worst possible outcomes. If the companies failed to act, he anticipated that "a dangerous consciousness among the mass of hungry men would exercise influence on the power of the dominant classes."[59] Magoon realized that the workers' consciousness was in the first place a product of the companies' incessant and unjust appropriation of their labor power, "working them from sun up." He reported "that some farms and mills have installed lights in the fields" so that work continued "well into the night." Magoon also mentioned how the workers' quality of life after the zafra further informed their identity:

> At the end of the zafra, little is to be done on the farms and in the mills, and so seventy-five percent of men employed during the zafra remain unemployed. The money that they were able to save from their work . . . is hardly enough for them to survive . . . Nearly all of the cane cutters remain unemployed for six months of the year and by August discover that they are broke, and without any way for them to survive along with their families. The most pressing economic problem in Cuba is to provide work for so many men during the six months in between each zafra.[60]

It is important to note that Magoon's exposition described for the most part the plight of Spanish and native Cuban workers at that time. Nonetheless, he was aware of how an individual's material condition shaped his consciousness and identity, and he revealed the inevitable processes that would encourage field workers, regardless of their nationality, race, or ethnicity, to construct an ideology of dissent. By recruiting black Caribbean workers to replace Spanish and black and white Cuban workers, the companies believed that they had solved the systemic problem that Magoon imagined engendering a militant workers' consciousness. When thousands of Haitians and Jamaicans went home after several harvests only to return to Cuba with their families and loved ones to settle permanently, however, the subordination and exploitation that gave rise to a consciousness among European and native field workers also inspired, by the mid-1920s, an identical response among the black Caribbean braceros. The significant drop in the price of sugar provided the context for their militant ideology of resistance to evolve.

In the fall of 1920, the collapse of the price of sugar affected not only the sugar companies but also the financial institutions of the island. During the war, most of the mills had borrowed millions of dollars from Cuban, Spanish, U.S., and Canadian banks located on the island. They used the loans to expand their footprint on the island and their production capacities. Meeting the Allies' demand for sugar between 1914 and 1919 resulted in unimaginable profits for everyone involved in the industry. Unfortunately, the financial activities of the sugar companies and their creditors were based upon speculation that the price of sugar would remain relatively high in the foreseeable future. This assumption had not only influenced the amount of capital and credit they borrowed but also the quantity of sugar produced. In fact, it was the overproduction of sugar that contributed to the dramatic decline in its price on the world market. When the sugar bubble burst and companies could sell only 10 percent of the 3.74 million tons they produced in 1920, customers and investors ran to their banks to close out their accounts. Meanwhile, the banks gave their borrowers a month to settle their debts. By January 1921, the sugar companies owed such banks as the Banco Nacional, the Banco Español, the Banco de la Habana, and the Royal Bank of Canada approximately $80 million, based upon the price of sugar, which was then selling at 15 to 20 cents per pound.[61] As a result, President Mario Menocal ordered a moratorium on the collection of all debts.

The banking crisis ruined dozens of mills. During 1921, the National City Bank of New York City alone acquired the debts and mortgages of sixty centrales.[62] Some of the larger mills survived by purchasing and absorbing smaller factories. The majority of foreign-owned companies, particularly U.S.-owned companies located in the central and eastern provinces, survived, however, and started the zafra on time. By February 1921, thirty-four mills had commenced grinding in Santa Clara, while twenty factories were operational in Camagüey. Thirty-eight more centrales began to receive cane from their macheteros and colonos in Oriente. In spite of the decline in the number of mills and the absence of available capital and credit, sugar experts and statisticians predicted that the 201 mills that remained financially sound would produce 3.9 million tons or 27,952,000 bags of raw sugar.[63]

In order to achieve this goal, the sugar companies required field laborers. Although the industry had a ready supply of workers to recruit from the mills that had gone bankrupt, and who now were unemployed, the companies instead petitioned the government to import more Caribbean workers. Between 1921 and 1925, 63,114 Haitians and 29,308 Jamaicans came to Cuba to cut and haul sugarcane.[64]

The black immigrant workers bore the brunt of the collapse of the price of sugar in the fall of 1920. After J. M. Burke, a Jamaican sugar planter from St. George Parish, returned home from traveling throughout the eastern provinces of Cuba, he tried to warn workers contemplating going to Oriente about the conditions they were sure to face: "The laboring classes are in the thousands walking about aimlessly with their hammocks on their backs. Where men do get work, sweating is the order of the day. A man cuts a ton of cane for one dollar.

He may just cut a trifle over during the day. Out of this, he pays the company's mess [hall] one dollar for boarding—leaving the worker nothing or next to nothing. Any attempts to protest against inadequate estimates of work done is visited with imprisonment."[65] The manager of the Manatí central, Eduardo Díaz Ulzurrun, reduced the pay of his macheteros to 80 cents for 100 arrobas in January 1921, noting that before 1920 the cane cutters had received $3 for the same amount of work. That his workers accepted less money surprised Ulzurrun, since other mills in the area offered better pay. Nevertheless, the high unemployment rate among the braceros caused some companies to refuse to give their workers a living wage. Manuel Rionda, owner of the Manatí, Francisco, Tacajó, and Tuinicú centrales, advised his managers to further cut the pay of cane cutters to 40 cents, new ratoon workers to 50 cents, and carreteros to between 40 and 50 cents, depending on the distance they hauled the cane for the mill during the zafra of 1922.[66] The Barbados Advocate signaled the alarm, publishing a travel advisory from that island's colonial secretary. After receiving a telegram from the British vice-consul in Santiago de Cuba, the colonial secretary announced that the colonos were refusing to pay their field workers, as well as denying them housing. The sugar companies were also neglecting the workers if they became ill. As a result, the vice-consul understood that a large number of men were dying.[67] In spite of the injustice, indignities, and malignant indifference suffered by the braceros, many Haitians and Jamaicans refused to heed the warnings not to travel to Cuba, as table 5 indicates:

TABLE 5. Antillean Immigration to Cuba, 1921–1925

	1921	1922	1923	1924	1925	Total
Haiti	12,042	848	10,966	20,415	18,843	63,114
Jamaica	7,868	5,016	6,127	5,372	4,925	29,308
Puerto Rico	452	304	549	581	448	2,334
Dominican Republic	290	265	66	297	243	1,161
British West Indies	171	6	7	15	3	202
French Antilles	52	—	22	—	—	74
Total	20,875	6,439	17,737	26,680	24,462	96,193

Source: ANC, Secretaria de la Presidencia, Leg. 121, Exp. 18, Expediente referente a la inmigración del quinquenales de 1921–1925, p. 17.

The braceros' marginal position, which the sugar and financial crisis intensified during the first half of the 1920s, contributed to the formation of a more radical consciousness. Their relations with the mills and the cane farmers resulted in numerous slights, injuries, and even deaths. These became, to borrow from Ken Post, the "substances" that led to a "class consciousness," which in time took "collective form." In these conditions, workers came to see themselves as "things, to be used or not according to the whims of others."[68] The braceros' evolving acceptance of the option of collective action stemmed not only from their self-conceptualization of becoming things, not people, but also from the indifference that the companies and farmers displayed after 1920. When the employers stopped paying, feeding, and lodging their field workers, they repudiated the agreement based upon the "principles of inequality" expressed in the braceros' work contracts, the terms of which were understood by the workers themselves as legitimate causes and grounds for their subordination. The mills' malfeasance gave the workers the right to challenge the power of the owners, managers, and farmers to dominate them.[69] Hugh Buchanan, a Jamaican bracero who lived and worked in Cuba during the sugar crisis of the early 1920s, and who in the late 1930s helped direct the labor protest movement in Jamaica, carried this conviction from Cuba when he stated that the organization of labor occurred when the elites lost their legitimacy to rule by not addressing "the desperate conditions of the poor."[70]

How the braceros were treated, humiliated, and dismissed after 1920 assisted the anarcho-syndicalists in fostering this consciousness. When they introduced the braceros to the doctrine of "internationalism" and explained that it was essential to mitigate the damaging effects of the segmented racial and color labor system that the companies employed to divide and control their work force, the braceros were receptive to their organizing activities.

Social revolutions are always based on ideas of social and economic equality or internationalism. This guiding principle led to the establishment of racially inclusive labor syndicates. In fact, racial and ethnic tolerance had become the dogma of the Spanish chapter of the International Brotherhood that met as early as 1870 in Barcelona. Meeting a year after Bakunin helped found the International Brotherhood, members of the International Workingmen's Association, as it was called, opened their conference with the solemn oath to work for the "complete emancipation of the proletariat, and the absolute extirpation of all injustices which have ruled and still rule . . . the millions of workers, white slaves and black slaves."[71] It is important to remember that during the sugar workers' strike of 1902 around Cruces, in Las Villas Province, as we saw in chapter 1, the mulatto leader of the Gremio de Braceros de Lejas, Evaristo Landa, expressed this notion of internationalism when he told his members that they could not question a worker's place of birth, and that what mattered most was the organization of all those who labored to reduce their poverty.[72]

It is interesting to note that the concept of internationalism before 1912 tended to weaken the Cuban labor movement as nationalist labor leaders fought to preserve all industrial and semi-industrial jobs for Cubans. But as an increasing number of Spanish workers arrived after 1912, the principle of internationalism began to resonate among native labor leaders, particularly in the sugar industry and its ancillary trades, such as maritime and railway. As a result, the animosity between Spanish and Cuban workers began to dissipate.[73] In order to organize the work force of the sugar industry, the anarcho-syndicalists had to share this philosophy with both white and black workers, particularly with the braceros. It took a series of events before they could offer the braceros an ideology to help them protect their rights.

A series of unsuccessful strikes in 1917 helped the anarchists gain adherents among workers in the sugar industry. The first strike was staged by the Association of Mechanics, Machinists, and Blacksmiths of Cienfuegos in September, and the strikers had fallen under the guidance of the reformers of the Socialist Party, particularly Francisco Domenech. The association included unions that represented potboilers, foundry men, carpenters, and masons. They demanded a 10 percent increase in wages and a reduction in the number of hours worked a day from twelve to eight. In October, they were joined by thousands of workers from a number of *centrales* in Santa Clara. The strike paralyzed 25 percent of the industry's sugar mills.[74] Responding as other presidents had when sugar workers went out on strike, President Menocal ordered the arrest of the leaders and the striking workers.

Although the strike eventually spread to a number of mills in Camagüey and Oriente, it finally failed after the government could not compel the sugar companies to meet the demands of the workers. More important, the exclusive composition of the strikers doomed the work stoppage from the start. In short, when the leader of the Workers' Association of Cienfuegos, Vicente Martínez, telegrammed Samuel Gompers, president of the American Federation of Labor, asking him to help explain to President Woodrow Wilson the general condition of workers in Cuba, hoping that Wilson would persuade the owners of the mills to reach some type of compromise with their work force, Martínez displayed the reformist nature of the strike and its aristocratic nature, as well as its racially exclusive composition. The strike failed because only a minority—the skilled and white Cuban workers of the industry—walked off the job.[75] Although their work was critical to the grinding and processing of cane, it was not as significant as that of the black Caribbean field workers, who were responsible for planting, harvesting, and delivering the cane to the mills. Their labor was essential for the mills to expand their production capacities.

The results of the strikes of 1917 convincingly demonstrated why the sugar companies adopted a segmented labor system that not only accentuated the divisions between manual and skilled laborers but also divided the power of labor according to race, ethnicity, and nationality. Some anarcho-syndicalists understood that the Socialist Party's efforts to racially and ethnically segregate and exclude certain workers would continue to fail. As a result, they decided to try to organize the agricultural workers in order to improve the lives and condition of all sugarcane workers.

The labor association that tried to organize the field workers emerged from La Hermandad Ferroviarria de Cuba (the Brotherhood of Railroad Workers of Cuba). Composed of a number of diverse trade unions and workers, including nonunion laborers, the Hermandad sponsored in 1916 the establishment of a permanent organization for railroad workers in Camagüey, La Unión de Camagüey, which represented the interests of not only the transportation workers but of factory laborers as well. Led by a number of reformers, the strike that it staged between November and December 1918 also failed.[76]

But a more radical labor organization had also appeared in Camagüey in 1916. Established in the northern coastal town of Morón, from which the majority of sugar mills exported their commodity, the Unión de Empleados de Ferrocarril de Norte de Cuba (Union of Railroad Workers of Northern Cuba) was led by a group of men who were influenced by the anarcho-syndicalist concept of internationalism. Their vision of the struggle between capital and labor caused them to organize and promote the interests of railway workers, dockworkers, porters, and workers in the sugar industry, including the macheteros and carreteros.[77] But in order for the Unión to do so, the reformist leadership of La Hermandad Ferroviarria de Cuba had to be discredited.

By the beginning of the 1920s, the moderates and reformers who guided most of the unions within La Hermandad Ferroviarria were, like the leadership of the Socialist Party of Cuba, influenced by Samuel Gompers and the American Federation of Labor. Before 1900, the AFL had advocated white and black worker solidarity. Later, however, its affiliated trade unions had constructed a color bar that banned black workers from joining them. Samuel Gompers's racial attitudes reflected this development: "For all of his eloquent pleas for unity among all of the workers regardless of race, color, or national origin, [Gompers] was basically a bigot. He referred repeatedly to white workers as superior to blacks . . . in his speeches and letters he used the common demeaning epithets of the day referring to blacks."[78] As a result, not only did La Hermandad's affiliation with the AFL reduce its effectiveness, but because the national leaders in Havana tolerated the presence of anarcho-syndicalists within their ranks, tensions between the two divergent labor philosophies prevented it from collectively challenging the company that controlled and monopolized the railroad system of Cuba, the Cuba Railroad Company, managed by H. C. Lakin. Lakin's company had come to monopolize many of the public and even private lines used by U.S. and Cuban sugar mills to transport their raw sugar to the coast. When the National Workers Congress convened in November 1920, a number of the Brotherhood's unions boycotted it, including the Union of Railroad Workers of Northern Cuba. As one of the meeting's organizers, Alfredo López, explained, their absence was based on a fundamental disagreement with Gompers and his aristocracy of workers as represented by the AFL. Viewing the AFL as reflecting "business unionism" that shunned the real concerns of the workers, López stated that the organizing model of the AFL and its policy toward black workers had sown the seeds of disunity and continued to weaken the national labor movement in Cuba.[79] The AFL's trade-union paradigm had encouraged white Cuban labor leaders not to recruit black workers on the grounds that their race and ethnicity made them inferior and insignificant. The Brotherhood's leaders purportedly saw blacks as "clumsy, lazy, and agents of contagious diseases, as well as natural strike-breakers since they only wanted to work when employers assured them special treatment."[80]

López's declaration changed the fundamental approach that organized labor took to protect and promote the rights of black workers. More important, in 1924 the Federation of Cuban Anarchist Groups, of which López was a founding member, insisted on establishing a campaign to organize Cuban, Haitian, and Jamaican workers on what they described as the feudal estates created by machinations between North American and Cuban elites.[81]

The first display of worker solidarity under the banner of internationalism occurred not in the sugar industry but at a factory outside Havana. While the railroad workers began challenging the Cuban Railroad Company on the eastern side of the island in the early months of 1921, thirty Jamaican braceros working at the El Moro de Mariel cement factory in Regla, across the Bay of Havana, went on strike after their company tried to cut their wages by 25 percent. It was a small strike, in both numbers and impact, but it made an impression: "the insolent spirit of the strikers has not changed since the Union of Railroad Workers joined in the brief boycott."[82] In addition, sensing the impact that this display of solidarity might have on the industry that employed the majority of black Caribbean braceros, the president of Cuba, Alfredo Zayas, in order to prevent the burning of sugarcane fields, instructed leaders of the national army and the rural guardsmen in the central and eastern provinces to take steps to preserve public order and increase their vigilance on all of the colonias and bateyes.[83]

When the island's economy had slightly improved by 1923, the railroad unions took the opportunity to advance their interests once more. Understanding their role in the sugar industry, the railroad workers in Camagüey challenged the Cuba Railroad Company. By the end of December 1923, the machinists, telegraph operators, and locomotive stokers had joined the protest. Together they called for a general strike and were soon joined by workers from the Railroad Line of Northern Cuba, who belonged to the Sindicato Ferroviario La Unión de Morón. During the general strike, the press reported how "Haitians, Jamaicans, and native cutters have joined hands in this concerted movement to secure increases in pay and the situation is becoming more acute every day."[84] The Zayas government immediately sent the army to Camagüey to crush the strikers after declaring martial law. The strike, however, lost steam because of dissension in the workers' ranks. To prevent discord among the workers, a number of railway labor leaders, such as Andres Otero Bosch, Abelardo Adán, and Juan Arévalo, traveled throughout the island to work on creating a national organization for railroad workers. Although their activities culminated in the organization of the Central de La Hermandad Ferroviaria de Cuba in February 1924, one union decided to remain outside the Central de La Hermandad, the Unión del Ferrocarril de Norte de Cuba's Unión de Morón.

Led by an exceptional anarcho-syndicalist, Enrique Varona González, the Unión de Morón attempted to build upon the multiethnic and class solidarity that the black Caribbean and native cane cutters had shown in 1923 by organizing all the sugarcane workers in Camagüey. This interest in organizing field workers and other laborers on the sugar estates of Camagüey stemmed not only from the Federation of Cuban Anarchist Group's campaign but also from Varona's background. Born in Pinar del Rio in 1888, Varona had worked in that province's tobacco industry, where anarcho-syndicalism informed its workers' consciousness.[85] After moving to Camagüey, Varona apprenticed as a locomotive stoker and later as a machinist for the Patria *central* near Morón. He qualified as a machinist for the Ferrocarril del Norte de Cuba in 1920. Although the Unión de Morón never associated itself with the Central de La Hermandad, it continued to work with and to support the other unions of railroad workers. Moreover, Varona and his associates assisted and fought for the rights of other laborers, particularly the longshoremen at the Puerto Tarafa and the workers whose sugar mills used the Railroad of Northern Cuba.

Their support caused workers to strike at several mills in order to protest being paid with company store scrip. The workers also walked out to demand an eight-hour day, and they insisted they be permitted to join the Unión de Morón. But the administrators of the Adelaida, Jaronú, Cunagua, and Lugareño *centrales* rejected their demands. Their foremen recommended turning down the workers' demands after realizing that they did not share the same goals as the strikers.[86] To support the sugar workers, Varona announced a boycott that took his men from their jobs. This resulted in the mills losing the work force that loaded and transported their raw sugar to the port of Morón. At the same time, the Unión de Morón clandestinely "proceeded to create a *comité obrero* [labor committee] to organize both the railroad and the sugarcane workers very slowly because of the fear among the braceros who still felt they could suffer from numerous reprisals at the hands of the managers, and the uncertainty of their economic future," remembered one cane cutter at the Jaronú *central*.[87] Another field worker at the Adelaida *central* near the town of Ranchuelos outside Morón recounted how "the mill became a hot-bed of agitation that Enrique Varona directed." The image of Varona at one of the meetings remained etched in the memory of this former machetero decades later. He continued: "The workers' struggle actually began in 1924 on the Adelaida when Varona had the opportunity to visit the *central*. He mobilized the workers there with exhortations of using the strike to demand increases in salaries and better living conditions." Varona worked painstakingly to unite the workers at the Adelaida with the larger sugar workers' movement—the Federation of Sugar Workers, as it would later be called—that was being organized throughout the region of Morón and elsewhere in Cuba. According to one source, "he had already established five syndicates around Morón among the sugar and train workers."[88] Although Varona and the Unión de Morón aggressively sought to mobilize all types of sugar workers, what made their organizing strategy effective was the purpose and objectives of the syndicates. Unfortunately, what he and other organizers may have revealed to the black sugarcane workers is not preserved in the historical record. Nonetheless, one may rely on the public texts left by a former Jamaican bracero radicalized by his Cuban experiences to illuminate the content of the ideology of dissent shared by the most effective labor syndicalists in the sugarcane-producing provinces of Camagüey and Oriente, areas where the majority of black Caribbean immigrants labored.

The organizers from Morón defined trade unionism and discussed its goals and strategies. Hugh Buchanan, who became a union organizer in Jamaica after leaving the sugar enclaves of Cuba in the 1930s, understood that unions needed to educate and advise the workers regarding their labor philosophy and strategy. He wrote: "Hand in hand with the organization on the industrial field . . . enlightened political action demands knowledge of the theory underlining labor unionism. This knowledge must be acquired by the leaders and passed on to the rank and file. The employers know what they want and where they are heading. Labor leaders must know where they are leading their followers. Without a definite labor philosophy the best intentions will lead no where and the masses are likely to be no better off than before they were organized."[89] The anarcho-syndicalist organizers also helped convinced Buchanan and other braceros that "strong labor unions demanded respect and it gives protection from every angle . . . it defends the rights of labor and humanity." Unionization afforded these protections, particularly to an individual's dignity, only after the workers themselves realized that "the religion of the poor could not assist in mitigating the effects of their subordination."[90]

In order to promote worker solidarity between whites and blacks and the skilled and unskilled, Varona and his cadre of organizers introduced the concept of internationalism. Emphasizing the role that class played in the workers' exploitation, Buchanan reminded his former mates in the cane fields of Cuba that "starting from fear of the deliberate exploitation of racial divisions by the capitalists . . . on no account must we fight race against race, for we are all one—Workers of the World Unite! . . . White workers are with us, [and] the black capitalist is just as oppressive as any other."[91] Emphasizing the IWW's call for workers' solidarity, first expressed among members of the International Brotherhood, the syndicates established at the sugar mills and farms in Camagüey and later in Oriente made the field workers and artisans inside the mills understand how the companies had used the categories of color, ethnicity, and nationality to exploit both blacks and whites. The organizers also rendered the segmented labor system as central to capitalism and imperialism.

Varona and his organizers undoubtedly applied Lenin's theories to deconstruct the exploitative nature of the segmented labor system. Lenin's interpretation of imperialism and how it affected the labor of foreign workers was detailed in *Imperialism: The Highest Stage of Capitalism*. He maintained that skilled and artisan laborers, the "aristocracy of workers," assisted in the exploitation of manual or unskilled workers. This hierarchy not only led to the subjugation of the lowest sections of the working class, but it also influenced neocolonial relations among hegemonic nations and their satellites, such as Cuba. Lenin stated:

> The exploitation of worse paid labor from backward countries is particularly characteristic of imperialism. On this exploitation rests, to a certain degree, the parasitism of rich imperialist countries which bribe a part of their workers with higher wages while shamelessly and unrestrainedly exploiting the labor of cheap foreign workers . . . The exploiters in civilized countries always take advantage of the fact that imported foreign workers have no rights.[92]

Alfredo López and other anarcho-syndicalists shared Lenin's thoughts on the experiences of immigrant workers and found them relevant. Lenin's ideas described Cuba's relationship with the U.S.-owned sugar mills, as well as the companies' relationships with native and black immigrant workers. As a result, his critique of imperialism provided Buchanan and other black Caribbean braceros with an explanation of their subordination.[93]

The Unión de Morón's organizing campaign proved successful because its organizers never compelled the sugarcane laborers to adopt their views and interpretations. This approach prompted the Federation of Sugar Workers to declare, "[T]he Ferrocarril del Norte is a symbol of progress. All of its workers are sowing the seeds of destruction in the furrowed fields of the wealthy in order to advance the interests of the largest number of workers of the country, a country that supports foreign and native businesses . . . On the other hand, the Ferrocarril cannot determine what sugar workers want. Only we can evaluate our conditions and decide which strategies to adopt to solve them. Sugar workers, do not sharpen your machetes and place them against your own throats!"[94]

The provincial government arrested Varona and other leaders of his organization in an effort to curb their unionizing activities. Varona, however, warned the provincial governor, Rogelio Zayas-Bazán, that if he and his men were not released within seventy-two hours, they would declare a general strike that would shut down the entire northern railroad system of Cuba.

As the strike continued into late October, it gained the attention of U.S. Ambassador Enoch Crowder. He believed that if the strike did not end immediately, it would not only affect the outcome of the Cuban general elections scheduled in November but also spread and damage the properties of U.S.-owned sugar companies in other parts of the island. His judgment may have been based upon information from the manager of the Chaparra central in Oriente. After reporting the dismissal of three labor agitators who worked in the warehouse and on the docks at the port of Manatí, Fernández Morrell wrote to Manuel Rionda that the "labor situation at Chaparra has recently taken a turn for the worse. From the mayor of Puerto Padre, Mr. Pérez Puelles, I have learned that not only have the colonos formed a union but also the factory and railroad laborers. Now it appears that efforts are being made in the direction of also unionizing the cane cutters."[95] Meanwhile in Oriente, the American consul in Santiago de Cuba, Francis Stewart, confirmed Crowder's suspicions when he reported that the strikes there eventually would include the macheteros and carreteros. His analysis underlined the workers' dire material condition. In September 1924, he wrote that along with the four railroad strikes that had stopped all transportation for nearly a month, "at present the workmen at several large sugarmills have struck and it is believed the trouble will spread. Apparently, a concerted effort is being made to unionize all labor on the island. Agitators work unhindered among the laboring classes, [particularly] cane cutters who are paid . . . eighty cents to one dollar per day."[96] Rumors of the recruitment and organization of the braceros had caused the American consul-general in Havana, Arthur C. Frost, to inform the State Department several months earlier that there was now an "objection to the entry of colored West Indian laborers" and that although efforts to bring them in persisted, "there is much sentiment at present time against the admittance of more such labor."[97] Compelled to resolve the work stoppage, the sugar mills accepted the demands of the workers on 28 October 1924.

Confident and empowered by the success of the sugarcane workers around Morón, in early November workers at the Florida, Céspedes, Jatibonico, Vertientes, Estrella, and Algodones *centrales* went on strike. Their demands were almost identical: an eight-hour workday and improved working conditions.[98] At the same time, in Oriente Francis Stewart received news from officials of the United Fruit Company in Banes that strikes might spread to the America, Oriente, and Palma sugar mills. Stewart informed Crowder that he expected the mills on the northern coast of Oriente to be affected shortly, "and the Miranda will probably be the next mill to become involved with the labor unions, and that the situation is bad." Stewart ended his report blaming the Railroad Brotherhood for organizing the sugarcane workers:

> That the Railroad Brotherhood is behind the sugarmill strikes is shown by the fact that Mr. Portuondo (a negro lawyer of this city and who is attorney for the Brotherhood) accompanied the governor's representative to Palma yesterday . . . In my opinion, every sugarmill on the island will become involved before the unions really talk business. The men are without doubt well organized and before many weeks the united unions will be in a position to and probably will declare a general strike throughout the country that will paralyze all industrial activity.[99]

The government responded to this series of strikes as it had before. It sent troops both to Camagüey and Oriente on the pretext of preserving order, while establishing an atmosphere of terror on the bateyes. In order to prevent the strikers from splintering into multiple, diverse, and competing factions, Varona had established the Sindicato Provincial de Trabajadores of Camagüey to promote worker solidarity. Composed of workers and labor leaders from the mills on strike, the strikers succeeded in sustaining their efforts into December. Afraid of what might happen on other sugar estates, U.S government officials insisted that the managers of the sugar mills consider the demands of the workers. The companies in Oriente were the first to respond. They told Stewart that their mills could not adopt an eight-hour workday and break even. And if they did, a more pressing problem would obtain—where were they going to find the necessary supply of workers?[100]

The mill owners decided instead to break the strikes by importing a few hundred black Caribbean braceros each. However, it appears that the braceros were not informed of the real purpose behind their contracts. Once they learned that they were intended to serve as strikebreakers, many decided that they did not want to be used as scabs. A Jamaican who was present in Camagüey at the time told a reporter of the *Daily Gleaner* that "the Cuban workers who are all unionized, by force sought to prevent the Jamaicans from working while the soldiers sent to help the estate owners with bayonets, machetes, and whips bludgeoned the poor unfortunate British subjects into working." The confused immigrant bracero observed: "The men are beaten for not going to work and the men are beaten for going to work."[101] Refusing to be used as strikebreakers, the Jamaicans left the fields. Other braceros at a different mill armed themselves in order not to be coerced to work as strikebreakers.[102]

The challenge that black Caribbean braceros mounted in refusing to be used as strikebreakers may be explained by the role that the Union of Antillean Workers played, particularly in Oriente. Led by a Jamaican organizer, Henry Shackleton, between 1920 and 1925, and composed of British West Indians, Haitians, and Cubans, the Union of Antillean Workers had established strong ties with a number of Cuban worker syndicates. At the same time, Shackleton and other black immigrant workers sought to end sectarian and ethnic strife between the braceros and Cubans. In doing so, they helped to strengthen the general labor movement. The relationship between Shackleton's organization and the anarcho-syndicalists was described by Rolando Alvarez Estévez as having "always been characterized by the honest principle of class solidarity, without deception, and with the long-term objectives of improving the bonds between the majority of starving, and iniquitously exploited workers of the movement."[103] Nonetheless, Shackleton and his members had to overcome the contempt that most Cubans had for the majority of black braceros, an attitude that emerged from the ideology crafted by the companies and the government that "transformed unfounded cultural attributes and behaviors into a pervasive naturalism."[104] Shackleton said that "Antillean workers were criticized by some governmental and labor officials for selling themselves to their exploiters like animals, and if solicited would even sell their own women for $10.00 in pesos."[105] Frustrated by such false and racist attitudes, and by the sugar companies' strategy of often using black Caribbean workers as strikebreakers to smash their workers' resistance, Shackleton used the same language that Lenin had used in describing the effects of imperialism on native and foreign workers. He reminded white and black Cuban workers that the black immigrants' experience included physical intimidation and terror at the hands of the army and rural guard. He also emphasized that the black braceros were the most exploited class of workers in Cuba and therefore could not be blamed for their status. They "were controlled by a few capitalists who manipulated their powerlessness to create their awful conditions." Ultimately, in order to show their dedication to the principle of class solidarity, once the Union of Antillean Workers had been amalgamated with the Sindicato del Obreros Azucareros, Shackleton and other union members would discourage black workers from emigrating.[106] The Union of Antillean Workers supported a ban on black emigration because it agreed with the anarcho-syndicalists' analysis that black Antillean emigration had engendered the suffering of thousands of Haitian and Jamaican workers.[107]

For his role and participation in the strikes of 1924 and 1925, Shackleton was selected to serve on the executive committee and, with Alfredo López and José García López, was charged with writing the constitution of the Third National Workers Congress of Cuba (CNOC). Meeting in August 1925 in the city of Camagüey, together with 160 delegates from 128 unions that represented an estimated 200,000 organized workers, members of the CNOC recognized the abhorrent circumstances that the braceros faced by offering a motion that confirmed the principle of worker solidarity. Prefacing the proposal with a declaration of hatred for foreign capital instead of foreign workers, "[T]his congress, understanding the horrors that are committed toward Antillean emigrants, agree with the executive board of the CNOC by protesting before the government those hateful offensives and insults that make victims of our compañeros."[108]

The series of work stoppages that occurred during the first half of the 1920s proved that the anarcho-syndicalists had realized the importance of organizing Caribbean braceros and incorporating them into the larger Cuban labor movement. Their numbers may have been relatively small compared to other Cuban workers, but Enrique Varona's campaign of 1924 and 1925 could not have been possible without the participation and cooperation of the black macheteros and carreteros. The timing of the work stoppages also suggests that black Caribbean workers who were permanently residing on the island participated in these protests. That skilled factory workers were involved in the strikes also suggests that some of the black Caribbean immigrants from Panama had lived up to their reputation as the most militant immigrant workers that the North American multinationals hired.[109] The material circumstances that Magoon and the Jamaican planter J. M. Burke described undoubtedly compelled the braceros to realize that they had nothing to lose. Rubén Martínez Villena noted their role and sacrifice. A leader of the Communist Party at the time, he observed that "the Antillean braceros, particularly the Haitians and Jamaicans at the start of the 1920s, began to acquire, in our country, deserving merit for their participation in the social struggle; for this reason they became an integral part in our own cause and contributed to the common fight of the Cuban proletariat, accumulating honor and respect among their brothers of the working class."[110] Unfortunately, the attempt to incorporate them into the Federation of Sugar Workers ended when Cuban President Gerardo Machado had Enrique Varona assassinated in front of his family outside a movie theater in Morón on 19 September 1925. As a result, it was not until 1933 that the Caribbean braceros again had the opportunity to participate fully in the Cuban labor movement.

Although the strikes had compelled the sugar mills to grant a number of concessions to the workers, the overall effects of the labor protests hardly improved the daily lives of the braceros. In fact, the strikes had gravely reduced their seasonal income. In a patronizing tone and language reflecting the hegemonic ideology of the sugar companies, and reminiscent of the manager's evaluation and response to the bracero's inquiry that began this chapter, Francis Stewart informed his superiors in Havana and later in Washington that for "the cane cutters, mostly Jamaican and Haitian and other West Indian negroes, the season of 1924–1925 was a lucrative one for this class of workers . . . Recently two small vessels plying between this port and Aux Cayes, Haiti took out a total of 360 natives, who, it is officially reported, had in their possession a total of $39,211."[111] Suggesting that the experience of these Haitian migrants was a prosperous one because they took home approximately $108 per worker during this tumultuous period, Stewart completely misrepresented their reality in a way that veiled the asymmetrical relationship between the braceros and the sugar companies. Nonetheless, they could only take their protests so far. They accepted their fate as macheteros and carreteros, took the miserable wages the companies offered, and after the zafra either stayed or returned home. In spite of the difficulties they endured, Haitians and Jamaicans still believed that Cuba was a land of opportunity. They involved themselves in trade unionism that claimed to protect the rights of all laborers. Others saw the ideology of Marcus M. Garvey as a philosophy to improve their lives as immigrant workers in Cuba.

5

GARVEYISM WITHOUT GARVEY

A Counter-Ideology in the Black Caribbean Communities

White people are no better than black people. Hear what I tell you! They are no better than us . . . The brain of a black man and of a black woman is greater than that of a white man.[1]

While working in Cuba for a total of five years, Enos McKenzie, a Jamaican bracero, heard the most important Pan-African nationalist leader of the first half of the twentieth century say the above words to his fellow immigrant workers. Another Jamaican machetero, a Mr. Fearon, proudly remembered:

In those days I went to Cuba [and] it was Marcus Garvey's days, and surprisingly I met him in Cuba . . . I met his brother in Cuba . . . [It was Marcus Garvey's] mission and those were the times when they had the Black Star Line business; I joined the Universal Negro Improvement Association . . . I lend them fifty pounds to carry the association; here the medal right in here now . . . And we usually keep meetings. Platform meetings for Garvey in Cuba, you know. In those days, I knew it and could speak the [Spanish] language fluently because if you can't read and write it, you couldn't speak as a platform speaker, for you have to talk exactly that the Spaniards or the Spanish speaking people can understand what you are saying, for you couldn't go have meetings and they don't hear what you saying, that would be against the law.[2]

In February 1921, Garvey visited Cuba hoping to convince people of African descent and sympathetic whites to join his movement, which sought to redeem Africa and the members of its diaspora. Their cooperation and assistance would include buying shares of stock in his commercial enterprises based in the United

States as well as joining his movement's main organization, the Universal Negro Improvement Association and African Community League (UNIA). As the agency that Garvey had designed to advance and protect the interests of all blacks regardless of ethnicity throughout the Americas, it seemed more than plausible that the UNIA would attract a large black enrollment in Cuba, given the history of race relations on the island as well as the current socioeconomic and political status of black Cubans. As someone who had been forced to leave Jamaica in order to find work and better wages, going first to Panama and later to Costa Rica, Garvey understood the causes and conditions associated with the subordination and exploitation of black Caribbean braceros. How black Cubans and Caribbean emigrant workers responded to Garvey's visit and overtures is explored in this chapter.

Garvey arrived in Cuba during the throes of an economic recession caused by the collapse in the price of sugar as well as the financial crisis that accompanied it. In these circumstances, how could blacks, regardless of nationality, find the energy and money to assist Garvey in making his movement an international one? After all, the financial crisis had led to widespread unemployment among black Cubans and whites. At the same time, the sugar companies had either stopped paying the braceros altogether or had suspended their wages until the price of sugar improved. How did the socioeconomic and political concerns of black Cubans inform their meetings with Garvey, and were these troubles similar to those of the black Caribbean workers? In what ways did the interpretation of the history of race relations in Cuba influence whether Garvey's ideology of resistance, which challenged the complex ideology and justification for the subordination of blacks, proved a success or a failure during and after his visit? Finally, how did blacks, specifically the black braceros, understand and adopt Garveyism to assist them as marginalized and exploited immigrants?

This chapter shows that Garvey's Pan-African nationalism could not match the intensity and importance of the Cuban nationalism articulated earlier by Martí, Maceo, and others of the Generation of 1895, a nationalism that resonated among some sectors of the black middle and working classes. As a result, they could not find common ground with Garvey, and his ideology of resistance failed to gain a footing among socially mobile urban black Cubans. They had come to pride themselves on being completely and faithfully Cuban. Moreover, urban black Cubans considered themselves already redeemed by their efforts to assimilate modern Hispano-Cuban culture. As a result, they saw Garvey's ideas, strategies, and movement as irrelevant. By failing to expose how the dominant white society's ideology obfuscated the role that race and ethnicity played in the island's history, Garvey failed to arouse the interest and support of black Cubans.

As a result, he redirected his efforts toward mobilizing and organizing the tens of thousands of black Caribbean braceros in the principal sugar-producing regions of Camagüey and Oriente. There, he was warmly received. It was there, among the most powerless class of workers in Cuba, that he was able to introduce his ideology and strategies. Employing the UNIA branches as mutual-aid societies and educational and religious sites, the black braceros seized on Garveyism to mitigate the physical as well as the psychological effects of their subordination. This was critical, given their status and condition as the sugar industry's primary work force.

In order to prevent his supporters and organizations from being perceived as threats to white hegemony and the island's security, Garvey publicly employed the elite's hegemonic narrative to speak glowingly about American and European civilization. Although many scholars have argued that this aspect of Garveyism made him seem opportunistic and an insincere admirer of African culture, one can also interpret his idealization of Western cultural concepts as a deceptive strategy to allay white fears about his movement while allowing his supporters to interpret for themselves the aspects of his counter-ideology that opposed the ideological hegemony of American and European whites. This was evinced by the proliferation, in a time of economic uncertainty, of UNIA branches in Cuba. These social sites, composed of black Caribbean braceros, inspired some of them to produce an explanation of their socioeconomic subordination in both racial and economic or class terms. Their interpretations were close to those of Enrique Varona and the anarcho-syndicalists. Finally, Garveyism converged with anarcho-syndicalism to challenge the racially and ethnically segmented labor system employed by the sugar companies. By the end of the 1920s, black Cubans, Haitians, and Jamaicans had developed a militant workers' consciousness that explained their material condition—an orientation suited for establishing a multiethnic alliance in the labor organizations and in the social sites of the UNIA in order to re-appropriate their honor and humanity.

Marcus Garvey landed in Havana on 28 February 1921.[3] Primitivo Ramírez Ros, a Conservative Party city councilman from Matanzas, greeted Garvey and his entourage, and graciously offered his home to the Pan-African leader while he toured Havana. Ramírez Ros also scheduled a number of meetings between

Garvey and influential people of the city, both black and white. Garvey's itinerary included visits with the Cuban president and his cabinet, some congressmen, and business leaders, as well as with officials from the societies of color. He also planned to speak with members of the city's black Antillean community. One of the city's newspapers, the Heraldo de Cuba, reported that Garvey's presence was a momentous occasion for the majority of British West Indians: "The arrival of Mr. Garvey in Havana has constituted an event which has given the black immigrants of this capital the reason to express from their hearts an enormous amount of energy and enthusiasm for him."[4] During the first two days of March 1921, they supported him at two public rallies in the Parque Santos y Artigas. At both events Garvey addressed large crowds of Jamaicans and North Americans, who paid fifty centavos each to hear him. At the end of each lecture, Garvey's assistants mingled with the audience in order to sell shares of stock in his numerous companies, such as the Black Star Steamship Line. Many of the braceros purchased stocks at twenty dollars a share on the promise that they could expect to earn 5 percent annually from their investment.[5] Garvey himself made it clear to his audiences that he hoped to use the profits from his businesses to redeem the stature of Africa. Solicitations to support the Black Star Steamship Line became a common occurrence during every speaking engagement that Garvey scheduled while on tour in Cuba and other parts of the Caribbean. During his visit to Belize (British Honduras) in July 1921, for example, the superintendent of police, H. S. Cavenaugh, reported that Garvey used the last ten minutes of every lecture to ask his audience to buy shares of stock in the "Line" and support his plan to settle Liberia.[6]

A reporter from the Heraldo de Cuba provided a description of both Havana rallies. Although Garvey spoke for a couple of hours, the paper gave only brief summaries of his speeches, in which he discussed the doctrine of Pan-Africanism. Garvey evidently emphasized the need for all blacks regardless of ethnicity to unite morally and economically, yet the paper omitted any discussion of how they were to accomplish this objective. According to the article, Garvey also made a number of references to Africa, yet it never explained the context in which the African continent was mentioned. The article's lack of specificity may have been caused by the reporter's attempt to withhold Garvey's counter-ideology from black Cubans as well as from black immigrants who could read Spanish. Instead, the reporter highlighted Garvey's impressive rhetorical skills. He was an "eloquent speaker who had mastered the art of speaking in a fashion that allowed him to hold his audience captive whenever he laughed, hollered, or sought to whip up their emotions at will," reported the journalist.[7]

Such scant reporting poses a problem for historians trying to evaluate the impact of Garvey's visit. As a result, the historian must look elsewhere to discern what Garvey might have said to persuade black Cubans and immigrants and others in attendance to join and support his movement. From a number of speeches later published by his wife, Amy Jacques Garvey, it appears that Marcus Garvey often discussed and covered the same themes and topics in his lectures and homilies.[8] If that is so, one can expect that the speeches he gave during his tour of the Caribbean during March and April 1921 identified the issues that concerned him. In addition, Garvey often spoke to constituencies similar to those who lived and worked in Cuba. In Central America, for instance, he addressed black immigrants working in Panama, Belize, and Costa Rica. In Jamaica, he traveled into the countryside to speak in front of crowds of peasants or workers employed by the sugar companies.

Garvey probably opened his speeches in Havana and elsewhere on the island by explaining the origins of his movement in Jamaica and later in the United States. He had arrived in New York City in 1914 with the hope of acquiring financial support for the first Jamaican Division of the UNIA, and to build a vocational or industrial school similar to Booker T. Washington's Tuskegee Institute, founded in Alabama in 1881. Unsuccessful in obtaining the support of black Americans for either project, Garvey left New York City to travel throughout the southern region of the United States. During this tour, he observed and recorded the dire socioeconomic conditions that the policies of Jim Crow had created for the majority of poor and rural blacks. Upon returning to New York City in 1917, Garvey along with a small number of followers established a branch of the UNIA that would later become the headquarters of his movement. He told his audiences that "within a month thirteen members grew to six hundred and in the space of six months, it improved to a membership of 10,000 . . . The Association that [I] started in New York four years ago has now a membership of four million."[9] By discussing his movement's humble and difficult origins, and how dramatically it had grown since 1917, Garvey not only attempted to demonstrate the level of support he had obtained but also the degree to which blacks throughout the Americas agreed with his philosophy and strategy to ameliorate their socioeconomic condition. His interpretation of black history informed his philosophy and approach.

During his tour of the Caribbean, Garvey often gave a brief history of the black experience in the Americas. In order to engender sentiments of Pan-African nationalism, he claimed that:

Africa, the land that God Almighty gave us, was robbed and despoiled by the nations of the world . . . [It] shall be redeemed by the four hundred million Negroes in the world . . . They robbed four million of us from Africa 300 years ago; they brought us in slavery to the Western Hemisphere; when the matter was brought before Queen Elizabeth it was represented that the Negroes were taken to be civilized and Christianized. After 300 years if they are civilized and Christianized, we will use that same civilization and Christianization to redeem the motherland.[10]

That Marcus Garvey usually extolled the virtues and attributes of Western culture has prompted one historian to claim that this reflected his lack of knowledge about the history and culture of pre-colonial Africa. Garvey, Richard Hart insists, "accepted fully the picture of 'darkest Africa' needing a civilizing western Christian influence" that the imperial powers had painted.[11] Other historians have argued that he was completely enamored with European culture and its social, political, and economic structures. Moreover, this affinity with European modernity, they argue, trivialized his commitment to Pan-African nationalism. As a result, some of his contemporaries and later a few of his biographers considered Garvey to be ideologically inconsistent, unprincipled, and an opportunist.[12] These writers, however, have failed to realize that this doctrine of Garveyism never overshadowed the other maxims that stressed his notions of racial equality. Garveyism deconstructed the concept of black inferiority on which Western European ideological hegemony rested. Advocating publicly that his supporters adopt certain aspects of Western culture allowed him to shroud this dangerous dogma while becoming a very influential and charismatic leader among blacks, even though the U.S. government kept a close watch on his movements. In his Caribbean tour, he sought to use the stature he had developed in the United States to transform his movement into one more international in scope.

One way to do this without drawing the suspicion of the elites was to encourage blacks to assimilate modern Western values. Their cultural refinement would not only create racial self-approbation but would also allow blacks to compete effectively with whites. To further lessen fears among whites, Garvey publicly announced that his intentions were not to disrespect any nation or race. The objectives of his tour were not to cause racial tensions but to inspire blacks and to unify those who lived and worked in these countries.

In order to construct a Pan-African consciousness, Garvey addressed the sociocultural legacy of slavery that left blacks fatalistically superstitious. "You Negroes . . . pray too much!" he frequently observed. "With all your prayers you [still] have hurricanes, earthquakes, droughts, and everything! You know why? You Negroes have not gotten into your heads the scientific idea of worshipping God! Emotion and sentiment does not count in a world like this . . . This world can only be moved by practical achievements. Unless you work with your prayers, you will be too late here or anywhere else. Along with your prayers, do some work and that is what the UNIA is here to advise you to do . . . We want you to do ennobling work."[13] Garvey's criticism of black religion has been interpreted as a philosophical difference that he had with the chaplain-general of the UNIA's New York branch, Dr. George A. McGuire. Garvey saw his movement and philosophy as being of secular importance, while Reverend McGuire believed that by catering to the religious and spiritual needs of black diasporans the movement could effectively recruit new members and obtain their financial support.[14] Garvey's position, however, does not reflect a rigid antireligious view. Instead, he argued that the adoption of a strong sense of religious faith along with a hardy work ethic would allow people of African ancestry to shape their own futures: "The time has come for Negroes to point themselves to a more glorious destiny. Will the members of the Race remain slaves and serfs? If there is nothing better for him but to be a lackey, let him die. No one [can] tell him that he must bow and cringe and scrape to be a man because that man [is] white."[15] This message undoubtedly could have made some black Cubans question the efficacy of remaining silent politically since the Race War of 1912 in the hope of garnering white patronage that would facilitate their integration. At the same time, Garvey's criticism may have inspired many black Caribbean workers to take control of their lives. They realized that they could stop being used as pawns and show a degree of agency by setting the cane fields on fire or refusing to be used as strikebreakers. Others could also shape their futures by participating in the labor movement that tried to organize all of the sugarcane workers.

To promote racial pride and solidarity, Garvey regularly emphasized that blacks already were equal to whites. During his speeches he often cited their contributions as workers to the economies of the Western nations as well as their role as soldiers during World War I. Regarding the latter, he reminded his audiences that "[W]hen the great war broke out . . . the British turned down the black men who applied for enlistment, but when the Germans had beaten them as well as the French and invaded France and Belgium they cried out for help and it was not until the black men, the supermen entered, that the Germans stopped and asked for peace. Had it not been for the men of the British West Indies and other black men the Kaiser would be drinking pea soup today in Buckingham Palace."[16] In spite of the significant role that black soldiers had played during the war, the European states under which they lived as colonial subjects refused to grant them the rights of citizens. This state of affairs demanded immediate action by the people. Garvey declared that "we are now going to make ourselves Africans. While the British, French, Americans and others failed to protect us in the past, the Red, Black, and Green would in a short time be able to give ample protection to all . . . The world belongs to all. God has created all men to be the lords of the earth and not some to be paupers and cringing beggars. Brothers . . . we should start to build a great African Empire. Better late than never."[17] Although Garvey argued that racial pride and solidarity were prerequisites for the acquisition of racial equality, it is interesting that his thoughts on this topic defined that equality in economic or class terms. Given the dire material circumstances of most braceros before and after the collapse of the price of sugar, the imagery that his statement invoked—that God had not preordained blacks to be simply poor vagabonds but the equals of whites—provided the sugarcane workers with a class analysis and perhaps the incentive to become political.

Garvey also tried to elevate the self-esteem of blacks. He tied the self-worth of blacks to racial equality. The role of black women proved critical in this process. He told black Caribbean females that they too needed to participate in the struggle for equality. Gender and their traditional status in society informed their role, however. They were simply required to help build the confidence of their husbands, sons, and brothers within the context of the home.[18] Garvey commanded black women to increase their own level of self-esteem and to create higher expectations for black men. He observed that "the women of the race [do] not appreciate themselves enough and . . . that [is] one of the chief reasons why the men up to the present had not advanced further. The progress of the race depends on the women, and if they, like the women of other races, would require much of the men, the men would be compelled to aim higher. If the woman would look for a Wellington or a Napoleon then there would have to be a Waterloo."[19]

To transform his U.S.-based movement into a truly international one, Garvey ended his rallies by urging the crowd to buy shares of the Black Star Line Corporation, "and be ready to get dividends in the next twelve months. Two million dollars is being raised for the purpose of building railroads, factories, and generally improving the country [Africa]. Any sum from five dollars up may be loaned for five, ten, or fifteen years, and will carry interest at the rate of five per cent per annum, and more than what can be obtained when [you] put money into the banks for others to benefit from."[20]

Because Garvey spoke on these and similar themes during his travels through the Caribbean, one can safely assume that he very likely reiterated them at the two public gatherings held in the Parque Santos y Artigas in Havana. His message resonated among the people there, convincing many of them to financially support his organizations and activities. Although it is impossible to know how much money Garvey collected during his stay in Havana, it has been reported that while visiting Colón, Panama, he raised $35,000 after speaking at six public rallies in his honor. He obtained a similar amount after speaking with black migrants working for the United Fruit Company near Limón, Costa Rica.[21]

On 3 March 1921, a reporter from the *Heraldo de Cuba* interviewed Garvey, who informed the journalist that Cuba was the first stop on a Caribbean tour that would allow him to visit the numerous branches of the UNIA. Twenty-five branches had already been established, and he was planning to meet with those located in Morón, Nuevitas, and Santiago de Cuba.[22] In order to calm the fears that his presence probably engendered among government officials and the representatives of the sugar companies, Garvey insisted that he had no intentions of interfering in the internal affairs of the island. He had come to Cuba "to seek the help of the black Cubans so as to unite all of the blacks in the world. In this way we can all enjoy the social and economic progress equally."[23]

Others saw Garvey's movement differently. In a letter dated 4 March 1920, Samuel Duncan, a dissatisfied former confidante of Garvey's inner circle from the UNIA branch in New York City, described Garvey and his organization as a menace to all the governments of the Americas. Garvey's Universal Negro Improvement Association and African Communities League are "not only antiwhite and anti-British," Duncan wrote, "but . . . engaged in the most destructive and pernicious propaganda to create disturbances between white and colored people in the British possessions."[24] Duncan's letter was circulated among the colonial governments of the British West Indies, and it is likely that agents of the British consulates in Cuba passed it along to Zayas and his ministers. Garvey's discussion with the reporter may very likely have been an attempt to defuse possible opposition from those who realized that his principle of racial unity challenged not only the racial hierarchy of Cuba but also the segmented labor system employed by the majority of sugar companies.

Studying the experiences of British West Indians on the banana plantations owned by the United Fruit Company surrounding Limón, Costa Rica, Aviva Chomsky argues that the company executives viewed organizations such as Garvey's "as a considerable threat."[25] As another historian has shown, in Costa Rica the company ensured that "class exploitation and ethnic domination were . . . closely intertwined on the plantation during this period." After "the demand for ethnic rights was raised" among the work force, "that of better working conditions and higher wages almost inevitably followed."[26] Garveyism, it seems, presented a similar threat to the sugar companies of Cuba.

Garvey insisted that his ideas and organization were relevant in Cuba. He acknowledged that the problems of blacks in the United States were fundamentally different from those of black Cubans. Yet he believed that the daily lives of both groups were influenced by the same common factors of racial prejudice and discrimination. Both fostered black inequality. To mitigate the effects of prejudice and discrimination, blacks needed an assortment of strategies based upon local and national circumstances. Nevertheless, he asserted that his general approach was relevant and useful for all blacks regardless of their nationality. Garvey informed the reporter from the *Heraldo de Cuba* that the social progress of black peoples was tied to their economic independence and self-reliance. This could be achieved by investing in "the Black Star and Factory Corporations that are essentially commercial enterprises. If they buy stock they will enjoy their dividends," Garvey claimed.[27] At the end of the interview, Garvey told the journalist that some of the black Cubans he had met were misinformed about the intentions of his visit. He had not come to convince them to return to Africa, as they believed. He wanted to tell them, however, that the creation of "an African state is important because it will help blacks in America and in Cuba to become full citizens in their own countries."[28]

Although Garvey consistently argued that establishing a strong nation-state in Africa was another prerequisite for black equality, believing that then and only then would the governments and societies of Europe respect the humanity of black people, he may have been speaking metaphorically when discussing the goal of creating an African state in this context. Garvey believed that the construction of a racial consciousness would solve the low levels of self-esteem that most blacks shared and that was engendered by African slavery and European colonialism. The reemergence of their self-respect and "consciousness of kind" would encourage blacks to organize, regardless of their socioeconomic differences, in order to collectively oppose their second-class status and demand their human rights. Considering themselves as citizens of an independent state in Africa—what William Edwards calls an "imagined state"—may have caused some black Caribbean workers in the sugar industry to collectively demand that the Haitian and British consuls protect their rights whenever the sugar companies and the Cuban authorities harassed or mistreated them.[29] The self-confidence they obtained with dual citizenship would allow them to navigate the appropriate diplomatic channels to protect their rights.

During the rest of his stay in Havana, Garvey briefly met with some officials of the societies of color, as well as with representatives of the government. Inexplicably, the Cuban press failed to record his conversation with the Cuban president. The reception that the societies of color gave Garvey, however, was reported. The published narrative of his meetings with the black Cuban organizations reaffirmed the dominant ideology of white Cubans. In brief, their conferences with the Pan-African nationalist consisted of acts and sentiments of admiration but also expressed indifference. The black Cuban leadership repudiated Garvey's message and found his strategies irrelevant.

On 3 March 1921, after members of the Club Abraham Lincoln and the Unión Fraternal had entertained Garvey for most of the day, he and his host, Ramírez Ros, arrived at the most distinguished society of color on the island, the Club Atenas. Composed of members of the black middle class, the Club Atenas was established to protect and enhance the civil rights of people of color. After Garvey was greeted by the president of the organization, Dr. Miguel Angel Céspedes, members of the club informed Garvey that they admired his work, which had resulted in the significant progress of blacks in the United States. Céspedes then summarized the objectives and activities of the Club Atenas. Because of this work, Céspedes believed that Garvey's Pan-African ideas could not gain new adherents in Cuba. In order to make Garvey feel utterly out of place, Céspedes emphatically told him that "in [our] view, the race of color in the island is Cuban, and fortunately by the order of the laws they enjoyed the same rights and privileges as Cubans belonging to the white race." Moreover, Céspedes stressed, "all of the roads to progress were open to them."[30]

Céspedes did not suggest that racial equality actually existed in Cuba; after all, the abolition of slavery had only occurred in 1886. "Nothing more could have taken place in the short space of forty years," he explained.[31] Believing that racial equality would be obtained in the near future, Céspedes told Garvey that civil equality had been achieved and that "the forces that favored their moral, intellectual, and material progress would continue to appear in order to make their differences disappear and be replaced with the feelings of brotherhood and equality based upon the common rights of a civilized state."[32]

The historical role that black Cubans had played since the 1860s informed Céspedes's optimism. He told Garvey that "black Cubans had had the power to liberate Cuba and create a republic where they could live with dignity and exercise all of the rights of free and civilized men." As a result, "[T]here is no need for us to create and join another nation. I am Cuban and do not share in the Pan-African identity. I do not possess a cosmopolitan human spirit."[33] The Cuban nationalism and identity that Céspedes and the members of the societies of color expressed were part of an emerging nativist ideology that the majority of the white Cuban middle and entrepreneurial classes had begun to articulate in the early 1920s. Cubans and second- and third-generation Spanish immigrants, who now considered themselves Cuban, sought to represent local and national interests in order to challenge the commercial and political power that the United States held over their country. This led some to organize around the notion that the island belonged only to the Cubans.[34] As I pointed out in an earlier chapter, this sector of society became highly xenophobic and worked to restrict and even ban the immigration of black workers. It is not surprising, then, that Céspedes and the societies of color publicly spurned the help of Marcus Garvey. The black Cuban leadership probably saw Garvey as just another foreigner who wanted to meddle in their affairs.

Finding their indifference to and rejection of his ideas and strategies inexplicable, Garvey cordially ended his visit with the Club Atenas. He announced that the club had provided "a vivid impression of the cultural development of blacks and the great harmony that exists between them and whites. The Club Atenas is an honorable institution in Cuba, and with such a distinguished organization, one can strongly declare that this nation is undoubtedly an exception."[35]

Garvey's attempt to establish a multiethnic and transnational coalition with black Cubans failed for a number of reasons. The attitude of the leaders of the black Cuban middle class toward Garveyism was prompted by their sincere belief that whites would eventually recognize and honor the historical contributions that blacks had made in liberating Cuba from Spain. Their role and loyalty during the wars of independence made them worthy of full Cuban citizenship.[36] Miguel Angel Céspedes's conversations with Garvey demonstrated the degree to which blacks had accepted Martí's interpretation and vision of Cuba as a raceless state. To speak out publicly about race would seem unpatriotic to many whites. The black middle class and the societies of color interpreted Garvey's strategy to deconstruct their identity as a prerequisite to contest their socioeconomic marginalization as a breach of faith in the "Fatherland." Finally, whites had never constructed apartheid in Cuba, making the black Cuban experience dissimilar to that of blacks in the United States, where Jim Crow made Garveyism relevant and effective. But not in Cuba.[37]

That a noticeable number of black Cubans had successfully climbed the socioeconomic ladder only supported their view that racial equality was inevitable.[38] Although the post–World War I depression and financial crisis impeded the mobility of a great number of blacks, they remained hopeful about the future. Moreover, the frightful images and experiences of the Race War of 1912 remained in the collective memories of both blacks and whites. The psychological repercussions of the 1912 war discouraged black leaders from revealing the role that race played in stifling their pursuit of equality. Their anxiety even precluded the adoption of Garvey's nationalist-economic plank to address their immiserization. Belisario Heureaux, director of the Committee for the Economic Interest of the Club Atenas, disingenuously claimed that their socioeconomic class rather than racial injustice explained the unacceptable rates of black unemployment and impoverishment.[39]

The analyses of Tomás Robaina, Marc McLeod, and Rosalie Schwartz partly explain why the societies of color rejected Marcus Garvey. A more important factor appears to have influenced the societies' encounter with the Pan-African nationalist leader. They rejected Garvey's philosophy and plans because, from their point of view, members of the black middle class had already rehabilitated themselves. The societies of color had made it a priority to refine the cultural characteristics and identity of people of color and former slaves immediately following the abolition of slavery in 1886. By 1920, their role and objectives had not changed. Therefore, the Club Atenas and other black Cuban groups sought to promote their members' civic and cultural progress. To Miguel Angel Céspedes, they were the most civilized representatives of the class of color and displayed as much "valor and force" as "any other Cubans in the making of the Republic." Moreover, history required the societies of color, such as the Club Atenas, to act as the vanguard in supervising the "progress . . . of Afro-Cubans in order to facilitate their integration into society as well as to promote the acceptance of blacks."[40] Their historic role made Garvey and the UNIA superfluous.

Representing the interests of the black middle class, the Club Atenas and the other societies of color took up the mantle of the mutual-aid organizations of the late nineteenth century. Organized and led by Juan Gualberto Gómez and composed of second- and third-generation Afro-Cubans, they renounced their African heritage and identity. When the Police Department of Havana alleged that a person of color had committed a series of murders while performing an African-based religious ritual during the summer of 1919, Céspedes not only denounced the crimes but also became infuriated at how quickly the authorities concluded that a black Cuban had committed them. In an open letter addressed to the citizens of Havana, he contended that this accusation was unwarranted at a time when blacks only sought "justice for our attempt to rehabilitate ourselves, for our promotion of the ideas and interminable desire for self-improvement and for our unlimited devotion to the well-being of our fatherland."[41]

Emphasizing that the history and experiences of black Cubans were different from those of blacks in the United States and Haiti, Céspedes ended his letter by questioning the sincerity of white Cubans and their commitment to constructing Martí's raceless Cuba. In Cuba, whites and blacks had fought for "the abolition of slavery and independence. From these events appeared a national identity linking whites and blacks together. Why can't whites have any confidence in the social, intellectual, and religious advancement of blacks?"[42] Unfortunately, white Cuban society ignored his plea. Since the start of the postwar depression, whites had constructed a "more stringent color line" to discourage and stifle the socioeconomic mobility of blacks.[43] Unable to demythologize the national narrative about the role that race played in their daily lives, the black Cuban middle and working classes continued to wait and hope for white largesse to ameliorate their socioeconomic and political marginalization.

Before Garvey reached Santiago de Cuba on 10 March 1921, he visited with black Caribbean sugar workers in Morón and Nuevitas in Camagüey Province.

The chaplain-general of the UNIA, the Reverend George McGuire, had visited these towns before Garvey and had successfully recruited new members and obtained their financial support.[44] Garvey's stay in Morón on 5 March 1921 included a number of rallies where he solicited support for his corporations and companies. As in Havana, his pleas for support followed a lecture that sought to contest the notion of black inferiority. It was here that Enos McKenzie heard Garvey speak of black racial superiority.[45] The socioeconomic background of his audiences also informed the themes and topics of Garvey's lectures. After a brief lesson on the history of the African diaspora, Garvey described the conditions in their own countries that forced them to work in Cuba. Speaking directly to the Jamaican braceros, he stated: "In all of my travels I have never come across a country that is more backward than Jamaica . . . Why must Jamaicans leave their country? Why is it that men have to leave and go abroad to make a living? It is because of the backward condition of the country. If you all had good statesmen in the island, Jamaica would be more prosperous."[46] He condemned Jamaica and the other islands for being politically and economically stagnant: "There are no factories, no industries . . . nearly everything you all need comes from abroad."[47]

At the same time, Garvey may have reiterated what many Haitian immigrants had come to believe about their home. He told them that their presence in Cuba was a result of a U.S. military occupation that was based on the notion of Haitian "savagery." That the United States remained in Haiti showed how the North Americans were still trying to convince the other Western nations that the Haitian people were not ready for self-government. American propaganda was falling on deaf ears. In order to enhance the self-esteem of the Haitian braceros, Garvey could have reminded them that white North Americans were the uncivilized people: "I want to bring to your attention also that before the landing of the American Occupational Force in Haiti nobody ever heard anything about the Haitians being cannibals. [You] are more civilized than those who want to civilize us. The burning and lynching of humans in the [U.S.] South are a palpable fact of what I am trying to say."[48]

Garvey demanded that the immigrants adopt the principles of self-help, cooperation, and progress in order to break their economic dependence. Speaking to the "Negroes of Jamaica," he proclaimed, "Don't allow yourselves to remain in a process of stagnation, arouse yourselves! Do not make a fool of yourselves . . . cease begging for what justly belongs to [you]. There is no reason why the Negro should not advance economically, socially and politically. And that hope will eventually be achieved when [we] set up the great republic in Africa."[49] Garvey informed them that the UNIA demanded economic cooperation from its members. To obtain this goal, the UNIA would have to change the psychology of Haitians and Jamaicans by introducing them to a counter-ideology that refuted the popularly held belief of black inferiority. Their sense of worthlessness caused blacks to hate themselves and prevented the assimilation of the principles of self-help and cooperation. Garvey emphasized that:

> A race that was ashamed of itself was a race that displeased God who created it. Were they going to continue in the same ignorance? That was what the UNIA set itself out to do, to change the current of thought and to make them realize that they belonged to one race and to one common destiny. If they rise, they must rise as a race and not as individuals. Individual effort had never yet done anything for humanity or saved any great situation; it took co-operative effort to save any situation.[50]

Garvey may have ended his lectures to the black braceros of Camagüey, of whom the majority were Haitians, with the request that they make the ultimate sacrifice to reform and liberate themselves. "Liberty was not gained without fighting. Liberty was not gotten by petitions, deputations, and mass meetings. You must be prepared to die for your liberty; I am one Negro prepared to die, even now on the spot, for this just and righteous cause," he insisted.[51] Understanding that many British West Indian emigrants had employed these strategies to compel their colonial officials to protect them, Garvey dismissed these methods, and in doing so possibly convinced the workers to do the same. Some of the braceros also could have viewed Garvey's sentiments as substantiating those of the anarcho-syndicalists Enrique Varona and Alfredo López, who had explained how European and North American elites employed their nation-states to appropriate their labor. Therefore, the black immigrants had to use direct action to reclaim their dignity and freedom. Afterward, Garvey departed for Banes to speak before crowds of workers from the Boston and Preston mills. From there, he traveled to Santiago de Cuba.

Referred to as "the Moses of the Black Race" by La Independencia, a daily newspaper in Santiago de Cuba, Garvey met with members of one of the more prestigious Cuban societies of color in that city, Club Aponte. He solicited its members for financial support, and in exchange he promised to assist them in their efforts to obtain racial equality. The leaders of Club Aponte, however, reiterated what Miguel Angel Céspedes had said more than a week earlier in Havana, but they also added, "The state of progress of the black man in Cuba, particularly within the political and social orders, has to occur by our own hands, within the cordial relationship between all of the elements of Cuban society as well as with the triumphant ideas of the Revolution that obtained the sanctity of the Republic."[52] With that response, Garvey proceeded to spend the rest of his visit in Santiago de Cuba meeting with British West Indian immigrants, "who cherished their time with him."[53]

The braceros who met Garvey included George Rawlins and Daniel Marden-borough, president and secretary of one of two UNIA divisions in the city. Founded on 23 February 1921 as a benevolent and recreational society, this UNIA branch stated in its *Reglamento* or constitution that it would promote "fellowship among its members . . . assist those in need, help find work . . . and offer and supervise in every possible way their instruction and education with the colleges, academies, and schools that it plans to establish."[54] The officers and the members of the city's other UNIA division, Number 194, undoubtedly welcomed him as well. This organization was established as early as October 1920.[55] It too reaffirmed a commitment to Garvey's philosophy of racial unity. Article 3 of its constitution reads: "The duty of the Association will be to establish universal fellowship among the members of the Negro race regardless of nationality, to spread the spirit of pride and love, and to reform, administer and assist the poor."[56] Similar to Rawlins's and Mardenborough's branch, Division Number 194 planned to establish a school and a college to educate and rehabilitate its members' character. In addition, Article 3 specifically emphasized the principle of economic nationalism. The organization hoped to develop and to participate in an expansive network of commerce and trade along with other UNIA branches in order to continue the material, moral, and intellectual rehabilitation of all blacks.[57]

Officials from one of the oldest Jamaican benevolent associations in Santiago de Cuba attended one of Garvey's conferences. Founded on 8 October 1919, the Asociación Sucursal de la Liga de Jamaica was created to cultivate sentiments of brotherhood and patriotism among its members, promote the spirit of unity within the community, and increase the number of individually owned and cooperative businesses. It shared a similar philosophy with the UNIA branches just mentioned. Article 1 of its Reglamento stated that the Liga de Jamaica hoped to advance the intellectual, economic, social, and moral dispositions of not only its members but also of other blacks in Cuba.[58] Primarily composed of British West Indian braceros eighteen years of age and older who had been living on the island for at least a month, the Liga de Jamaica also accepted anyone who wanted to join the association regardless of nationality. It often granted honorary membership to Cuban and Haitian workers who demonstrated an interest in the history and people of Jamaica, and who could help accomplish its stated goals. Its fundamental objective was to assist in improving the lives of black Caribbean immigrants.

The existence of the UNIA branches as well as La Liga de Jamaica in Santiago de Cuba suggests that Garvey's philosophy had become a recognizable paradigm among black immigrants before his arrival. Its dissemination became the responsibility of an emerging class of black West Indian leaders who represented, protected, and promoted the socioeconomic interests of their communities. These activists gained experience while governing their respective organizations. Confidence in men like T. Higginson, a tailor by trade, H. Hector, a shoemaker, J. Francis, a dry-cleaner, J. Watkins, a bookseller, and J. Sharpe, a public speaker, caused the twenty-nine braceros who labored on the San Germán central in Holguín, and who sat in their UNIA's General Assembly, to elect them to the offices of president, vice-president, secretary, and treasurer respectively of Division Number 123.[59] Together, these officers approved and admitted new members, set the agendas for their meetings, and conducted all the financial activities of the association. In addition, they acted as intermediaries, representing the interests of their association before provincial and municipal authorities.

Higginson, Hector, Francis, Watkins, and Sharpe were elected because of their socioeconomic backgrounds. It appears that the UNIA branch officials in Cuba were often the most educated members of their divisions and labored in the skilled crafts. The rank-and-file members believed that these men had the time and the resources to govern their associations. They also had a history of publicly conducting themselves in a moral and exemplary fashion. Anyone with a criminal record was disqualified from serving on the consejos directivos (board of directors). Their tenure lasted as little as six months or as long as two years.[60] Similarly, the social and economic status of Andrew McClarity, William Minott, Richard Harris, George Douglass, and John James prompted the black braceros who worked on the Boston central and who were members of UNIA Division Number 52 to elect them to the board of directors. McClarity was a watchmaker,

Minott and Harris were tailors, Douglass worked as a bookbinder, and James taught school. The organization's chaplain, Charles Clark, was a bricklayer. On the other hand, four of the five executive officers of the Women's Division of Number 52—Elizabeth Rhoden, Adella Remmie, Sarah Fletcher, and Florance Burton—were domestic servants, while Ester Cunningham worked as a cook for the mill's manager and white office staff. They helped administer a UNIA branch that consisted of over two hundred members.[61] The occupations of the female officers reflected the only vocations available for black Antillean women.

The General Assembly of La Liga de Jamaica used similar criteria to elect Alfredo Grizzelle its president, Frederick C. Smith second vice-president, and Henry Shackleton secretary. This was the same Henry Shackleton who had organized the Union of Antillean Workers and incorporated it into the larger Sindicato de Obreros Azucareros, and who later participated in the Third Cuban National Labor Congress of 1925.[62] Shackleton undoubtedly used his position in the Asociación Sucursal de la Liga de Jamaica to consider the possibility of recruiting and organizing Caribbean braceros, including Haitians, for his syndicate in the future. Its Reglamento was written to create a transnational or multiethnic organization, permitting Cubans and any black Caribbean bracero to join, although they were to be honorary members. He probably also designed the Union of Antillean Workers along the lines of the Asociación de la Liga de Jamaica after it was established in October 1919 during the last months of the tiempo muerto. Most labor unions in the sugar industry acted as benevolent, cultural, and educational centers, particularly those established by the anarcho-syndicalists. The Union of Antillean Workers was no different. Although it is impossible to know, Shackleton may have even considered Garvey's black nationalism, as well as his interpretation of black history, as important doctrines to support his own class analysis of the black migrant workers' experiences in Cuba. That Shackleton met a Garveyite by the name of Dave Davidson two years later in 1921, while working in the People's Committee that provided mutual aid to unemployed braceros, allows one to assume that he was familiar with Garveyism. After working in the People's Committee with Davidson, Shackleton finally may have realized the importance of establishing the Union of Antillean Workers.[63] Working with the anarcho-syndicalists to mobilize and organize black Caribbean sugarcane workers, Shackleton had also been introduced to the concept that the braceros' subordination and exploitation were rooted in their powerlessness as immigrant laborers.

Such ideological convergence between anarcho-syndicalism and Garveyism engendered a militant workers' consciousness. Robert Palmer deconstructed Garveyism in this fashion. Living in Cuba for twelve years, Palmer became a member of the UNIA because Garveyism was practical and helped him and others make sense of their socioeconomic experiences. Palmer remembers that during the meetings "we talk about how the whites have treaded on top of us, and how they have treated us. That is Garvey[ism]. So we adopted what he said."[64] Richard Hart believes that this circumspect explanation may indeed explain Garvey's popularity. In other words, "although Garvey made his appeal in exclusively racial terms, the overwhelming majority of his audiences processed his analysis in terms of class. To them the betterment of the black man meant improvement in the conditions of the working class."[65] How workers like Palmer were interpreting Garvey's ideology while he met with them in April 1921 prompted officials of the U.S. State Department to instruct their consular agents stationed throughout the Caribbean to deny Garvey a visa. In a confidential memorandum sent by Charles L. Latham, the U.S. consul in Kingston, to the U.S. consul in Port-au-Prince, Latham stated that Garvey had "lately become well known as a speaker of a radical type, [and] the leader of a new movement to gather Negroes all over the world into a nation . . . the refusal of [a] visa is in view of the activities of Garvey in political and racial agitation."[66]

It is not surprising then that some black West Indian labor leaders in places like Panama had earlier used Garveyism and the UNIA to support their organizing activities during the strikes of 1919 and 1920.[67] Nonetheless, the qualifications and dedication of the black Caribbean leaders of the first Cuban UNIAs ensured that after Garvey left to travel to Jamaica, Costa Rica, and later Panama, his philosophy would continue to spread throughout the island.

But the attempt to mobilize and organize the black braceros proved difficult. The financial crisis, which crippled the sugar industry at the start of 1921, discouraged many black immigrants from joining. The majority of Haitians and Jamaicans faced unemployment and oppressive working conditions during the first half of the 1920s. As a result, during the 1920s the socioeconomic circumstances of the braceros limited the effectiveness of the UNIA. More important, their general situation may have impeded the development of an immigrant workers' consciousness.

Unable to count on the financial support of their members, some associations closed their doors between 1921 and 1922. For example, in March 1923,

Florence C. Williams, a member of Morón Division Number 374, explained that the Black Cross Nurses' Women's Arm had been reorganized because "the past two years have been most hazardous in this country, thus compelling us to lay down arms."[68] The president of Banes Division Number 52, Robert S. Blake, blamed his organization's inactivity during 1922 and 1923 on the fact that many of its male members were unemployed and had moved in search of work. Nevertheless, he believed that the rest of the members would now keep the division's doors open for "the race-loving Negroes of Banes . . . and so continue to be the model division of Cuba."[69] Aubrey Jones, the president of the UNIA division in Camagüey, concurred. He reported that "after a long and bitter struggle to prevent the disintegration which threatened [us] during the last months of 1922, when the terrible economic depression that prevailed made the disbandment of the division a strong probability, the [Camagüey] Division has come to life with a renewed vigor and is prepared to climb the winding paths of progress with enthusiasm."[70] The president of the division on the Florida batey in Camagüey also mentioned how his group had been hampered by a lack of financial support.

In order to create a financially sound movement, many UNIAs staged membership drives. In December 1923, the UNIA of the city of Camagüey held its regular Sunday assembly. The division's secretary, Herman Angus, described the gathering as an extraordinary turnout caused by the interest that the ideological program of the UNIA generated. After the meeting opened with a series of songs and a sermon by its chaplain, Mr. P. Murray of Banes Division Number 52 took the stage to discuss a range of topics, including the progress the UNIA had made in Cuba. His request for new members resulted in three new affiliates. Then Angus himself took the stage to point out "the new spirit of enthusiasm existing among the members and the friends of the organization." He later "appealed for the continuance of the same and advised those who were outside of the fold to come in and help strengthen and fortify the work."[71] Efforts to recruit new members for the UNIA division on the batey of the Vertientes central in Camagüey included introducing the principles of Garveyism to black Cubans along with the black Caribbean immigrants. While visiting his colleagues during a meeting of the Vertientes association, the former president of the division of the Francisco central, John Samuels, told the Cubans that the objectives and activities of the UNIA were not only for the Jamaicans and Haitians, but for all black people of the world. His recruiting efforts led the Vertientes division's secretary, W. M. Warner, to comment that "Samuels' instructions have enthused the people here and slowly but steadily the spirit of Garveyism is growing in the hearts of our people here."[72] Once the workers of the sugar industry realized the role that Garveyism could play in their lives, they joined to take advantage of the benefits that the organization offered.

Although faced with financial difficulties, in August 1922 black sugar workers established one of the first documented UNIA divisions in the town of Banes, Division Number 52.[73] Meeting three times a week, this division also scheduled two recreational and cultural fetes each month. Sometimes these events marked a special holiday, yet they combined pleasure with business. For example, when Division Number 52 celebrated Mother's Day on 18 February 1923, the event included readings and music performed by the Liberty Hall Choir and the children of its members. R. G. Murray, secretary of the association, witnessed the procession and observed that:

> Everything was well prepared and the children acquitted themselves fine for the occasion. Recitations and songs were duly practiced and all the mothers turned out to hear the children and to receive from them presents of flowers . . . The program was quite a long one . . . All of the officers were in regalia. The Major of the African Legions led the procession, after which the other officers followed in succession to their respective place, while the Liberty Hall choir sang the hymn "Shine on Eternal Light." . . . At this stage the president, Mr. R. S. F. Blake, in his usual forceful manner delivered a most lovely address and several speakers delivered inspiring addresses mostly on the love of mothers and their duties toward the little ones . . . The National Anthem brought the day's functions to a close.[74]

The Mother's Day celebration of 1923 altered the usual activities that Division Number 52 planned on Sundays. Those afternoons saw its Liberty Hall act as a school so that the members' children could receive an education. Religious themes and topics often made up the curriculum of their Sunday school.

Not only did Banes Division Number 52 commemorate women as mothers, but it also assisted in defining black Caribbean womanhood. It afforded its female members the opportunity to assist in the administration of the association. Acting as the general secretary of the Ladies Division, Mrs. N. A. Ingleton recruited new members, arranged and scheduled guest speakers, disseminated information about Garveyism, and governed the association. The visibility of its women members and the active role they played in the UNIA proved to be among the more important characteristics of the association. In Cuba and elsewhere, the UNIA provided black women with the opportunity to leave the household. Many female members used the space of their associations to educate themselves, perform volunteer work, and contribute to the struggle for racial equality.[75] As a result, black immigrant women became some of the strongest advocates of Garveyism in Cuba. Writing to the movement's newspaper, the Negro World, Mrs. Ingleton informed other UNIA chapters how the ideas of racial pride and unity had affected her organization: "As we sit in Liberty Hall, Banes . . . [as] Negro men and women we can't but think that we are the best race on God's earth. Every interested member of this division is anxious to do something to push the cause along . . . Not only is our membership roll being enlarged, but our people are understanding more of their race and what is meant by the UNIA. And never shall the UNIA fail till Africa is redeemed and Negroes feel the joy of true happiness, riches, freedom, and a well-protected government in the sunny land of Africa."[76]

At the same time, the traditional role of women as caregivers served the mutual-aid organization with the establishment of the Society of the Black Cross. As an appendage of the Ladies' Division of the organization, the Black Cross Nurses' Women's Arm provided social work and became responsible for taking care of sick members.[77] The role that Black Cross members performed often took them into places where the braceros were mistreated. Some of the nurses of the UNIA divisions in Oriente Province cared for Jamaican and Haitian braceros who fell ill while quarantined in January 1924. Victor Rodríguez, a member of one of the UNIA divisions of Santiago de Cuba, recounted the activities of the nurses of the Black Cross at that time. He wrote that "on a recent trip to some of the towns in the interior, I visited some of the hospitals there to find quite a number of our brethren who had recently left their health resort [the quarantine station] in a deplorable state . . . They suffered from severe colds, cramps, and many other ailments. Very fortunately for them on nearly all of the sugar plantations the dispensers of the hospitals are Jamaicans and members of the UNIA, thus affording them superior assistance in recuperating."[78] That the women of the Black Cross provided "superior" medical care for the recently arrived braceros demonstrated the quality of their training and their commitment to the principles of racial unity and fellowship.

This was not the first time that the UNIA divisions of Oriente had provided mutual aid to the braceros. In the autumn of 1921, faced with an unexpectedly large number of immigrants, government officials in Santiago de Cuba, along with J. W. Sheridan, the Jamaican immigration official, decided to detain over one thousand Jamaican braceros at the quarantine barracks in order to house and feed them. In time, space became so acute that the government had to move most of the men to an empty warehouse on the docks. There, the provincial governor ordered that each migrant receive only one meal a day. He then charged the president and the members of the local UNIA division with the responsibility of feeding the black immigrants. The distribution of food became problematic, however. Acting on their own accord, the UNIA volunteers offered the braceros more food than the governor had specified, reported city officials.[79] The objective of providing mutual assistance to their members, as well as to nonmembers at a time when the Cuban economy made the lives of most black immigrants tenuous at best, reflected the impact that Garveyism had on their communities.

In the early 1920s, the Garveyites used their admission fees and monthly dues, which ranged from twenty-five to thirty-five centavos, to subsidize the cost of members' funerals and burials. After 1923, some UNIA divisions charged as much as seventy-five centavos monthly and stipulated a six-month waiting period before an associate could enjoy these benefits.[80] Nonetheless, to diminish the shock of conditions exacerbated by the crisis of the sugar industry, the UNIA divisions offered their members unemployment benefits. Like many associations, Division Number 194 in Santiago de Cuba charged its members fifteen centavos per month to subsidize a small stipend of a few pesos when they fell ill or lost their jobs. The amount of money that the associates received, however, gradually declined the longer they remained out of work.[81] The members of Division Number 323 on the batey of the Jobabo *central* in Las Tunas who fell ill obtained health insurance at a cost of sixty centavos each month.[82] The organization subsidized the cost of a doctor's appointment, a visit, and a stay at a medical clinic or hospital, as well as the care offered by the Black Cross nurses.

The UNIA sought to ease its members' alienation as immigrant laborers in other ways as well. Besides offering them fellowship based on the principles of Pan-African nationalism, particularly the tenets of racial solidarity, pride, and love, these associations sought to change the character and behavior of black immigrants. The UNIA instructed its members in Garvey's theology, which was called Christian materialism. Evolving from the conception of Black Liberation Theology, Christian materialism promoted the idea that "matter cannot be separated from the spirit." In his attempt to raise the moral consciousness of blacks, Garvey insisted that they try to emulate the exemplary life of Jesus Christ. At the same time, blacks were not to rely on biblical Scripture to explain their lives in fatalistic terms. Instead, Garvey told his followers that Christ was the first reformer who attempted to balance the spiritual with the worldly actions and rights of mankind, and he demanded that members become responsible for their own behavior, experiences, and lives. They could not blame others, particularly whites, for their socioeconomic problems. In this way, the Garveyites realized that the principle of self-determination could be germane to improving the morality of both the individual and the race. They assumed that "no hungry man can be a good Christian, no dirty and naked man can be a good Christian, for he is bound to have bad wicked thoughts, therefore, it should be the duty of religion to find physical as well as spiritual food for the body of man."[83] The UNIA offered activities to its members that combined the secular with the spiritual, with the goal of creating a sense of community. This also explains why many UNIA leaders were clergymen.[84]

All of the UNIA divisions in Camagüey and Oriente provinces regularly opened their meetings by singing the hymn "Onward, Christian Soldiers" or "Shine on, Eternal Light," while the officers and members of the General Assembly marched into their Liberty Halls. A series of prayers offered and directed by a chaplain often followed these processions. Members of the consejos directivos then gave a series of addresses and lectures that touched upon the socioeconomic status of blacks and on the ideas and programs necessary to rehabilitate the character of black people and the stature of Africa. For example, Robert Blake, president of Banes Division Number 52, declared that in spite of having been taught to believe that they were the natural servants of others, exploited as slaves and now ill-treated as immigrant workers, while at the same time having their wives and daughters abused and taken from them, "Negroes of the world, God made you men, and as men you have had a past, and as men launch out for the future . . . Can such a movement perish, can a few selfish scoundrels destroy such an inspiration? No, for from this race shall come forth princes to teach to the nations of the earth the true principles of the doctrine of the lowly man of Galilee."[85] The rituals and speeches at UNIA meetings have been compared to religious revivals. The intent of most UNIA meetings in Costa Rica, however, was political, "address[ing] the profound psychological oppression of blacks in the diaspora . . . [and] exorcis[ing] the debilitating trauma of internalized racism in an apocalyptic messianic manner."[86] Undoubtedly that was the objective of Blake's speech in Banes.

Enhancing their self-esteem encouraged the workers to help change the socioeconomic conditions that the sugar companies and the state fostered. In late December 1923, at another meeting of Banes Division Number 52, a lecture given by the president of Division Number 194 in Santiago de Cuba, John Taylor, included information about the treatment and conditions that many black immigrants suffered while being quarantined. Having presented the same lecture at other UNIA branches in Camagüey and Oriente, Taylor explained that another reason for his trip to Banes was to obtain moral and financial support for the creation of the West Indian Defense Club. According to Taylor, this organization sought to compel the Cuban government to protect the lives and rights of the immigrants and to annul the quarantine policy.[87] The political nature of Taylor's visit and speech violated Article 2 of the Reglamentos that both the Banes association and Division Number 194 had submitted to the governor of Oriente. That clause explicitly prohibited UNIA divisions from engaging in the political affairs of the country. Ignoring this proviso, Taylor and his hosts demonstrated a level of racial and class solidarity that was international in breadth. In 1923, the majority of black migrants incarcerated in Santiago de Cuba were Haitians. The decision of Taylor and his hosts to voice their opposition to the inhumane treatment of the braceros and persuade the authorities to end the mass detention of Haitian workers suggests that they recognized that it was their responsibility to help all of their migrant brothers and sisters. Unable to rely on the British and Haitian consuls for assistance and protection, they were empowered by the principles of self-help and cooperation to defy racial injustice.

This racial and class consciousness became apparent during Richard Bachelor's meeting in 1925 with members of Division Number 608 on the batey of the Miranda central. As the UNIA commissioner of Cuba, Bachelor had traveled throughout the island to recruit new members. While at Miranda, he discussed the nature of race relations in Cuba, particularly between black Caribbean workers and white Cubans. The details of his talk have not been found. However, he compared the braceros' social and economic status with that of black Cubans and Chinese immigrants during the sugarcane workers' strikes of 1924 and 1925, which suggests that he may have discussed the role and impact that the segmented labor system had in their lives. Bachelor concluded that black

Caribbean workers could improve their condition by continuing to pool their resources so as to make their UNIA organizations more responsive to their needs. To show their economic independence, he wanted them to open their own grocery and retail stores and shops. Bachelor also recommended that they try to find employment in other industries besides sugar. Undoubtedly because of their involvement in the strikes of 1924 and 1925, he reported meeting with representatives of Cuban president Gerrado Machado to discuss how the government could help improve their employment opportunities.[88] Uncertain about the future, the black braceros promised to apply the principles of self-help and cooperation.

In spite of the financial difficulties that the black immigrants experienced, archival records prove that many black braceros helped to establish UNIA branches in the bateyes and towns built by the sugar companies. Mr. Fearon remembered lending fifty pounds to the UNIA on the batey of the Ermita *central* near Guantánamo, "to carry on the association for Garvey in Cuba."[89] Workers from many of the occupations of the colonia, central, and batey joined Garvey's movement. When they were in need, they realized that the UNIA would help. Their strong commitment to the principle of racial and class solidarity guaranteed a response.

As early as July 1921, a machetero named Irvine Sandiford informed other British West Indian immigrants that some braceros were routinely being physically assaulted and even killed by members of the rural guard that patrolled the hinterland of the Chaparra and Delicias *centrales* near Puerto Padre, Oriente. To make the situation worse, many of the macheteros and carreteros found themselves in dire straits after having been promised a daily wage of one dollar, only to receive instead forty to sixty cents from the sugar companies. According to Sandiford, "[A]ll of the West Indians, even those who are getting something to do and can supply themselves a meal, are praying day and night to get out of this place."[90] Appealing for help, Sandiford counted on the Garveyites in Cuba to come and rescue the braceros: "I hope you will take part and do your best, because although all of us are not members of the UNIA we are all brethren of the race and will become members whether it be soon or late."[91] That Sandiford couched his solicitation in racial terms reflected the degree to which Garveyism resonated among the class of black Caribbean workers regardless of their occupation or ethnicity. More important, the fact that Sandiford, a worker earning less than a dollar per day, promised that he and others like him would soon join the UNIA movement proves that Garveyism was not just a bourgeois philosophy that appealed to the black immigrant artisan class that governed these associations. Indeed, by July 1922 many of the migrant field laborers at the Chaparra and Delicias had joined the UNIA in Puerto Padre.[92] There and elsewhere, the UNIA influenced the daily lives of many black Caribbean and Cuban workers in the provinces of Camagüey and Oriente. They employed Garveyism to assess their position in Cuba and to realize that individual self-respect, along with racial and class solidarity, was critical to their socioeconomic advancement.

Informed by Garvey's ideology, S. N. Gordon, a bracero and member of the UNIA division established on the Florida *central* in Camagüey, voiced his frustration after a conversation with the son of the mill's white Cuban manager. Gordon became very upset when the young Cuban failed to acknowledge his people's physical sacrifice and work on the island. The young man raised Gordon's ire when he told the bracero that Cubans would never extend equality to them, or even friendship, because the field workers were all black men. Gordon's conversation with the manager's son caused him to candidly assess the black immigrants' experience in Cuba: "The Negro today is being ignored after laying the foundation of the white governments of the world. Think of the Republic of Cuba. Who felled the forests, laid the railroads, planted the canes, and reaped the crops? West Indian Negroes! And today the white folks who inherit the wealth of this country, which amounts to millions of dollars, look upon Negroes and style them as undesirables."[93] By intersecting race and class to interpret the exploitation of the black immigrants, Gordon's analysis and conclusions had a universal dimension, shared by the majority of black workers throughout the Americas. Although Garvey warned his supporters not to become members of organized labor, at least in Cuba, his philosophy undoubtedly supplemented the interpretation of the anarcho-syndicalists who emphasized "internationalism" or class solidarity to diminish the role that imperialism and capitalism played in the subordination of people of African ancestry. The idea that international capitalism had alienated black as well as white workers with the deliberate use of racial and ethnic ideologies may have made it less problematic for Enrique Varona and Henry Shackleton to recruit and organize the black Caribbean field workers and others of the sugar industry. Undoubtedly some black immigrants developed a militant workers' consciousness after deconstructing Garveyism and discovering its economic or class-based analysis, which explained and called for collective action.

Working on the Manatí *central*, Zephaneah Nicholas observed: "Our men and women are mere stepping stones for others on to progress. How long will this continue? How long will the Negro allow himself to be converted into such a tool?" In order to end the exploitation of blacks, Nicholas called for action: "The world is undergoing a change, and the survival of the fittest is the burning question or factor of the present moment. If you do not care to line up with the onward march of humanity you will be found wanting or be obliterated from the map of the races of men."[94] The activism that the UNIA fostered among members of black immigrant communities included the rehabilitation of the individual's self-esteem. This too became a prerequisite for collective action.

Writing from Victoria de Las Tunas, Joseph Lloyd pointed out that he became an active member of the movement after regaining his race consciousness. This process helped him realize that "there is no height to which I cannot aspire if I depend on the God-given power of my mind, body and soul . . . I have a lineage of which I may be proud . . . [and] there is no reason why I should remain a slave because my forefathers were."[95] This identity, reflective of the "New Negro" movement centered in Harlem, New York, during the renaissance of black literary and intellectual life of the 1920s, engendered a sense of confidence among black immigrants. They believed that with hard work anything was possible in Cuba. Working in Nuevitas, Camagüey, C. D. Austin believed that the followers of Garvey never made any excuses nor did they become discouraged when faced with discrimination, injustice, and exploitation. Instead, their trials and tribulations made them resilient. To defeat the forces that opposed their progress, Austin insisted on racial solidarity to assist in strengthening the determination and desire for freedom and equality.[96] Garveyism in Cuba became a transnational movement that included Haitians and black Cubans. Their cooperation was viewed as essential if all blacks were to obtain racial justice.

According to Benjamin Small, a bracero of the Macareño *central* in Santa Cruz, Camagüey, Garveyism had improved relations between Haitians and Jamaicans. Arriving in Cuba during World War I, he reported that in 1918 the two groups did not like each other. Competition for work between these immigrant groups caused them to often fight and injure one another. Living in the cramped quarters of the barracones had exacerbated the ethnic tension between them. According to Small, "[A]s common laborers, Jamaicans and Haitians lived in large open houses arranged in such a way that one hundred or more men lived together within an area of about two yards each in which to live and prepare his meals."[97]

195

The animosity that each group held for the other was often expressed in the cane fields as they refused to help one another or treat their co-workers with respect. The idea of providing a simple cup of water to a thirsty Haitian was rejected by the Jamaican cane cutters. Any act of camaraderie became alien for Haitian macheteros as well, observed Small. But the relations between the two immigrant groups gradually changed as Garvey's doctrines took root, informing their lives after sowing "the seeds of unity." By 1928, Small could see dramatic changes:

> Today I have seen Jamaicans wed with Haitians. I have seen the Haitian fellow politely offer his seat to a Jamaican lady. In times of hardships, I have seen them divide a dime for lunch. Yet more loyal they seem to me when I have seen quite a number of them lay their tools down today to join with us on the 1st of August to celebrate our Liberation day. Let those who experienced the past days in Cuba and are now enjoying these today ask ourselves if Garveyism has made such a change in Cuba what else will it not do? I say Garveyism has done for Haitians and Jamaicans in a few years what Christianity has failed to do for centuries.[98]

The UNIA also introduced Garvey's principles to black Cubans. In doing so, they were included in the multiethnic coalition that sought to advance the socioeconomic interests and rights of all blacks.

By the late 1920s, the ideology of Marcus Garvey resonated among black Cubans living in Santiago de Cuba. In March 1927, Cayetano Monier and Felix Machado, president and secretary general respectively of UNIA Capitulo Cubano Numero 71, notified the governor that the honorable delegate of the General Office of New York City, Herrieta Vinton Davis, had come to Santiago de Cuba. There, Davis promised to attend to the city's children as a nurse of the Black Cross. She would also "spread the idea of the redemption of Africa and the progress of the race of Ethiopia in the world."[99]

Vinton Davis's meeting with Monier's group entailed discussing how to disseminate and furnish black Cubans "with a common identity to establish their own industries, commerce, and banks as well as to defend those enterprises and win the appreciation and consideration of the other races." According to Monier, Vinton Davis's visit was a special occasion. It was scheduled while Marcus Garvey sat in a prison cell in Atlanta, Georgia, where he had been held since February 1925. The U.S. government had taken away his freedom for "defending these principles and supporting their goals."[100] Monier's activism and support of Garveyism suggest that, at least in Santiago de Cuba, it had become a competing ideology with that articulated by the leaders of the societies of color in Cuba. They also suggest that Garveyism resonated among black Cubans because it offered a racial and class paradigm to interpret and alleviate their socioeconomic marginalization. Charged with the responsibility of disseminating his philosophy and soliciting the support of other black Cubans, Monier drafted a circular that detailed the movement's progress and agenda in Cuba:

> The parental Body of our Association has taken into consideration that the Republic of Cuba is inhabited by more than 1,320,370 people of the race of color including foreigners and natives according to the census of the country. It has constituted more than forty-two divisions, chapters and branches in the island with the determination of establishing an intimate union and fellowship among the brothers who speak English, French, and Spanish, in order to work together for the advancement and progress of the Race. We envision a free and happy Africa organized as an independent and sovereign Republic that represents all of the descendants of Ethiopia.[101]

The UNIA's call for racial unity and fellowship among blacks in Cuba proved to be a critical strategy that threatened the elites and commercial classes. During the 1920s, black immigrants confronted intense xenophobia. Newspaper editors, government officials, and some citizens made the immigrants the object of a national debate that centered on issues of citizenship, nationalism, and modernity. Emphasizing their racial, national, and ethnic differences, these Cubans helped to define the braceros as "undesirables" who endangered the stability and progress of the Republic. Some citizens and critics of black immigration concluded that their presence jeopardized the cordial relations among the races and even the diplomatic and commercial ties that Cuba had with England and Haiti. Cuban nationalists also saw them as symbols of North American imperialism. Meanwhile, the sugar companies, along with their colonos, intensified the appropriation of their labor. This state of affairs had encouraged the braceros to join the labor protests led by Enrique Varona, Henry Shackleton, and other labor leaders who defied the racial and ethnic ideologies that controlled and exploited black and white workers in the sugar enclaves. As a result, many Cubans demanded that the government reduce the presence of the black immigrants and prohibit their entrance.

6

MULTIPLE DOMINANT IDEOLOGIES

Xenophobia and Cuban Nationalism in the Neocolonial Context

of Black Caribbean Immigration

> It had been out of necessity for the sugar industry to increase the importation of African slaves before the abolition of slavery, then the importation of Chinese braceros, and now Haitian and Jamaican workers. Nevertheless, these peoples have brought only superficial benefits to the developers of sugarcane. By staying and living in Cuba they have become a grave source of racial and moral conflict, the consequences of which we will suffer from now on . . . everyone including future generations will discover themselves in unimaginable circumstances.[1]

This assessment of the origins, nature, and impact that black Caribbean immigration had and would continue to have in the future is taken from the article "El alza del azúcar" (The Rise of Sugar). Published by the Comisión de la Asociación de Hacendados y Colonos (Commission of the Association of Sugar Estate Owners and Farmers) in January 1924 and edited by the public historian of the city of Camagüey, Jorge Juarez Cano, the critique represented one of the multiple ideologies that Cuban and North American sugar producers had constructed to show the citizens of Cuba that they supported an end to black immigration. This ideology also was designed to stifle any attempts at solidarity between white and black Cuban workers and the braceros. Although the elites had produced this narrative for the Cuban public earlier and had articulated it since the 1910s when thousands of Haitians and Jamaicans arrived, by the mid-1920s they realized that they had to revise their anti-black-immigrant discourse during the labor protests and strikes. Their earlier words had failed to persuade the braceros and the Cuban and Spanish workers to accept and foster the black immigrants' marginalization and exploitation. The solidarity of the sugarcane workers convinced the Cuban government that some of the black immigrant macheteros and carreteros would reject their fate. However, their immediate repatriation could not take place without alienating the power of the North American sugar companies. It was apparent that immigration reform had to occur gradually.

How the Cuban political elites amended the anti-black Caribbean narrative is one topic of this chapter. Who was responsible for this ideology and what did it emphasize? How did the companies respond to public attacks on the labor power that had facilitated the expansion of the industry and of the sugar mills' fortunes? More important, what strategies and actions did the braceros employ to counter the discourses of both the Cuban and the North American elites?

Addressing these questions will illuminate how the divergent and contradicting ideologies that the political and commercial elites developed often took into consideration the multiple audiences or constituencies that they wished to persuade. Appearing immediately before the height of black Antillean agency in the cane fields, this process continued during the last half of the 1920s as the Cuban economy failed to recover sufficiently from the decline in the price of sugar. The companies' narratives were designed for Jamaican and British functionaries whose duty was to ameliorate the marginalization, exploitation, and abuse of their workers. Convincing these officials that the workers' well-being had always been their goal, the companies' message was crafted to allow them to retain a surplus of bracero labor. In exchange, the sugar mills claimed that they provided the workers with remittances that they sent or carried home. It is interesting that the companies were never concerned about losing their Haitian workers. Because of the Haitian government's duplicity in the workers' emigration, the sugar companies continued to show contempt for these workers, using their Haitian ethnicity or identity to explain their submissiveness and exploitation. Concurrently, when Cuban leaders had to address these same foreign officials, they corroborated the narrative of the companies.

The position and opinions expressed by Cuban leaders regarding black Caribbean immigration changed in front of Cuban audiences, however. Informed by the populist and nativist beliefs that "Cuba was for Cubans," they directed a campaign opposing Jamaican and Haitian immigration in order not to alienate a broad coalition of nationalists who had come to resent the impact of North American political and economic power on their country. Making the criminality of some braceros into a universal trait of all Haitians and Jamaicans, the government adopted measures against black immigrants to slow their arrival. When the social and economic conditions that had inspired the braceros collectively to defy their marginalization and exploitation reemerged during the late 1920s and early 1930s, the government quickly took steps to prevent the workers' newfound activism by classifying them as illegal immigrants upon the completion of the zafra and their work contracts. This designation gave the authorities legal grounds to repatriate the Jamaicans and Haitians, to the dismay of the sugar companies. Some officials realized that the workers would no longer accept their immiserization caused by the sugar mills' continuous efforts to increase the surplus of field workers while shortening the length of the zafra. This repatriation policy continued even after native and black Caribbean workers participated in the strikes that once again shocked the sugar industry during the early 1930s. The workers' articulation of "internationalism," however, failed to convince a new group of Cuban elites to abandon the anti-black-immigrant ideology that Cuban nationalism had produced.

The cases of intimidation and violence against black immigrants that were reported before the sugarcane workers' strikes of 1924–25 prompted Godfrey Haggard, head of the British Legation in Havana, to send a series of letters of inquiry to the Cuban secretary of state, Carlos Manuel de Céspedes. Citing the reports of unjustified homicides and abuses at the hands of certain Cuban functionaries, taken from the testimonies of a noticeable number of Jamaican and West Indian witnesses, Haggard also protested the inhumane conditions that British subjects suffered while detained at the quarantine station in Santiago de Cuba. This latter issue stemmed from the decision of the Cuban government to continue its quarantine policy six years after the influenza and pneumonia epidemics of 1918 and 1919 had ended in Jamaica. By the mid-1920s, the provincial government of Oriente had transformed the quarantine station into a site using similar symbols and metaphors of subordination that the braceros would face in the "nowhere spaces" of the sugar enclaves. The black Caribbean workers reported that government officials were unprepared to lodge and feed the hundreds of Jamaicans and Haitians who steadily arrived. The quarantine station at Santiago de Cuba proved to be too small and lacked potable water, food, and even beds. Men and women usually slept in the same rooms and on the dirty cement floors of the building. As a result, some Jamaican officials viewed the detention of the immigrants in Santiago de Cuba as an effective strategy for abusing the workers while prohibiting their entrance in order to ensure that they would not strain the treasury of the nation by becoming public charges.[2] In addition, the braceros told their consular officials that the Cuban authorities had failed to arrest and prosecute the police officers and rural guards who had killed their co-workers. According to them, this iniquity demonstrated that the Cuban authorities were not serious about providing justice for the victims and their families. Haggard ended his dispatch insisting that if the Cuban government refused to take immediate action, its silence and lassitude would jeopardize diplomatic and economic relations between the two countries.[3]

In response, Céspedes apologized for his failure to inform the British consul of the improved sanitary conditions at the quarantine station. His brief response concluded with assurances that the Cuban authorities had extended "to His Britannic Majesty's West Indian subjects all of the protection in our power."[4] Céspedes then drafted a lengthy written explanation to assuage Haggard's concerns. After consultation with President Zayas and representatives of the sugar companies, Céspedes told Haggard that the contents of his earlier note had been based on old and inaccurate information. He reported that conditions at the quarantine station had improved—specifically, that immigrant men and women had beds to sleep on as well as their own rooms. In reference to Haggard's concern that a dozen or more braceros had been discharged for demanding their pay at the Candelaria *central*, he mentioned that because the economy's recovery remained on schedule, the majority of braceros were now paid on time in either Cuban or United States currency.

Céspedes also addressed the nature and cause of the general mistreatment and status of the braceros since the beginning of the financial crisis in the sugar industry in the winter of 1921. Perhaps influenced by the strong nativist sentiments shared by so many citizens, Céspedes responded with an undertone of rancor and condescension. Emphasizing the role that the economy played in Cuban–black Caribbean relations, as well as the workers' conditions on the sugar enclaves, he claimed:

> Your government cannot be ignorant of the very severe economic crisis through which this country passed a short time ago . . . with the principal banks in liquidation, with a large number of sugar mills and plantations under embargo . . . and with more than 1,200,000 tons of sugar unsold at the end of the year of 1921

and the beginning of 1922 . . . it is not surprising that some [business] concerns, national as well as foreign, should find themselves obliged to close down and to dismiss their laborers in the face of the absolute impossibility of paying them.[5]

Céspedes also questioned the accuracy of the reports of abuse that Haggard had received. If the British West Indians were treated as poorly as they claimed, why would they continue to come in large numbers, he asked. The Cuban government's policies were benevolent and took into consideration the well-being of the immigrants. Moreover, their wages allowed the immigrants to return home to take care of their families and communities. Céspedes then questioned Haggard's sincerity. Responding to the British consul's threat to unilaterally end black West Indian emigration unless the Cuban authorities swore to prevent abuses and attacks in the future, Céspedes advised Haggard that if the British government believed that Cuba appeared incapable of protecting the lives of British subjects, then both governments needed to cooperate in order to prohibit black West Indian immigration. He also suggested that Britain negotiate with the Association of Sugar Estate Owners and Farmers if it desired to implement this policy.

Céspedes was right to examine the motives of the British agents in and outside of Cuba. The abuse that Jamaicans and other black workers from the British Antilles experienced earlier in the decade undoubtedly was a result of the conflict of interest that some officials in the British consulates had developed. In Santiago de Cuba, some of them had clandestinely become labor brokers, bonding and delivering large numbers of immigrant workers to the sugar mills. But the Jamaican government was to blame as well. It believed that the finances of the colony prevented it from spending the necessary resources to protect the rights of Jamaicans in Cuba. Between March and July 1922, this issue prompted Governor Probyn to discuss with Colonial Secretary Winston Churchill whether or not they should request assistance from the U.S. consular officers in order to help "distressed Jamaicans in exceptional cases, and at the cost of this government." Probyn informed Churchill that although they probably could persuade U.S. officials to help subsidize the cost of protecting British workers, and even give them the discretion to assist the macheteros and carreteros, he was convinced that "to change policy and give U.S. Consular officials this power would inevitably lead to costly expenditures elsewhere."[6] It appears that Probyn was looking for an excuse not to help British subjects living in Cuba. He could have obtained much of the money needed to defend the rights of Jamaicans from the Emigrants Deposits held by the island's treasury. As the fee or tax that every emigrant had to pay the government before leaving the island, the tax principally served to cover the cost of the workers' repatriation. Some £145,070 were deposited in this account in 1922 alone. In a later dispatch, Probyn reported to Churchill "that ten to fifteen percent of this sum would remain permanently unclaimed." Probyn also revealed that he had other ideas for the workers' deposits, because he was considering introducing legislation that would give him the power to appropriate and use as "General Revenue such deposits as have not been claimed for a period of years," in order to reduce the colony's debt, which totaled £2,936,291.[7] It is because of such fiscal priorities that the lives and rights of Jamaican workers were neglected by those responsible for protecting them. As a result, Jamaican braceros continued to be abused and harassed.

News of the British government's attempt to mediate and temper the subordination and exploitation of the braceros angered and frustrated representatives of the sugar companies and Cuban provincial authorities. It was in this context that the pamphlet published by the Comisión de la Asociación de Hacendados y Colonos in January 1924 and edited by Jorge Juarez Cano appeared. At the same time, officials of the Cuban Trading Company, such as Higinio Fanjul, Manuel E. Rionda, and B. Braga Rionda, who owned the Tuinicú, Manatí, Francisco, and Tacajó mills, responded to Godfrey Haggard's inquiries into the braceros' reports of violence and intimidation by cynically describing them as "unimaginable cases of abuses." As important representatives of the sugar industry, they selected a close associate, Aurelio Portuondo, to draft a memorandum that Céspedes was to hand to the British consul. The message sought to obfuscate the nature of the living and working conditions that the braceros faced. First, Fanjul and Rionda agreed that they could not deny that during the economic crisis some sugar companies had paid their workers with vales. However, Jamaican braceros were not the only workers paid in scrip. The companies also gave vales to Haitian and Cuban workers. Moreover, they admitted that they would pay their workers with vales again in the event of another economic crisis.

Second, the memorandum blamed the braceros for publicly exposing the violations of the 1909 Arteaga Law that prohibited the use of paper scrip as money. The mill owners' accusation had been confirmed earlier when both the secretary of state and the secretary of agriculture issued Circular Number 5930 on 19 September 1923—a year before the series of work stoppages rocked the industry. Sent to all of the city councils of Camagüey and Oriente, this decree had reminded the sugar companies that they were still prohibited from using vales to pay their field and day laborers. The government had announced this ban only in "response to the petitions from the braceros who reported having been frequently paid in vales and IOUs in order to buy merchandise at the company stores located on the bateyes."[8] The circular had also warned the mill owners that if they violated the Arteaga Law, they would be prosecuted. The representatives of the sugar industry, however, believed that if one group of braceros accepted the vales as wages, then so should other workers, regardless of their nationality. They concluded that the Haitians had accepted the scrip "because they are so simple and ignorant. The Jamaicans, however, whose culture is so superior to the Haitians, demanded not only real money but also insisted upon setting the terms of their daily work routines when other workers throughout the island anxiously took what they could get."[9] That members of the Association of Sugar Producers deliberately tried to pay black Caribbean workers with counterfeit money because of their race and ethnicity shows their level of contempt for the law as well as their scorn for the workers responsible for the expansion of their industry and its prosperity. To them, "Haitianness" continued to connote an uncivilized and submissive worker. Meanwhile, "Jamaicanness" implied an insolent bracero whose refinement allowed him to articulate not only his right to be paid in U.S. or Cuban currency but also the privilege of negotiating the terms of his employment. Portuondo disingenuously dismissed the claim that the Jamaicans' forceful utterances, which were part of an evolving radical worker's consciousness, had caused their dismissal and expulsion from the farms and mills. Instead, he cited the role of the unscrupulous emigrant brokers to explain why many Jamaican braceros, along with some Haitian braceros, were evicted and discharged. The owners argued that these agents, who were Haitians and Jamaicans themselves, convinced their contracted workers that it was to their benefit to move from mill to mill to obtain better wages. Misled, the workers gained nothing. Frustrated and dissatisfied by the constant movement and unsuccessful search for better wages and conditions, the Jamaican braceros in particular had fabricated the stories of being dismissed without receiving their wages that they told to their British consuls, according to Portuondo.

Blaming the emigrant brokers for the mistreatment and dismissal of the braceros was an act of pure deception on Portuondo's part. These labor agents, after all, worked for the sugar companies. They sent brokers throughout the

Caribbean in search of a surplus of macheteros and carreteros. The companies' recruiters had lured black immigrants to Cuba with promises of better pay, housing, and medical care. For instance, on the British island of Dominica, as reported by its newspaper, the Guardian, an agent from the Chaparra sugar mill in Puerto Padre, Oriente, had placed posters and placards throughout the city of Roseau announcing that the sugar mill needed cane cutters to harvest three tons of cane per man per day. Workers would receive $1.20 per ton of cut cane. The advertisements emphasized that Puerto Padre's newly built quarantine stations and hospital were in excellent condition. The barracones on the Chaparra's batey were "first-class, and sweet potatoes are to be given to all of the laborers free; [and] that the average cost of living is fifty cents per day . . . and the Chaparra Company which require the men will send them back after the crop finishes, free of cost to them." The Guardian, however, advised its readers not to believe the posters because it had obtained firsthand accounts from a number of returning braceros who had endured harsh economic conditions. Yet it concluded that since times were also hard in Dominica, where "there is no money . . . the poorer people are suffering much, the plantations have reduced expenditures thereby throwing a good many laborers out of work . . . the offer of the company to give employment to West Indian laborers might turn out to be a blessing in disguise to our own people, especially if they can save money over that way, and on their return would reinvest in land in their own homeland."[10] The alleged benevolence "of the company to give employment" to the braceros not only became the basis of their subordination, but also shows how British colonial authorities were complicit in the marginalization and exploitation of their subjects abroad.

Finally, representing the sentiments of the Association of Hacendados and Colonos, Portuondo's memorandum concealed the fact that the black immigrant workers were the most marginalized and exploited class of laborers. He emphasized that everyone on the island had suffered during the recent periods of economic and political crises. According to Portuondo, the economic crisis of 1920 touched the lives of many Spanish immigrants and of the Cuban people as well as of the Caribbean workers. Understanding that the companies could no longer degrade, humiliate, and exploit the Jamaican braceros without their challenging the power of the sugar mills and farmers, Portuondo produced the following compassionate narrative for Haggard and his functionaries in Kingston and London: "The industrialists and agriculturalists of the island never intended to hurt the Antilleans. On the contrary, we wish to provide them with better wages and conditions in order to convince them to stay in Cuba where their generous work is valued . . . If they were poorly treated and compensated, then this current wave of immigration would have decreased since these factors would cause the Antilleans to return to their respective countries."[11] Portuondo's conclusion veiled the desire of his cohorts to keep a surplus of workers that they could continue to exploit. This ideology placed the Association of Sugar Producers in direct opposition to many Cubans, who saw the black Caribbean workers as "undesirables": "The hacendados and colonos of Oriente and Camagüey do not share the specific opinions expressed by the press and by the people of the country who are not directly interested in the sugar industry concerning the restrictions or prohibitions of Antillean emigration nor whether it is desirable for Cuba. The sugar mill owners and farmers are disposed to put in effect necessary measures to maintain better conditions for the Antillean braceros in order to guarantee their well-being and the commodities that they produce."[12] It appears that the sugar companies were more concerned about producing their profitable merchandise than alleviating the abuse and exploitation of their workers.

The revenue that the companies earned from the zafra of 1924 influenced the sympathetic nature and tone of their correspondence with British officials. Using the labor power of the black Caribbean immigrants, the sugar companies produced over four million tons of sugar worth $352 million. Although the harvest was smaller than that of 1923, they still obtained $110 million more than the previous year.[13] Yet the companies never constructed their narrative in favor of black immigration for Cuban consumption. Nor was it designed to dissuade the Zayas government from ignoring the will of the people. After the zafra of 1924 ended, and while the industry experienced a number of strikes led by the anarcho-syndicalists, the president and the Cuban Congress started to discuss how to ban black immigration.

In June 1924, a congressman introduced a resolution to ban Jamaican laborers from entering Cuba. Although it was tabled, some of his colleagues supported the bill in order to show the British consul that he could not intimidate the Cuban people. In fact, some congressmen argued that Haggard's charges of the braceros' mistreatment were false and misleading. Following the congressional resolution, the Association of Sugar Estate Owners and Farmers asked President Zayas to establish a commission to study the problem. Composed of the owners of the sugar companies, their colonos, and others associated with the industry, the commission would share its work with Congress so that the latter could draft legislation to ensure that the braceros would not affect the island's socioeconomic development.[14] A group of industry representatives later met with Zayas to inform him that the mills still needed the estimated 65,000 Jamaicans who traveled to Cuba every year to participate in the zafra.[15]

Meanwhile, the Cuban press kept the controversy alive. In August, the *Avisador Comercial* published an article titled "Undesirable Immigration." Like the other Havana dailies, it fueled the flames of xenophobia and blamed the black immigrants for the tensions between Cuba and Great Britain. The immigrants were also blamed for a series of minor outbreaks of smallpox in Oriente. The presence of these black foreigners upset the editorial staff of the *Avisador Comercial*, who believed that the personal behavior, character, and culture of the black braceros made them undesirable: "It is a well-known fact that the Antillean immigrants in Cuba live in great promiscuity and do not follow even the most elemental mandates of hygiene. It is quite true that the Jamaicans and Haitians work cheaper than the Cubans, but due to their customs and peculiarities they are not at all a favorable kind of immigrant for our republic. No patriotic and far-thinking government would allow the entry of this kind of immigration, but on the contrary would keep them out of our territory."[16] The paper claimed that British enmity toward Cuba would never be resolved as long as this type of immigration continued. Finally, the *Avisador Comercial* stated that it considered black Caribbean immigration the most important issue in the next general elections, and it suggested that both the Conservative and Liberal parties include in their platforms the exclusion of "Antillean" immigration.

In mid-July 1924, the British Foreign Office leaked Haggard's correspondence with Céspedes in "The White Paper." It was published in both the *Jamaican Gazette* and the *Daily Gleaner* in August. Almost immediately, President Zayas announced from the floor of Congress that he favored imposing further restrictions and if necessary the total exclusion of Jamaican immigrants from Cuba.[17] He also stated that Haggard's claims were unjustifiable and that "it is quite natural that incidents take place among the 65,000 Jamaicans now residing in Cuba, but that the civil and judicial authorities take care of these cases." Zayas concluded his speech by insisting that any policy that led to a complete ban on Jamaican immigration would be a result of cordial negotiations with Britain.[18] Cloaked in nationalism, Zayas's speech was disingenuous. It was intended to hide from public gaze the influence of the North American sugar companies. Hudson Stroude argued that while Zayas trumpeted his nationalist slogan, "Cuba for Cubans," he was "dealing secretly and thickly with foreign corporations, and giving them excessive privileges in his beloved fatherland."[19] This type of collaboration between the government and the predominantly U.S.-owned companies became the fundamental element that defined the political culture of the island. Usually after coming to power, both Conservative and Liberal politicians used the influence and resources of the government to obtain personal wealth and status. Since their endeavors occurred within the neocolonial system that the United States had imposed on the island with the 1902 Platt Amendment, the political leaders of Cuba tended to protect and enhance the power of foreign capital in exchange for the right to loot the national treasury. As a result, the amount of wealth they ultimately acquired, Louis A. Pérez has argued, allowed them to challenge the power of North American businessmen. This state of affairs led to the creation of "strategic alliances" when a cohort of Cuban politicians and their families became partners in North American enterprises. Others were appointed managers or administrators of the numerous U.S.-owned businesses, especially the sugar mills.[20] Many Cuban nationalists, including students, intellectuals, workers, and members of the middle class, interpreted the government's relationship with North American interests as corrupt and treasonous. They had come to imagine Cuba as a nation exclusively for those born on the island who spoke Spanish, practiced Catholicism, and venerated the leaders, intellectuals, and activists of the generations of 1868 and 1895. As a result, they demanded that the political class of the 1920s reform the political culture and economy. The resources of the island, particularly its land and labor, were to be reserved for Cubans and no one else, they claimed. The emergence of this nationalist movement explains Zayas's deception on the floor of Congress in August 1924. In the fall of 1924, the presidential campaign between the Conservative candidate, Mario Menocal, and the Liberal candidate, Gerardo Machado, also assured that Congress would slowly begin to adopt measures to discourage braceros from entering Cuba. Machado's victory signaled that his "Platform of Regeneration," or program of national rejuvenation, would include not only the political and economic reforms that most nationalists desired in order to end corruption but also measures to curtail the hegemony of the North American commercial class. The obvious step to take to obtain the latter was to prohibit black Caribbean immigration.

During the strikes of 1924 and 1925, the government began to strictly enforce the clause included in the immigration laws of 1917 and 1921 that required braceros to give thirty dollars to Cuban customs and immigration officials. This amount would be deposited and used to repatriate them at the conclusion of the harvest. However, the sugar industry's dependence on black immigrant labor, particularly during World War I, had encouraged most port officials simply to ask for two dollars from the migrants before they gained entry. Some Jamaican and Panamanian newspapers believed that the decision to enforce this part of the immigration law would reduce the number of black immigrants because "very few if any of the laborers who go to Cuba could possibly show thirty dollars if called upon. It is not an uncommon thing for a man to set out for Cuba with his steamship ticket and a couple of dollars in his pocket." The emigrants often left their homeland virtually broke after buying their passports, paying departure taxes, and purchasing passage permits, according to immigration officials in Jamaica and Panama.[21] Ironically, when the government began to enforce this requirement, the sugar companies decided to pay the thirty dollars in advance before they were permitted to import the workers.

During this same period, Cuban legislators introduced two bills that reflected the strength of the country's dominant nationalist ideology. Passed in May 1924, the first act amended the immigration laws by prohibiting the entrance of all single women. This bill repealed the article of the Immigration Law of 1917 that permitted black single females to immigrate. In addition, the law banned married women as well unless they could show documentation that their spouses were in Cuba and had requested their presence. These decrees made it difficult for the braceros to reassemble their homes in Cuba. Six months later, the lower house of Congress passed the Native Labor Bill. Cubans had to make up at least 75 percent of the workers hired by all industrial and agricultural businesses. In addition, the bill required that the sugar companies place the same percentage of native workers in skilled occupations and clerical positions. However, the Native Labor Bill was defeated in the upper chamber. Nevertheless, the bill sought to reverse a recently developed trend involving a large number of braceros who, after completing their work contracts, left the enclaves and successfully found employment on the docks and the coffee estates, as well as on the railroads. Work in these industries had once been reserved for Cuban laborers.[22]

The Congress's dominant ideology, which tried to diminish the presence and role of the black immigrants, was supplemented by state-sponsored terror.

In March 1924, a bracero was shot in the back by a rural guard. The victim and several witnesses claimed that his hands were tied behind his back at the time of the assault. Refuting the migrant's assertion, the guard told civil officials that the black worker had attacked him with a knife and that he shot the machetero in self-defense. In May, a bracero from Barbados, after being stabbed by a Haitian, was approached by a policeman. While the Barbadian was recounting how he had been assaulted, the officer ordered him to accompany him to the police station. As he gathered his belongings from the pavement of the street, the officer shot the bracero in the face and ran off.[23] Then in June, while traveling by train through Camagüey Province, a Jamaican wearing his war medals on his chest was confronted by a number of rural guards. To humiliate him, they ordered that he take off his badges of honor and throw them overboard. When he refused, they attacked him. At the next station, the Jamaican was arrested and taken to jail. There, he informed the authorities that the guardsmen had robbed him of thirty dollars. Such violence against braceros occurred as the mild economic recovery slowed, and the Cuban elites altered their narrative to heighten their citizens' xenophobia.

By 1926, the price of sugar had declined steadily, dropping from 5 cents a pound in 1923, to 3.82 cents in 1924, to 2.22 cents in 1926.[24] Yet that year the sugar companies produced a record quantity of 4.9 million tons. Their revenue, however, was less than it had been in 1925. This state of affairs dramatically affected the lives of the braceros. Some Cuban newspapers reported that once again the black migrant workers and their families were facing starvation and abject misery. It was in this context that Cuban authorities revised the narrative against black immigrants. They added a subplot that stressed Haitian and Jamaican criminality, portraying them as a danger to Cuban society and civilization. They also described the unemployed workers as animals who preyed on one another. Between April 1926 and December 1927, police arrested the Haitian Andres Juan several times for robbing other Haitian braceros. Jobless himself, Juan used the aliases Mariano Acosta and Mariano y Royal to evade the authorities as he assaulted, swindled, and victimized Haitians who had arrived to work the harvest. The Santiago de Cuba police described Juan as a "dangerous parasite who constantly required the vigilance of the authorities."[25] Although Juan had spent time in jail in April and October 1926, it was not until December 1927 that the government ordered his deportation. Roberto Marter Nisois, Fernándo Martel, and Enrique Martínez Speck, nationals from Guadalupe, were arrested and charged with the robbery and assault of "people from their own country as well as workers that come from Jamaica and Haiti. The authorities realized that their criminal activity increased during the zafra when most of their victims are other West Indians and Cubans."[26] The police of Santiago de Cuba also charged Martínez Speck with operating a prostitution ring. He was deported in January 1928.

Many unemployed and stranded black Caribbean women also turned to a life of crime, according to the authorities. For example, the police arrested and later charged Elena Osorio, an "English" female from Kingston, Jamaica, with prostitution. Osorio was described as an unemployed "mulatta" who had left her husband, who worked as a dentist, and her children in Kingston. She came to Cuba and immediately married another man. Together they began to rob their countrymen. Osorio also recruited and persuaded teenage girls from her country to work as prostitutes.[27] It was in this context that the issue of prostitution among Haitian women discussed earlier became a concern for the authorities of Oriente.

By the late 1920s, government officials viewed all black Caribbean women as harlots who threatened not only civil society but also, and more importantly, the sugar mills. The secretary of state telegraphed the governor of Oriente insisting that he and the city councils move to eradicate "the presence of such women from the sugar centers. Their stay has extremely negative repercussions. These women not only are exploited by the workers but also are weak and infirm . . . [But] the problems they have produced by associating themselves with the worst specimen . . . compels the authorities to take the necessary steps to protect and defend our society."[28] Ultimately, the secretary of state envisioned the menacing epidemiological impact that black Caribbean women could have beyond the borders of the bateyes. He recommended that Article 126 of the Municipal Law be applied to prevent "dangerous diseases from being introduced to society that are carried by these unhappy women who are directly attacking the fundamental foundation of our progress, that is, our increasing native population."[29] Addressing black immigrant prostitution from moral, criminal, and epidemiological perspectives allowed Cuban elites to emphasize the multiple ways that the blacks' ethnicity threatened the Republic while reinserting this interpretation into the nationalist discourse on immigration. As the governor of Oriente concurred with the secretary of state's recommendation, he also pronounced that "it is your patriotic duty to end this profession when and where it is taking place." As a result, by 1926 law enforcement officials at the local and provincial levels as well as the Department of Immigration cooperated to end prostitution among black immigrant females.[30]

The persuasive effects of this specific rhetoric of difference allowed President Gerardo Machado (1924–33) publicly to announce even before the zafra of 1926 ended in May that he planned to prohibit black immigration. He singled out the economic role and ethnicity of the immigrants for his decision: "The dangerous Antillean aliens . . . [coming] here have caused so much protest from our natives residing in the interior . . . they are terrible to compete with as laborers and therefore [must] be stopped. Due to the graft of former administrations they have been allowed here but the present government will not permit it."[31] Although Machado had permitted the sugar companies to import black workers so they could finish the zafras of 1925 and 1926, he now promised that they "will be the last people in the future to penetrate our national territory . . . These laborers do not have the least moral sentiments, are uneducated . . . [they] are actually savages and for a plate of food will cause the greatest troubles in our fields."[32] Before the harvest of 1927 began, however, Machado changed his position after his secretary of agriculture, Juan Delgado, met with members of the Association of Sugar Producers. Delgado had received petitions from some of the mill owners asking for permission to import more black workers, and he convinced Machado to allow the Central Fruit Company to bring in 4,000 Antilleans for its Cunagua, Jaronú, and Tánamo *centrales.* In addition, the government allowed the United Fruit Company to disembark 10,500 braceros for its Preston and Boston mills. Table 6 shows the official flow of black Caribbean immigration between 1926 and 1930. The Haitians, who were recruited exclusively to perform field work and were viewed as more accepting of their subordination, continued to disembark in relatively high numbers until the start of the North American economic depression. Meanwhile, the drop in Jamaican workers was a result of the hostile atmosphere that many advocates of black immigration, particularly Jamaican officials, believed had been engendered by the government's rhetoric and measures against black immigrants. This decline reflected the sugar companies' realization that the Jamaican workers' consciousness, demands, and protests made them less exploitable.

Machado worried that the presence of Jamaicans would reignite protests in the cane fields. Conditions had worsened in the wake of the economic downturn after 1925. From the San Germán *central,* A. E. Wilmot, a Jamaican machetero, wrote to the British consul in Havana, William G. Ewan, that he had observed

TABLE 6. Immigrants Classified by Nationality, 1926–1930

	1926	1927	1928	1929	1930	Total
United States	484	674	866	1,028	795	3,847
South American	51	247	167	115	111	691
Antillean	886	559	—	—	—	1,445
Haitian	12,346	14,312	14,353	4,339	5,126	50,476
Jamaican	2,508	2,348	974	243	38	6,111
Spanish	9,644	8,572	6,689	7,475	4,243	36,623
Total	25,919	26,712	23,049	13,200	10,313	99,193

Source: ANC, Fondo: Donativos y Remisiones, Leg. 403, No. 11, "Estadísticas impresa, editada por la sección de Estadística de la Secretaria de la Hacienda relativa a inmigración y movimiento de pasajeros años de 1930 y comparaciones con el año 1929–editado en 1931," Cuadro 9.

hundreds of men wandering from mill to mill in the provinces of Camagüey and Oriente, "loafing through want of occupation and at times on the verge of starvation for the past five months, beginning in June 1926." Wilmot believed that the companies were at fault for his compatriots' misery since the sugar mills sought to recruit an additional 14,500 braceros, a figure that would further swell the pool of surplus workers.[33] He advised the British and Jamaican authorities to warn the people of the West Indies not to risk coming to Cuba. The desperation and humiliation that the braceros experienced followed them beyond the confines of the fields, bateyes, and rural Cuba in general.

Braceros returning home also faced worsening conditions at sea. For example, the Chaparra Sugar Company hired an individual named Cezano to deliver 990 black Caribbean workers to its Chaparra and Delicias mills to work the 1926 harvest. Cezano also was obligated to supervise the repatriation of his workers. According to his contract, Cezano promised to obtain a couple of ships to carry these workers home over two separate voyages. But because his contract with the Chaparra Sugar Company was soon to expire, Cezano decided to rent a fifty-passenger steamer that had once sailed the Hudson River in New York in order to transport the 990 workers home in just one trip. Not only did the SS *Angelita* run out of food and water during the voyage to St. Lucia and Barbados, where most of the workers came from, but in order to prevent the ship from capsizing, "it was necessary to keep the passengers well distributed over the deck which was done by the crew in no gentle manner." As a result, the ship had to be diverted to Puerto Plata in the Dominican Republic. Notified by the British Legation in Havana about what had happened, the undersecretary of state of the Colonial Office, C. H. Grimshaw, considered "black-listing" Cezano, the owner of the SS *Angelita*, along with the McCormack Steamship Company of Tampa, Florida, and the Chaparra Sugar Company for violating Barbados's Merchant Shipping Act Number 1898-2 and Great Britain's Imperial Merchant Shipping Act of 1906. In late August 1926, the manager of the Chaparra Company apologized and offered his cooperation to ensure that workers would never again be tightly packed on board the vessels employed for their repatriation.[34] Nevertheless, emigrant brokers such as Cezano continued to mistreat the black immigrants. In January 1927, both the Haitian and British consuls in Santiago de Cuba sent the governor of Oriente Province letters detailing the abuses that labor agents had committed.[35] The governor thanked the consuls and promised that the authorities would prosecute those agents who committed crimes against the field workers. They never did. Episodes such as this as well as the miserable circumstances in which the braceros lived and worked made them reconsider whether Cuba was still a place they could call home and work to earn money for themselves and their families. As a result, many began to look toward the United States as their next destination.

Aware of the difficulties they would continue to confront by either staying or leaving, some braceros decided to emigrate to the United States. In May 1925, the Jamaicans Claudius Spied of Banes, an employee at the Boston sugar mill, and Frank Shakespeare of the Tánamo *central*, petitioned the U.S. consul in Antilla, Oriente, for visas to enter the United States. The purpose of their trip was similar to that of the hundreds of Jamaicans who had left for Cuba during the 1910s—both desired to be reunited with their families. Another Jamaican bracero, Richard Valentine of the San Germán sugar mill, explicitly stated this common wish to "pass to the states" because "[I] have ten cousins and two uncles in the states who [are] urg[ing] me very much to come to them." Before the consul could issue the visas, the men had to present letters written by the sugar mills' administrators verifying their employment and proving that they had relatives living in the United States. Finally, the consul told both Spied and Shakespeare that he could grant them only a six-month visa, and at the end of this term they would have to return to Cuba.[36] If they could not demonstrate conclusively that they would return to Cuba, the men would have to apply for visas with the American consulate in London. Stipulated under the 1924 immigration treaty between the United States and Britain, this requirement subjected all British West Indians who applied for a visa or passport to a very restrictive quota. Confronted with the economic uncertainties in Cuba and the desire to reunite their families, some workers, particularly Jamaican females, were not discouraged and applied for visas at the American consulate in London.

With the recommendation from the manager of the Preston, Daisy Garrison applied for a visa so that she and her fourteen-month-old son could be reunited with her husband, who was living in New York City. Since 1920, she had worked as a seamstress for the United Fruit Company. Meanwhile, Clementine Bartley, also of Preston, applied for her visa after spending five years "employed by a number of the best families of that city as a laundress, and house keeper," according to the mill's manager. Although Bartley was employed, she was now divorced and had to rely on allowances from her two grown children as well as from her sister and brother residing in New York. This fact, according to the manager, made "it extremely necessary that she join the other members of her family as soon as possible."[37]

Ernest and Mildred Weeks of New York City requested a visa for their son George, who worked for the Chappara in Oriente. Convincing the U.S. consulate in London to grant their twenty-four-year-old son a visa, the Weekses retained a notary public to assist them with their application. According to their sworn affidavit, they were gainfully employed as a building superintendent and as a dressmaker. The Weekses earned sixty-two dollars a week, and their income made them "capable of taking care of their child who will never be a charge either upon the Government of the City of New York; nor yet upon the United States; that they have a home prepared for their son." The Weekses petitioned the American official as parents and patriots. George was "their only living child and they are both desirous to have him with them in order that their family might be complete; that the United States of America is their home and for this very reason their son should be with them . . . both are desirous of seeing their son soon take out his citizen's papers in order to enjoy the privileges that they both now enjoy in the City of New York and the United States."[38] That some black Caribbean workers attempted to leave Cuba through the American consulate in London shows the degree to which their lives had become more precarious after

1925. Unable to improve their situation with the arts of resistance, including protest, sabotage, trade unionism, and the assistance of the UNIA, some workers, particularly Jamaicans, believed that it was time to emigrate to the United States. Such motives are typical of peasant laborers as well as of part-time or seasonal workers. They try to "search not only for the best possible remuneration for a given amount of work, but for the opportunity to do as much work as possible. No efforts are spared, no sacrifice is too great, when the absolute amount of income can be increased," states John Kulczycki.[39] For those who could not leave Cuba, the employment situation had become volatile and dangerous, influenced by multiple dominant ideologies that produced immeasurable uncertainty. Nonetheless, the North American sugar producers still told the authorities that they required the labor power of Haitians and Jamaicans.

Countering the anti-immigrant rhetoric of the government and the press, in March 1928 the administrator of the Atlantic Fruit and Sugar Company, Eardley G. Middleton, submitted a report to the government that justified the recruitment and exploitation of Haitian and Jamaican workers. His remarks centered on the effects that banning these immigrants would have on a company like his, as well as other policies the government had adopted that proved disastrous to the sugar industry. He emphasized that besides producing sugar, particularly at the Tánamo *central* in Sagua de Tánamo in Oriente, the Atlantic Fruit and Sugar Company also grew tobacco on its estates. This commodity could only be grown and harvested when the company had a surplus of sugarcane workers. Often the company lacked those workers, however. As a result, it had to petition the government for permission to import 4,000 Haitians annually. The cost of labor for the Tánamo amounted to forty dollars for every contracted bracero. The mill also paid the U.S.-controlled Haitian government fifteen dollars per migrant. That Haitian emigration generated revenue for the government suggests that its decision to ban the emigration of its nationals in 1928 was just a ploy by the North Americans and their Haitian collaborators to assuage the fears and concerns of friends of the Haitian migrant workers. They had shown the U.S. Congress how corrupt the bracero trade had become. Nonetheless, since it had become a source of revenue for the Haitian government, U.S. officials in Haiti, proving that the military occupation was successful, also became complicit in the subordination and exploitation of the braceros.[40] The inability to recruit and import an excess supply of workers caused the Atlantic Fruit and Sugar

Company to limit production on its own accord, stated Middleton. Attempting to portray the level of black immigration as slight and inconsequential to Cuban society and its economy, he misled Cuban officials by stating that the sugar companies operating in Cuba annually imported only 10 percent of their work force. The Commission on Cuban Affairs' statistics refuted the claim. Using data from the Cuban Department of Agriculture, Commerce, and Labor, the commission reported that the sugar companies employed 514,000 field workers throughout the year of 1934. During a harvest season, they required 230,000 macheteros and another 50,000 carreteros, guards, inspectors, and skilled mill workers. The commission concluded that "possibly as many as 100,000 of these workers are Haitians or Jamaicans."[41] This means that at the height of the Great Depression and after the sugar companies had to shorten the length of the harvest season in order to meet the quotas set by the Cuban government, black Caribbean workers represented 20 to 30 percent of the industry's work force. Such was the case even though the Depression had visited the island as early as 1924, according to the commission. As a result, it is safe to conclude that the percentage of braceros remained either constant or was slightly higher before the Machado government ordered the companies to reduce their output in 1929 with the goal of stabilizing and increasing the price of sugar.[42]

José M. Cortina, a senator from Camagüey Province, responded to Middleton's claims in a letter to Machado. His correspondence reveals the multiple narratives that characterized the divergent elements of the dominant ideology of the North American and Cuban elites. Cortina informed the president that since the beginning of March 1928, 21,972 Haitians and Jamaicans had been processed by Cuban Customs and Immigration at the port of Santiago de Cuba. Many arrived sick and threatened the city's sanitation and health conditions. He believed that although the braceros usually came only to work the zafra and then returned home, some 150,000 black Antilleans had settled in Cuba since 1908. As a result, "it is false to say that we need to import more. They have increased the colored population by five percent, with men who know nothing and feel nothing about our history. But today, they have integrated themselves into the economy by doing other things than sugar." Undoubtedly citing the militancy of some Jamaican braceros, Cortina could not believe that "they prefer to be paid on a daily basis. Even white and black Cubans, who can make a living by doing other things or by operating a piece of machinery for the industry, are not that lucky."[43] Underlining the role of North American political and commercial power and the ideological conflict between Cuban and U.S. elites, he also opposed black immigration because he believed that the people who supported it were not concerned with the island's future. Although Cortina admitted to using Jamaican and Haitian workers on his own sugar plantation, where he "paid them well," he insisted that the time had come to end it. Reiterating what "Billiken," the anti-black-immigrant opinion writer, had said in 1916 at the beginning of this national debate to dissuade black Cubans from establishing a multiethnic alliance with the braceros, Cortina claimed: "On account of the black race of Cuba, I think that enough is enough. The noble black Cuban has been harmed and humiliated by the immigration of so many uncultured men. It has endangered their attempt to become a patriotic and cultural force, and has ruined their work to obtain absolute social equality."[44] Cortina's rhetoric demonstrates how Cuban nationalism intersected with the fear and paranoia that black Caribbean immigration could transform Cuba into a black nation. The race and ethnicity of the braceros made their presence threatening as well as untenable for whites and blacks.

Beginning in February 1928, the Cuban secretary of immigration informed the governor of Jamaica that the Machado government had reformed the laws that governed the entry of immigrants into the country. Two months later, the *Daily Gleaner* published the travel requirements for anyone wishing to go to Cuba. Besides a passport, the bracero needed to carry fifteen dollars that he would immediately hand to customs and immigration officials, to be deposited with the Cuban treasury. Braceros also had to possess thirty dollars to cover the cost of their return passage home. All immigrants had to be twenty-one years of age. Minors arriving without adult supervision required written permission from their parents, notarized by the Cuban consul in Jamaica. They were to be physically fit and free from contagious diseases. The same qualifications applied to all female immigrants.[45] The new rules were to take effect in June 1928.

The intensity of the migration of black Caribbean men and women gradually declined over the next few years. As U.S. trade policies with the island reduced the amount of Cuban sugar shipped to the United States, the desire to increase the capacity of the mills by importing more black labor declined. For example, the number of Haitians declined from 14,353 in 1928 to 4,339 in 1929. Meanwhile, the total number of Jamaicans who entered Cuba dropped from 974 in 1928 to 243 in 1929.[46]

The political crisis that the repressive regime of President Machado created also affected the number of braceros returning to Jamaica and Haiti. Violence and intimidation became the cornerstones of the Republic's political culture when in 1928 Machado used force and bribery to convince both Liberal and Conservative political elites that he was the only individual capable of being president. *Cooperativismo*, the compact between all the political parties, as it was called, resulted in Machado winning re-election unopposed, for a six-year term. When members of the professional and middle classes took to the streets to protest Machado's ineffectiveness at solving the desperate economic problems of the country, he used martial law to abolish habeas corpus and establish a police state. When the working class joined the protest movement, Machado ordered the police and army to silence his critics. Many of his opponents, including labor leaders, students, professors, journalists, and politicians, were murdered, imprisoned, or deported.[47] Given this state of affairs, by the end of the 1920s even the Haitians refused to stay. For example, although 5,126 Haitians arrived to work the zafra in 1930, 4,537 left immediately after the harvest. Concurrently, the sugar companies only imported 38 Jamaican braceros in 1930, while 5,208 Jamaicans decided to leave once their work had been completed in May 1930.[48] The state of the sugar industry and its commercial ties with the United States also helped to reduce further the number of black braceros entering Cuba.

———≈———

The official repatriation of black immigrants gradually occurred following passage of the Smoot-Hawley Tariff Act by the U.S. Congress in May 1929. After considerable debate in the Senate and lobbying from U.S. beet producers, the U.S. government levied a duty of two cents per pound on all Cuban sugar entering the country.[49]

The Smoot-Hawley Act had several consequences. Besides slightly increasing the price of Cuban sugar entering the U.S. market from 1.76 cents to 2.02 cents, it prompted the Cuban government to order most sugar mills to cut production in order to stabilize the price of the commodity on the world market. Announced by Dr. Viriato Gutiérrez of the Cuban government, the plan to reduce the amount of cane the mills could process into raw sugar and sell abroad also permitted the companies to export 2,800,000 tons of a total harvest of 3,118,000 tons to the United States in 1931.[50] In addition, under Gutiérrez's plan, the companies were allowed to increase their production in the future only if demand warranted it, and if the other sugar-producing islands competing for the U.S. market—Puerto Rico, Hawaii, and the Philippines—agreed to limit their output to the levels of 1930.[51]

The sugar companies of Cuba, however, soon realized that reducing output did not stabilize nor dramatically increase the price of sugar. Overproduction throughout the world had glutted the sugar market. As a result, Cuban sugar continued to sell below the 1929 price of 1.72 cents per pound, dropping to 0.71 cents by 1932. Moreover, the Cuban share of the U.S. market declined sharply, dropping from 49.4 percent in 1930 to 25.3 percent in 1933.[52] The sugar mills attempted to compensate for this loss by increasing domestic consumption. Cuban consumption climbed by 16.1 percent to 47.9 percent in 1933. Nevertheless, between 1932 and 1933 the sugar companies continued to reduce their production and exports.[53] This development was not enough to persuade the Machado government to restrict the importation of black braceros. In fact, it continued to allow "anyone who wished to enter Cuba to apply through the Cuban Consulate in Kingston or [Port-au-Prince] to obtain a Landing Permit from the Cuban Immigration Department." Nevertheless, fundamental changes in the economy and industry caused official Haitian immigration to decline sharply from 5,126 in 1930 to 22 in 1931. In addition, between 1930 and 1934, only 5,899 Jamaicans traveled to Cuba to work during the harvests. It also is important to note that 28,459 Jamaicans left Cuba under the supervision of the government.[54]

Finally, Gutiérrez's plan to cut production in order to stabilize the price of Cuban sugar discouraged North American banks from servicing the debt of numerous centrales. The inability to secure credit to cover the costs associated with the harvest also resulted in a decrease in the need for black Caribbean workers. In short, the owners and managers of the centrales responded to the financial crisis of the 1930s just as the Commission for the Association of Sugar Producers said its members would if another crisis emerged—they either suspended or shortened the harvest. In addition, their workers went unpaid for months or received vales that were redeemable only at the company stores. Other owners dismissed their braceros altogether. As unemployed workers, the braceros became public charges of the state, making them subject to deportation under Article 1 of Decree Number 1404 of the Immigration Law of 1921.[55]

Although the collapse of the global economy made it possible to repatriate black immigrants on a larger scale than ever before, President Machado continued to use the rhetoric of differences to demonize Haitian and Jamaican workers while promising to end black immigration once and for all. To demonstrate how important this issue had become to most Cubans and how this ideology converged with Cuban nationalism, Machado also decided to host the Second International Conference on Emigration and Immigration. Doing so would give him credibility in formally ridding the island of braceros during the first years of the 1930s.

Held in Havana between 31 March and 17 April 1928, the conference was attended by officials from Latin America, Europe, and Asia. Participants examined a range of issues and difficulties that immigrants confronted. The conference considered the means of transportation that foreign workers used; the sanitary conditions that immigrant workers faced during transit and upon their arrival; the health care provided by the sugar companies; levels of cooperation among the immigrants themselves and whether they established mutual-aid societies; and the strategies that immigrants employed to adapt to their new surroundings.

The conference adopted a number of resolutions that sought to ensure the health of immigrants. They agreed that all emigrating workers should be vaccinated before they traveled, and should receive medical examinations and additional vaccinations administered either by government officials of the host countries or by the medical personnel of the companies who recruited them. They determined that host countries were obligated to supervise the recruitment process and to intervene when the actions of emigrant brokers resulted in the abuse and exploitation of migrant workers. President Machado publicly expressed his support for the resolutions aimed at protecting foreign workers who entered Cuba as well as improving their sanitary conditions.[56] But it appears that the resolutions were to be applied only to European immigration. The government was unwilling to extend those safeguards to the black braceros.

In August 1928, just four months after the conference ended, the Haitian consul in Havana sent a series of reports and inquiries to the Cuban government that detailed the incarceration of hundreds of braceros in the town of Ciego de Avila in Camagüey Province. Over the next several months, he repeatedly condemned the arrest and detention of his fellow citizens who had not been charged with any crimes. The consul also learned that the braceros were forced to work on public-works projects for the town and that "only the Haitian prisoners were subjected to these illegal measures."[57] He demanded that the practice be stopped immediately. Cuban officials initially denied his claims and even stated that Haitians had never been compelled to work. But following an investigation by Leopoldo Ruíz, captain of the rural guard of Ciego de Avila, functionaries in Havana admitted that many Haitians had indeed been forced to labor for the city. But Ruíz emphasized that this was not a controversial policy, because the town's judiciary had ordered other individuals, including Spanish immigrants and Cuban nationals, to work even before they had been prosecuted and sentenced, "in accordance with the legal precepts of the state."[58] The Haitian consul rejected Ruíz's explanation and continued to insist that Haitian citizens be released if they had not violated the laws of Cuba. The Cuban government ordered another investigation, hoping to placate the Haitian consul. Directed by Manuel Arango of the National Secret Police, the second inquiry dubiously confirmed Ruíz's findings: Haitian braceros who had not been convicted of a crime were, he concluded, never forced to work.

Race clearly played a role in the adoption of this convict-labor system in the central and eastern provinces. It was given legitimacy when the Emigration and Immigration Conference failed to address the status and rights of "illegal" immigrants. This indifference was informed by the argument that every country operated under its own laws regarding this category of foreign worker. In Cuba the term illegal had always been used synonymously with undesirable. Ever since the zafra of 1913, during which thousands of black Haitians and Jamaicans landed in Cuba, the companies along with the government had defined and manipulated the workers' racial and ethnic differences to naturalize their status as "undesirable." The concept also reinforced their subordination and exploitation. Their formal condition made them even more susceptible to the whims of the host society. Government officials as well as representatives of domestic and foreign sugar companies could and did systematically degrade, humiliate, and exploit their black foreign laborers, who were regarded as immigrants without any rights.[59] In addition, the economically depressed state of the sugar industry during the 1920s, as well as the seasonal labor that thousands of braceros performed, worsened their position in society. Once the macheteros' and carreteros' work contracts expired at the end of the zafras, they were categorized as undocumented foreigners. The sugar quotas that the government imposed upon the companies compounded the problem by reducing the length of contracts and therefore the workers' wages. When the harvest season was shortened after 1928, greater numbers of black migrant workers entered the swollen ranks of a reserve army of unemployed men and women, as they had done during most of the 1920s. This time, however, they became undocumented aliens sooner and for a longer period of time. Subject to arrest and imprisonment, these poverty-stricken migrants were not only incarcerated by Cuban authorities but compelled to work on various public-works projects before they were deported. Concurrently, the government sought to repatriate the unemployed braceros, who if allowed to stay would compete for work with locally born laborers. For this reason, the Cuban Congress proposed legislation in 1930 to restrict not only the immigration of black workers, but also of Chinese laborers. The 1930 act, however, exempted skilled workers and professionals. Many observers believed that proponents of the 1930 law sought to restrict and reduce the number of Haitian and Jamaican macheteros or carreteros, but not of British West Indians who worked in some skilled occupation for the sugar companies. In the end, President Machado publicly refused to support the bill. His opposition to a restriction on black immigration was influenced by a number of developments.

As the economic depression grew worse, native workers demanded that the state intervene in order to protect their lives and increase their employment opportunities. Responding to these workers' nationalist sensibilities, immigration officials studied the nature and impact of black immigration, especially its effects on rural workers. Their investigation began in 1931 when the price of sugar hovered around 2 cents per pound, and at a time when the industry was experiencing a decline in output. Antonio José Molina sent one of the lengthiest and most comprehensive reports to the Immigration Commission in Havana. As the military supervisor of the Department of Immigration of Oriente Province, Molina informed the commission that the tendency of the sugar companies to violate the immigration law of 1921 had considerably diminished. Their involvement in the illegal trafficking of braceros had stopped. No longer were they clandestinely hiding the arrival of stowaways or using fraudulent passenger manifests to disembark field workers in Santiago de Cuba or in their own private ports. Although there were still some companies intent on making a mockery of the law, most of the mills now realized that they could successfully complete their harvests in the future without large numbers of imported braceros. He believed that the companies finally were attracting a surplus of locally born workers after constructing better homes for their laborers. Molina observed that "the native workers and other residents have been happy with their new homes constructed by the mills [and] as a result, the zafra will go on as normal."[60]

Undoubtedly, Molina was referring to the United Fruit Company's decision to construct 1,700 new homes. The construction of these "rustic" dwellings, which were often made with palm leaves, clay, and corrugated steel and tin, began as early as 1928. In order to reduce its dependence on the black braceros, the United Fruit Company also persuaded some 14,299 Cubans along with their families to migrate from the western regions of the island to the bateyes and sugarcane fields surrounding the Boston and Preston *centrales*. In spite of its internal colonization scheme, however, the United Fruit Company continued to import hundreds of Haitians to cut cane for its mills.[61]

According to Molina, the sugar mills had begun to hire more Cuban workers instead of blacks from the Caribbean islands as early as 1927. His data clearly contradicts that of other official sources, particularly the ones quoted in Table 6 above. Molina claimed that the number of black foreign workers arriving in Oriente had declined from 40,000 in 1926 to 18,000 in 1927. Their numbers continued to drop steadily; only 7,000 arrived for the harvest of 1928–29. The following year saw only 2,548 disembarked in Santiago de Cuba and other ports of the province.[62] The decline in the number of braceros entering Cuba undoubtedly convinced President Machado that a law restricting black immigration was unnecessary in 1930. It seemed that the sugar mills had cut their labor costs in response to the decision to cap production levels.

The hiring of predominantly Cuban workers was also a result of the Department of Immigration's strict enforcement of Decree Number 1404 of 1921. For example, in January 1931 Molina's office repatriated 2,706 Haitians and 6,830 Jamaicans because they could not find work. As public charges of the state, "this measure was necessary since the large contingent of Antilleans . . . constituted a serious danger to the development of Oriente, its economy and public order."[63]

> At the same time, in the city of Santiago de Cuba, and in other parts of the province, they have come to work in prostitution . . . As prostitutes many foreign women find themselves living and being exploited by men of different nationalities in official zones of tolerance . . . [Although] they are harassed by the police, in most cases, even the latter are extremely lenient toward them. These foreign women are also involved in the drug trade, controlling the drugs which they sell among the black population of the cities and who have relations with them in order to easily obtain the drugs.[64]

Molina described the majority of braceros as "unemployed, rotten and undesirable foreigners" who ought to be expelled. He recommended that the Immigration

Commission persuade Congress to enact new legislation to control the level of black immigration and prescribe their behavior upon arrival.

Molina ended his report with an economic assessment of black immigration. His conclusions echoed the dominant narrative of the Cuban elites. He stressed that Haitians and Jamaicans had taken jobs from locally born workers, and he blamed the powerful foreign companies and their cane farmers for this situation. For too many years, they had preferred foreign braceros to Cubans for cutting and hauling cane. In addition, the fact that the black braceros often sent their wages to their families back home or carried most of their earnings with them to their own countries after the zafras galled Molina. He insisted that his office would continue to enforce the immigration law in Oriente. As far as Molina was concerned, there still were too many braceros in the province. In January 1931, there were 65,664 Antilleans in the province; of that number, 55,892 were Haitians, and 1,872 Jamaicans.[65]

Molina's exaggerated assessment of the impact of black immigration on Cuban society persuaded the government to restrict the arrival of black emigrants and expel those already living there in order to take better care of its own rural workers. In June 1931, even the British Legation in Havana realized what was in store for the majority of Jamaicans and other workers from its Caribbean colonies when it began to negotiate with the United Fruit Company, the Atlantic Fruit Company, and the Standard Fruit Company the cost of shipping them home. These companies owned a fleet of steamships and so monopolized the lucrative business of repatriating the black braceros.[66] On 16 October 1931, the Cuban press reported: "No permits will be issued to the sugar mills at the beginning of the next crop in order to bring Haitian and Jamaican labor, according to the Secretary of Interior, Octavio Zubizarreta, who is seeking to provide employment for thousands of Cubans."[67] Less than a month later, the Cuban Senate, led by Dr. Francisco María Fernández, drafted an immigration bill that superseded all existing laws. It prohibited immigration to Cuba for two years. Regarding contracted workers, Article 2 of the bill stated: "The immigration of imported labor is absolutely prohibited . . . Tribunals shall impose a penalty of $500 and five to six months detention on persons breaking this rule." Another article created a permanent Immigration Commission composed of senators, congressmen, civil servants, and businessmen.[68] The adoption of the new immigration law shows that, unlike the debates that surrounded the arrival of the braceros between 1913 and 1928, curtailing the immigration of black Caribbean workers was best achieved if framed in economic, moral, cultural, and nationalist terms. The latter was a dramatic departure from the past. The economic depression and the financial weakness of the sugar industry prevented the companies from influencing the island's immigration policies.

During December 1932, a conference sponsored by the National Organization of Cuban Workers was held in Santa Clara Province. Attended by delegates representing workers from thirty-two mills, the conference called for a work stoppage. The following month, some 20,000 sugarcane workers, including Haitian and Jamaican braceros, went out on strike. The effects of their actions were felt immediately. An estimated one hundred cane farmers failed to deliver their crop. In addition, the twenty-five mills dependent upon these colonos for their sugarcane either suspended the start of the zafra or operated at a lesser level than they had planned.

The workers struck in order to improve their wages and working conditions. The price of sugar and the decline in output had caused most of the companies to reduce their workers' wages by 20 to 25 percent annually. In 1932, the companies generally paid their black braceros 60 cents per 100 arrobas of cut cane. Skilled artisans working inside the mill factories earned one peso per day.[69] The length of the harvest period also influenced the total amount of their wages. By 1932, some mills had decided to grind their cane for only one or two months. As mentioned earlier, since the end of the war the harvest period had been shortened to five months. Rather than a zafra lasting from January to either June or July, in 1932 the harvest season usually lasted until the middle of April. As a result, thousands of unemployed workers and their families were forced to survive a much longer dead season with substantially less income.

The braceros responded to this situation as they had done after the collapse of the price of sugar in the autumn of 1920. In order to survive, most field workers became panhandlers or received assistance from other sugar workers, particularly the skilled artisans of the mill factories. Other field laborers traveled through the countryside looking for work at the mills that continued to grind cane or searching for other ways to subsist. Some companies gave their workers permission to grow food in the cane fields or on land located close to the mills. According to one Cuban worker, "conucos appeared in just about every area and almost all of the cane fields were covered with fruit, malanga, yams, and wheat. Thanks to these items, a large number of families were able to survive."[70] But a growing number of British West Indians who either collectively bought land to cultivate or individually squatted on small pieces of ground were defrauded of their plots and evicted by the companies or their colonos. According to Francis O'Meara, acting consul general of the British Legation in Havana, this usually occurred after the black migrants had "placed the land under cultivation . . . [only then] were the unfortunate men evicted so the Cubans could take possession of the fruits of their labor."[71] Because of these conditions, the workers decided to organize a strike.

Anarcho-syndicalists and Communist labor leaders directed the effort. One organizer, Rodolfo Díaz, realized that the racially segmented work force of the sugar industry made it difficult to unionize both the field and industrial workers. Black Caribbean and Spanish immigrants composed nearly half of the industry's work force. As previously mentioned, at the end of December 1932, delegates from thirty-two mills met in Santa Clara to establish the Sindicato Nacional de Obreros de la Industria Azucarera (SNOIA).[72] Representing the interests of both industrial and agricultural workers in the sugar industry, the SNOIA demanded a minimum wage of 50 cents per 100 arrobas of cut cane for the macheteros, and 40 cents to 70 cents for every 100 arrobas of hauled cane for the carreteros. Unskilled day laborers were to receive a minimum of one peso per day for work performed inside the mill factories. The organization also demanded an eight-hour day without a decrease in salary for all sugar workers, and the establishment of three shifts for mill workers. Some field workers, other than macheteros and carreteros, were no longer to be paid for performing piece-meal work, but instead were to receive a daily salary for planting and hoeing. SNOIA organized a work stoppage in January 1933 to obtain extra work shifts and hours for unemployed and underemployed workers.

As an expression of internationalism, leaders of the SNOIA demanded, in recognition of the contributions and sacrifices made by the black Caribbean braceros, "all forms of discrimination in salary and treatment against Jamaicans and Haitians end. The principle of equal pay for equal work regardless of occupation ought to be a right for all blacks including Jamaicans and Haitians."[73] Several Jamaicans—A. G. S. Coombs, H. C. Buchanan, and Alexander Clarke, among others— assisted with the strike. Buchanan had been introduced to the principles of anarcho-syndicalism during the strikes of 1924–25. He and the others would become important leaders in the trade union movement in Jamaica's sugar industry after they returned home in 1934. Three years later, in

1937, Coombs and Buchanan collaborated with Clarke, who had changed his surname to Bustamente, to form the Jamaican Workers and Tradesmen Union (JWTU), which led the strike and rebellion of April 1938 against the West Indian Sugar Company's mills.[74]

Reminiscent of the syndicates established by Enrique Varona during the strikes of 1924–25, the striking workers established self-governing committees at all the mills to direct the work stoppage. "White, black, native and foreign, Haitian, Jamaican, Chinese, young and old, men and women," agricultural and industrial workers were elected to the committees.[75] They ensured that the workers of the Niquero, Media Luna, Romelie, Esperanza, Baguanos, Santa Lucía, Tacajó, and Preston centrales in Oriente, the Jatibonico in Camaguey, and the Nazabal, Purio, Hormiguero, Constancia, Santa Isabel, and Carmita centrales in Santa Clara walked out of the cane fields and mill factories. Some of the strikers armed themselves to force the mills to close, to press for their demands, and to defend themselves against the rural guard. By the end of February, most of the companies had accepted the demands of the workers. The strike that suspended the start of the zafra had immediate political effect. Viewed as one of the most important challenges to the power of North American capital, the strike weakened Machado's support among representatives of the sugar industry and the entrepreneurial class in general. The activities of the SNOIA persuaded other labor unions to use the strike to protest the repressive and corrupt dictatorship, as well as U.S. imperialism. It is not surprising that the general strike that occurred between July and August 1933 caused the government to collapse. On 12 August 1933, President Machado resigned and left the island for the Bahamas.

The political vacuum created by Machado's departure was filled by a number of Cuban nationalists. Most were aware of the role that Haitian and Jamaican braceros had played in the syndicalist movement of the first half of the 1920s, as well as in the strike in the sugar industry in 1933. But officials of the revolutionary and nationalist government of Dr. Ramón Grau San Martín (September 1933–January 1934) ignored their contributions and quickly forgot the role they had played in the labor movement. Governing the country with the aid of his minister of the interior, Antonio Guiteras, less than a month after taking office President Grau San Martín announced, on 18 October 1933, Decree Number 2232, which prohibited the disembarkation of Haitian and Jamaican braceros. The decree also ordered the repatriation of all foreigners considered to be illegal aliens.[76] Less than one month later, on 8 November, the government published

Decree Number 2583, the Law for the Nationalization of Work. Similar to the labor law that Congress had sought to pass during the Zayas government, and directed at both Cuban and foreign businesses, this law stipulated that 50 percent of industrial and commercial jobs be filled by locally born workers. The law, however, included a couple of exceptions that allowed enterprises such as the sugar companies to retain their foreign workers. First, it precluded immigrants from working in technical positions even if there were no qualified Cubans available. The decree also extended the same rights that Cubans enjoyed to those foreigners who had served in the U.S. and British armed forces during World War I and who were residing in Cuba before the passage of the decree of 8 November 1933. But on 20 December 1933, Grau issued Decree Number 3282, instructing immigration officials to detain and repatriate only Haitians who were indigent and unemployed. The law also called for the Cuban army to enforce all of the decrees relating to black immigration.[77] The enforcement of the latter law resulted in the repatriation of some 5,907 Haitians by 25 May 1934. In addition, immigration officials detained another 3,000 Haitians, who faced immediate expulsion as soon as the authorities determined their status.

The Cuban government deported not only indigent and unemployed black immigrants, but even those who owned property and livestock. Black braceros who had established permanent homes in Cuba since the 1910s were required to sell their possessions before being expelled. Some took their time in order to postpone the inevitable. For example, when the municipal authorities of Mayarí, located on the northern coast of Oriente near Nipe Bay and the Preston mill, notified the Haitian Cantariso Dumas that he was to be repatriated, Dumas showed that he owned four chickens, three turkeys, a three-bedroom house for his family, "and even a horse of good quality that he purchased recently by handing a deposit to a Cuban by the name Manuel González."[78] As a result, officials gave Dumas one month to sell his belongings. When Dumas failed to sell his livestock, provincial authorities in Santiago de Cuba decided to give him another month to get rid of all of his belongings, which he finally did.

Black braceros who believed that repatriation would harm their families petitioned the authorities to have their status reevaluated. Many hoped for asylum. Antonio Pierre, a Haitian from Alto Songo in Oriente Province, pleaded with immigration officials to let him stay in his adopted country. Pierre insisted that he did not wish to violate the immigration and labor laws of Cuba. Emphasizing that his circumstances no longer made him a Haitian, Pierre claimed, "I do not harvest coffee or cut cane. I have dedicated myself as a farmer, something that I have done for more than twenty years." He continued, "I have eight Cuban children and a Cuban wife."[79] For these reasons, Pierre believed that his case deserved special consideration, and that he should be granted permanent residency. Attempting to gain sympathy from the authorities, Pierre ended his deposition stating, "I do not wish to abandon my eight children and wife who are Cuban and destroy a life that I have had for some twenty years."[80]

The examples of Dumas and Pierre suggest that the repatriation of black workers was a dramatic and stressful event. Yet it occurred in a timely and orderly fashion. By the middle of the 1930s, the government had processed thousands of Haitians and Jamaicans. One cohort of nine hundred expelled Haitians ranged in age between fourteen and sixty-five. Nearly 60 percent of this contingent of deportees, however, were between the ages of thirty and fifty. In January 1937, the government deported another group of nine hundred Haitians. As with the previous group, the majority of workers ranged in age from thirty-four to sixty-five. Of that nine hundred, forty-five were children under the age of fourteen. All of the deportees were classified as Haitians and as agricultural workers.[81]

Meanwhile, the government of Jamaica established policies that sought to facilitate the repatriation of its workers and their families. In order to keep families intact, as well as cover the cost of transporting their dependents, in November 1936 the government lowered the age of Jamaican children classified as minors from sixteen years to fourteen, particularly girls, "who are absolutely dependent on their parents and are unlikely for one cause or another to be able to earn a living in Cuba." Immigrant children over the age of sixteen who sought to accompany their parents had to petition the authorities for financial assistance. Three years earlier, in December 1933, the government permitted both Jamaican men and women who had Cuban spouses to bring them home at the expense of the government. In addition, legitimate and illegitimate children born to Jamaican women were repatriated at the cost of the government. Finally, at its expense, the government also retrieved the sick and infirm, men as well as women.[82]

As the Cuban government enforced the immigration laws, some sugar companies and coffee farmers reported a shortage of field workers. They informed the government that they could not complete their harvests without the labor of the black immigrants. T. M. Snow, an official of the British Legation in Havana, questioned this assessment. He wrote to the governor of Jamaica, John Simon: "There are no shortages of labor in Cuba," and he reported that "the grinding season of 1935 ended during the last week of March." To discourage Jamaicans from traveling to Cuba and from believing the promises of the emigrant brokers, both the *Daily Gleaner* and the *Jamaican Times* published this notice: "Intending emigrants are warned that it is unlikely that they will be able to obtain employment in Cuba and that it is most unwise for anyone to proceed to that Republic in the hope of securing employment."[83]

EPILOGUE

The experiences of the black Caribbean immigrants in Cuba, especially Haitians and Jamaicans, during the 1910s and 1920s show how they attempted to challenge and resist the ideologies of race, ethnicity, and class that the Cuban and North American sugar companies used to subjugate and exploit them. These ideologies were revealed as soon as the black immigrants arrived and were transported to the colonias, bateyes, and centrales. The immigrants encountered symbols, structures, and biases that made them feel inferior and questioned their humanity. The braceros were denied dignity and experienced an assortment of humiliating abuses.

Once the black immigrant workers were situated in the enclaves, in order to control them company officials defined and manipulated racial and ethnic conceptions that depreciated their color, cultural identity, and nationality. The workers confronted what Philippe Bourgois called "conjugated oppression," as these categories determined among other things the quality of their housing, diet, and medical care. All were less than adequate, reinforcing the workers' marginalization vis-à-vis the status of white Cubans and North Americans, as well as of Spanish immigrants. The workers felt "conjugated oppression" in the cane fields and in the mill factories. For example, the majority of Haitians allegedly were natural-born macheteros and nothing more, whereas most Jamaicans also cut, loaded, and hauled cane to the mills. The Jamaicans' knowledge of English and their deferential comportment toward whites—a public personality contrived as a strategy to counter the racial and ethnic ideologies of the sugar companies—sometimes provided them with the opportunity to work inside the mills as skilled artisans.

The companies consistently reserved every administrative and supervisory position in the enclaves for whites. Together with the segmented division-of-labor paradigm, "conjugated oppression" encouraged competition among the workers and discouraged worker protest, activism, and solidarity. As a result, the companies' ideologies, which established the socioeconomic structures and arrangements on the bateyes, were hardly the paternalistic ones that some scholars have claimed. They were explicitly designed to subjugate, control, and exploit the black Antillean braceros.

The companies' racial and ethnic definitions and ideologies were supported and augmented by the political elites, including municipal and provincial bureaucrats, police, journalists, and some white and black citizens. Together they framed the debate over black Antillean immigration that engendered anti-immigrant intimidation and violence. Employing the rhetoric of differences to produce narratives that transformed the braceros into "undesirables," the elites incorporated race, ethnicity, and class into the discourse on Cuban national identity. After 1912, Cuban nationalism included nativist and xenophobic elements. According to the political class and the general public, citizenship was reserved only for Cubans.

The socioeconomic structures and arrangements that the companies and elites produced with these ideologies were successful up to a point. Similar to the industrial plantation model that consisted of North American and European capital along with an inexhaustible supply of black labor to produce sugarcane and other tropical staples under the institution of African slavery, worker protest and solidarity were restrained but never destroyed.

During the 1910s, when the labor power of the braceros was responsible for the resuscitation and expansion of the sugar industry, these workers developed useful ideologies and strategies to resist their subjugation and exploitation. For example, after completing their first sugar harvest many braceros returned home. They did so in order to spend the meager wages they had earned to help support their families. More important, they went home to retrieve their spouses, children, or loved ones. Familial obligations explain why so many braceros frequently moved back and forth to Cuba during the 1910s and 1920s. With their families in tow, many black Caribbean workers decamped to Camagüey and Oriente hoping to reconstitute their homes in Cuba, including cultural and spiritual worldviews and structures like those in Haiti and Jamaica. That a large number of braceros decided to stay in Cuba also shows how they came to feel a sense of affinity for the Republic of Cuba. By the 1930s, many had married Cubans and had children. Undoubtedly these black immigrants thought of themselves as Cuban citizens.

Jamaican workers created numerous benevolent societies that became autonomous sites where they could encourage fellowship and the retention of their culture. These associations also offered their members health insurance and even funeral and burial benefits. These latter services were critical, given the dangerous work that black Caribbean workers performed as well as the lack of sanitation in the barracones and the inadequate medical care they received in the enclaves. Some organizations also served as venues where workers could secretly develop useful narratives to contest their marginalization. This was evinced when, after having been introduced to the nuances of Jim Crow, an ideology that the sugar mills brought from the United States to Cuba, some Jamaicans adopted a singular public personality, an exaggerated sense of deference toward all whites regardless of nationality. At the same time, the spiritual worldviews of the Haitians and Jamaicans and their status as immigrant field workers encouraged the braceros in all likelihood to establish "communities of fate." They understood that as macheteros and carreteros they were obligated to trust only themselves and other black workers from the Caribbean to survive and resist. They never revealed this conviction publicly.

Ultimately, the black Antillean braceros identified the anarcho-syndicalist principle of internationalism and Garveyism as ideologies they could use to resist their subjugation and exploitation. These insightful interpretations explained how race, ethnicity, and class informed their daily lives. Some braceros reimagined and merged the two paradigms in order to construct a radical or militant worker's consciousness and identity. As the level and intensity of their marginalization increased after the dramatic drop in the price of sugar and the financial crisis that ensued, the braceros decided to take part in the series of strikes that hit the sugar industries of Camagüey and Oriente. This study has revealed factors previously unknown to some scholars who believe that the braceros' class would have discouraged them from playing an active role in the Cuban labor movement.

Many labor leaders and the rank-and-file at the time recognized and acknowledged the exemplary role that the braceros performed. Cuban nationalists, however, were unwilling to extend them the dignity, respect, and gratitude they deserved. Instead, as the financial crisis of the 1930s approached, they continued to criticize and punish the braceros as the source of the Republic's social and economic ills, demonstrating again how nativism and xenophobia intersected with the nationalistic narrative of the Cuban elites. Cuban citizenship remained as elusive as ever for the majority of black Caribbean workers. At this critical moment, the competing ideology of the sugar mills became subordinate and delegitimized. At the beginning of the 1930s, unable to influence the debate on black Antillean immigration, the sugar companies saw the Cuban government pass and enforce a host of anti-black-immigration laws that preceded the repatriation of thousands of braceros by the mid-1930s.

———≈———

Returning to their country during the 1930s, Haitians like Dumas and Pierre encountered a society that had been governed by U.S. military officials since 1915. Foreign businesses had taken advantage of the occupation, seizing the small plots of land that the peasantry had used for subsistence. Prior to 1915, the nation's constitution had prohibited foreigners from owning property. During the presidency of Philippe Sudre Dartiguenave (1915–22), however, the constitution was amended to nullify the ban. As a result, by 1927 foreign businesses had acquired an estimated 43,000 acres of land that had been previously settled and worked by peasants.[1]

The dispossession and displacement of the Haitian peasantry occurred while the overall population of the nation continued to increase. In 1935, the country's population reached 3 million. The rural peasantry made up 95 percent of this total and continued to live in hopeless desperation. Haiti's demographic density of three hundred individuals per square mile was three times greater than that of the Dominican Republic and two times that of Cuba.[2] As a result, the economic depression of the 1930s made buying or renting a small plot of land nearly impossible. The braceros who returned at this time were forced to subsist on smaller and marginally inferior plots of land, usually in the mountains, or to move into the towns and cities to survive. Haitians who could not survive left once again, this time migrating to the Dominican Republic to cut and haul sugarcane. Those who stayed faced a shortage of schools and hospitals. After the U.S. occupation ended in 1936, socioeconomic immobility and sickness remained common experiences for the majority of rural workers. Their lives were also disrupted by droughts and hurricanes, which further reduced their resources.

Competition for land and food among the peasantry became a common occurrence. Manuel, the fictional Haitian migrant in Roumain's *Masters of the Dew*, who had been repatriated from Cuba, commented on conditions in the early 1940s: "I left for foreign lands . . . and when I returned, I found my village pillaged by drought and plunged into the deepest kind of poverty . . . I found the peasants divided up and quarrelling."[3]

Haiti's export-oriented economy exacerbated the poverty of the rural peasantry. Although the peasants grew notable quantities of coffee, bananas, sugar, and cotton for the North Atlantic economy, they did so according to terms set by the Standard Fruit Company and other foreign companies. In fact, North American and European companies, merchants, and middlemen not only determined the prices of these commodities but also the amounts they could sell on the world market. This economic model exploited the peasantry as the foreign commercial class, and their businesses appropriated a substantial percentage of the profits by controlling the export sector of the economy. As a result, during the depression of the 1930s, "If peasants were fortunate they ate one or two meals a day of red beans and rice, yams, and bananas . . . few ever ate any meat . . . Their days were thus spent trying to extricate themselves from the consequences of a never-ending crisis of impoverishment—not with politics—and attempting to amass capital (in order to buy land and animals) by successfully growing marketable cash crops."[4]

Jamaican braceros returned to their island to face circumstances similar to those that confronted their Haitian counterparts. By 1929, much of the countryside's 270,240 cultivable acres had been seized by the United Fruit Company and the West India Sugar Company (WISCO). These multinationals controlled one-third of the island's sugar and fruit industries. Controlling 43,605 acres to grow cane sugar alone on vast tracts of land in the south-central and northwestern regions that included the parishes of Hanover, Westmoreland, and St. Catherine, their sugar mills and cane farms denied the peasantry access to sufficient amounts of land to establish small plots. Lacking the opportunity to either own or rent land, as many as 42,000 rural wage workers, or 4 percent of the total population, worked as seasonal laborers on the sugar estates. Meanwhile, an estimated 100,000 peasants and workers harvested bananas.[5] Often employed by "big" Jamaican banana farmers who owned their land, and whose role and status were similar to those of the Cuban colonos, these peasants and workers ironically confronted nearly the identical socioeconomic arrangements and conditions that characterized the Cuban plantation model of development that they had left.

Charged by the British Parliament in 1929 to investigate the sugar industry in its Caribbean colonies, the West Indian Sugar Commission discovered that the poor housing sugar planters and later companies such as WISCO provided for estate workers was a result of willful negligence. Not even the presence of indentured East Indians could convince the companies to improve the standards in estate housing. The commission suggested that the race and ethnicity of the workers helped explain the poor housing on the estates: "On many estates on which indentured coolies were settled, the old long ranges of single rooms [or barracks] with floors [of] traditional compost of cow dung and clay remain, ruinous, decrepit, and full of dirt and vermin. Their survival, like that of the old estate laborers' cottages, perpetuates a low standard of living which there is a common tendency to regard as being all that the West Indian laborer, whether Indian or Creole, needs or desires."[6] WISCO did attempt to improve housing for its workers, influenced by the United Fruit Company's decision to provide its workers, particularly on its banana plantations, with rebuilt and new housing that included raised two-room houses with wooden floors.

The low wages and poor living conditions of cane workers prompted many Jamaican peasants to enter the banana industry. At the outset of the economic depression of the 1930s, the relatively stable price of bananas did not affect demand abroad, particularly in the United States. As a result, "smaller" farmers and peasants began to plant bananas not only on new land but also in areas once reserved for sugar and other tropical staples like coconuts. Many sold their crops to the United Fruit Company. In order to improve their relationship with this foreign company, in 1929 the majority of farmers and some peasants established the Jamaican Banana Producers Association. This cooperative organization not only sold its members' crops to the United Fruit Company but also negotiated favorable trade agreements with the governments of Great Britain and Canada. In 1932, the Ottawa Agreement permitted banana producers to export their crop to England and Canada at around two pounds sterling per ton. Banana producers lost much of the U.S. market while they increased exports to Great Britain and Canada.[7]

Prosperity for the banana farmers and peasants, however, was short-lived. As early as 1931, the Panamanian banana disease appeared in Jamaica and began to ruin the crop. That year saw producers lose over 12,000 acres of their fruit crop in the parish of St. Mary and another 12,000 acres in Portland. The destruction wrought by this disease prompted the United Fruit Company to sell its banana plantations in these two parishes. But Mother Nature had just begun its ravages. Hurricanes in 1933 and 1934 destroyed half of the industry's crops in 1933 and 1935. In fact, Lester Brooks described the hurricane of 1933 "as the greatest disaster outside of [the one] of 1912."[8] As a result, the daily lives of banana growers, including farmers and peasants, declined dramatically. Undoubtedly this state of affairs compelled many of them, particularly the peasants, to split their time as seasonal and part-time workers for the sugar industry.

The impacts of the Depression, crop diseases, and hurricanes made life precariously fragile for most rural workers in Jamaica. By the late 1930s, their existence had come to resemble that which many Jamaican emigrants had experienced in Cuba before their expulsion. As seasonal workers for the sugar industry, many had to rely on small plots of land for their subsistence. Neither occupation—seasonal work nor farming—even when the peasants combined the two, could guarantee an adequate standard of living. As a result, the Jamaican and Haitian braceros returned from Cuba to face conditions that mirrored those of the mid-to-late nineteenth century. Many remained on marginal lands to either eke out a living or produce a tropical commodity for export, while being lured by low wages attached to seasonal employment on the sugar estates. By 1938, it was undoubtedly these circumstances that would cause them to protest their conditions and participate in the trade workers' movement.

NOTES

INTRODUCTION

1. Fernando Ortiz Fernández, *Hampa afro-cubanos, los negros esclavos: Estudio sociológico y de derecho público* (Havana, 1916), 58; Maturin Murray Ballou, *History of Cuba; or Notes of a Traveller in the Tropics* (Boston, 1854), 180–82; Miguel Barnet, *Biography of a Runaway Slave*, trans. W. Nick Hill (New York, 1994), 37; Sidney Mintz and Richard Price, *The Birth of African-American Culture: An Anthropological Perspective* (Boston, 1976), 2.

2. Lisa Yun, *The Coolie Speaks: Chinese Indentured Laborers and African Slaves in Cuba* (Philadelphia, 2008); José Baltar Rodriguez, *Los chinos de Cuba* (Havana, 1997); Juan Pérez de la Riva, *Los Culies chinos en Cuba* (Havana, 2000).

3. Matt D. Childs, *The 1812 Aponte Rebellion in Cuba and the Struggle against Atlantic Slavery* (Chapel Hill, 2006); Robert L. Paquette, *Sugar Is Made with Blood: The Conspiracy of La Escalera and the Conflict between Empires over Slavery in Cuba* (Middleton, CT, 1988); Manuel Barcia, *The Great African Slave Revolt of 1825: Cuba and the Fight for Freedom in Matanzas* (Baton Rouge, 2012); Michele Reid-Vázquez, *The Year of the Lash: Free People of Color in Cuba and the Nineteenth-Century Atlantic World* (Athens, GA, 2011).

4. Philip A. Howard, *Changing History: Afro-Cuban Cabildos and Societies of Color in the Nineteenth Century* (Baton Rouge, 1998).

5. See James C. Scott, *Domination and the Arts of Resistance: Hidden Transcripts* (New Haven, 1990).

6. When using the term *ideology*, I am not only referring to its traditional construction as the content of a set of beliefs and ideas, but also to its broader definition, which includes the social processes, institutions, and arrangements manufactured by a society's culture. L. Althusser, "Ideology and Ideological State Apparatuses," in *Lenin and Philosophy* (London, 1971); R. Johnson, "Three Problematics: Elements of a Theory of Working-Class Culture," in *Working Class Culture*, ed. J. Clarke, C. Critcher, and R. Johnson (London 1979); Göran Therborn, *The Ideology of Power and the Power of Ideology* (London, 1980).

7. Arthur Stinchcombe, "Organized Dependency Relations and Social Stratification," in *The Logic of Social Hierarchies*, ed. Edward O. Laumann et al. (Chicago, 1970). The socioreligious beliefs of Haitians and Jamaicans were fundamental attributes of their ethnicity and therefore of their identity. When using the term *ethnicity*, I mean beliefs, customs, and behavior, or the cultural identity

239

of the braceros. At this time and in this context, not only were "Culture and racial identity . . . the foundation of ethnicity," but I believe that nationality was too. See Mervyn C. Alleyne, *The Construction and Representation of Race and Ethnicity in the Caribbean and the World* (Barbados, 2005), 9.

8. César Ayala, *American Sugar Kingdom: The Plantation Economy of the Spanish Caribbean, 1898–1934* (Chapel Hill, 1999); Alan Dye, *Cuban Sugar in the Age of Mass Production: Technology and the Economics of the Sugar Central, 1899–1929* (Stanford, 1998).

9. Manuel Moreno Fraginals, *The Sugarmill: The Socioeconomic Complex of Sugar in Cuba* (New York, 1976), 15.

10. Ramiro Guerra, *La industria azucarera en Cuba* (Havana, 1940), 114–15.

11. Ibid., 124, 127.

12. Jorge Ibarra, *Cuba, 1898–1921: Partidos politicos y classes socials* (Havana, 1992); Jorge Ibarra, *Prologue to Revolution, Cuba, 1898–1958* (London, 1998); Gillian McGillivray, *Blazing Cane: Sugar Communities, Class, and State Formation in Cuba, 1868–1959* (Durham, 2009).

13. Karl Marx, *Das Kapital*, Vol. 3 (London, 1960), 853.

14. For a vivid description of a cane worker's life, see Sidney Mintz, *Worker in the Cane: A Puerto Rican Life History* (1960; repr., New York, 1974).

15. Barnet, *Biography of a Runaway Slave*, 101–102.

16. John D. Kelly, "The Other Leviathans: Corporate Investment and the Construction of a Sugar Colony," in *White and Deadly: Sugar and Colonialism*, ed. Pal Ahluwalia, Bill Ashcroft, and Roger Knight (Cammack, NY, 1999), 104.

17. Barry Carr, "'Omnipotent and Omnipresent'? Labor Shortage, Worker Mobility and Employer Control in the Cuban Sugar Industry," in *Identity and Struggle at the Margins of the Nation State*, ed. Aviva Chomsky and Aldo Lauria-Santiago (Durham, 1998), 275.

18. Ibid., 274. Carr believes the easy and accessible credit that the sugar mills' company stores provided the braceros to purchase food and other necessities is proof of such paternalism. McGillivray cites a number of examples where some cane farmers employed paternalism to convince the braceros that they shared the same financial interests. McGillivray, *Blazing Cane*, 175.

19. John Dumoulin, "El primer desarrollo del movimiento obrero y la formación del proletariado en el sector azucarero Cruces," *Islas* 48 (May–August 1974): 3–66; Rebecca Scott, "The Lower Class of Whites and the Negro Element: Race, Social Identity and Politics in Central Cuba, 1899–1909," in *La Nación soñada: Cuba, Puerto Rico y Filipinas antes el 98*, ed. Consuelo Naranjo Orovio, Miguel Angel Puig-Samper, and Luis Miguel García Mora (Madrid, 1995); Rebecca J. Scott, "Fault Lines, Color Lines, and Party Lines: Race, Labor, and Collective Action in Louisiana and Cuba," in *Beyond Slavery: Explorations of Race, Labor, and Citizenship in Post-Emancipation Societies*, ed. Frederick Cooper, Thomas C. Holt, and Rebecca J. Scott (Chapel Hill, 2000).

20. Instituto de Historia del Movimiento Comunista, *Historia del movimiento obrero cubano, 1865–1958*, Vol. 1 (Havana, 1987); Carlos Del Toro, *El movimiento obrero cubano en 1914* (Havana, 1969); John Dumoulin, *Azúcar y lucha de clases, 1917* (Havana, 1980); Evelio Telleria, *Los congresos obreros en Cuba* (Havana, 1973). All of these writers have tended to place the black Antillean braceros on the margins of the Cuban labor movement, portraying them as inanimate objects. Aleida Plasencia Moro completely ignores them in her article "Historia del movimiento obrero en Cuba," in *Historia del movimiento obrero en América Latina*, ed. Pablo González Casanova (Mexico City, 1984).

21. Philippe I. Bourgois, *Ethnicity at Work: Divided Labor on a Central American Banana Plantation* (Baltimore, 1989); Aviva Chomsky, "Laborers and Smallholders in Costa Rica's Mining Communities," in Chomsky and Lauria-Santiago, eds., *Identity and Struggle at the Margins of the Nation State,* 169–95; Ken Post, *Arise Ye Starvelings: The Jamaican Labour Rebellion of 1938 and Its Aftermath* (The Hague, 1978).

22. Franklin W. Knight, "Jamaican Migrants in the Cuban Sugar Industry, 1900–1934," in *Between Slavery and Free Labor: The Spanish-Speaking Caribbean in the Nineteenth Century,* ed. Manuel Moreno Fraginals et al. (Baltimore, 1985); Elizabeth McLean Petras, *Jamaican Labor Migration: White Capital and Black Labor, 1850–1930* (Boulder, CO, 1988).

23. Marc McLeod, "Undesirable Aliens: Race, Ethnicity, and Nationalism in the Comparison of Haitian and British West Indian Immigrant Workers in Cuba, 1912–1939," *Journal of Social History* 31, no. 3 (1998): 599–623. McLeod discovered that thousands of Jamaicans survived the Cuban government's forced repatriation program of 1933 until the end of the decade. Jorge L. Giovannetti, "Historia visual y etnohistoria en Cuba: Inmigración antillana e identidad en los hijos de Baraguá," *Caribbean Studies* 30, no. 2 (July–December 2002): 216–52; Michael Conniff, *Black Labor on a White Canal: Panama, 1904–1981* (Pittsburgh, 1985); Bourgois, *Ethnicity at Work;* Aviva Chomsky, *West Indian Workers and the United Fruit Company in Costa Rica, 1870–1940* (Baton Rouge, 1996).

24. Marc C. McLeod, "Sin dejar ser Cubanos: Cuban Blacks and the Challenges of Garveyism in Cuba," *Caribbean Studies* 31, no. 1 (Jan.–June 2003): 75–105.

1. ADOPTING BLACK CARIBBEAN WORKERS

1. "Jamaica: Labour Shortage in St. Thomas," *Jamaican Times,* 22 November 1919, reprinted in *The Workman* 7, no. 25 (24 January 1920): 6.

2. John R. Brook, *Civil Report of Major-General John Brooke, U.S. Army Military Governor, Island of Cuba, 1900* (Washington, D.C., 1900), 285, 320.

3. Ramiro Guerra, *Azúcar y población en las Antillas* (1927; repr., Havana, 1970), 66; Alan Dye, "Tropical Technology and Mass Production: The Expansion of Sugarmills, 1899–1929" (PhD diss., University of Illinois, 1991), 6.

4. Dye, "Tropical Technology," 44.

5. Hugh Thomas, *Cuba: The Pursuit of Freedom* (New York, 1971), 274. Also see Fe Iglesias García, "The Development of Capitalism in Cuban Sugar Production, 1860–1900," in Manuel Moreno Fraginals et al., eds., *Between Slavery and Free Labor,* 70.

6. Dye, "Tropical Technology," 57, 5.

7. Ibid., 8–9.

8. Between 1882 and 1894, some 224,000 Spanish immigrants and Canary Islanders arrived in Cuba, according to Devon C. Corbitt. Of that total, a little more than half, or 142,000, returned to their country during this same period. Those who came with their families and stayed, however, became colonos themselves. See Devon C. Corbitt, "Immigration in Cuba," *Hispanic American Historical Review* 22 (May 1942): 304.

9. Cleona Lewis, *America's Stake in International Investments* (Washington, D.C., 1938); Mira Wilkins, *The Emergence of Multinational Enterprise: American Business Abroad from the Colonial Era to*

1914 (Cambridge, MA, 1970). The Brookings Institution sponsored Lewis's study. The signing of the U.S.-Cuban Reciprocity Treaty of March 1903 encouraged the arrival of American businessmen and their capital. This treaty reduced the U.S. tariff on Cuban sugar by 20 percent, from 1.685 to 1.348 cents per pound. In exchange, the Cuban government gave U.S. shippers a reduction of between 25 and 40 percent of the standard. American lawmakers viewed the Reciprocity Treaty of 1903 as a mechanism to revive the Cuban economy as well as to meet the growing demand of sugar in the Unitd States, according to Hugh Thomas. The treaty gave Cuban sugar producers access to a society where its citizens annually consumed sixty-three pounds of sugar per person in 1899, seventy-five pounds in 1904, and by 1914 on the eve of World War I, eighty-one pounds. See U.S. Tariff Commission, *Sugar: Report to the President of the United States* (Washington, D.C., 1934), 172–73, quoted in César Ayala, *American Sugar Kingdom*, 65; Thomas, *Cuba*, 469.

10. Benjamin Allen, *A Story of Growth of E. Atkins & Co. and the Sugar Industry in Cuba* (Boston, 1926), 21.

11. Thomas, *Cuba*, 274.

12. Lewis, *America's Stake*, 267; Allen, *A Story of Growth*, 27. Havemayer and his cousin Charles Senff, a prominent stockholder in several East Coast refineries who had invested substantial funds in the Trinidad Sugar Company, appointed Edwin Atkins as president. Also see Thomas, *Cuba*, 275; Julio Le Riverend, *Historia económica de Cuba* (Havana, 1967), 217.

13. Le Riverend, *Historia económica de Cuba*, 217.

14. Ayala, *American Sugar Kingdom*, 91. After 1902 the government of Cuba changed the name of the province of Puerto Príncipe to Camagüey.

15. Charles Berchon, *A través de Cuba: Relativo geográfico descriptivo y económico* (Madrid, 1910), 139.

16. *The Louisiana Planter and Sugar Manufacturer* 22, no. 8 (25 February 1899): 115. This weekly periodical published news articles, financial and commercial data, and scholarly reports on the American, Asian, Caribbean, and European sugar industries. Hereafter cited as *Louisiana Planter*.

17. Leland Jenks, *Our Cuban Colony: A Study in Sugar* (New York, 1928), 179.

18. Le Riverend, *Historia económica de Cuba*, 217.

19. Watt Stewart, *Keith and Costa Rica: The Biography of Minor Cooper Keith* (Albuquerque, 1964); Ariel James, *Banes: Imperialismo y nación en una plantación azucarera* (Havana, 1976), 57–59. The Cuban government changed the name of Santiago de Cuba Province to Oriente following the war with Spain in 1898.

20. James, *Banes*, 71.

21. Ibid., 93; Le Riverend, *Historia económica de Cuba*, 217; Oscar Zanetti et al., *United Fruit Company: Un caso del dominio imperialista en Cuba* (Havana, 1976), 6.

22. Lewis, *America's Stake*, 267; Le Riverend, *Historia económica de Cuba*, 217.

23. Lewis, *America's Stake*, 268; Le Riverend, *Historia económica de Cuba*, 218.

24. Rolando Alvarez Estévez, *Azúcar e Inmigración, 1900–1940* (Havana, 1988); Alberto Arredondo, *El Negro en Cuba* (Havana, 1939); Knight, "Jamaican Migrants"; Elizabeth M. Thomas-Hope, "The Establishment of a Migration Tradition: British West Indian Movements to the Hispanic Caribbean in the Century After Emancipation," in *Caribbean Social Relations*, ed. Colin G. Clarke (Liverpool, 1978).

25. James, *Banes*, 174.

26. Reynaldo Cruz Ruíz, "La Inmigración antillana en los primeros años del siglo XX" (unpublished manuscript in its author's possession, n.d., Santiago de Cuba, Cuba), 80–81.

27. Quoted in Hortensia Pichardo, ed., *Documentos y artículos para el estudio de la historia de Cuba*, Vol. 2 (Havana, 1979), 199–201. Also quoted in Alvarez Estévez, *Azúcar e inmigración*, 22–23. Alvarez Estevez provides figures for not only West Indians but also Asians, Africans, Puerto Ricans, French, and South Americans.

28. Alvarez Estévez, *Azúcar e inmigración*, 27. Magoon arrived in Cuba after frustrated and angry members of the Liberal Party led a rebellion against Estrada Palma for fraudulently winning the presidential election in November 1905.

29. Secretaria de Hacienda de la República de Cuba, Sección de Estadísticas, *Inmigración y movimiento de pasajeros* (Havana, 1903–1930).

30. Cruz Ruíz, "La Inmigración antillana," 83.

31. El Secretario de Hacienda to Gobernador de la Provincia de Oriente, 7 June 1911, Archivo Histórico Provincial de Santiago de Cuba, Legajo 785, no. 33, Materia: Inmigración. Henceforth, the Archivo Histórico Provincial de Santiago de Cuba will be referred to as AHPSC.

32. Quoted in "Illegal Entry," *Cuban Review* (New York) 10, no. 2 (December 1912): 9.

33. *La Independencia*, date n.a. Quoted in *Louisiana Planter* 48, no. 5 (3 February 1912): 79.

34. Zanetti et al., *United Fruit Company*, 65; James, *Banes*, 113.

35. *Louisiana Planter* 48, no. 17 (27 April 1912): 301.

36. *Avisador Comercial*, date n.a., quoted ibid., 48, no. 1, (6 January 1912): 14. The *Avisador* was founded in Havana in 1869. Eduardo Anillo Rodríguez, *Cuatro siglos de vida, desde Pedro Barba hasta Varona Suarez* (Havana, 1919), 156.

37. *Louisiana Planter* 48, no. 17 (27 April 1912): 301.

38. Dumoulin, "El primer desarrollo," 3–66; Scott, "The Lower Class of Whites," 179–91; Scott, "Fault Lines, Color Lines."

39. Dumoulin, "El primer desarrollo," 18.

40. Ibid., 28; Scott, "Fault Lines, Color Lines," 90–91.

41. *Louisiana Planter* 34, no. 2 (14 January 1905): 28.

42. Ibid.

43. Ibid.

44. George L. Beckford, *Persistent Poverty: Underdevelopment in Plantation Economies of the Third World* (New York, 1972), 74. Also see Eric R. Wolf and Sidney W. Mintz, "Haciendas and Plantations in Middle America and the Antilles," *Social and Economic Studies* 6, no. 3 (September 1957): 380–412.

45. *Louisiana Planter* 34, no. 2 (14 January 1905): 28.

46. Jenks, *Our Cuban Colony*, 164.

47. Ibid., 164–65.

48. H. P. Starrett, "Cost of a Sugar Estate in Cuba," *Cuban Review* 10, no. 12 (November 1912): 28. Starrett served as U.S. Deputy Consul General in Havana.

49. Quoted in Ayala, *American Sugar Kingdom*, 80.

50. Alvarez Estévez, *Azúcar e inmigración*, 33.

51. Quoted in Thomas, *Cuba*, 514.

52. J. P. Sanger, *Informe sobre el Censo de Cuba, 1899* (Washington, D.C., 1900), 436–47; Victor H. Olmsted, *Censo de la República de Cuba: Bajo la administración provisional de los Estados Unidos, 1907* (Washington, D.C., 1908), 508–10.

53. Thomas, *Cuba*, 514; Aline Helg, *Our Rightful Share: The Afro-Cuban Struggle for Equality, 1880–1912* (Chapel Hill, 1995), 172–74.

54. Gobernador de Oriente to Francisco López Levia, Secretaria de Gobernación, Havana, 30 March 1910, AHPSC, Fondo: Gobierno Provincial, Leg. 1790, no. 10 (1910), Expediente: Partido de Color.

55. AHPSC, Fondo: Gobierno Provincial, Leg. 1790, no. 30 (1910), Materia: Partido de Color.

56. Alcalde Municipal de Guantánamo to Provincial Gobernador Manduley del Rio, Santiago de Cuba, 27 April 1910, AHPSC, Fondo: Gobierno Provincial, Leg. 1790, no. 3 (1910), Expediente: Partido Independiente de Color.

57. AHPSC, Fondo: Gobierno Provincial, Leg. 1790, no. 3, (1910), 27 April 1910. Aline Helg discovered that Guantánamo's officials uncovered a plot by Emilio Wilson and Evaristo Negret to organize five hundred blacks to kill the whites. Helg, *Our Rightful Share*, 174.

58. Louis A. Pérez Jr., *Lords of the Mountain: Social Banditry and Peasant Protest in Cuba, 1878–1918* (Pittsburgh, 1989).

59. Quoted in Helg, *Our Rightful Share*, 165.

60. "Hidrofobia, odio y mal fé," *Libertad*, 15 February 1912, 1, AHPSC, Fondo: Gobierno Provincial, Leg. 1790, no. 5, 1911–12.

61. AHPSC, Fondo, Gobierno Provincial, Leg. 1790, no. 5, 1911–1912.

62. Gobernador to El Alcalde Municipal de Santiago de Cuba, 27 February 1912, AHPSC, Fondo: Gobierno Provincial, Leg. 1790, no. 5, 1911–12. Some leaders of the PIC discussed their program with a group of socialists and anarchists in the town of Baracoa.

63. Academia de Ciencias de Cuba, *Indice histórico de la provincial de Camagüey, 1899–1952* (Havana, 1970), 57.

64. Gobernador de Oriente to Secretaria de Gobernación, 27 May 1912, AHPSC, Fondo: Gobierno Provincial, Leg. 1790, no. 10, 1912; *Louisiana Planter* 48, no. 22 (1 June 1912): 386–87.

65. Alcalde Municipal de Banes to Mayor General Jefe de las fuerzas armas de la República, Santiago de Cuba, 5 June 1912, AHPSC, Fondo: Gobierno Provincial, Leg. 1790, no. 10, 1912.

66. Jefe de Policía gubernativa to Gobierno Provincial, 31 May 1912, AHPSC, Fondo: Gobierno Provincial, Leg. 1790, no. 10 (1912).

67. Quoted in Helg, *Our Rightful Share*, 209.

68. Gobernador to Fiscal de la Audencia, Santiago de Cuba, 27 May 1912, AHPSC, Fondo: Gobierno Provincial, Leg. 1792, no. 3 (1912).

69. Ibid.

70. Bourgois, *Ethnicity at Work*, 215.

71. Only sixteen soldiers were killed between May and July. Helg, *Our Rightful Share*, 210–22.

72. Jefe de Policía Gobernativa Florentino Masa to Gobernador de Santiago de Cuba, 25 June 1912, AHPSC, Fondo: Gobierno Provincial, Leg. 1790, no. 12 (1912); Dominga Gonzalez Sánchez, "La inmigración negra y la situación socioeconomic de negros y mulattos en el campo," *Economía y Desarrollo* 3 (May–June 1988): 108.

73. Bourgois, *Ethnicity at Work*, 218–19.

74. Ibid., chs. 5–7; Chomsky, *West Indian Workers*; Ronald N. Harpelle, *The West Indians of Costa Rica: Race, Class, and the Integration of an Ethnic Minority* (Montreal, 2001).

75. Quoted in Zanetti et al., *United Fruit Company*, 212.

76. Thomas-Hope, "The Establishment of a Migration Tradition," 66. The socioeconomic context that caused Jamaicans to leave home is explored in Petras, *Jamaican Labor Migration*, chs. 1 and 2.

77. "Migrant Worker," in Erna Brodber, ed., "Life in Jamaica in the Early Twentieth Century: A Presentation of 90 Oral Accounts" (Kingston, 1980), Vol.: Parish of St. Elizabeth 58SteMb, 16. Housed in the Sir Arthur Lewis Institute of Social and Economic Research on the campus of the University of West Indies, Mona, these unpublished transcripts of ninety interviews were tape-recorded by a team of ethnographers during the early 1970s. Their research methodology included "the practice of the free association school of Psycho-Therapists." Hereafter cited as "Life in Jamaica."

78. "Clock Tower Man," ibid., Vol.: Parish of Westmoreland 87Wma, (recorded November 1975), 9–10.

79. Michelle Harrison, *King Sugar: Jamaica, The Caribbean and the World Sugar Industry* (New York, 2001), 22–23, 63. Although Harrison examines the sugar industry of Jamaica since the island's independence in the 1960s, she interviewed a number of male and female cane cutters who first began to cut cane in Cuba.

80. "Happy Struggle but Not Much Mobility," in "Life in Jamaica," Vol.: Parish of St. Mary 68STmFc, 11.

81. "Rev. John B.," in "Life in Jamaica," Vol.: Parish of St. Thomas 75StTMa, 7.

82. "A Droger's Daughter," in "Life in Jamaica," Vol.: Parish of Hanover 9HFc, 16.

83. "West Indian in Cuba Writes Encouraging Letter," *The Workman* 7, no. 35 (3 April 1920): 4.

84. Sydney Olivier, *White Capital and Coloured Labour* (New York, 1929), 63. Olivier was governor of Jamaica between 1897 and 1913. He also spent thirty-five years traveling throughout the British Empire, including Africa, Latin America, and the Caribbean, as an agent in the British Colonial Office.

85. "The Labor Rush to Cuba," *The Workman* 7, no. 49 (10 July 1920): 4.

86. "United We Stand," *The Workman* 6, no. 17 (26 April 1919): 4.

87. "Position of Jamaicans in Cuba," *Daily Gleaner* (Kingston), 25 January 1919, 16.

88. "Sam Burt," in "Life in Jamaica," Vol.: Parish of Westmoreland 88Wmb, 3.

89. "Mr. Bert: I Don't agree to Settle in the Western Hemisphere at All, Always want to go to Africa," in "Life in Jamaica," Vol.: Parish of St. Thomas 76St Tmb, 1, 9.

90. Elizabeth Thomas-Hope, "Population Mobility and Land Assets in Hill Farming Areas of Jamaica," *Caribbean Geography* 4, no. 1 (March 1993): 50, 60.

91. Sidney W. Mintz, "The Jamaican Internal Marketing Pattern," *Social and Economic Studies* 4 (1955):95–103; Woodville K. Marshall, "Peasant Development in the West Indies since 1838," in *Rural Development in the Caribbean*, ed. P. I. Gomes (London, 1985), 4–5. See also Post, *Arise Ye Starvelings*, 120.

92. Gisela Eisner, *Jamaica, 1830–1930: A Study in Economic Growth* (Manchester, UK, 1961), 220.

93. "A Man of Jewish Ancestry," in "Life in Jamaica," Vol.: Parish of Manchester b29MMb (recorded July 1973), 1. Identified as "Mass A," the ethnographer described this individual as "an old black man, who was born in 1894." Also see "Mr. Sam," in "Life in Jamaica," Vol.: Parish of West Moreland 88WMb (recorded November 1975), 3; "Mona in Retrospect," in "Life in Jamaica," Vol.: Parish of Kingston 22KMd, (recorded January 1973), 3.

94. George W. Roberts, The Population of Jamaica (Cambridge, UK, 1957) 65.

95. Eisner, Jamaica, 134.

96. "Man Boy," in "Life in Jamaica," Vol.: Parish of Clarendon 5Cmb (recorded April 1975), 12.

97. "Aunt D," in "Life in Jamaica," Vol.: Parish of St. Catherine, 49StcFb (recorded March 1975), 9–10.

98. Judith Blake, Family Structure in Jamaica: The Social Context of Reproduction (New York, 1961), 70. Blake's study is based upon the field survey and interviews of one hundred peasant women and men. Questions asked focused on Jamaican social and family life. Her study began in August 1953 and ended in January 1954. Although the views and attitudes of her respondents were recorded some twenty years beyond the scope of this study, they reveal the values that were undoubtedly handed down by members of the segment of society that lived and worked in Cuba.

99. "A Cart Driving Mother," in "Life in Jamaica," Vol.: Parish of Kingston 16KFd (recorded January 1973) 3–4. Mrs. Bennett's sister continued to live in Cuba until she died in 1973.

100. Blake, Family Structure in Jamaica, 110–27; Edith Clarke, "Land Tenure and the Family in Four Selected Communities in Jamaica," Social and Economic Studies 1, no. 4 (1966): 81–118; Michael Horowitz, Morne-Paysan: Peasant Village in Martinique (Prospect Heights, IL, 1992).

101. Blake, Family Structure in Jamaica, 141.

102. "Miss Lyn," in "Life in Jamaica," Vol.: Parish of Portland 32PFb (November 1973) 7; "A Droger's Daughter," in "Life in Jamaica," Vol.: Parish of Hanover 9HFc (May 1975), 6–8. Hilda Durrant was born in January 1894. Before she left for Cuba, she was studying to be a teacher, until people told her that she could not make any money: "The teaching profession—the money was too cheap so they didn't encourage me to go." P. 6. "Droger" means "old-time people."

103. M. Douglass, "The Idea of Home: A Kind of Space," Social Research 58, no. 1 (1991): 290.

104. John Berger, And Our Faces, My Heart, Brief as Photos (London, 1984); Andrew Dawson, "Cultural Identity and Economic Decision Making in Three Peripheral Areas of Europe," in Constraints on Competitiveness in EC Agriculture: A Comparative Analysis, ed. J. Phelan and M. Henchion (Brussels, 1994); N. J. Rapport, "Busted for Hash: Common Catchwords and Individual Identities in a Canadian City," in Urban Lives: Fragmentation and Resistance, ed. V. Amit-Talai and H. Lustiger-Thaler (Toronto, 1994); N. J. Rapport, "Migrant Selves and Sterotypes: Personal Context in a Postmodern World," in Mapping the Subject: Geographies of Cultural Transformation, ed. S. Pile and N. Thrift (London, 1995).

105. "A Woman Come Down in the World," in "Life in Jamaica," Vol.: Parish of Clarendon 2CFb (recorded April 1975), 14–15.

106. "Happy Struggle but Not So Much Mobility," in "Life in Jamaica," Vol.: Parish of St. Mary 68STm Fc, 11.

107. "Uncle B.: A Miraculous Healing," in "Life in Jamaica," Vol.: Parish of St. Thomas 77St TMc (recorded November 1973), 3, 10.

108. See Beckford, *Persistent Poverty*, 76–77; Sidney Mintz, "The Caribbean as a Socio-Cultural Area," in *Peoples and Culture of the Caribbean*, ed. Michael Horowitz (Garden City, NJ, 1971), 38–39; Charles Wagley, "Plantation-America: A Cultural Sphere," in *Caribbean Studies: A Symposium*, ed. Vera Rubin (Seattle, 1960), 8–9.

109. Sir Spenser St. John, *Hayti, or The Black Republic* (London, 1889), 140.

110. James G. Leyburn, *The Haitian People* (New Haven, 1941), 88–98; Patrick Bellegarde-Smith, *Haiti: The Breached Citadel* (Boulder, CO, 1990), 55–56; Jean Price-Mars, "Class ou Caste?" *Revue de Société d'Histoire et de Géographie d'Haiti* 13, no. 46 (July 1942): 1–50.

111. Benoit Joachim, *Les Racines du Sous-Développement en Haiti* (Port-au-Prince, 1979), 133–35.

112. Alex Dupuy, *Haiti in the World Economy: Class, Race, and Underdevelopment since 1700* (Boulder, CO, 1989), 100.

113. Ibid., 102.

114. Ibid., 103.

115. Mats Lundahl, *Peasants and Poverty: A Study of Haiti* (New York, 1979), 191.

116. See Emily Greene Balch, *Occupied Haiti* (New York, 1972); Bellegarde-Smith, *Haiti*; Suzy Castor, *La ocupación norteamericana de Haiti y sus consecuencias, 1915–1934* (Mexico City, 1971); Joachim, *Les Racines de Sous-Développement*; Kethly Millet, *Les Paysans haïtiens et l'occupation américaine d'Haïti, 1915–1930* (Québec, 1978); David Nicholls, *From Dessalines to Duvalier: Race, Colour and National Independence in Haiti* (Cambridge, UK, 1979).

117. Quoted in Bernarda Sevillano Andrés, *Trascendencia de una cultura marginada: Presencia haitiana en Guantánamo* (Guantánamo, 2007), 62. Between 2000 and 2004, Sevillano Andres interviewed a small number of Cubans of Haitian ancestry whose grandparents or parents came to Cuba during the 1910s and 1920s.

118. Jacques Roumain, *Masters of the Dew* (Oxford, 1944), 44.

119. Samuel Martínez, *Peripheral Migrants: Haitians and Dominican Republic Sugar Plantations* (Knoxville, 1995), 61; Maurice Dartigue, *Conditions rurales en Haiti* (Port-au-Prince, 1938), 30, 38.

120. Martínez, *Peripheral Migrants*, 87.

121. Ibid., 88. Also see Alfred Métraux, *Making a Living in the Maribal Valley (Haiti)* (Paris, 1951), 19; Gerald F. Murray, "The Evolution of Haitian Peasant Land Tenure," 2 vols. (PhD diss., Columbia University, 1977), Vol. 2, 385–86.

122. Murray, "Evolution of Haitian Peasant Land Tenure," 528–32; Ira Lowenthal, "Marriage Is 20 and Children 21: The Cultural Construction of Conjugality and the Family in Rural Haiti" (PhD diss., Johns Hopkins University, 1987), 232.

123. Ira Lowenthal, "Labor, Sexuality and the Conjugal Contract in Rural Haiti," in *Haiti—Today and Tomorrow: An Interdisciplinary Study*, ed. Charles R. Foster and Albert Valdman (Lanham, MD, 1984), 29.

124. Sevillano Andrés, *Trascendencia de una cultura marginada*, 53–54, 64.

125. Ibid., 70.

126. Select Committee on Haiti and Santo Domingo, *Inquiry into the Occupation and Administration of Haiti and Santo Domingo: Hearing before a Select Committee on Haiti and Santo Domingo*, U.S. Senate, 67th Congress, 1st and 2nd Sessions, Senate Report, Vol. 1 (Washington, 1922), 163–64.

127. Ibid., 164.

128. Ibid., 165.

129. Ibid., 262.

130. Ibid., 560.

131. Ibid., 1293.

132. Sevillano Andrés, *Trascendencia de una cultura marginada*, 70.

133. Alberto Pedro Díaz, "Guanamaca: Una comunidad Haitiana," *Etnologia y Folklore* 1 (Jan.–June 1966): 36. As a euphemism, "limpiar botellas" meant performing the sexual act of fellatio. Chati remembers that a large number of women believed this propaganda. As a result, "many women wanted to leave Haiti in order to become rich 'cleaning bottles.'" In addition, the agents used force to keep them in Cuba after they learned the real purpose for their trip to the island.

134. Lara Putnam, *The Company They Kept: Migrants and the Politics of Gender in Caribbean Costa Rica, 1870–1960* (Chapel Hill, 2002), 81.

135. Bonham C. Richardson, *Igniting the Caribbean's Past: Fire in British West Indian History* (Chapel Hill, 2004), 34.

136. Roberts, *The Population of Jamaica*, 136–37. The Jamaican divisions of both the United Fruit Company and the Atlantic Fruit Company announced in the local newspaper that several of their ships sailed from Port Antonio to Santiago de Cuba weekly. See the advertisement page of *The Gleaner*, 8 February 1919, 23. Many Jamaican emigrants also came from the rural towns and villages surrounding Spanish Town and Montego Bay, as well as from the parishes of St. Ann, St. Elizabeth, St. James, St. Mary, and Westmoreland. See Maria Eugenia Espronceda Amor, "La estructura de parentesco del inmigrante bajo una concepción dinámica, el caso jamaicano," *Del Caribe* 31 (2000), 26–32.

137. H. G. de Lisser, *In Jamaica and Cuba* (Kingston, 1910), 149–50.

138. Giovannetti, "Historia visual y etnohistoria," 252.

139. Select Committee on Haiti and Santo Domingo, *Inquiry into the Occupation*, A. Pierre-Paul to A. J. Maumas, letters of 1, 6, and 13 August 1919, S. Rep. Vol. 2, 1356–57; ibid., Maumas to the Haitian Minister of Finance and Commercial Ministerial Palace, 6 July 1921, 1382.

140. Ibid., Vol. 2, (1922), 1307.

141. Robert B. Hoernel, "A Comparison of Sugar and Social Change in Puerto Rico and Oriente, Cuba: 1898–1959" (PhD diss., Johns Hopkins University, 1977), 137; Balch, *Occupied Haiti*, 77–78; confidential report dated 10 September 1925, prepared by Maurice Dunlop, National Archives Branch Depository, College Park, MD, Record Group 84, U.S. Consular Posts Reports, Port-au-Prince, Haiti, Vol. 114, 1925. References to the National Archives, College Park, will hereafter be cited as NA/CP.

142. See AHPSC, Fondo: Gobierno Provincial, Leg. 309, nos. 10–18, 1926. This legajo contains numerous letters from a large number of managers of Oriente sugar mills written to the provincial government requesting passports and other travel documents so that their employees could go abroad to locate workers to cut cane. Many of the letters from these managers include passport pictures of their recruiters, their names, occupations, tenure at the mill, and the frequency of previous trips abroad.

143. Quoted in Díaz, "Guanamaca," 32–33.

144. B. Dartiguenave, Secretary of State for the Interior to the Secretary of State for Finance, 13 July 1921, in Select Committee on Haiti and Santo Domingo, *Inquiry into the Occupation*, S. Rep. Vol. 2, 1386.

145. Eduardo Díaz Ulzurrun to Manuel Rionda, 10 August 1917, Rionda-Braga Papers, Record Group II, Series 1, Box 26 (1897–1917), Smathers Library, University of Florida, Gainesville, Florida. Hereafter cited as Rionda-Braga Papers.

146. *Daily Gleaner*, 8 February 1919, 23. In accordance with the Immigration Law of 1905, Section 2, police permits were issued to British subjects and others residing on the island and who emigrated as laborers. Besides a passport, the permit was a legal document that demonstrated that its holder was a British subject. The British consuls in Cuba recognized these permits, and immigrant workers used them to gain access to their treasury receipts, which covered the cost of their repatriation. See Governor Manning, Kingston, to L. Harcourt, Secretary of State for the Colonies, London, 9 April 1913, National Archive of Jamaica, Record Series: CSO, Governor of Jamaica Dispatches to the Colonial Secretary of State, Reference Code: 1B/5/18/68–1913. Henceforth the National Archive of Jamaica will be cited as NJA.

147. Zanetti et al., *United Fruit Company*, 213.

148. "Gemini," in "Life in Jamaica," Vol.: Parish of St. James 64STjMb (recorded October 1975), 8.

149. See Expedient "contiene communicaciones manuscritos . . . referente al consul de Haiti en Guantánamo informandole al Sr. Gobernador de Oriente sobre el mal trato del vigilante," AHPSC, Fondo: Gobierno Provincial, Leg. 375, no. 27, 1920, Materia: Consulados. Also see the newspaper article "Protection for Jamaicans in Cuba: Engage Attention of Legislative Council," *The Workman* 7, no. 38, 24 April 1920, 1. Established in Panama in 1912, this weekly newspaper was read by British West Indian workers who emigrated to construct the Panama Canal. It published articles and editorials taken from news sources first published in the countries where the workers originated, including Antigua, Barbados, Dominica, Jamaica, St. Lucia, and Trinidad and Tobago. It also published articles from the local presses of the countries to which members of the black diaspora emigrated, such as Cuba, Haiti, the Dominican Republic, and the Unitd States. Initially the organ of the United Brotherhood of Canal Workers, it became a principal source of information for members of the black diaspora living in Panama.

150. Dye, *Cuban Sugar*, 70.

151. Academia de Ciencias de Cuba, *Indice histórico de Camagüey*, 16; Díaz Ulzurrun to M. Rionda, 10 August 1917, Rionda-Braga Papers, RG II, Ser. 1, Box 26 (1897–1917); Hoernel, "A Comparison of Sugar and Social Change," 120.

152. James, *Banes*, 178; Leon Primelles, *Cronica Cubana, 1915–1918: La Reelección de Menocal y la Revolución de 1917. La Danza de los Milliones. La Primera Guerra Mundial* (Havana, 1955), 64, 183, 365, 471; Leon Primelles, *Cronica Cubana, 1919–1922: Menocal y la Liga Nacional Zayas y Crowder, Fin de la Danza de los Milliones y reajuste* (Havana, 1957), 63.

153. "Rev. John B." in "Life in Jamaica," Vol.: Parish of St. Thomas in the East, 75StTMa (recorded February 1975), 7.

154. "Mona in Retrospect," in "Life in Jamaica," Vol.: Parish of Kingston 22KMd (recorded January 1973), 6–7.

155. Quoted in Díaz, "Guanamaca," 30–31.

156. Quoted in Matthew Casey, "Haitians' Labor and Leisure on Cuban Sugar Plantations: The Limits of Company Control," *New West Indian Guide* 85, no. 1–2 (2011): 8–10.

157. Díaz Ulzurrun File, Rionda-Braga Papers, RG II, Ser. 1, Box 26 (1897–1917), Díaz Ulzurrun File. By 1918, the Manatí *central* had decided to spend $15 for every Haitian bracero it recruited to cut sugarcane in its fields. Correspondence of Díaz Ulzurrun, 4 December 1918, ibid., Ser. 10-a-c, Box 9 (1911–43).

158. "Man Boy," in "Life in Jamaica," Vol.: Parish of Clarendon 5CMb (recorded April 1975), 14.

159. "Cuba May Keep Out Jamaicans: Thousands of Our Labourers Are Pouring into the Big Island," *Daily Gleaner*, 13 April 1916, 1.

160. *Louisiana Planter* 53, no. 3 (18 July 1914): 45.

161. "John B.," in "Life in Jamaica," Vol.: Parish of St. Thomas 75StTMa (recorded February 1975), 8.

162. Quoted in James, *Banes*, 179.

2. SUBJUGATION OF THE BRACEROS: LIFE AND WORK ON THE SUGAR ESTATES

1. Ursinio Rojas, *Las luchas obreras en el central Tacajó* (Havana, 1979), 23–24.

2. *Louisiana Planter* 60, no. 8 (23 February 1918): 122.

3. Carr, "'Omnipotent and Omnipresent'?" 264.

4. Letter from Nan Atkinson Risely, Francisco Central, n.d., Rionda-Braga Papers, RG II, Ser. 17, Box 1 (1901–1921); E. Díaz Ulzurrun to Manuel Rionda, Manatí, 3 June 1917, Rionda-Braga Papers, RG II, Ser. 1, Box 26 (1897–1917).

5. Mintz, *Worker in the Cane*, 16.

6. *Louisiana Planter* 62, no. 23 (7 June 1919): 362, and 48, no. 16 (20 April 1912): 281.

7. Mintz, *Worker in the Cane*, 16.

8. Moreno Fraginals, *The Sugarmill*, 94; "Rev. John B.," in "Life in Jamaica," Vol.: Parish of St. Thomas, 75StTMa, 10.

9. Mintz, *Worker in the Cane*, 16; Moreno Fraginals, *The Sugarmill*, 94.

10. *Louisiana Planter* 53 (18 July 1914): 46. The writer's assessment of the skill required of loaders and carreteros to bundle and haul cut cane to the mills means that the black Caribbean braceros should have been considered skilled workers along the lines of the craftsmen who worked in the mill factories processing sugarcane into sugar.

11. "Man Boy," in "Life in Jamaica," Vol.: Parish of Clarendon 5CMb, 27–28.

12. "Mona in Retrospect," in "Life in Jamaica," Vol.: Parish of Kingston 22KMd, 7.

13. Moreno Fraginals, *The Sugarmill*, 73–74.

14. Teresa Casuso, *Cuba and Castro*, trans. Elmer Grossberg (New York, 1961), 54.

15. Alvaro Reynoso, *Ensayo sobre el cultivo de la caña de azúcar* (Havana, 1862); Moreno Fraginals, *The Sugarmill*, 89–91. Moreno Fraginals also mentions that Reynoso's method had been adopted by other sugar producers around the world and was still being used in 1903. Mintz, *Worker in the Cane*, 16–17. Mintz has described Reynoso's planting system, which remained a fundamental element of the sugar industry in Puerto Rico until after World War II. Mintz states that it took hoe men and seeders ten to twelve hours to perform their jobs. E. Díaz Ulzurrun Correspondence, 22 June

1917, Rionda-Braga Papers, RG II, Ser. 1, Box 26 (1897–1917). During the dead season, immigrant laborers also worked inside the mill repairing old equipment or installing new machinery.

16. Ibarra, Cuba, 1898–1921, 166.

17. Zanetti et al., United Fruit Company, 241; Hoernel, "A Comparison of Sugar and Social Change," 124; Louisiana Planter 49, no. 26 (28 December 1912): 435.

18. E. Díaz Ulzurrun Correspondence, 10 January 1916, Rionda-Braga Papers, RG II, Ser. 1, Box 10 (1890–1917). Díaz Ulzurrun informed Manuel Rionda that he had to raise the wages of the cane cutters on the Manatí to eighty cents per 100 arrobas because other companies "around the neighborhood" were paying that price. By the end of the zafra of 1917, the cost of 100 arrobas of cut cane had nearly doubled at the mill, and Ulzurrun reported that his cane cutters were now being paid $1.50. He hoped that this wage rate would help solve the labor shortage. See Díaz Ulzurrun to M. Rionda, 26 July 1917, ibid., Box 26 (1897–1917).

19. Governor Manning to Walter H. Long, Secretary of State for the Colonies, London, 14 April 1917, NJA, Record Series: CSO, Ref. Code 1B/5/18/72, 1917.

20. Louisiana Planter 58, no. 17 (28 April 1917): 265.

21. "News of the Cuban Sugar Industry," Facts About Sugar 5 (11 August 1917): 102; Louisiana Planter 60, no. 2 (12 January 1918): 23. The Senado central was located on the northern coast of Camagüey Province near the port town of Nuevitas.

22. Díaz Ulzurrun to M. Rionda, 30 October 1917, Rionda-Braga Papers, RG II, Ser. 1, Box 26 (1897–1917); Louisiana Planter 60, no. 4 (26 January 1918): 54, and no. 1 (12 March 1918): 184.

23. Gaceta Oficial de la República de Cuba, 4 August 1917, 1941–42. A copy of the Gaceta Oficial may be found in the Manuscript and Rare Books Collections of the Instituto de Literatura y Lingüística de Cuba, Havana, Cuba.

24. Ibid., 1941–1942, Law of 4 August 1917, Articles 1 and 2.

25. Ibid., Article 2.

26. Ibid., Article 5.

27. Zanetti et al., United Fruit Company, 215.

28. James Howard Kunstler, The Geography of Nowhere: The Rise and Decline of America's Man-Made Landscape (New York, 1993), quoted in Samuel Martínez, Decency and Excess: Global Aspirations and Material Deprivations on a Caribbean Sugar Plantation (Boulder, CO, 2007), 33.

29. Carr, "'Omnipotent and Omnipresent'?" 262.

30. Francisco Pérez de la Riva, La habitación rural en Cuba (Havana, 1952), 8.

31. Ibid., 12. Also see Moreno Fraginals, The Sugarmill.

32. Barnet, Biography of a Runaway Slave.

33. Martínez, Decency and Excess, 36.

34. Ibid., 36–37.

35. La historia del central Brasil (entrevista a trabajadores antiguos del central por los años 1917–1935), Archivo Provincial de Camagüey, Anuario Azucarero de Cuba del Año 1956. Henceforth the Archivo Provincial de Camagüey will be referred to as APC.

36. Ana Nuñez Machin, Memoria amarga del azúcar (Havana, 1981), 28–29, 19. How the company stores and moneylenders in Cuba treated the braceros is reminiscent of the patterns of deceit that

similar institutions used to make black sharecroppers indebted to white landlords after emancipation in the United States. See Leon F. Litwack, *Trouble In Mind: Black Southerners in the Age of Jim Crow* (New York, 1998), 130–42. Could the American sugar companies have taken this white southern strategy to Cuba in order to control and appropriate the labor of their black Antillean workers?

37. La legación de la Republique d'Haiti to Orestes Ferrera, Archivo Nacional de Cuba, 1930, Fondo: Donativo y Remisiones, Leg. 390, no. 1. Henceforth the Archivo Nacional de Cuba will be referred to as ANC.

38. "La historia del central Brasil," APC, Anuario Azucarero de Cuba del Año 1956.

39. Nuñez Machin, *Memoria amarga del azúcar*, 18.

40. "Migrant Worker: We Africa, We Africa You Know," in "Life in Jamaica," Vol.: Parish of St. Elizabeth 58SteMb (recorded April 1974), 18–19.

41. "Gemini," in "Life in Jamaica," Vol.: Parish of St. James 64STjMb (recorded October 1975), 7.

42. Academia de Ciencias de Cuba, *Indice histórico* (Havana 1970), 49–50. The Ley Arteaga was considered one of the first victories won by the working class of Cuba. Also see Expediente . . . relativo a la circular expedida por la Secretaria de Gobernación acerca de la total prohibición de pagarla a los obreros y jornaleros de ingenio con vales y fichas, AHPSC, Fondo: Gobierno Provincial, Leg. 308, no. 9, 1923.

43. Wolf and Mintz, "Haciendas and Plantations," 390–91.

44. Martínez, *Decency and Excess*, 36.

45. Pérez de la Riva, *La habitación rural*, 65–66. Also see Harrison, *King Sugar*, 8.

46. Pérez de la Riva, *La habitación rural*, 77; *Louisiana Planter* 53, no. 3 (18 July 1914): 45; Martínez, *Decency and Excess*, 37.

47. Díaz Ulzurrun to the Directors, 12 May 1919, Rionda-Braga Papers, RG II, Ser. 10a-c, Rionda Subfiles, Box 9 (1911–43).

48. Gerard Smith to M. Rionda, 5 January 1919, ibid., Box 8 (1911–1943).

49. Ibid.

50. Sevillano Andrés, *Transcendencia de una cultura marginada*, 65.

51. "Position of Jamaicans in Cuba," *The Gleaner*, 25 January 1919, 16.

52. "Mi historia es tu historia," APC, Informe [histórico] de la industria azucarera de Camagüey.

53. Quoted in James, *Banes*, 179–80.

54. "La historia del central Brasil," APC, Anuario Azucarero de Cuba del Año 1956.

55. Nuñez Machin, *Memoria amarga del azúcar*, 30–32, 33–35. The great influenza pandemic of 1918 killed millions worldwide.

56. "La historia del central Brazil," APC, Anuario Azucarero de Cuba del Año 1956.

57. M. Rionda to G. Smith at Francisco, Camagüey, 27 October 1919, Rionda-Braga Papers, RG II, Ser. 10a-c (1911–43), Box 8; C. H. Forbes Lindsay, *Cuba and Her People of To-Day* (Boston, 1911), 177–78. Also see Primelles, *Crónica Cubana, 1915–1918*, 539.

58. Martínez, *Decency and Excess*, 37.

59. According to the Secretaria de Hacienda de Cuba, *Inmigración y movimiento de pasajeros*, black Antillean immigration peaked dramatically between 1917 and 1921. That period saw 79,247 Haitians and 80,817 Jamaicans officially disembark in Cuba.

60. Hilda Durrant of Hanover Parish, Jamaica, who traveled to Cuba in 1914 to be with her brothers and sister, described the batey on which she worked as a "whole parish—district like." She also referred to the administrator of the mill as the batey's mayor. See "A Droger's Daughter," in "Life in Jamaica," Vol.: Parish of Hanover 9HFc (recorded May 1975), 7.

61. Carr, "'Omnipotent and Omnipresent?'" 275.

62. Louisiana Planter 53, no. 3 (18 July 1914): 45.

63. Robert T. Hill, Cuba and Porto Rico: With Other Islands of the West Indies (New York, 1909), 77.

64. "La historia del central Brasil," APC, Anuario azucarero de Cuba del Año 1956.

65. "Mi historia es tu historia," APC, Informe [histórico] de la industria azucarera de Camagüey.

66. "La historia del central Brazil," APC, Anuario azucarero de Cuba del Año 1956.

67. United Fruit Company, Some Facts Regarding the Development and Operation of the United Fruit Company Sugar Properties in the Republic of Cuba (Preston, Oriente, Cuba, 1944), 44.

68. Quoted in Louisiana Planter 62, no. 17 (26 April 1919): 270.

69. Bourgois, Ethnicity at Work, x.

70. Ibid.

71. "La historia del central Brasil," APC, Anuario Azucarero de Cuba del Año 1956. During the 1920s, the Brasil central was named the Jaronú. It was part of the Compañía Azucarera Cubana, a subsidiary of the American Sugar Refining Company under Cuban administration and direction.

72. "Mi historia es tu historia," APC, "Informe [histórico] de la industria azucarera de Camagüey." George L. Beckford believes that the central objective of the governments of all plantation colonies was to enhance and protect the interests of the plantations within its borders. They therefore never decided to assist in the general welfare of plantation workers. See Beckford's Persistent Poverty, 39–41. However, the United Fruit Company provided the children of its workers with educational facilities, but not until the 1930s and 1940s. See United Fruit Company, Some Facts, 63.

73. Erna Fergusson, Cuba (New York, 1946), 238–39.

74. Ibid., 239.

75. James, Banes, 152–53.

76. "Going Home from Cuba," The Workman 8, no. 10 (9 October 1920): 1.

77. "La historia del central Brazil," APC, Anuario Azucarero de Cuba del Año 1956.

78. Ibid.

79. United Fruit Company, Some Facts, 63; Fergusson, Cuba, 238.

80. Roumain, Masters of the Dew, 50–51.

81. "Mi historia es tu historia," APC, Informe [histórico] de la industria azucarera de Camagüey.

82. Quoted in Chomsky, West Indian Workers, 52–53.

83. Conniff, Black Labor on a White Canal.

84. Juan Pérez de la Riva, "La inmigración antillana en Cuba durante el primer tercio del siglo XX," Revista de la Biblioteca Nacional José Martí 42 (May–August 1975): 84.

85. Juan Jerez Villarreal, Oriente: Biografía de una provincia (Havana, 1960), 312.

86. Carlos Martí, El país de la riqueza (Madrid, 1918), 215.

87. Kenneth F. Kiple, The Caribbean Slave: A Biological History (Cambridge, UK, 1984), 178.

88. Kenneth F. Kiple and Virginia H. King, *Another Dimension to the Black Diaspora: Diet, Disease, and Racism* (Cambridge, UK, 1981), 176–82.

89. Kiple, *The Caribbean Slave*, 179. Also see Alejandra Bronfman, *Measures of Equality: Social Science, Citizenship, and Race in Cuba, 1902–1940* (Chapel Hill, 2004), 1–67; Aline Helg, "Race in Argentina and Cuba, 1880–1930: Theory, Policies, and Popular Reaction," in *The Idea of Race in Latin America, 1870–1940*, ed. Richard Graham (Austin, 1990).

90. "Emigration to Big Island: Cuban Officials Alarmed at the Growing Invasion of Jamaicans," *The Gleaner*, 20 December 1916, 6.

91. "El peligro negro," in "Arreglando el mundo," *La Prensa* (Havana), 25 March 1916, 8.

92. Paul Gordon and David Rosenberg, *Daily Racism: The Press and Black People in Britain* (London, 1989), 24.

93. Ibid., 3.

94. "Calamar en tinta," in "Palpitaciones de la Raza de Color,"*La Prensa* (Havana), 15 March 1916, 4. A copy of this article may be found in the Rionda-Braga Papers, RG II, Ser. 10a-c (1911–43), Box 54. Tristán was the essayist Ramón Vasconceles, who commented on black issues.

95. *La Prensa*, 15 March 1916, 4.

96. *Havana Evening News*, 11 November 1922, page n.a. This paper was published for the English-speaking community of Havana. The authorities initially covered up the massacre, which finally came to light after the editor of the afternoon daily, A. D. Roberts, discovered documents related to the army's investigation and published an account of the crime on 8 November 1922. News of the alleged murders caused a couple of former army officers to later break into the office of the newspaper and ransack it, damaging the press and the type-setting equipment. The men also attacked and beat up Roberts while he tried to protect his property.

97. Administrador del central Palma Soriano to Sr. Gobernador de Oriente, 5 Marzo 1919, AHPSC, Fondo: Gobierno Provincial, Leg. 304, no. 21, 1919.

98. Bourgois, *Ethnicity at Work*, x.

99. Ibid.

100. Fe Iglesias García, "Caracteristicas de la inmigración Española in Cuba, 1904–1930," *Económia y Desarrollo* 2 (March–April 1988): 94.

101. *Louisiana Planter*, 65, no. 23 (4 December 1920): 360.

102. Iglesias García, "Caracteristicas de la inmigración," 96.

103. Report on the Blue Book of Jamaica, 1918–1919, Section VII, Vital Statistics and Public Health, 8 November 1919, from Acting Governor H. Bryan to the Viscount Milner, NAJ, Record Series: CSO, Governor of Jamaica Dispatches to the Colonial Secretary of State, Ref. Code: 1B/5/18/74-1919; "The Tide of Emigration in Jamaica," *Daily Gleaner*, 28 August 1920, page n.a.

104. "Secretaria de agricultura ejecutaré La Ley de inmigración," *Diario de la Marina* (Havana), 16 December 1922. The census of 1919 revealed that 10,136 Haitians and 23,754 Jamaicans arrived that year, out of a total of 39,925 immigrants. Where the editors of the paper obtained the annual figure of 72,855 black immigrants is anyone's guess. If the same number of Haitians and Jamaicans entered the island in 1920 as in 1919, their total number only would have been 67,780. See Cuba, Dirección del Censo, *Census of the Republic of Cuba, 1919* (Havana, 1922), 184.

105. *Diario de la Marina*, 16 December 1922.

106. Godfrey Haggard, British Legation, Havana, to Carlos Manuel de Céspedes, Secretary of State for Foreign Affairs of Cuba, 3 January 1924 to 8 March 1924, National Archive of Great Britain at Kew Gardens, Foreign Office, Cuba No. 1 (1924), Correspondence Between His Majesty's Government and the Cuban Government Respecting the Ill-Treatment of British West Indian Labourers in Cuba. The correspondence of Haggard and Céspedes may also be found in the British Parlimentary Papers, 1924 (Cmd. 2158), Vol. 26. For the circumstances surrounding the murder of Oscar Taylor, see E. Brice, British Consul in Santiago de Cuba, to the Governor of Oriente, José Barcelo, 18 March 1923, AHPSC, Fondo: Gobierno Provincial, Leg. 786, no. 31, 1923, Expediente: Inmigración.

107. "Un Jamaicano fue herido gravemente en Bayate," La Independencia (Santiago de Cuba), 12 March 1921.

108. Godfrey Haggard to Carlos Manuel de Céspedes, 3 January 1924, GB, FO, Cuba, No. 1.

109. David Theo Goldberg, The Racial State (Malden, MA, 2002), 129.

110. Consul de Haiti en Guantánamo to Sr. Gobernador de Oriente, 21–26 January 1920, AHPSC, Fondo: Gobierno Provincial, Leg. 375, no. 27, 1920.

111. Ibid. During the colonial period as well as under apartheid, the Dutch of South Africa used the term kaffir derogatively to refer to the indigenous people.

112. "Haitiano herido en Cabonica," La Independencia (Santiago de Cuba), 12 March 1921.

113. Consul del Haiti en Santiago de Cuba to Gobernador Provincial, 12 January–9 March 1923, AHPSC, Fondo: Gobierno Provincial, Leg. 376, no. 4, 1923. Fis was killed on Sunday, 31 December 1922. The fact that the police buried his body the night of his death raised Laporte's suspicions and caused him to request the formal investigation.

114. "Sucesos de Policía," El Cubano Libre (Santiago de Cuba), 12 January 1924.

3. SOCIAL STRATEGIES OF RESISTANCE: THE DISCLOSED AND UNDISCLOSED LIVES OF BLACK CARIBBEAN BRACEROS

1. "La historia del central Brasil," APC, Anuario Azucarero de Cuba del Año 1956.

2. Sub-Secretario en la Habana to Gobernador Provincial de Oriente, 30 August 1913, AHPSC, Fondo: Gobierno Provincial, Leg. 786, no. 2.

3. Scott, Domination and the Arts of Resistance, 65. Scott believes that such assemblies can be compared to working-class cafés and to the "hush arbors" of African slaves. As privileged social sites, the autonomous assemblies reflect the efforts among subordinates to resist their inferiority.

4. James, Banes, 180.

5. Leslie G. Desmangles, The Faces of the Gods: Vodou and Roman Catholicism in Haiti (Chapel Hill, 1992), 64.

6. Ibid.

7. G. Smith to Fanjul, 12 October 1917, Rionda-Braga Papers, RG II, Ser. 1, Box 22 (1897–1917).

8. Labor Conditions in Port-au-Prince, report by Maurice P. Dunlop, American Consul, August 16–22, 1924, NA/CP, RG 84, Record of Consular Posts, Port-au-Prince, Haiti, Vol. 112, 1924.

9. Unreliability of Haitian Birth Certificates, Maurice P. Dunlop, American Consul, August 3, 1925, ibid., Vol. 114.

10. Sevillano Andrés, Trascendencia de una cultura marginada, 57–58.

11. Ibid.; Samuel Martínez, *Peripheral Migrants*, 121–22.

12. Sevillano Andrés, *Trascendencia de una cultura marginada*, 70.

13. Martínez, *Peripheral Migrants*, 123.

14. Gobernador de Oriente to Secretario de Agricultura, Commercio y Trabajo, 3 August, 1921, AHPSC, Fondo: Gobierno Provincial, Leg. 2228, no. 15, 1910–1925, Materia: Prostitución. In order to underscore the impact that prostitution had on the sugarcane workers and on society in general, the governor added to his report two articles from *El Cubano Libre* (Santiago de Cuba) and *Diario del Pueblo* (Guantánamo) that discussed the role of Haitian women in this occupation.

15. Martínez, *Decency and Excess*, 83.

16. "Estampas de Barracón," oral interview of Orlando González by Oscar E. Arbesón Estévez, in José Zurita Fadraga, Informe [histórico] de la Industria de Azucarera de Camagüey, La historia del central Algodones, 1917-30 (mimeograph copy 28 August 1968), APC. Gonzalez worked on the colonia San Miguel attached to the Algodones. Academia de Ciencias de Cuba, *Indice histórico de Camagüey*, 70. It is important to note that the former Cuban president José Miguel Gómez was one of the partners who owned the Algodones. In 1917, politics seem to have trumped economics when the liberal forces led by Miguel Gómez attacked the mill in March, disrupting its harvest and suspending its operation until April. Nevertheless, once the Algodones started grinding again, it was able to produce 40,000 sacks of raw sugar from the harvest of 1917, according to González.

17. Jesús Guanche and Dennis Moreno, *Caidije* (Santiago de Cuba, 1988), 28; Sevillano Andrés, *Trascendencia de una cultura marginada*, 65.

18. Guanche and Moreno, *Caidije*, 29.

19. Joel James, José Millet, and Alexis Alarcón, *El Vodú en Cuba* (Santiago de Cuba, 1998), 70.

20. Guanche and Moreno, *Caidije*, 29; Select Committee on Haiti and Santo Domingo, S. Rep., Vol. 2, 9 March 1922, 1284.

21. "Mi historia es tu historia," APC, "Informe [histórico] de la industria de azucarera de Camagüey." This is the third document found in this "Informe [histórico]." It is a transcription of another interview by Oscar E. Arbesón Estévez with an unnamed field worker who also labored on the San Miguel colonia attached to the Algodones mill.

22. Rojas, *Las luchas obreras*, 23.

23. "Mi historia es tu historia," APC, "Informe [histórico] de la industria de azucarera de Camagüey."

24. James, *Banes*, 180.

25. M. Dunlop to U.S. State Department, Washington, D.C., 16 August 1924, NA/CP, RG 84, U.S. Consular Posts, U.S Consul, Port-au-Prince, Haiti, Vol. 112, 1924, file no. 844; Dunlop to U.S. State Department, 10 September 1925, ibid., RG 84, U.S. Consular Posts, Vol. 114, 1925, file no. 856.

26. Dunlop to the State Department, 10 September 1925, NA/CP, RG 84, U.S. Consular Posts, Vol. 114, 1925, file no. 856. Because of the poor condition of the documents in Record Group 84, some include file and page numbers, while the majority do not. Most records can be located according to the volume number and the date of the correspondence.

27. Rojas, *Las luchas obreras*, 35.

28. Incoming correspondence of Gerard Smith, 12 October 1919, Rionda-Braga Papers, RG II, Ser. 1, Box 22 (1897–1917).

29. "Man Boy," in "Life in Jamaica," Vol.: Parish of Clarendon 5CMb, 28. Mr. Fearon mentioned that the amount of a carretero's wages and savings were determined by whether the driver owned or rented a team of oxen. If they were rented, the driver had to give a portion of his salary to the owner of the oxen. "If they belonged to you then the $40.00 one earned that day is yours."

30. Rojas, Las luchas obreras, 35.

31. Miguel Barnet, Afro-Cuban Religions, trans. Christine Renata Ayorinde (Kingston, 2001), 82.

32. Michel S. Laguerre, Voodoo Heritage (London, 1980), 28.

33. Quoted in Maureen Warner-Lewis, Central Africa in the Caribbean: Transcending Time, Transforming Cultures (Kingston, Jamaica, 2003), 232–33.

34. Guanche and Moreno, Caidije, 103.

35. John V. Taylor, The Primal Vision: Christian Presence amid African Religion (Philadelphia, 1963), 65–66. Also cited in Desmangles, The Faces of the Gods, 64.

36. Desmangles, The Faces of the Gods, 86.

37. Guanche and Moreno, Caidije, 109.

38. Barnet, Afro-Cuban Religions, 117.

39. Laguerre, Voodoo Heritage, 184; Desmangles, The Faces of the Gods, 69.

40. Desmangles, The Faces of the Gods, 69.

41. Roumain, Masters of the Dew, 87–88. Legba, the principal deity, or loa, in the Vodun religion, sits atop the pantheon of gods. According to Harold Courlander, he is a Dahomean god "characterized as a limping old man. [A person] possessed by Legba may cavort about on a kind of cane-crutch called a Legba stick." Harold Courlander, The Drum and the Hoe: Life and Lore of the Haitian People (Berkeley, 1960), 21–22. Legba's Catholic identity is Saint Anthony. Legba is empowered to patrol the plane that separates the divine from the ordinary worlds. He opens the door for his followers to encounter the other loa. Legba is also charged with protecting the faithful while at home and during their journeys. As a result, he is known as the Master of the Crossroads. See Alfred Métraux, Haiti: Black Peasants and Voodoo (New York, 1960), 60–61.

42. Métraux, Haiti, 70.

43. Warner-Lewis, Central Africa in the Caribbean, 221; Guanche and Moreno, Caidije, 112.

44. "Estampas de Barracón," subfile, APC, Informe [histórico] de la industria azucarera de Camagüey.

45. Jualynne E. Dodson, Sacred Spaces and Religious Traditions in Oriente Cuba (Albuquerque, 2008), 116.

46. Laguerre, Voodoo Heritage, 17; Barnet, Afro-Cuban Religions, 18.

47. Melville J. Herskovits, Life in a Haitian Valley (1937; repr., New York, 1975), 17–24.

48. Métraux, Haiti, 70.

49. For the years 1921 to 1925, see Expediente referente a la inmigración del quinquenales de 1921–1925, ANC, Fondo: Secretaria de la Presidencia, Leg. 121, Exp. 18; for the 1926–1930 period, see Estadisticas impresa, editada por la sección de Estadística de la Secretaria de Hacienda relativa a inmigración y movimiento de pasajeros años de 1930 y comparaciónes con el año 1929, ANC, Fondo: Donativos y Remisiones, Leg. 403, no. 11.

50. Sergio Valdes Bernal, "La inmigración en Cuba: Estudio lingüístico-histórico," Anales del Caribe 7–8 (1987–1988): 224.

51. See Howard, Changing History.

52. William Safran, "Deconstructing and Comparing Diaspora," in *Diaspora, Identity and Religion: New Directions in Theory and Research*, ed. Wlatraud Kokot and Khachig Toloyan (London, 2004), 13–17.

53. See McLeod, "Undesirable Aliens," 599–623.

54. James, Millet, and Alarcón, *El Vodú en Cuba*, 74–76.

55. Casey, "Haitians' Labor and Leisure," 11; Díaz, "Guanamaca," 30.

56. Julio Corbea, "La comunidad Cubana-Haitiana de la Caridad," *Del Caribe* 1, nos. 3–4 (Jan.–June 1984): 62. Cubans often used *pichón* (squab) to refer to the child of a Haitian born on the island.

57. Díaz, "Guanamaca," 34; Estampas de Barracón, APC, Informe de la historia de la central Algodones. The Haitian informants that Díaz interviewed in 1966 had arrived in Cuba in 1910. Felipe García and Pablo Pérez worked as macheteros on the Uruguay plantation. Amado Fernández also worked as a machetero, but on the Jaronú. He remained a cane cutter after the Jaronú became the Brasil in 1921.

58. Guanche and Moreno, *Caidije*, 22–23.

59. See Richard D. E. Burton, "Names and Naming in Afro-Caribbean Cultures," in *New West Indian Guide* 73, nos. 1–2 (1999): 35–58, quoted in Jean Besson, *Martha Brae's Two Histories: European Expansion and Caribbean Culture-Building in Jamaica* (Chapel Hill, 2002), 23–24.

60. See Jerome S. Handler and JoAnn Jacoby, "Slave Names and Naming in Barbados," *William and Mary Quarterly*, 3rd Ser., 53, no. 4 (1996): 685–726.

61. Díaz, "Guanamaca," 34.

62. Alcalde municipal de Baracoa to Gobernador de Oriente, 5 February 1918, AHPSC, Fondo: Gobierno Provincial, Leg. 786, no. 8, Expediente: Inmigración, 1918.

63. Secretaría de Agricultura, Comercio y Trabajo, *Legislación obrera de la República de Cuba. Leyes y disposiciones vigentes* (Havana, 1919), 210–23. The 3 August 1917 law became effective under Decree Number 1707 of 29 October 1917.

64. Díaz, "Guanamaca," 34.

65. Valdes Bernal, "La inmigración en Cuba," 225.

66. Sub-Secretario, La Habana, to Gobernador Provincial de Oriente, 30 August 1913, AHPSC, Fondo: Gobierno Provincial, Leg. 786, no. 2, Expediente: Inmigración.

67. Alcalde municipal, Palma Soriano, to Provincial Governor, 15 September 1913, AHPSC, Fondo: Gobierno Provincial, Leg. 786, no. 2.

68. Giovannetti, "Historia visual y etnohistoria," 227.

69. Espronceda Amor, "La estructura de parentesco," 29.

70. Blake, *Family Structure in Jamaica*, 71.

71. "Man Boy," in "Life in Jamaica," Vol.: Parish of Claredon 5CMb (recorded April 1975), 9–10. A pupil-teacher was qualified to give exams to persons who sought the same amount of education as they had, according to Mr. Fearon.

72. Conniff, *Black Labor on a White Canal*, 39, 69; United Fruit Company, *Some Facts*, 63.

73. "A Highly Protected Mother," in "Life in Jamaica," Vol.: Parish of Claredon 1Cfa (recorded June 1975), 6; "Aunt D," in "Life in Jamaica," Vol.: Parish of St. Catherine 49STcFb (recorded March 1975), 9.

74. Blake, *Family Structure in Jamaica*, 71.

75. Jorge L. Giovannetti, "The Elusive Organization of 'Identity': Race, Religion, and Empire among Caribbean Migrants in Cuba," *Small Axe* 19, no. 1 (March 2006): 4. The Episcopal and Methodist churches also catered to the spiritual needs of British West Indians working in Guantánamo.

76. Robert J. Stewart, *Religion and Society in Post-Emancipation Jamaica* (Knoxville, 1992), xviii.

77. Warner-Lewis, *Central Africa in the Caribbean*, 145.

78. Ibid., 147; Monica Schuler, "Myalism and the African Religious Tradition in Jamaica," in *Africa and the Caribbean: The Legacies of a Link*, ed. Franklin Knight and Margaret E. Crahan (Baltimore, 1979), 72–76.

79. Stewart, *Religion and Society*, xix.

80. Warner-Lewis, *Central Africa in the Caribbean*, 148–53.

81. Karl Laman, *The Kongo*, Vol. 3 (Uppsala, 1962), 177.

82. Schuler, "Myalism," 66.

83. Quoted in Stewart, *Religion and Society*, 132.

84. "Rev. John B.," in "Life in Jamaica," Vol.: Parish of St. Thomas 75StTMa, 8. Ms. Laura McKenzie of Kellits in Clarendon Parish discussed how when she was seventeen years old, her father sold all of his possessions and property in order to take his wife and children to Cuba in 1915. Although she had to stay in Clarendon to take care of her older sister, she eventually joined her parents in Cuba. See "A Woman Down in the World," in "Life in Jamaica," Vol.: Parish of Clarendon, 2CFb, (recorded April 1975), 15.

85. Quoted in Espronceda Amor, "La estructura de parentesco," 28.

86. Gloría Rolando, *My Footsteps in Baraguá* (documentary film), Images of the Caribbean (1996).

87. Giovannetti, "Historia visual y etnohistoria," 230, 234–37.

88. Rob Ruch, "Three Kings Day in Consuelo: Cricket, Baseball, and the Cocolos in San Pedro de Macoris," in *Sport in Latin America and the Caribbean*, ed. Joseph L. Arbena and David G. La France (Wilmington, DE, 2002), 76, 79, 80.

89. Reglamento de La Estrella Naciente de Cuba, 1917–24, AHPSC, Fondo: Gobierno Provincial, Leg. 914, no. 8, 1918, Materia: Logias. This organization existed until 1953.

90. Scott, *Domination and the Arts of Resistance*, 56. Scott argues that the subordinate class's organizations had to present a public façade to prove their nonthreatening nature to the dominant class.

91. Ibid., 118–23. Scott argues that subordinate groups tend to create places where they are able to meet outside the watchful eyes of the dominant group in order to "formulate patterns of resistance."

92. "Master Carpenter," in "Life in Jamaica," Vol.: Parish of St. Ann 46STAMa (recorded 1975), 11–12.

93. Chomsky, *West Indian Workers*, 187.

94. La Estrella Naciente de Cuba, AHPSC, Fondo: Gobierno Provincial, Leg. 914, no. 8, 1918.

95. La Estrella de Belen Central Numero Uno, AHPSC, Fondo: Gobierno Provincial, Leg. 914, no. 15, 1920.

96. Stewart, *Religion and Society*, 62–63.

97. AHPSC, Fondo: Gobierno Provincial, Leg. 916, no. 2, 1927, Materia: Logias.

98. Giovannetti, "The Elusive Organization of 'Identity,'" 3. Giovannetti argues that black Caribbean workers developed certain identities to address and solve a number of problems in Cuba.

99. "Migrant Worker: We a Africa, We a Africa You Know," in "Life In Jamaica," Vol.: Parish of St Elizabeth 58Ste Mb (recorded April 1974), 18.

100. "Mona in Retrospect," in "Life in Jamaica," Vol.: Parish of Kingston 22KMd (recorded in 1973), 7.

101. Reglamento de La Brillante Estrella de Cuba,"
AHPSC, Fondo: Gobierno Provincial, Leg. 914, no. 13, 1911, Materia: Logias.

102. Ibid.

103. Ibid.

104. Scott, *Domination and the Arts of Resistance*, 132–33.

105. Chomsky, *West Indian Workers*, 188–89.

106. West Indian Star: Instruction and Sport, 21 October 1930, ANC, Fondo: Registro de Asociaciones, Leg. 313, Expediente 9093, no. 54.

107. Ibid.

108. Harpelle, *The West Indians of Costa Rica*, 50.

109. "What Others Think About the Negro," *The Workman* 7, no. 23 (10 January 1920): 4.

110. Ibid.

111. Ibid.

112. "Mr. Bert: I don't agree to settle in the Western Hemisphere at All. Always want to go to Africa," in "Life in Jamaica," Vol.: Parish of St. Thomas 76StTMb (recorded November 1973), 1.

113. Conniff, *Black Labor on a White Canal*, 65.

114. El Correro del Atlantico (Limón, Costa Rica), 18 February 1915, 1. Quoted in Jeffrey Casey, *Limón, 1880–1940: Un estudio de la industria bananera en Costa Rica* (San Jose, 1979), 125.

115. Nancy Foner, "Towards a Comparative Perspective on Caribbean Migration," in *Caribbean Migration: Globalised Identities*, ed. Mary Chamberlain (London, 1998), 51.

116. Marcus Garvey, "The Race Question in Jamaica," in *Consequences of Class and Color: West Indian Perspectives*, ed. David Lowenthal and Lambros Comitas (Garden City, 1973), 4–5.

117. "All Aboard for Cuba," *The Workman* 7, no. 51 (24 July 1920): 4.

4. THE EVOLUTION AND EXPRESSION OF A WORKER CONSCIOUSNESS: BLACK CARIBBEAN PROTEST, RESISTANCE, AND THE CUBAN LABOR MOVEMENT

1. *The Workman* 6, no. 24 (14 June 1914): 1.

2. See Secretaria de Hacienda de Cuba, *Inmigración y movimiento de pasajeros*, for the 1917–21 figures; Expediente referente a la inmigración del quinquenales de 1921–1925, ANC, Fondo: Secretaria de la Presidencia, Leg. 121, Exp. 18. For the year 1926, consult ANC, Fondo: Donativos y Remisiones, Leg. 403, no. 11.

3. *Louisiana Planter* 60, no. 10 (9 March 1918): 150–51.

4. Ibid., 60, no. 2 (12 January 1918): 23; "Barbados Recruiting Agency, Cuba's Rival Attractions," The Workman 7, no. 34 (27 March 1920): 2.

5. "Rev. John B," in "Life in Jamaica," Vol.: Parish of St. Thomas 75St Tma (recorded 1975), 8–9.

6. Barry Carr, "Identity, Class, and Nation: Black Immigrant Workers, Cuban Communism, and the Sugar Insurgency, 1925–1934," in Marginal Migrations: Circulation of Culture Within the Caribbean, ed. Shalini Puri (Oxford, 2003), 77–108. Carr argues that large numbers of Haitians sought better wages and working conditions on the coffee farms of Oriente after the mid-1920s. It appears that their display of power began when their labor was viewed as critical to the expansion of the sugar industry.

7. Carr, "'Omnipotent and Omnipresent'?" 265, 262.

8. Quoted in Louisiana Planter 62, no. 12 (22 March 1919): 185.

9. Ibid.

10. Sir Leslie Probyn, Governor of Jamaica to Secretary of State of the Colonies, 3 April 1919, "Alleged Ill-Treatment of Jamaicans in Cuba," NAJ, Ref. Code, 1B/5/18/74, 1919, CSO.

11. Louisiana Planter 62, no. 12 (22 March 1919): 185.

12. "Protection for Jamaicans in Cuba," quoted in The Workman 7, no. 38 (24 April 1920): 1.

13. "Mi historia es tu historia," and "La historia del central Algodones," APC, Informe [histórico] de la Industria de Azúcar de Camagüey.

14. Telegrams to Señor Gobernador Provincial de Santiago de Cuba from Ramón Ros, Administrador de Distintos Ingenios de la Jurisdición de Manzanillo, 25 March 1916 to 4 April 1916, AHPSC, Fondo: Gobierno Provincial, Leg. 307, no. 1, Materia: Centrales.

15. E. F. Torres, Jefe de Regimiento No. 3, to Gobernador de Santiago de Cuba, 4 April 1916, AHPSC, Fondo: Gobierno Provincial, Leg. 307, no. 1.

16. Louisiana Planter 60, no. 8 (23 February 1918): 119.

17. Ibid., 60, no. 7 (16 February 1918): 103.

18. Communications from Sr. Federico Fernández, administrador de la central America, to Sr. Gobernador, comunicado el incendio intencional en sus caña verales, AHPSC, Fondo: Gobierno Provincial, Leg. 307, no. 20, 1919.

19. Office of the Commandant U.S. Naval Station, Guantánamo Bay, Cuba, to Edward Wise, American Consul, 1 April 1918, NA/CP, RG 84, Record of Foreign Service Posts, Guantánamo, Cuba, Vol. 19, 1918; AHPSC, Fondo: Gobierno Provincial, Exp. Inmigración, Leg. 787. Tallon was considered an agent of the Industrial Workers of the World.

20. Kirwin R. Shaffer, Anarchism and Countercultural Politics in Early Twentieth-Century Cuba (Gainesville, FL, 2005), 56.

21. Communications from Gobernador to Alcalde Municipal de Santiago de Cuba y los todos centrales de la Provincia, 4 January 1918 to 14 December 1918, AHPSC, Fondo: Gobierno Provincial, Leg. 307, no. 16, 1918.

22. Ibid., 6 January 1918.

23. Ibid., 7 January 1918.

24. Caña quemada en todo la provincia desde el comienzo de la zafra en Decembre 1924 hasta 28 Febrero 1925, AHPSC, Fondo: Gobierno Provincial, Leg. 2877, no. 5, 1921–29.

25. Bonham Richardson, *Igniting the Caribbean's Past: Fire in British West Indian History* (Chapel Hill, 2004), 1–4.

26. Instituto de Historia del Movimiento Comunista, *Historia del movimiento obrero Cubano, 1865–1958*, I, 197.

27. Ibid., 197.

28. U.S. Commission on Cuban Affairs, *Problems of the New Cuba* (New York, 1935), 82–83.

29. Ibid., 82.

30. Ibid., 82–83.

31. Joseph Buck to the American Minister in Havana, 14 January 1918, 17 January 1918, NA/CP, RG 84, Record of Foreign Service Posts, Consular Posts, Antilla, Cuba, Vol. 37, 1918–19, Doc. No. 850, 4.

32. Harold Harty, manager, United Fruit Co. Banes Division, to Joseph F. Buck, 19 February 1918, 20 March 1918, and 25 April 1918, American Vice Consul, Antilla, Oriente, ibid.

33. Scott, *Domination and the Arts of Resistance*, 95.

34. *Louisiana Planter* 52, no. 22 (31 May 1919): 350.

35. W. B. Houston to H. Clum, 7 May 1919, NA/CP, RG 84, Vol. 25.

36. *Louisiana Planter* 52, no. 22 (31 May 1919): 350.

37. Ibid., 351.

38. Richardson, *Igniting the Caribbean's Past*, 5–6.

39. Harpelle, *The West Indians of Costa Rica*, 45; Giovannetti, "Historia visual y etnohistoria en Cuba," 234–35.

40. Probyn to Milner, 3 April 1919, Governor of Jamaica Dispatches to Colonial Secretary of the Colonies, NAJ, Ref. Code 1B/5/18/74-1919, Record Series: CSO.

41. Probyn to Viscount Milner, 2/ December 1919, ibid. Also see *Louisiana Planter* 62, no. 16 (19 April 1919): 250.

42. Instituto de Historia del Movimiento Comunista, *Historia del movimiento obrero Cubano 1865–1958*, I, 178–79.

43. H. C. Prinsen Geerlings, *Cane Sugar and Its Manufacturing*, 10.

44. Mintz, *Sweetness and Power*, 187.

45. "Protection for Jamaicans in Cuba: Engage Attention of Legislative Council," quoted in *Daily Gleaner*, 10 April 1920, 1. This news story was the paper's main headline. The matter of sending special Jamaican government officials to Cuba in order to protect the interests and rights of their emigrants appeared as early as 1913. Governor Manning had raised this subject during discussions with members of the Legislative Council in December. The Council rejected Manning's appeal to provide special protection for Jamaican emigrants in Cuba on the grounds that the Council "had refused to do so for laborers in Central America." See W. H Manning to Lewis Harcourt, 5 December 1919, NAJ, Governor of Jamaica Dispatches to the Colonial Secretary of State for the Colonies, Ref. Code 1B/5/18/68-1919, Record Series: CSO.

46. McGillivray, *Blazing Cane*, 114; Harpelle, *The West Indians of Costa Rica*, ch. 3; Giovannetti, "Historia visual y etnohistoria en Cuba," 233–35.

47. *Daily Gleaner*, 10 April 1920, 1.

48. Eisner, *Jamaica*, 149–50.

49. "British Emissary Arrives at Havana," The Workman 8, no. 7 (18 September 1920): 1; "With Cuban Republic Somewhat Strained," The Workman 8, no. 2 (24 August 1920): 1. Both articles were taken from several news reports of 6 July published in the Havana Evening News, El Mercurio, and El Heraldo.

50. Shaffer, Anarchism and Countercultural Politics, 3. There were other Cuban anarchists who supported the ideas of the Russian anarchist Peter Kropotkin. They were called anarcho-communists and believed in the principle of "from each according to his ability to each according to his need."

51. Meaker, The Revolutionary Left in Spain, 6–7.

52. Forman, Nationalism and the International Labor Movement, 37.

53. Quoted in Ibarra, Cuba: 1898–1921, 145.

54. Ibid.

55. Ibid.

56. Quoted in Post, Arise Ye Starvelings, 3. Huiswoud made this statement in Kingston, Jamaica, in 1929 while he debated the Pan-African nationalist leader Marcus M. Garvey.

57. Ibid., 133.

58. Ibarra, Cuba: 1898–1921, 148.

59. Magoon, Report of the Provisional Governor, 47.

60. Ibid., 49.

61. Thomas, Cuba, 544–46; Jenks, Our Cuban Colony, 213–14.

62. Jenks, Our Cuban Colony, 285.

63. Louisiana Planter 66, no. 6 (5 February 1921): 90, and no. 9 (26 February 1921): 134.

64. Expediente referente a la inmigración del quinquenales de 1921–25, ANC, Fondo: Secretaria de la Presidencia, Leg. 121, Exp. 18.

65. "Emigration to Cuba, Strongly Condemned by One Who Returns," The Workman 8, no. 52 (30 July 1921): 1.

66. Eduardo Díaz Ulzurrun, Manatí central, to Manuel Rionda, New York City, 5 January 1921, Rionda-Braga Papers, RG II, Ser. 10a-c (1911–43), Subfiles Box 75; M. Rionda to E. Ulzurrun, 28 December 1921, ibid., RG II, Ser. 10a-c, Box 15, 1911–43. Ratoons were cane saplings grown from the roots of old cut canes. Ordinary laborers who worked around the batey received 80 cents to $1.00 per day during the 1922 zafra.

67. "Conditions in Cuba," The Workman 8, no. 51 (23 July 1921): 2.

68. Post, Arise Ye Starvelings, 175; Scott, Domination and the Arts of Resistance, 111.

69. See Scott, Domination and the Arts of Resistance, 103.

70. Quoted in Post, Arise Ye Starvelings, 177.

71. Quoted in Murray Bookchin, The Spanish Anarchists: The Heroic Years, 1868–1936 (New York, 1977), 46–51.

72. Instituto de Historia del Movimiento Comunista y de la Revolución Socialista de Cuba, El movimiento obrero Cubano: Documentos y articulos, Vol. 1 (1865–1925) (Havana, 1981), 143.

73. Ibarra, Cuba: 1898–1921, 144.

74. Dumoulin, Azúcar y lucha, 13; Instituto de Historia del Movimiento Comunista, El movimiento obrero Cubano, I, 183.

75. Dumoulin, Azúcar y lucha, 181–82. Dumoulin argues that the leaders of the 1917 strike in the sugar industry decided to focus on the skilled industrial workers because they shared a number of

traits that made their organization less problematic, namely their shared ethnicity and language, their concentrated numbers inside the mill factories, and their alledged collective discipline.

76. Primelles, *Cronica Cubana*, 1915–1918, 499–500.

77. APC, Fondo: Gobierno Provincial, Leg. 46, Exp. 12, 1916.

78. Philip S. Foner, *Organized Labor and the Black Worker*, 1916–1981 (New York, 1974), 75.

79. Telleria, *Los congresos obreros*, 76; Shaffer, *Anarchism and Countercultural Politics*, 57.

80. Foner, *Organized Labor and the Black Worker*, 75; Keith P. Griffler, *What Price Alliance? Black Radicals Confront White Labor, 1918–1938* (New York, 1995), 19–20.

81. See *¡Tierra!* (Havana), 27 November 1924, 1; El *Progreso* (Havana), 29 November 1924, 3.

82. "Los jamaiquinos abandonaron el trabajo en el Mariel," El *Mundo*, 8 March 1921, 1; Primelles, *Cronica Cubana*,1915–1918, 412.

83. "La vigilancia en las fincas azucareras," El *Mundo*, 14 March 1921, 2.

84. Quoted in Giovannetti, "The Elusive Organization of 'Identity,'" 6.

85. Oscar Zanetti et al., *United Fruit Company*; Alejandro García Álvarez, *Caminos para el azúcar* (Havana, 1987), 300; Instituto de Historia del Movimiento Comunista, *Historia del movimiento obrero Cubano 1865–1958*, I, 218.

86. *Louisiana Planter* 73, no. 13 (27 September 1924): 253.

87. "La historia de central Brasil," APC, Anuario Azucarero de Cuba del Año 1956. The Brasil was called the Jaronú during the 1920s.

88. "Historia del central Adelaida," 1917, APC, Anuario Azucarera de Cuba del Año 1956.

89. Quoted in Post, *Arise Ye Starvelings*, 355. Vladimir I. Lenin discussed these aspects of trade unionism in his pamphlet *What Is to Be Done?*, in the section entitled "Trade Unionist Politics and Social Democratic Politics." See V. I. Lenin, *What Is to Be Done?* (1901; rept., Peking, 1973), 66–122.

90. Quoted in Post, *Arise Ye Starvelings*, 177.

91. Quoted ibid., 355.

92. Quoted in Griffler, *What Price Alliance?* 17. Lenin first explored how imperialism affected both native and foreign-born workers in his pamphlet *Imperialism: The Highest Stage of Capitalism* (1916; repr., New York, 1939), 105–106. Kirwin Shaffer suggests that the Cuban anarchist press not only published news about their cohorts in Europe, Latin America, and the United States, but also encouraged readers to support the Mexican Revolution, and the political prisoners Sacco and Vanzetti and Enrique Flores Magon in the United States. Therefore it is clear that Lenin's writings became influential among anarcho-syndicalists in Camagüey and Oriente. Shaffer, *Anarchism and Countercultural Politics*, 6, 9, 184, 191. According to Shaffer, this probably occurred among those anarchists who contributed financially to their newspapers and the causes that they supported, as well as when those from "Morón, Cienfuegos, Manatí, Holguin and Cruces also shared [their] copy of the newspaper with others, by either passing it along to others or reading it aloud." P. 152.

93. Olga Cabrera, *Alfredo López: Maestro del proletariado Cubano* (Havana 1985), 51. In 1922, López and his groups not only called for the solidarity of workers but also reached the important conclusion that the sugar workers of the interior had to be organized. This was to be done with the establishment of schools, reading rooms, libraries, and workers' centers. See ibid., 101, 104 n. 9.

94. Manifesto impreso expedido por la Federación de Obreros del Azúcar a todo el pueblo Camagüeyano, APC, Fondo: Centrales Azucareros, Leg. 20, no. 774.

95. F. Morrell to M. Rionda, 18 October 1924, Rionda-Braga Papers, BBC Ser. 10, Box 10.

96. Francis Stewart, American Consul, Santiago de Cuba, to Frank Tierney, New York, 26 September 1924, NA/CP, RG 84, Records of the U.S. Foreign Service Posts, Vol. 251, 1924, Santiago de Cuba.

97. Arthur C. Frost, Consul General in Charge, Havana, to U.S. State Department, 20 June 1924, ibid., Havana Cuba, Vol. 522, 1924.

98. Heraldo de Cuba (Havana), 7 November 1924, 8.

99. Francis Stewart to Enoch Crowder, American Ambassador, Havana, 7 November 1924, NA/CP, RG 84, Record of Foreign Service Posts, Consular Posts, Santiago de Cuba, Vol. 250, 1924.

100. Stewart to Crowder, 7 November 1924, ibid., Vol. 250, Santiago de Cuba, 1924.

101. "West Indians Still Mistreated in Cuba," quoted in The Workman 13, no. 23 (17 January 1925): 1.

102. Rubén Martínez Villena, "Las contradicciones internas del imperialismo yanqui en Cuba," in Documentos para la historia de Cuba, ed. Hortensia Pichardo (Havana, 1973), 543–53.

103. Alvarez Estévez, Azúcar y Inmigración, 150.

104. Paul E. Willis, Learning to Labour: How Working Class Kids Get Working Class Jobs (Farnborough, UK, 1977), 162. Willis argues that in order for dominant groups to defend their power and privilege, they construct a body of ideas that falsely portray those whom they wish to subjugate and exploit. The false consciousness that the government and the companies sought to promote among native workers included the image of the braceros as "undesirable" aliens. This helps to explain the anti-black-immigrant violence that some Cubans had expressed.

105. Congreso Obrero Nacional, Memorias (Cienfuegos, 1925), 44–45.

106. Ibarra, Cuba: 1898–1921, 157; Instituto de Historia del Movimiento Comunista, El movimiento obrero Cubano, I, 434.

107. See Nueva Luz, 11 January 1923, 6. This anarchist organ called for a ban on black Antillean immigration because of the oppressive conditions that immigrant workers experienced as soon as they arrived in Cuba. It described the unhealthy train cars that transported them to the mills, the overcrowded barracones, and their low piece-rate wages.

108. Quoted in Ibarra, Cuba: 1898–1921, 157.

109. Harpelle, The West Indians of Costa Rica, 49.

110. Martínez Villena, "Las contradicciones internas del imperialismo," 543–53.

111. "Sugar Production in the Santiago de Cuba Consular District: Zafra of 1924–1925," 10 August 1925 and 13 August 1925, prepared by Francis Stewart, NA/CP, RG 84, Records of Foreign Posts, Consular Posts, Santiago de Cuba, Vol. 260, 1925.

5. GARVEYISM WITHOUT GARVEY: A COUNTER-IDEOLOGY IN THE BLACK CARIBBEAN COMMUNITIES

1. "Clock Tower Man," in "Life in Jamaica," Vol.: Parish of West Moreland 87 Wma (recorded November 1975), 27.

2. "Man Boy," in "Life in Jamaica," Vol.: Parish of Clarendon 5Cmb (recorded April 1975), 31.

3. La Discusión (Havana), 1 March 1921, 7. Also cited in Pedro Pablo Rodríquez, "Marcus Garvey en Cuba," Anales del Caribe 7–8 (1987–88): 279; Bernardo García Dominguez, "Garvey and Cuba," in Garvey: His Work and Impact, ed. Rupert Lewis and Patrick Bryan (Trenton, NJ, 1991), 300; Sandra Estévez Rivero, La sombra de Marcus Garvey sobre el oriente Cubano (Santiago de Cuba, 2005), 48.

4. "Marcus Garvey, Moises de la raza negra expone al Heraldo sus apleos planes sobre la futura República del Africa," Heraldo de Cuba (Havana), 4 March 1921, 1.

5. Ibid., 3.

6. Peter Ashdown, "The UNIA and the Black Cause in British Honduras, 1914–1949," Journal of Caribbean History 15 (1981): 47–48.

7. "Marcus Garvey," Heraldo de Cuba, 4 March 1921, 3. Belize's superintendent of police, Cavenaugh, made similar statements about Garvey's performance. He said, "In his moments of animal ferociousness . . . he knew how to get to his hearers and was cheered heartily time and time again." Quoted in Ashdown, "The UNIA and the Black Cause," 48.

8. Amy Jacques Garvey, Garvey and Garveyism (New York, 1978); E. U. Essien-Udom and Amy Jacques Garvey, eds., More Philosophy and Opinions of Marcus Garvey, Vol. 3 (London, 1977).

9. Daily Gleaner (date and page numbers not available), cited in "Honorable Marcus Garvey Given Big Reception by the UNIA and ACL," The Workman 8, no. 35 (2 April 1921): 1.

10. Ibid. Garvey used a portion of this passage in a speech entitled "The Case of the Negro for International Racial Adjustment" at Royal Albert Hall in London on 6 June 1928. See Essien-Udom and Garvey, eds. More Philosophy and Opinions, III, 44–45.

11. Richard Hart, "The Life and Resurrection of Marcus Garvey," Race 9 (1967): 229.

12. See John Hope Franklin, From Slavery to Freedom: A History of Negro Americans (New York, 1974), 365–67; Theodore Draper, The Rediscovery of Black Nationalism (New York, 1969); Judith Stein, The World of Marcus Garvey: Race and Class in Modern Society (Baton Rouge, 1986). They document how several black leaders, such as W. E. B. Du Bois and A. Philip Randolph, criticized Garvey for his inconsistencies as the leader of a black nationalist movement. Edmund David Cronon's Black Moses: The Story of Marcus Garvey and the Universal Negro Improvement Association (Madison, WI, 1959) also takes Garvey to task for creating an inherently weak movement.

13. Daily Gleaner, cited in The Workman 8, no. 36 (9 April 1921): 6.

14. Giovannetti, "The Elusive Organization of 'Identity,'" 14–15.

15. Daily Gleaner, cited in The Workman 8, no. 36 (9 April 1921): 6.

16. "Marcus Garvey Speaks to Vast Crowd in Liberty Hall, Colón," The Workman 8, no. 39 (30 April 1921): 1.

17. Ibid.

18. Honor Ford-Smith, "Women and the Garvey Movement in Jamaica," in Garvey: His Work and Impact, ed. Rupert Lewis and Patrick Bryan (Trenton, NJ, 1991), 75. In spite of this assigned role, black women became active leaders in the movement and involved themselves in the day-to-day operation of the UNIA organizations, according to Ford-Smith, 76–78.

19. The Workman 8, no. 39 (30 April 1921): 8.

20. Ibid.

21. Conniff, Black Labor on a White Canal, 71.

22. *Heraldo de Cuba*, 4 March 1921, 3.

23. Ibid. Amy Jacques Garvey argues that the objective of Garvey's tour of the Caribbean in 1921, including his visit to Cuba, was to gain financial support to pay for the "fourth ship of the Black Star Line . . . the S.S. Phillis Wheatley." Garvey, *Garvey and Garveyism*, 61–62.

24. Ibid., 45. A dissatisfied former member of the UNIA branch in New York, Duncan left the movement in 1918. Two years later, he wrote his letter as the executive secretary of the West Indian Protective Society of America, "the only society in the U.S. looking out after the interest of colored people of foreign birth." Duncan was born in the British West Indies and became a naturalized citizen of the United States sometime before 1918. Ibid., 45–47.

25. Chomsky, *West Indian Workers*, 203–204. Chomsky discovered that the government of Costa Rica as well as the United Fruit Company—the same company that owned and operated the Boston and Preston *centrales* near Banes, Oriente—were very suspicious of Garveyism because of the principle of racial solidarity that the UNIA promoted on the banana plantations surrounding the Caribbean coastal town of Limón.

26. Bourgois, *Ethnicity at Work*, 99.

27. *Heraldo de Cuba*, 4 March 1921, 3.

28. Ibid.

29. William A. Edwards, "Garveyism: Organizing the Masses or Mass Organization?" in *Garvey: His Work and Impact*, ed. Rupert Lewis and Patrick Bryan (Trenton, NJ, 1991), 216–17.

30. *Heraldo de Cuba*, 4 March 1921, 3, 10.

31. Ibid.

32. Ibid., 10.

33. Ibid.

34. Louis A. Pérez Jr., *Cuba: Between Reform and Revolution* (Oxford, 1988), 174–78.

35. *Heraldo de Cuba*, 4 March 1921, 3, 10.

36. Tomás Fernández Robaina, "Urrutia, Cubans, and Black Nationalism," in *Between Race and Empire: African Americans and Cubans before the Revolution*, ed. Lisa Brock and Digna Castañeda (Philadelphia, 1998), 120–25.

37. Ibid. Also see McLeod, "'Sin dejar ser Cubanos,'" 94–95; Lillian Guerra, *The Myth of José Martí: Conflicting Nationalisms in Early Twentieth-Century Cuba* (Chapel Hill, 2005), ch. 7.

38. Rosalie Schwartz, "Cuba's Roaring Twenties: Race Consciousness and the Column 'Ideales de una Raza,'" in *Between Race and Empire: African Americans and Cubans before the Revolution*, edited by Lisa Brock and Digna Castañeda (Philadelphia, 1998), 105; McLeod, "'Sin dejar ser Cubanos,'" 86–87.

39. Quoted in Schwartz, "Cuba's Roaring Twenties," 113–14. Marc McLeod argues that black Cubans had become dependent on white patronage to obtain some socioeconomic advancement. McLeod, "'Sin dejar ser Cubanos,'" 93.

40. Carta abierta del Club Atenas dirigida al País, Havana, July 1919, ANC, Fondo: Secretaria de la Presidencia, Caja, 89, no. 66, 1919.

41. Ibid.

42. Ibid.

43. Schwartz, "Cuba's Roaring Twenties," 105.

44. Giovannetti, "The Elusive Organization of 'Identity,'" 14–15.

45. "Clock Tower Man," in "Life in Jamaica," Vol.: Parish of Westmoreland 87 Wma (recorded November 1975), 26–27.

46. "Hon. Marcus Garvey Continues to Address," quoted in The Workman 8, no. 36 (9 April 1921): 6. During his visit to Jamaica, Garvey discussed political and economic conditions to the rural peasants of the island. It was this sector of the Jamaican population that the sugar companies pulled to Cuba to labor in the fields and work in the mills.

47. Quoted ibid.

48. "Voodooism in Haiti," Negro World 14, no. 8 (7 April 1923): 10.

49. Quoted in The Workman 8, no. 36 (9 April 1921): 1.

50. Quoted ibid., 6.

51. Quoted ibid., 8.

52. "Ecos Sociales," La Independencia, 12 March 1921, 4.

53. Ibid.

54. Universal Improvement and Association Communities League, 23 February 1921, Santiago de Cuba, AHPSC, Fondo: Gobierno Provincial, Leg. 2689, no. 2, 1921, Materia: Sociedades Recreo. Daniel Mardenborough served as secretary, while Rawlins acted as president. The letterhead on this organization's stationary included the word Negro, in its title, as did the stationary for all of the UNIA organizations in Oriente.

55. Reglamento de Asociación universal para el adelanto de la raza negra Division no. 194 en el domicillo provincial Jesus Rabi, 18 February 1921, AHPSC, Fondo: Gobierno Provincial, Leg. 2689, no. 2, 1921; "Division 194 of Santiago de Cuba," Negro World 14, no. 5 (17 March 1923): 8.

56. AHPSC, Fondo: Gobierno Provincial, Leg. 2689, no. 2, 18 February 1921.

57. Ibid.

58. Reglamento de la Asociación de la Liga de Jamaica, 1919, AHPSC, Fondo: Gobierno Provincial, Leg. 2623, no. 12, 1919. Also cited in Estévez Rivero, La sombra de Marcus Garvey, 25.

59. Expediente: Sociedades universal para el Adelanto de la raza negro división no. 123, en San Germán, Holguín, AHPSC, Fondo: Gobierno Provincial, Leg. 2452, no. 6, 1926. Cuban law required that every benevolent and recreational association have a group of officers to govern their confraternities. These officers comprised the board of directors. They were nominated and elected by their general assemblies, which were comprised of the dues-paying members.

60. AHPSC, Fondo: Gobierno Provincial, Leg. 2689, no. 2, 1921. Both Rawlins and Mardenborough were elected to two-year terms. The officers of the UNIA Division No. 52, located in the town of Banes, usually served six months as officers of what they called their Junta Directiva. AHPSC, Fondo: Gobierno Provincial, Leg. 2452, no. 2, 1922. Expediente, Banes: Sociedad de instrucción y cultura "Asociación universal para adelanto de la Raza negra división no. 52, de Banes."

61. AHPSC, Fondo: Gobierno Provincial, Leg. 2452, no. 2, 1922.

62. AHPSC, Fondo: Gobierno Provincial, Leg. 2623, no. 12, 1919; Instituto de Historia del Movimiento Comunista, El movimiento obrero Cubano, 417, 433–34.

63. Giovannetti, "The Elusive Organization of 'Identity,'" 7.

64. "Gemini," in "Life in Jamaica," Vol.: Parish of St. James 64STjMb (recorded October 1975), 4.

65. Hart, "The Life and Resurrection," 226. Hart worked closely with Hugh Buchanan in Jamaica before and during the labor protest of 1938.

66. Charles L. Lathan, American Consul, Kingston, Jamaica, 7 April 1921, NA/CP, Record Group 84, Record of Foreign Service Posts, Port-au-Prince, Haiti, Vol. 106.

67. Conniff, Black Labor on a White Canal, 55–59. Between 1,200 and 1,500 longshoremen struck in May 1919 for better wages. Although the workers returned to their jobs after a couple of weeks, the Colón Federal Labor Union sought the help of the local UNIA to organize additional dockworkers, who were paid in silver rather than gold. In January, Garvey sent one of his top assistants, Herrieta V. Davis, to support the organizing work of the CFLU and the United Brotherhood of Canal Workers. In February 1920, the latter called for a strike. Garvey himself sent $500 to support the workers.

68. "Black Cross Division, Morón Branch, no. 374, Camagüey, Cuba," Negro World 14, no. 4 (10 March 1923).

69. "A Rising Message from Banes, Oriente, Cuba," Negro World 14, no. 9 (14 April 1923): 4.

70. "The UNIA in Camagüey, Cuba Surmounts Difficulties," Negro World 14, no. 15 (26 May 1923): 7.

71. "Camagüey Cuba," Negro World 15, no. 19 (22 December 1923): 7.

72. "Vertientes, Camagüey, Cuba," Negro World 19, no. 9 (10 October 1925): 6.

73. Asociación universal para Adelanto de la Raza negra división no. 52 de Banes, AHPSC, Fondo: Gobierno Provincial, Leg. 2452, no. 2, 1922, Expediente Banes: Sociedad de instrucción y cultura.

74. Ibid.; "Big Day at Banes, Oriente, Cuba," Negro World 14, no. 6 (24 March 1923): 4.

75. Ford-Smith, "Women and the Garvey Movement," 77–78.

76. "The Future Lies before Us, Says the Banes Div. No. 52, of Cuba," Negro World 14, no. 7 (31 March 1923): 7.

77. AHPSC, Fondo: Gobierno Provincial, Leg. 2452, no. 2, 1922.

78. "Haitians and Jamaicans Fare Badly in Cuba," Negro World 15, no. 25 (2 February 1924): 2.

79. "Jamaica: Our Labourers in Cuba," The Workman 9, no. 24 (21 January 1922): 2.

80. UNIA de la Raza Negra en Guantánamo, contiene reglamento, cartas, resoluciones . . . 18 July 1922, AHPSC, Fondo: Gobierno Provincial, Leg. 2452, no. 2, 1922; ibid., Leg. 2452, no. 3, 1922. Exp. The governor of Oriente approved the constitution of Division Number 164 on 18 July 1922. The president of the branch, C. A. Thomas, and his secretary, W. Alexander Charley, submitted the appropriate petition and reglamento to the government. Also see "Información general," Negro World 15, no. 18 (15 December 1923): 9. In addition, every member had to purchase a copy of the UNIA constitution for 25 centavos and the organization's insignia for another 15 centavos.

81. AHPSC, Fondo: Gobierno Provincial, Leg. 2689, no. 2, 1921.

82. AHPSC, Fondo: Gobierno Provincial, Leg. 2452, no. 7, 1927.

83. Ernle P. Gordon, "Garvey and Black Liberation Theology," in Garvey: His Work and Impact, ed. Rupert Lewis and Patrick Bryan (Trenton, NJ, 1991), 140–41.

84. Giovannetti, "The Elusive Organization of 'Identity,'" 14. Giovannetti believes that the UNIAs in Cuba were more religious in nature than political. At the same time, he admits that

black religion had always been used politically to help blacks resist and protest their subjugation and exploitation. Ibid., 17. Evidence suggests that Garveyism was malleable and interpreted in multiple ways by his followers. As a result, some used it to interpret their exploitation in class terms as well.

85. "A Ringing Message from Banes, Oriente," *Negro World* 14, no. 9 (14 April 1923): 4.

86. Bourgois, *Ethnicity at Work*, 98.

87. "Banes Cuba," *Negro World* 15, no. 22 (12 January 1924): 7.

88. "Miranda, Oriente," *Negro World* 18, no. 14 (16 May 1925): 8.

89. See AHPSC, Fondo: Gobierno Provincial, Leg. 2452, numbers 1–10. This very large bundle of documents includes the reglamentos, correspondence, and resolutions of the Universal Negro Improvement Association and African Community Leagues located in Banes, Guantánamo, Jobabo, Victoria de las Tunas, Segua de Tánamo, Puerto Padre, San Germán, Santiago de Cuba, and Antilla. Fondo: Gobierno Provincial, Leg. 2453, no. 1 contains the records for the UNIA in Río Cauto, Bayamo. Fondo: Gobierno Provincial, Leg. 2689, no. 2, has the reglamento and other documents for the UNIA Division led by Rawlins and Madenborough of Santiago de Cuba. Also see "Man Boy," in "Life in Jamaica," Vol.: Parish of Clarendon 5CMb, 31.

90. "Pathetic Letter from the Island of Cuba," quoted in *The Workman* 9, no. 7 (24 September 1921): 1.

91. Ibid.

92. AHPSC, Fondo: Gobierno Provincial, Leg. 2452, no. 4, 1922. The provincial government of Oriente licensed the UNIA of Puerto Padre on 18 July 1922. Its acting president was Joseph Osbourne.

93. "It Irks Him That Negroes Are Underlings," *Negro World* 24, no. 22 (7 July 1922): 8.

94. "Negro Remains the Tool of Other Races," *Negro World* 24, no. 25 (28 July 1928): 8.

95. "Why I Am a Garveyite," *Negro World* 21, no. 22 (8 January 1927): 3.

96. "Opposition Ought to Increase Our Progress," *Negro World* 22, no. 9 (9 April, 1927): 10.

97. "What Garveyism Has Done in Cuba," *Negro World* 24, no. 30 (1 September 1928): 8.

98. Ibid.

99. Expediente: UNIA de Santiago de Cuba, correspondencia entre el presidente Cayetano Monier y secretario general Felix Machado y el gobernador provincial, 17 March 1927, AHPSC, Fondo: Gobierno Provincial, Leg. 2452, no. 9, 1927.

100. Ibid.

101. Ibid.

6. MULTIPLE DOMINANT IDEOLOGIES: XENOPHOBIA AND CUBAN NATIONALISM IN THE NEOCOLONIAL CONTEXT OF BLACK CARIBBEAN IMMIGRATION

1. "El alza del azúcar," in "Palpitaciones de la vida nacional," January 1924, pp. 139–50, APC, Fondo: Jorge Juarez Cano, Leg. 68, no. 68.

2. Bryan to Milner, Report on the Blue Book of Jamaica, 1918–19, 8 November 1919, NAJ, Ref.Code: 1B/5/18/74–1919, Record Series: CSO, Governor of Jamaica Dispatches to the Colonial

Secretary of State. President Zayas continued to quarantine immigrants from Jamaica after learning that diphtheria or foot and mouth disease had broken out on the island. See Acting Governor Bryan to Secretary of State for the Colonies Winston Churchill, 7 August 1922, ibid., Ref.Code: 1B/5/18/76—1922, Record Series: CSO. By September, fifty adult deaths had been attributed to the disease. By late September, it had spread to the parishes of St. Elizabeth and Westmoreland. See ibid., dispatches of 7 and 25 September 1922.

3. Godfrey Haggard, British Legation, Havana, to Carlos Manuel de Céspedes, Secretary of State for Foreign Affairs of Cuba, 3 January 1924 to 8 March 1924, in National Archive of Great Britain at Kew Gardens, British Foreign Office, Cuba No. 1 (1924): Correspondence Between His Majesty's Government and the Cuban Government Respecting the Ill-Treatment of British West Indian Labourers in Cuba (London, 1924).

4. Céspedes to Haggard, 23 January 1924, ibid.

5. Céspedes to Haggard, 24 January 1924, ibid.

6. Probyn to Churchill, 13 June 1922, NAJ, Ref. Code: 1B/5/18/76-1922, Record Series: CSO, Governor of Jamaica Dispatches to the Colonial Secretary of State, Dispatch No. 80, 7 March 1922, and Dispatch No. 256, 5 June 1922.

7. Probyn to Churchill, 27 June 1922, NAJ, Ref. Code: 1B/5/18/76-1922, Governor of Jamaica Dispatches to the Colonial Secretary of State. Jamaica's 1922 budget amounted to £200,000 pounds. Prior to 1925, every emigrant had to deposit £5 pounds with the government before being permitted to leave Jamaica.

8. Expediente: Relativo a la circular expedida por la Secretaria de Gobernación acerca de la total prohibición de pagarle a los obreros y jornaleros de ingenios con vales y fichas, 4 October 1923 to 5 December 1923, AHPSC, Fondo: Gobierno Provincial, Leg. 308, no. 9, 1923.

9. Memorandum para El Sr. Secretario de Estado Aurelio Portuondo, Havana, 25 January 1924, Rionda-Braga Papers, RG II, Ser. 10a-c (1911–43), Box 58, Subfiles, No. 7.

10. "Dominica Labourers for Cuba," *Guardian*, 5 April 1923, quoted in *The Workman* 10, no. 40 (12 May 1923): 7.

11. Rionda-Braga Papers, RG II, Ser. 10a-c (1911–43), Box 58.

12. Ibid., Box 58, 25 January 1924.

13. Thomas, *Cuba*, 556–58.

14. *Louisiana Planter* 73, no. 1 (5 July 1924): 12.

15. "Jamaican Labour Necessary in Cuba Says Delegation of Sugar Men," *The Workman* 13, no. 3 (30 August 1924): 1.

16. "Indeseable Inmigración," *Avisador Comercial*, 2 August 1924.

17. Acting Governor Bryan to Secretary of State J. H. Thomas, 22 July 1924, NAJ, Ref. Code: 1B/5/18/78-1924, Record Series: CSO, Governor of Jamaica Dispatches to the Colonial Secretary of State.

18. *Louisiana Planter* 73, no. 8 (23 August 1924): 154.

19. Hudson Stroude, *The Pageant of Cuba* (New York, 1934), 259. Stroude observed Cuban politics first-hand during the regimes of Menocal, Zayas, and Machado.

20. Louis A. Pérez Jr., *Cuba under the Platt Amendment, 1902–1934* (Pittsburgh, 1986), 228–29. Pérez states that President José Miguel Gómez (1908–12) served on the board of directors of the

Cuba Cane Sugar Company after leaving office. Zayas's vice-president, Miguel Arango, had been a manager of several Cuba Cane mills. Orestes Ferrara, Speaker of the House and later ambassador of Cuba to the United States, had served as secretary of the Violet Sugar Company and served on the board of directors of Cuba Cane and of the De Georgio Fruit Company. President Mario Menocal (1912–20) had managed the Chaparra and Delecias centrales before being elected twice, in 1912 and again in 1916.

21. "Emigration of Jamaicans to Cuban Republic," The Workman 13, no. 5 (13 September 1924): 7.

22. "The Republic of Cuba Bans Female Immigration," Daily Gleaner, 6 June 1925; "The Native Labor Bill," Havana Post, 29 May 1926, 3. See "Los Jamaiquinos abandonaron el trabajo en el Mariel," El Mundo, 8 Marzo 1921. At least thirty Jamaicans had been hired at the cement factory at Mariel.

23. "Labourers in Cuba," Jamaican Herald, 11 October 1924.

24. Thomas, Cuba, 556–58.

25. Expediente: Inmigración, AHPSC, Fondo: Gobierno Provincial, Leg. 787, no. 5, 1927.

26. Expediente: Carta de Riguel por Jefe Policía Secreta, 24 November 1927, AHPSC, Fondo: Gobierno Provincial, Leg. 787, no. 6, 1927.

27. Expediente: Policía Secreta de Oriente, no. R.S. 2198, 24 November 1927, AHPSC, Fondo: Gobierno Provincial, Leg. 787, no. 3, 1927.

28. Telegrama de Secretaria de Gobernación por el Gobernador Provincial de Oriente, 8 June 1923, AHPSC, Fondo: Gobierno Provincial, Leg. 2228, no. 16, 1923.

29. Ibid.

30. AHPSC, Fondo: Gobierno Provincial, Leg. 2228, no. 18, 8 June 1925, and No. 20, 25 October 1927. In June 1925, the secretary of state applied Article 12, Paragraph 19, of Public Order 213, decreed in 1900, and Article 594, Number 2, of the Penal Code to attack prostitution and to promote public morality and good customs in society. It gave the police the responsibility and power to eradicate this "immoral activity." Article 12 permitted the police to close all establishments, cafés, restaurants, and brothels. In October 1927, the Department of Immigration arrested Consuelo P. Gómez after she disembarked from a ship that had arrived from Kingston, Jamaica. Reportedly she had come to work as a prostitute in a brothel called La Casa de Lola. The authorities deported Gómez back to Jamaica.

31. "No inmigración Antillana," Heraldo de Cuba, 22 May 1926.

32. "No inmigración en la futura," ibid.

33. "Sugar Cane Crisis," quoted in The Workman 15, no. 15 (27 November, 1926): 1, 8.

34. British Legation, Santo Domingo, DR, to Secretary of State, 21 July 1926, and British Legation, Havana, to Sir Austen Chamberlain, 24 August 1926, NAJ, Ref. Code: 1B/5/77/17-1926, Record Series: CSO, Governor of Jamaica Dispatches to the Colonial Secretary of State.

35. Expediente: Cartas enviadas al Consulado Ingles y al de Haiti por el Gobernador Provincial relativo a una resolución hecha por el Gobierno de la Provincia con vistas a que censen los abusos cometidos por los reclutadores de obreros inmigrantes, Santiago de Cuba, 3 Enero 1927, AHPSC, Fondo: Gobierno Provincial, Leg. 377, no. 10, 1927. As early as 1925, the American consul in Antilla, Oriente, insinuated to his superiors in Havana and Washington, D.C., that some

Jamaican braceros had their birth certificates, visas, and passports taken by the emigrant brokers as well as by the agents of the sugar mills as soon as they arrived. As a result, when they sought to leave Cuba, they found it impossible to do so. See Report on the Undue Hardship upon Prospective Immigrants, 3 March 1925, Antilla, Cuba, NA/CP, RG 84, Records of Foreign Service Posts, Antilla, Cuba, Vol. 77, 1925.

36. Horace Dickinson, American Consul, Antilla, Cuba, to Claudius Spied, 6 May 1925, and to Frank Shakespeare, 6 May 1925; Richard Gordon Valentine, San Germán, Oriente, Cuba, to the American consul, 29 June 1925, all ibid.

37. Manager, Preston mill, to Horace L. Washington, American Consul General, London, England, 31 January 1925, ibid.

38. Julia Liggan, Notary Public, NY County, No. 187, to the American Consulate, London, England, 29 July 1925, ibid.

39. John J. Kulczycki, "Scapegoating the Foreign Worker," in *The Politics of Immigrant Workers: Labor Activism and Migration in the World Economy since 1830*, ed. Camille Guerin-Gonzalez and Carl Strikwerda (New York, 1998), 152.

40. Report on the Restriction and other factors Affecting the Sugar Industry of Cuba, including the Restrictions on the Zafra and Haitian and Jamaican Immigrants, Eardley Middleton to President G. Machado, 22 March 1928, ANC, Fondo: Secretaria de la Presidencia, Caja 121, no. 66, 1928.

41. Commission on Cuban Affairs, *Problems of the New Cuba*, 285.

42. Ibid., 52, 215.

43. Cortina to Machado, 29 May 1928, ANC, Fondo: Secretaria de la Presidencia, Caja 121, no. 66, 1928.

44. Ibid.

45. Emigration to Cuba: Rules Governing Entrance of Immigrants, 23 February 1928, NAJ, Ref. Code: 1B/5/77/101-1928, Record Series: CSO, Governor of Jamaica Dispatches to the Colonial Secretary of State. See "Rules Governing the Entry of Emigrants," *Daily Gleaner*, 14 April 1928.

46. Estadísticas impresa., Editada por la Sección de Estadística de la Secretaria de Hacienda relativa a inmigración y movimiento de pasajeros años de 1930 y comparaciones con el año 1929, editado en 1931, ANC, Fondo: Donativos y Remisiones, Leg. 403, no. 11.

47. Copia de un articulo escrito por Cosme de la Torriente y al parecer publicado, explicando las causas de la Revolución en Cuba contra el Gobierno de Machado, ANC, Fondo: Secretaria de la Presidencia, Caja 100, no. 44, n.p. Also see Luis E. Aguilar, *Cuba 1933: Prologue to Revolution* (New York, 1974), 88–115.

48. ANC, Fondo: Donativos y Remisiones, Leg. 403, no. 11.

49. Robert F. Smith, *The United States and Cuba: Business and Diplomacy, 1917–1960* (New York, 1960), 53–66.

50. Dirección de Demografía del Comité Estatal de Estadística, *Memorias inéditas del censo de 1931* (Havana, 1978), 40.

51. Smith, *The United States and Cuba*, 69.

52. Commission on Cuban Affairs, *Problems of the New Cuba*, 236.

53. Le Riverend, *Historia económica de Cuba*, 237.

54. Governor of Jamaica Dispatches to the Colonial Secretary of State for the Colonies, 1 November 1929, NAJ, Ref. Code: 1B/5/77/179-1929, Record Series: CSO; Eisner, *Jamaica*, 147. For the Haitian figures, see *Estadística impresa . . . de la Secretaria de hacienda relativa a inmigración y movimiento de pasajeros años de 1930*, ANC, Fondo: Donativos y Remisiones, Leg. 403, no. 11, which reports two sets of numbers for the immigration of Haitians in 1930—5,126 and 2,769. The Cuban Census of 1931 uses the larger figure of 5,126. See Dirección de Demografía, *Memorias inéditas del censo de 1931*, 290.

55. "Decreto No. 1404," 22 Julio 1921, *Gaceta Oficial de La República de Cuba*, 1445–46.

56. Alvarez Estévez, *Azúcar e inmigración*, 159–61.

57. Expediente . . . relacionado con el escrito del Ministerio de Haiti en Cuba quejandose de que a los subditos Haitianos presos se las somete a trabajos forzados, 30 August–3 October 1928, ANC, Fondo: Secretaria de la Presidencia, Caja 44, no. 32, 1928.

58. Ibid.

59. See Alejandro Portes, "Towards a Structural Analysis of Illegal (Undocumented) Immigration," *International Migration Review* 12 (Winter): 469–84.

60. Expediente referente a inmigración y emigración, Santiago de Cuba y Havana, 2 October 1931, un informe a La Comisionado de Inmigración, ANC, Fondo: Secretaria de la Presidencia, Leg. 121, Exp. 68.

61. Informe sobre la inmigración Haitiano y Jamaicano, Havana, 29 June 1934, ANC, Fondo: Secretaria de la Presidencia, Leg. 121, Exp. 84. Also see "Sin un jornal decoroso," *Diario de la Marina*, 8 Julio 1934, 11.

62. ANC, Fondo: Secretaria de la Presidencia, Leg. 121, Exp. 68.

63. Ibid.

64. Ibid.

65. Ibid. Molina also counted 4,500 Barbadians, 1,900 Puerto Ricans, 950 Dominicans, and 550 immigrants from the Virgin Islands living in Oriente.

66. Repatriate from Cuba-UFCO offers ships, NAJ, Ref. Code: 1B/5/77/91—1931, Record Series: CSO, Governor of Jamaica Dispatches to the Colonial Secretary of State for the Colonies. See J. G. Kieffers, UFCO Division Manager, to Acting Colonial Secretary of State A. R. Dignum, 26 June 1931, ibid. Because of the large number of British West Indian workers in Cuba, these companies started a bidding war with one another to see who could dominate this trade. The British government was able to make the United Fruit Company lower its price per passenger from $11 to $8. The Atlantic Fruit Company agreed to lower its price from $10 to $9.50 per worker. In a letter of 6 August 1931, Dignum notified the Standard Fruit Company that he had accepted its offer of $8 per worker. Ibid.

67. Cuban Immigration Regulations, Vol. I and Vol. II, ibid., Governor of Jamaica Dispatches to the Colonial Secretary of State for the Colonies; British Minister in Havana to the Governor of Jamaica, 28 October 1931, NAJ, Ref. Code: 1B/5/77/7-1931, Record Series: CSO.

68. Cuban Immigration Regulations, Vol. I and Vol. II, and J. Joyce Broderick, British Legation in Havana, to Governor of Jamaica, 6 November 1931, 2 December 1931, NAJ, Ref. Code:

1B/5/77/7-1931, Record Series: CSO, Governor of Jamaica Dispatches to the Colonial Secretary of State. Broderick reported that the Machado government permitted the sugar companies to import 2,500 black migrant workers for the sugar crop of 1929–30. The Cuban Immigration Department estimated that there were 40,000 Haitians, Jamaicans, Barbadians, and other West Indians now living in Cuba.

69. See Rojas, Las luchas obreros, 40–53.

70. Ibid., 44.

71. Francis O'Meara, British Consulate General, to Governor of Jamaica, 17 October 1930, NAJ, Ref. Code: 1B/5/77/153-1930. O'Meara reported that such practices had been experienced by two Jamaicans, Samuel Brown and Richard Smith. Because the British Consulate in Havana did not have any money to retain a lawyer for these workers, O'Meara wrote to the governor requesting "a modest expenditure for legal advice." On 25 October 1930, the governor responded to O'Meara: "We are already spending large sums on Jamaicans who have emigrated to Cuba . . . There are no funds at present from which expenditure for legal assistance could be used and we should have to ask Legislative Council for a vote . . . It is already doing enough for Jamaicans in Cuba." NAJ, Ref Code: 1B/5/77/153-1930.

72. Plasencia Mora, "Historia del movimiento obrero," 123.

73. Instituto de Historia de Movimiento Communista, Historia del movimiento obrero Cubano, I, 273.

74. Post, Arise Ye Starvelings, 2–6. Bustamente's life as a young adult is unclear. As so many Jamaican braceros had done, he traveled to Cuba several times, working for the last time in the railroad industry. Two years after returning to Jamaica, in 1936 Bustamente became involved in the political life of the country. Of the many issues he addressed, the mistreatment of Jamaicans in Cuba became one of the most pressing. Ibid., 252–53. Also see Abigail B. Bakan, Ideology and Class Conflict in Jamaica: The Politics of Rebellion (Montreal, 1990), 100–103.

75. Instituto de Historia del Movimiento Communista, El movimiento obrero Cubano, I, 274.

76. Aguilar, Cuba 1933, 174.

77. Informe sobre la inmigración Haitiano y Jamaicano, Havana, 29 July 1934, ANC, Fondo: Secretaria de la Presidencia, Leg. 121, Exp. 84.

78. Carta de F. Sánchez del Guardia Rural de Mayarí por José Marrero, ANC, Fondo: Donativo y Remisiones, Caja 702, no. 21, 1938.

79. ANC, Fondo: Donativo y Remisiones, Caja 702, no. 21, 1938, Documento 33.

80. Ibid.

81. Ibid.

82. Repatriation from Cuba—Instruction as to Wives of Jamaicans, Children, age of Children, medicine for Sick Repatriates, and letters of 19 November 1936, NAJ, Ref. Code: 1B/5/77/375-1933, Record Series: CSO, Governor of Jamaica Dispatches to the Colonial Secretary of State. These rules took effect on 13 December 1933.

83. T. M Snow to Sir John Simon, Governor of Jamaica, 29 November 1935, NAJ, Ref. Code: 1B/5/77/7-193, Record Series: CSO, Dispatches to the Colonial Secretary of State, in reference to Notice No. 905.

EPILOGUE

1. David Nicholls, *Haiti in Caribbean Context: Ethnicity, Economy and Revolt* (Oxford, 1985), 117.

2. Robert I. Rotberg, *The Politics of Squalor* (Boston, 1971), 150.

3. Roumain, *Masters of the Dew*, 149.

4. Rotberg, *The Politics of Squalor*, 151.

5. Great Britain Parliament, House of Commons, *Report of the West Indian Commission* (London, 1930), 113. Also see Post, *Arise Ye Starvelings*, 119. The number of individuals involved in the banana industry is for the year 1938. This probably is a low estimate, given the fact that the price of bananas tended to be more stable than sugar during the depression era of the 1930s.

6. Great Britain Parliament, House of Commons, *Report of the West India Commission*, 52.

7. Post, *Arise Ye Starvelings*, 87.

8. "Mass L-Gentleman Farmer," in "Life in Jamaica," Vol.: Parish of St. Elizabeth 57SteMa (recorded August 1975), 1. Mr. Brooks believed that the hurricane of 1933 was the greatest disaster since the 1912 storm because it totally destroyed the logwood industry as well.

BIBLIOGRAPHY

MANUSCRIPT SOURCES

Cuba

Archivo Histórico Provincial de Camagüey, Anuario Azucarero de Cuba del Año 1956 (APC).
Archivo Histórico Provincial de Santiago de Cuba (AHPSC).
Archivo Nacional de Cuba (ANC).
Biblioteca Nacional de José Martí.
Biblioteca Provincial Elvira Cape de Santiago de Cuba.
Instituto de Literatura y Lingüística de Cuba, Manuscript and Rare Books Collections, Havana.

Great Britain

National Archive of Great Britain at Kew Gardens
  Parliamentary Papers. House of Commons. Correspondence Between His Majesty's Government and the Cuban Government Respecting the Ill-Treatment of British West Indian Labourers in Cuba. London, 1924.

Jamaica

Erna Brodber, ed. "Life in Jamaica in the Early Twentieth Century: A Presentation of 90 Oral Accounts." Kingston, 1980. Housed at the Sir Arthur Lewis Institute of Social and Economic Research on the campus of the University of West Indies, Mona.
National Archive of Jamaica (NAJ).
Sir Arthur Lewis Institute of Social and Economic Research, University of the West Indies, Mona.

United States

National Archives Branch Depository, College Park, MD, Record Group 84, U.S. Consular Posts Reports, Port-au-Prince, Haiti, Vol. 114, 1925.

Rionda-Braga Papers, Record Group II, Series 1, Subject Files 1897–1917, Boxes 22 and 26; Series 10, Subject File 1924, Box 10; Series 10a-c, Subject Files 1911–1943, Boxes 8, 15, 32, 52, 54, 74, 75, 87, 115, 129; Series 12, Subject Files 1904–25, Boxes 2 and 3; Series 17, Subject Files, Box 1. Smathers Library, University of Florida, Gainesville, Florida.

PUBLISHED PRIMARY SOURCES

Academia de Ciencias de Cuba. Índice histórico de la provincia de Camagüey, 1899–1952. Havana, 1970.

Ballou, Maturin Murray. History of Cuba; or Notes of a Traveller in the Tropics. Boston, 1854.

Brook, John R. Civil Report of Major-General John Brooke, U.S. Army Military Governor, Island of Cuba, 1900. Washington, D.C., 1900.

Congreso Obrero Nacional. Memorias. Cienfuegos, 1925.

Cuba. Dirección del Censo. Census of the Republic of Cuba, 1919. Havana, 1922.

Great Britain Parliament, House of Commons. Report of the West Indian Commission. London, 1930.

Magoon, Charles. Report of the Provisional Governor of Cuba. Washington, D.C., 1907.

Núñez Machin, Ana. Memoria amarga del azúcar. Havana, 1981.

Olmsted, Victor H. Censo de la República de Cuba: Bajo la administración provisional de los Estado Unidos, 1907. Washington, D.C., 1908.

Pichardo, Hortensia, ed. Documentos para la historia de Cuba. Vol. II. Havana, 1979.

Sanger, J. P. Informe sobre el Censo de Cuba, 1899. Washington, D.C., 1900.

Secretaría de Agricultura, Comercio, y Trabajo. Legislación obrera de la República de Cuba: Leyes y disposiciones vigentes. Havana, 1919.

Secretaría de Hacienda de la República de Cuba, Sección de Estadísticas. Inmigración y movimiento de pasjeros. Havana, 1903–1930.

Select Committee on Haiti and Santo Domingo. Inquiry into the Occupation and Administration of Haiti and Santo Domingo: Hearing before a Select Committee on Haiti and Santo Domingo, U.S. Senate, 67th Congress, 1st and 2nd Sessions, Senate Report, Vol. 1. Washington, D.C., 1922.

U.S. Commission on Cuban Affairs. Problems of the New Cuba. New York, 1935.

U.S. Tariff Commission. Sugar: Report to the President of the United States. Washington, D.C., 1934.

BOOKS

Aguilar, Luis E. Cuba 1933: Prologue to Revolution. New York, 1974.

Allen, Benjamin. A Story of Growth of E. Atkins & Co. and the Sugar Industry in Cuba. Boston, 1926.

Alleyne, Mervyn C. *The Construction and Representation of Race and Ethnicity in the Caribbean and the World*. Barbados, 2005.

Alvarez Estévez, Rolando. *Azúcar e Inmigración, 1900–1940*. Havana, 1988.

Anillo Rodríguez, Eduardo. *Cuatro siglos de vida, desde Pedro Barba hasta Varona Suarez*. Havana, 1919.

Arredondo, Alberto. *El Negro en Cuba*. Havana, 1939.

Ayala, César. *American Sugar Kingdom: The Plantation Economy of the Spanish Caribbean, 1898–1934*. Chapel Hill, 1999.

Bakan, Abigail B. *Ideology and Class Conflict in Jamaica: The Politics of Rebellion*. Montreal, 1990.

Balch, Emily Greene. *Occupied Haiti*. New York, 1972.

Baltar Rodriguez, José. *Los chinos de Cuba*. Havana, 1997.

Barcia, Manuel. *The Great African Slave Revolt of 1825: Cuba and the Fight for Freedom in Matanzas*. Baton Rouge, 2012.

Barnet, Miguel. *Afro-Cuban Religions*. Translated by Christine Renata Ayorinde. Kingston, 2001.

———. *Biography of a Runaway Slave*. Translated by W. Nick Hill. 1968. Reprint, Willimantic, CT, 1994.

Beckford, George L. *Persistent Poverty: Underdevelopment in Plantation Economies of the Third World*. New York, 1972.

Bellegarde-Smith, Patrick. *Haiti: The Breached Citadel*. Boulder, CO, 1990.

Berchon, Charles. *A través de Cuba: Relativo geográfico descriptivo y económico*. Madrid, 1910.

Berger, John. *And Our Faces, My Heart, Brief as Photos*. London, 1984.

Besson, Jean. *Martha Brae's Two Histories: European Expansion and Caribbean Culture-Building in Jamaica*. Chapel Hill, 2002.

Blake, Judith. *Family Structure in Jamaica: The Social Context of Reproduction*. New York, 1961.

Bookchin, Murray. *The Spanish Anarchists: The Heroic Years, 1868–1936*. New York, 1977.

Bourgois, Philippe I. *Ethnicity at Work: Divided Labor on a Central American Banana Plantation*. Baltimore, 1989.

Bronfman, Alejandra. *Measures of Equality: Social Science, Citizenship, and Race in Cuba, 1902–1940*. Chapel Hill, 2004.

Cabrera, Olga. *Alfredo López: Maestro del proletariado cubano*. Havana, 1985.

Casey, Jeffrey. *Limón, 1880–1940: Un estudio de la industria bananera en Costa Rica*. San Jose, 1979.

Castor, Suzy. *La ocupación norteamericana de Haiti y sus consecuencias, 1915–1934*. Mexico City, 1971.

Casuso, Teresa. *Cuba and Castro*. Translated by Elmer Grossberg. New York, 1961.

Childs, Matt D. *The 1812 Aponte Rebellion in Cuba and the Struggle against Atlantic Slavery*. Chapel Hill, 2006.

Chomsky, Aviva. *West Indian Workers and the United Fruit Company in Costa Rica, 1870–1940.* Baton Rouge, 1996.

Conniff, Michael. *Black Labor on a White Canal: Panama, 1904–1981.* Pittsburgh, 1985.

Courlander, Harold. *The Drum and the Hoe: Life and Lore of the Haitian People.* Berkeley, 1960.

Cronon, Edmund David. *Black Moses: The Story of Marcus Garvey and the Universal Negro Improvement Association.* Madison, WI, 1955.

Dartigue, Maurice. *Conditions rurales en Haiti.* Port-au-Prince, 1938.

Del Toro, Carlos. *El movimiento obrero cubano en 1914.* Havana, 1969.

Desmangles, Leslie G. *The Faces of the Gods: Vodou and Roman Catholicism in Haiti.* Chapel Hill, 1992.

Dirección de Demografía del Comité Estatal de Estadística. *Memorias inéditas del censo de 1931.* Havana, 1978.

Dodson, Jualynne E. *Sacred Spaces and Religious Traditions in Oriente Cuba.* Albuquerque, 2008.

Draper, Theodore. *The Rediscovery of Black Nationalism.* New York, 1969.

Dumoulin, John. *Azúcar y lucha de clases 1917.* Havana, 1980.

Dupuy, Alex. *Haiti in the World Economy: Class, Race, and Underdevelopment since 1700.* Boulder, CO, 1989.

Dye, Alan. *Cuban Sugar in the Age of Mass Production: Technology and the Economics of the Sugar Central, 1899–1929.* Stanford, 1998.

Eisner, Gisela. *Jamaica, 1830–1930: A Study in Economic Growth.* Manchester, UK, 1961.

Essien-Udom, E. U., and Amy Jacques Garvey, eds. *More Philosophy and Opinions of Marcus Garvey.* Vol. 3. London, 1977.

Estévez Rivero, Sandra. *La sombra de Marcus Garvey sobre el oriente cubano.* Santiago de Cuba, 2005.

Fergusson, Erna. *Cuba.* New York, 1946.

Foner, Philip S. *Organized Labor and the Black Worker, 1916–1981.* New York, 1974.

Forbes-Lindsay, C. H. *Cuba and Her People of To-Day.* Boston, 1911.

Forman, Michael. *Nationalism and the International Labor Movement: The Idea of the Nation in Socialist and Anarchist Theory.* University Park, PA, 1998.

Franklin, John Hope. *From Slavery to Freedom: A History of Negro Americans.* New York, 1974.

García Álvarez, Alejandro. *Caminos para el azúcar.* Havana, 1987.

Garvey, Amy Jacques. *Garvey and Garveyism.* New York, 1978.

Goldberg, David Theo. *The Racial State.* Malden, MA, 2002.

Gordon, Paul, and David Rosenberg. *Daily Racism: The Press and Black People in Britain.* London, 1989.

Griffler, Keith P. *What Price Alliance? Black Radicals Confront White Labor, 1918–1938.* New York, 1995.

Guanche, Jesús, and Dennis Moreno. *Caidije.* Santiago de Cuba, 1988.

Guerra, Lillian. *The Myth of José Martí: Conflicting Nationalisms in Early Twentieth-Century Cuba*. Chapel Hill, 2005.

Guerra, Ramiro. *La industria azucarera en Cuba*. Havana, 1940.

———. *Azúcar y población en las Antillas*. 1927. Reprint, Havana, 1970.

Harpelle, Ronald N. *The West Indians of Costa Rica: Race, Class, and the Integration of an Ethnic Minority*. Montreal, 2001.

Harrison, Michelle. *King Sugar: Jamaica, the Caribbean and the World Sugar Industry*. New York, 2001.

Helg, Aline. *Our Rightful Share: The Afro-Cuban Struggle for Equality, 1886–1912*. Chapel Hill, 1995.

Herskovits, Melville J. *Life in a Haitian Valley*. 1937. Reprint, New York, 1975.

Hill, Robert T. *Cuba and Porto Rico: With Other Islands of the West Indies*. New York, 1909.

Horowitz, Michael. *Morne-Paysan: Peasant Village in Martinique*. Prospect Heights, IL, 1992.

Howard, Philip A. *Changing History: Afro-Cuban Cabildos and Societies of Color in the Nineteenth Century*. Baton Rouge, 1998.

Ibarra, Jorge. *Prologue to Revolution: Cuba, 1898–1958*. London, 1998.

———. *Cuba, 1898–1921: Partidos políticos y classes socials*. Havana, 1992.

Instituto de Historia del Movimiento Comunista y de la Revolución Socialista de Cuba. *El movimiento obrero Cubano: Documentos y articulos*. Vol. 1 (1865–1925). Havana, 1981.

———. *Historia del movimiento obrero Cubano 1865–1958*. Vol. 1 (1865–1935). Havana, 1987.

James, Ariel. *Banes: Imperialismo y nación en una plantación azucarera*. Havana, 1976.

James, Joel, José Millet, and Alexis Alarcón. *El Vodú en Cuba*. Santiago de Cuba, 1998.

Jenks, Leland. *Our Cuban Colony: A Study in Sugar*. New York, 1928.

Jerez Villarreal, Juan. *Oriente: Biografía de una provincia*. Havana, 1960.

Joachim, Benoit. *Les Racines du Sous-Développement en Haiti*. Port-au-Prince, 1979.

Kiple, Kenneth F. *The Caribbean Slave: A Biological History*. Cambridge, UK, 1984.

Kunstler, James Howard. *The Geography of Nowhere: The Rise and Decline of America's Man-Made Landscape*. New York, 1993.

Laguerre, Michel S. *Voodoo Heritage*. London, 1980.

Laman, Karl. *The Kongo*. Vol. 3. Uppsala, 1962.

Lenin, V. I. *What Is to Be Done?* 1901. Reprint, Peking, 1973.

———. *Imperialism: The Highest Stage of Capitalism*. 1916. Reprint, New York, 1939.

Le Riverend, Julio. *Historia económica de Cuba*. Havana, 1967.

Lewis, Cleona. *America's Stake in International Investments*. Washington, D.C., 1938.

Leyburn, James G. *The Haitian People*. New Haven, CT, 1941.

Lisser, H. G. de. *In Jamaica and Cuba*. Kingston, 1910.

Litwack, Leon F. *Trouble in Mind: Black Southerners in the Age of Jim Crow*. New York, 1998.

Lundahl, Mats. *Peasants and Poverty: A Study of Haiti*. New York, 1979.

Martí, Carlos. *El país de la riqueza*. Madrid, 1918.

Martínez, Samuel. *Decency and Excess: Global Aspirations and Material Deprivations on a Caribbean Sugar Plantation.* Boulder, CO, 2007.

———. *Peripheral Migrants: Haitians and Dominican Republic Sugar Plantations.* Knoxville, 1995.

Marx, Karl. *Das Kapital.* Vol 3. London, 1960.

McGillivray, Gillian. *Blazing Cane: Sugar Communities, Class, and State Formation in Cuba, 1868–1959.* Durham, 2009.

Meaker, Gerald H. *The Revolutionary Left in Spain, 1914–1923.* Stanford, 1974.

Métraux, Alfred. *Haiti: Black Peasants and Voodoo.* New York, 1960.

———. *Making a Living in the Maribal Valley (Haiti).* Paris, 1951.

Millet, Kethly. *Les Paysans Haïtiens et l'Occupation Américaine d'Haïti, 1915–1930.* Quebec, 1978.

Mintz, Sidney W. *Sweetness and Power: The Place of Sugar in Modern History.* New York, 1985.

———. *Worker in the Cane: A Puerto Rican Life History.* 1960. Reprint, New York, 1974.

Mintz, Sidney, and Richard Price. *The Birth of African-American Culture: An Anthropological Perspective.* Boston, 1976.

Moreno Fraginals, Manuel. *The Sugarmill: The Socioeconomic Complex of Sugar in Cuba.* New York, 1976.

Nicholls, David. *From Dessalines to Duvalier: Race, Colour and National Independence in Haiti.* Cambridge, UK, 1979.

———. *Haiti in Caribbean Context: Ethnicity, Economy and Revolt.* Oxford, 1985.

Olivier, Sydney. *White Capital and Coloured Labour.* New York, 1929.

Ortiz Fernández, Fernando. *Hampa afro-cubanos, los negros esclavos: Estudio sociológico y de derecho público.* Havana, 1916.

Paquette, Robert L. *Sugar Is Made with Blood: The Conspiracy of La Escalera and the Conflict Between Empires over Slavery in Cuba.* Middleton, CT, 1988.

Pérez de la Riva, Francisco. *La habitación rural en Cuba.* Havana, 1952.

Pérez de la Riva, Juan. *Los Culies chinos en Cuba.* Havana, 2000.

Pérez, Louis A., Jr. *Lords of the Mountain: Social Banditry and Peasant Protest in Cuba, 1878–1918.* Pittsburgh, 1989.

———. *Cuba: Between Reform and Revolution.* Oxford, 1988.

———. *Cuba under the Platt Amendment, 1902–1934.* Pittsburgh, 1986.

Petras, Elizabeth McLean. *Jamaican Labor Migration: White Capital and Black Labor, 1850–1930.* Boulder, CO, 1988.

Primelles, Leon. *Cronica Cubana, 1919–1922: Menocal y la Liga Nacional Zayas y Crowder, Fin de la Danza de los Milliones y reajuste.* Havana, 1957.

———. *Cronica Cubana, 1915–1918: La Reelección de Menocal y la Revolución de 1917. La Danza de los Milliones. La Primera Guerra Mundial.* Havana, 1955.

Post, Ken. *Arise Ye Starvelings: The Jamaican Labour Rebellion of 1938 and Its Aftermath.* The Hague, 1978.

Prinsen Geerligs, H. C. *Cane Sugar and Its Manufacture.* Altricham, 1919.

Putnam, Lara. *The Company They Kept: Migrants and the Politics of Gender in Caribbean Costa Rica, 1870–1960*. Chapel Hill, 2002.

Reid-Vázquez, Michele. *The Year of the Lash: Free People of Color in Cuba and the Nineteenth-Century Atlantic World*. Athens, GA, 2011.

Reynoso, Alvaro. *Ensayo sobre el cultivo de la caña de azúcar*. Havana, 1862.

Richardson, Bonham. *Igniting the Caribbean's Past: Fire in British West Indian History*. Chapel Hill, 2004.

Roberts, George W. *The Population of Jamaica*. Cambridge, UK, 1957.

Rojas, Ursinio. *Las luchas obreras en el central Tacajó*. Havana, 1979.

Rotberg, Robert I. *The Politics of Squalor*. Boston, 1971.

Roumain, Jacques. *Masters of the Dew*. 1944. Reprint, Oxford, 1978.

Scott, James C. *Domination and the Arts of Resistance: Hidden Transcripts*. New Haven, 1990.

Sevillano Andrés, Bernarda. *Trascendencia de una cultura marginada: Presencia haitiana en Guantánamo*. Guantanamo, 2007.

Shaffer, Kirwin R. *Anarchism and Countercultural Politics in Early Twentieth-Century Cuba*. Gainesville, FL, 2005.

Smith, Robert F. *The United States and Cuba: Business and Diplomacy, 1917–1960*. New York, 1960.

St. John, Sir Spenser. *Hayti, or The Black Republic*. London, 1889.

Stein, Judith. *The World of Marcus Garvey: Race and Class in Modern Society*. Baton Rouge, 1986.

Stewart, Robert J. *Religion and Society in Post-Emancipation Jamaica*. Knoxville, 1992.

Stewart, Watt. *Keith and Costa Rica: The Biography of Minor Cooper Keith*. Albuquerque, 1964.

Stroude, Hudson. *The Pageant of Cuba*. New York, 1934.

Taylor, John V. *The Primal Vision: Christian Presence amid African Religion*. Philadelphia, 1963.

Telleria, Evelio. *Los congresos obreros en Cuba*. Havana, 1973.

Therborn, Göran. *The Ideology of Power and the Power of Ideology*. London, 1980.

Thomas, Hugh. *Cuba: The Pursuit of Freedom*. New York, 1971.

United Fruit Company. *Some Facts Regarding the Development and Operation of the United Fruit Company Sugar Properties in the Republic of Cuba*. Preston, Oriente, Cuba, 1944.

Warner-Lewis, Maureen. *Central Africa in the Caribbean: Transcending Time, Transforming Cultures*. Kingston, Jamaica, 2003.

Wilkins, Mira. *The Emergence of Multinational Enterprise: American Business Abroad from the Colonial Era to 1914*. Cambridge, MA, 1970.

Willis, Paul E. *Learning to Labour: How Working Class Kids Get Working Class Jobs*. Farnborough, UK, 1977.

Yun, Lisa. *The Coolie Speaks: Chinese Indentured Laborers and African Slaves in Cuba*. Philadelphia, 2008.

Zanetti, Oscar, et al. *United Fruit Company: Un caso del dominio imperialista en Cuba*. Havana, 1976.

ARTICLES, ESSAYS, FILMS, AND DISSERTATIONS

Althusser, L. "Ideology and Ideological State Apparatuses." In *Lenin and Philosophy, and Other Essays*, ed. Louis Althusser and Ben Brewster. New York, 1971.

Ashdown, Peter. "The UNIA and the Black Cause in British Honduras, 1914–1949." *Journal of Caribbean History* 15 (1981): 41–55.

Burton, Richard D. E. "Names and Naming in Afro-Caribbean Cultures." *New West Indian Guide* 73, nos. 1–2 (1999): 35–58.

Carr, Barry. "'Omnipotent and Omnipresent'? Labor Shortage, Worker Mobility and Employer Control in the Cuban Sugar Industry." In *Identity and Struggle at the Margins of the Nation State*, edited by Aviva Chomsky and Aldo Lauria-Santiago. Durham, 1998.

———. "Identity, Class, and Nation: Black Immigrant Workers, Cuban Communism, and the Sugar Insurgency, 1925–1934." In *Marginal Migrations: Circulation of Culture within the Caribbean*, edited by Shalini Puri. Oxford, 2003.

Casey, Matthew. "Haitians' Labor and Leisure on Cuban Sugar Plantations: The Limits of Company Control." *New West Indian Guide* 85, nos. 1–2 (2011): 5–30.

Chomsky, Aviva. "Laborers and Smallholders in Costa Rica's Mining Communities." In *Identity and Struggle at the Margins of the Nation State*, edited by Aviva Chomsky and Aldo Lauria-Santiago. Durham, 1998.

Clarke, Edith. "Land Tenure and the Family in Four Selected Communities in Jamaica." *Social and Economic Studies* 1, no. 4 (1966): 81–118.

Corbea, Julio. "La comunidad Cubana-Haitiana de la Caridad." *Del Caribe* 1, nos. 3–4 (Jan.–June 1984): 61-64.

Corbitt, Devon C. "Immigration in Cuba." *Hispanic American Historical Review* 22 (May 1942): 280–308.

Cruz Ruíz, Reynaldo. "La inmigración antillana en los primeros años del siglo XX." Unpublished article loaned to the author.

Dawson, Andrew. "Cultural Identity and Economic Decision-Making in Three Peripheral Areas of Europe." In *Constraints on Competitiveness in EC Agriculture: A Comparative Analysis*, edited by J. Phelan and M. Henchion. Brussels, 1994.

Díaz, Alberto Pedro. "Guanamaca: Una comunidad Haitiana." *Etnologia y Folklore* 1 (Jan.–June 1966): 25–39.

Douglass, M. "The Idea of Home: A Kind of Space." *Social Research* 58, no. 1 (1991): 287–307.

Dumoulin, John. "El primer desarrollo del movimiento obrero y la formación del proletariado en el sector azucarero Cruces." *Islas* 48 (May–August 1974): 3–66.

Dye, Alan. "Tropical Technology and Mass Production: The Expansion of Sugarmills, 1899–1929." PhD diss., University of Illinois, 1991.

Edwards, William A. "Garveyism: Organizing the Masses or Mass Organization?" In *Garvey: His Work and Impact*, edited by Rupert Lewis and Patrick Bryan. Trenton, NJ, 1991.

Espronceda Amor, Maria Eugenia. "La estructura de parentesco del inmigrante bajo una concepción dinamica, el caso jamaicano." *Del Caribe* 31 (2000): 26–32.

Fernández Robaina, Tomás. "Urrutia, Cubans and Black Nationalism." In *Between Race and Empire: African Americans and Cubans before the Revolution*, edited by Lisa Brock and Digna Castañeda. Philadelphia, 1998.

Foner, Nancy. "Towards a Comparative Perspective on Caribbean Migration." In *Caribbean Migration: Globalised Identities*, edited by Mary Chamberlain. London, 1998.

Ford-Smith, Honor. "Women and the Garvey Movement in Jamaica." In *Garvey: His Work and Impact*, edited by Rupert Lewis and Patrick Bryan. Trenton, NJ, 1991.

García Dominguez, Bernardo. "Garvey and Cuba." In *Garvey: His Work and Impact*, edited by Rupert Lewis and Patrick Bryan. Trenton, NJ, 1991.

Garvey, Marcus. "The Race Question in Jamaica." In *Consequences of Class and Color: West Indian Perspectives*, edited by David Lowenthal and Lambros Comitas. Garden City, 1973.

Giovannetti, Jorge L. "The Elusive Organization of 'Identity': Race, Religion, and Empire among Caribbean Migrants in Cuba." *Small Axe* 19, no. 1 (March 2006): 1–27.

———. "Historia visual y etnohistoria en Cuba: Inmigración antillana e identidad en Los hijos de Baraguá." *Caribbean Studies* 30, no. 2 (July–December 2002): 216–52.

Gonzalez Sánchez, Dominga. "La inmigración negra y la situación socioeconomica de negros y mulattos en el campo." *Economía y Desarrollo* 3 (May–June 1988): 105–15.

Gordon, Ernle P. "Garvey and Black Liberation Theology." In *Garvey: His Work and Impact*, edited by Rupert Lewis and Patrick Bryan. Trenton, NJ, 1991.

Handler, Jerome S., and JoAnn Jacoby. "Slave Names and Naming in Barbados." *William and Mary Quarterly*, 3rd Ser., 53, no. 4 (1996): 685–726.

Hart, Richard. "The Life and Resurrection of Marcus Garvey." *Race* 9 (1967): 217–37.

Helg, Aline. "Race in Argentina and Cuba, 1880–1930: Theory, Policies, and Popular Reaction." In *The Idea of Race in Latin America, 1870–1940*, edited by Richard Graham. Austin, 1990.

Hoernel, Robert B. "A Comparison of Sugar and Social Change in Puerto Rico and Oriente, Cuba: 1898–1959." PhD diss., Johns Hopkins University, 1977.

Iglesias García, Fe. "Caracteristicas de la inmigración Española in Cuba, 1904–1930." *Económia y Desarrollo* 2 (March–April 1988): 76–101.

———. "The Development of Capitalism in Cuban Sugar Production, 1860–1900." In *Between Slavery and Free Labor: The Spanish-Speaking Caribbean in the Nineteenth Century*, edited by Manuel Moreno Fraginals et al. Baltimore, 1985.

Johnson, R. "Three Problematics: Elements of a Theory of Working-Class Culture." In *Working Class Culture*, edited by J. Clarke, C. Critcher, and R. Johnson. London 1979.

Kelly, John D. "The Other Leviathans: Corporate Investment and the Construction of a Sugar Colony." In *White and Deadly: Sugar and Colonialism*, edited by Pal Ahluwalia, Bill Ashcroft, and Roger Knight. Cammack, NY, 1999.

Knight, Franklin W. "Jamaican Migrants in the Cuban Sugar Industry, 1900–1934." In *Between Slavery and Free Labor: The Spanish-Speaking Caribbean in the Nineteenth Century*, edited by Manuel Moreno Fraginals et al. Baltimore, 1985.

Kulczycki, John J. "Scapegoating the Foreign Worker." In *The Politics of Immigrant Workers: Labor Activism and Migration in the World Economy since 1830*, edited by Camille Guerin-Gonzalez and Carl Strikwerda. New York, 1998.

Gordon, Ernle P. "Garvey and Black Liberation Theology." In *Garvey: His Work and Impact*, edited by Rupert Lewis and Patrick Bryan. Trenton, NJ, 1991.

Lowenthal, Ira. "Labor, Sexuality, and the Conjugal Contract in Rural Haiti." In *Haiti—Today and Tomorrow: An Interdisciplinary Study*, edited by Charles R. Foster and Albert Valdman. Lanham, MD, 1984.

———. "Marriage Is 20 and Children 21: The Cultural Construction of Conjugality and the Family in Rural Haiti." PhD diss., Johns Hopkins University, 1987.

Marshall, Woodville K. "Peasant Development in the West Indies since 1838." In *Rural Development in the Caribbean*, edited by P. I. Gomes. London, 1985.

Martínez Villena, Rubén. "Las contradicciones internas del imperialismo yanqui en Cuba." In *Documentos para la historia de Cuba*, edited by Hortensia Pichardo. Havana, 1973.

McLeod, Marc C. "'Sin dejar ser Cubanos': Cuban Blacks and the Challenges of Garveyism in Cuba." *Caribbean Studies* 31, no. 1 (Jan.–June 2003): 75–105.

———. "Undesirable Aliens: Race, Ethnicity, and Nationalism in the Comparison of Haitian and British West Indian Immigrant Workers in Cuba, 1912–1939." *Journal of Social History* 31, no. 3 (1998): 599–623.

Mintz, Sidney. "The Caribbean as a Socio-Cultural Area." In *Peoples and Culture of the Caribbean*, edited by Michael Horowitz. Garden City, NJ, 1971.

———. "The Jamaican Internal Marketing Pattern." *Social and Economic Studies* 4 (1955): 95–103.

Murray, Gerald F. "The Evolution of Haitian Peasant Land Tenure." 2 vols. PhD diss., Columbia University, 1977.

Pérez de la Riva, Juan. "La inmigración antillana en Cuba durante el primer tercio del siglo XX." *Revista de la Biblioteca Nacional José Martí* 42 (May–August 1975): 75–88.

Plasencia Moro, Aleida. "Historia del movimiento obrero en Cuba." In *Historia del movimiento obrero en América Latina*, edited by Pablo González Casanova. Mexico City, 1984.

Portes, Alejandro. "Towards a Structural Analysis of Illegal (Undocumented) Immigration." *International Migration Review* 12 (Winter): 469–84.

Price-Mars, Jean. "Classe ou Caste?" *Revue de Société d'Histoire et de Géographie d'Haiti* 13, no. 46 (July 1942): 1–50.

Rapport, N. J. "Migrant Selves and Stereotypes: Personal Context in a Postmodern World." In *Mapping the Subject: Geographies of Cultural Transformation*, edited by S. Pile and N. Thrift. London, 1995.

———. "'Busted for Hash': Common Catchwords and Individual Identities in a Canadian City." In *Urban Lives: Fragmentation and Resistance*, edited by V. Amit-Talai and H. Lustiger-Thaler. Toronto, 1994.

Rodríquez, Pedro Pablo. "Marcus Garvey en Cuba." *Anales del Caribe* 7–8 (1987–88): 279–301.

Rolando, Gloría. *My Footsteps in Baraguá*. A documentary film, Images of the Caribbean. 1996.

Ruch, Rob. "Three Kings Day in Consuelo: Cricket, Baseball, and the Cocolos in San Pedro de Macoris." In *Sport in Latin America and the Caribbean*, edited by Joseph L. Arbena and David G. La France. Wilmington, DE, 2002.

Safran, William. "Deconstructing and Comparing Diaspora." In *Diaspora, Identity, and Religion: New Directions in Theory and Research*, edited by Wlatraud Kokot and Khachig Toloyan. London, 2004.

Schuler, Monica. "Myalism and the African Religious Tradition in Jamaica." In *Africa and the Caribbean: The Legacies of a Link*, edited by Franklin Knight and Margaret E. Crahan. Baltimore, 1979.

Schwartz, Rosalie. "Cuba's Roaring Twenties: Race Consciousness and the Column 'Ideales de una Raza.'" In *Between Race and Empire: African Americans and Cubans before the Revolution*, edited by Lisa Brock and Digna Castañeda. Philadelphia, 1998.

Scott, Rebecca J. "Fault Lines, Color Lines, and Party Lines: Race, Labor, and Collective Action in Louisiana and Cuba, 1862–1912." In *Beyond Slavery*, edited by Frederick Cooper, Thomas C. Holt, and Rebecca J. Scott. Chapel Hill, 2000.

———. "The Lower Class of Whites and the Negro Element: Race, Social Identity and Politics in Central Cuba, 1899–1909." In *La Nación soñada: Cuba, Puerto Rico, y Filipinas antes el 98*, edited by Consuelo Naranjo Orovio, Miguel Angel Puig-Samper, and Luis Miguel García Mora. Madrid, 1995.

Stinchcombe, Arthur. "Organized Dependency Relations and Social Stratification." In *The Logic of Social Hierarchies*, edited by Edward O. Laumann et al. Chicago, 1970.

Thomas-Hope, Elizabeth. "Population Mobility and Land Assets in Hill Farming Areas of Jamaica." *Caribbean Geography* 4, no. 1 (March 1993): 49-63.

———. "The Establishment of a Migration Tradition: British West Indian Movements to the Hispanic Caribbean in the Century After Emancipation." In *Caribbean Social Relations*, edited by Colin G. Clarke. Liverpool, 1978.

Valdes Bernal, Sergio. "La inmigración en Cuba: Estudio lingüístico-histórico." *Anales del Caribe* 7–8 (1987–88): 220–33.

Wagley, Charles. "Plantation-America: A Cultural Sphere." In *Caribbean Studies: A Symposium*, edited by Vera Rubin. Seattle, 1960.

Wolf, Eric R., and Sidney W. Mintz. "Haciendas and Plantations in Middle America and the Antilles." *Social and Economic Studies* 6, no. 3 (September 1957): 380–412.

NEWSPAPERS AND PERIODICALS

Costa Rica
El Correro del Atlantico (Limón)

Cuba
Avisador Comercial (Havana)
Diario de la Marina (Havana)
Diario del Pueblo (Guantánamo)
El Cubano Libre (Santiago de Cuba)
El Heraldo (Havana)
El Mercurio (Havana)
El Mundo (Havana)
El Progreso (Havana)
Evening News (Havana)
Gaceta Oficial de la República de Cuba (Havana)
Havana Evening News
Havana Post
Heraldo de Cuba (Havana)
La Discusión (Havana)
La Independencia (Santiago de Cuba)
La Prensa (Havana)
Nueva Luz (Havana)
¡Tierra! (Havana)

Jamaica
Daily Gleaner (Kingston)
Jamaican Herald
Jamaican Times

Panama
The Workman

United States

Cuban Review

Facts about Sugar (New York, Domestic Sugar Producers)

Louisiana Planter and Sugar Manufacturer

The Negro World

INDEX

239n7; Garvey movement and, 170, 193; government's rhetorical use of, 91, 211, 212, 218; of Haitians, 17, 64, 99, 110–15, 117, 199; of Jamaicans, 59, 87, 118–23, 126, 132; and labor resistance, 16, 156; and living conditions, 86, 87, 237; sugar companies' use of, 5, 6, 45, 84, 161, 204; as tool to divide, 6, 45, 156

eugenics, 2, 91–92

evangelical movement, 121–22

Evans, L. Ton, 56–57

Ewan, William G., 212

Fanjul, Higinio, 90, 203

Faure, Sabastien, 148

Federation of Cuban Anarchist Groups, 157–58, 159

Federation of Sugar Workers, 160, 161–62, 166

Fergusson, Erna, 86

Fernández, Amado, 258n57

Fernández, Federico, 140

Fernández, Francisco María, 225

Ferrera, Orestes, 77, 272n20

Fis, Eduardo, 100, 255n113

Fletcher, Sarah, 185

Florida central, 73, 163, 194

Francis, J., 184

Francisco central, 27, 62–63, 80, 103

Francisco Sugar Company, 60, 61

Freemasons, 125

Fritze and Company, 26

Frost, Arthur C., 162–63

García, Calixto, 116

García, Felipe, 64, 258n57

García López, José, 165

Garrison, Daisy, 215

Garvey, Amy Jacques, 171, 267n23

Garvey, Marcus M.: black Cubans and, 18–19, 176, 177–80, 196–97; on black pride and self-esteem, 173–74, 177; black religion criticized by, 173; and braceros, 169, 180–

83; Cuba tour of, 7, 10, 167–68, 169–71, 175; hegemonic narrative employed by, 169, 172–73; in Jamaica, 268n46; objectives of in Cuba, 175, 267n23; oratorical skills of, 170–71, 266n7; on origins of movement, 171; political inconsistency of, 172, 266n12; promotion of Black Star Line Corporation by, 170, 175, 267n23; seen as threat, 175–76, 267n25; support for workers' struggles by, 186, 269n67; theology of, 190–91; U.S. imprisonment of, 196; view of Africa by, 176–77

Garveyism: anarcho-syndicalism's convergence with, 7, 10–11, 169, 182, 185–86, 194; black Cubans and, 18–19, 168–69, 179, 196–97; black inferiority deconstructed by, 172; black women and, 185, 188–89, 266n18; braceros' receptivity to, 88, 113–14, 124, 169, 183–84, 186, 187–88, 194, 234; and Haitian-Jamaican relations, 195–96; as transnational movement, 195. See also Universal Negro Improvement Association (UNIA)

Gayle, S. O., 46, 81

Giovannetti, Jorge L., 16, 17–18, 19, 124

Gobineau, Arthur de, 2, 91–92

Gómez, Consuelo P., 272n30

Gómez, José Miguel: and importation of braceros, 4, 43, 92; and Liberal Rebellion of 1917, 72, 90, 125, 147; and Partido Independiente de Color, 37, 38, 39, 40; ties to sugar industry of, 256n16, 271–72n20

Gómez, Juan Gualberto, 180

Gómez, Máximo, 116

Gompers, Samuel, 155, 157

González, Manuel, 229

González, Orlando, 106, 113, 116, 256n16

Gordon, S. N., 194

Grau San Martín, Ramón, 11, 228–29

Gray, Josephine, 128–29

Green, Ethel, 127–28

Gremio Braceros de Cruces, 33

59, 64, 74, 204–5, 212; shipping resources used for, 31, 59, 62, 63; from Spain and Canary Islands, 1–2, 4, 32, 34, 83, 86, 96, 155, 241n8; sugar industry's dependence on, 209, 216, 233; to United States, 214–16; Zayas and, 201, 206–8, 271n2. See also anti-immigrant sentiment; Haitian immigrants; Jamaican immigrants

immigration brokers. See labor brokers

immigration laws, 29–30, 209; of 1906, 30, 43, 97; of 1917, 74–75, 117, 209; of 1921, 209, 220, 223; of 1924, 209; of 1928, 218; of 1930, 223; of 1931, 225–26

immigration statistics: during 1900s, 30; during 1910s, 65, 82, 97, 134, 252n59, 254n104; during 1920s, 96, 97, 114, 134, 152, 153, 213, 217, 218, 224, 254n104; during 1930s, 220, 274n54, 275n68

El Imparcial, 84

imperialism, 161, 164, 194

Imperialism: The Highest Stage of Capitalism (Lenin), 161, 264n92

incendiarism, 135, 137–39, 140, 141, 143–44

La Independencia, 31, 182

Industrial Workers of the World (IWW), 140, 161, 261n19

influenza, 81

informal economy, 104–5

Ingleton, N. A., 188–89

internationalism, 160–61, 227, 234; about ideology of, 154–55; anarcho-syndicalist movement and, 4, 6–7, 34

International Workingmen's Association, 154–55

Isabel central, 38, 63

Ivonet, Pedro, 37, 38, 39–40, 41, 42

Jamaica, 268n46, 271n7; banana industry in, 59, 236–38, 276n5; and braceros in Cuba, 202, 230, 262n45; conditions in, 236–38; debt of, 203; education system in, 48–49;

hurricane of 1933 in, 238, 276n8; immigration brokers in, 61, 62, 63; land ownership in, 46–47; peasantry in, 47–48

Jamaica (town), 38–39

Jamaican Gazette, 207

Jamaican immigrants, 118–33; artisan laborers among, 118; beliefs and practices of, 122–23, 126; British Consulate and, 118–19, 145–47, 200–202, 214, 249n146, 275n71; and British West Indies identity, 18, 124; churches of, 121–22, 123, 259n75and Garvey movement, 181–82, 195–96; and Haitians, 87, 123–24, 131–32, 195–96; initial importation to Cuba of, 4–5, 29; labor brokers' abuses toward, 272–73n35; and labor unions, 129; motives for emigrating, 16–17, 22, 43–51, 96–97; mutual-aid and benevolent societies of, 8, 99, 125–30, 234; public persona of, 132–33; racism and xenophobia against, 59, 92, 93, 131; re-creation of home in Cuba by, 8, 50–51; repatriation of, 230–31, 241n23; sailing to Cuba by, 31, 63; schools of, 120–21, 258n71; as squatters, 118–19; statistics on immigration of, 17, 114, 152, 212, 217, 218, 220, 254n104; and United States, 59, 216; violence against, 95, 147–48, 254n96. See also ethnicity: of Jamaicans

Jamaican Times, 231

James, John, 184

Jaronú central, 83, 85, 101, 113, 115–16, 159, 212, 253n71

Jatibonico central, 64, 163, 228

Jim Crow, 130–31, 171; Cuba's adoption of elements of, 91, 131, 234

Jobabo central, 95, 147, 190, 270n89

Jones, Aubrey, 187

Juan, Andres, 210

Juarez Cano, Jorge, 198, 203

Keith, Minor C., 25, 27

Kelsey, Carl, 57–58, 60, 107, 108

Santa Clara Province, 16, 25, 33–34, 39, 58, 90, 116, 152, 155. *See also* Las Villas Province

Santa Lucia *central*, 81, 228

Santiago de Cuba, 81, 141, 162, 200–201, 202, 210–11, 224; British consulate in, 101, 118, 137, 145, 146, 153, 202; Garvey movement in, 175, 182–85, 189, 190, 192, 196–97, 268n54; Partido Independiente de Color in, 39; population of, 97; port of, 62, 217, 223, 224; violence against braceros in, 95, 98

Sarria, Juan, 25

Saturnino, 107

schools, 85, 120–21, 253n72, 258n71

Schwartz, Rosalie, 179

Scott, James C., 5, 143, 255n3, 259nn90–91

Scott, Rebecca, 16, 33

Scott, Robert, 123

scrip. See *vales*

Second International Conference on Emigration and Immigration (1928), 221

segregation, 85, 86–88, 89–90

Senado *central*, 73–74, 106, 251n21

Senff, Charles, 242n12

Septembre, Septema, 41

Sevillano Andrés, Bernarda, 55, 80

Shackleton, Henry, 164–65, 194, 197

Shaffer, Kirwin R., 264n92

Shakespeare, Frank, 214

Sharpe, J., 184

Sheridan, J. W., 190

Simon, John, 231

Sindicato Nacional de Obreros de la Industria Azucarera (SNOIA), 227, 228

Sindicato Provincial de Trabajadores of Camagüey, 163

Sindicato del Obreros Azucareros, 165

slavery, 3–4; braceros' situation compared to, 65–66, 72, 76, 136–37

Small, Benjamin, 195–96

Smith, Frederick C., 185

Smith, Gerard, 80

Smith, Richard, 275n71

Smoot-Hawley Tariff Act, 219

Snow, T. M., 230–31

Socialist Party of Cuba, 155, 156, 157

"social territories," 15, 68

Society of the Black Cross, 189

Soledad *central*, 25–26, 63

Spain: immigrants from, 2, 4, 32, 34, 83, 86, 96, 241n8; War of Independence from, 2, 27

Spied, Claudius, 214

Spreckels, Claus, 26

squatters, 103–4, 118–19

Standard Fruit Company, 225, 236, 274n66

Starrett, H. P., 36

Stewart, Francis, 163, 166

Stinchcombe, Arthur, 8

St. John, Sir Spenser, 52

Stone, William Preston, 119–20, 124

Stoute, William, 130

strikes, 16, 33, 155, 158; of 1919–20, 186, 269n67; anarcho-syndicalists and, 16, 33, 34, 227; general strike of 1923, 158; by railroad workers, 150, 156; strikebreakers used against, 163–64; of sugar workers (1918), 142–43; of sugar workers (1924), 159–64; of sugar workers (1933), 226–28; of sugar workers (1917), 155–56, 263–64n75. *See also* labor unions

Stroude, Hudson, 208

sugar companies: *bateyes* of, 8, 75–76, 83–84, 85, 252–53n60; domination of U.S.-owned, 11, 22, 24, 25–29, 37, 130, 208; ethnicity used by, 5, 6, 45, 84, 161, 204; labor brokers work for, 60, 61, 204–5; and labor shortages, 30, 72, 97–98, 216–17; labor surplus sought by, 24–25, 30, 62, 64, 72, 74, 103, 145, 199, 200, 203–4, 206, 213, 216; municipal governments' relationship to, 85–86; profits of, 9, 22, 23, 109, 151; whites' position in, 82–84, 88–89, 233. *See also* United Fruit Company

sugar enclaves, 15, 29, 80, 85, 232–34

301

sugar industry, Cuban: black Cubans and, 32–33, 42; Britain's dependence on, 145–46; cane-cutting labor in, 69–70, 71, 250–51n15; cane-loading labor in, 70; capital investment and technology in, 24, 36, 37; Chamebelona Rebellion impact on, 72–73; colonos' role in, 12–13; connection between fields and mill in, 24; crisis of in 1920–21, 6, 96, 134, 135, 151–52, 186–87; and Cuban domestic consumption, 220; dependency on immigrant labor of, 72, 209, 216, 233; labor shortages in, 30, 32, 72, 97–98, 216–17; labor strikes in, 16, 142–43, 155–56, 159–64, 263–64n75; piece-rate wage system of, 110, 141–42, 144; and railroads, 23–24, 84; seasonal work nature of, 141–42; shipping routes of, 58–59; Smoot-Hawley Tariff Act impact on, 219–20; U.S. companies' domination of, 11, 22, 25–29, 37, 130, 208; and U.S.-Cuban Reciprocity Treaty, 242n9; under U.S. military occupation, 2, 23; work force of, 2–3, 12, 24–25, 217, 224–25; during World War I, 25, 83, 85, 109. See also centrales

sugar prices: in 1912–21, 73; in 1923–26, 210; in 1929–31, 220; in 1931, 223; collapse of (1920), 6, 96, 134, 135, 151–52

sugar production, 28, 90, 152, 220

T., Benjamin, 43

Tacajó central, 98, 108, 109, 110, 113, 228

Tánamo central, 212, 216

Taylor, John, 192

Taylor, Oscar, 98

Ten Years' War (1868–78), 4

Teresa central, 81, 138

Thomas, C. A., 269n80

Thomas, Hugh, 242n9

tiempo muerto, 105, 250–51n15; braceros' food growing during, 103, 226–27; workers' situation during, 109, 142, 151

Tinguaro central, 28

tobacco workers, 148, 149, 150

transculturation, 110

Trinidad central, 26

Trinidad Sugar Company, 26, 242n12

Tuinicú Cane Sugar Company, 27

Tuinicú central, 63, 90

Tuskegee Institute, 171

unemployment, 153, 168, 179, 186

Unión de Empleados de Ferrocarril de Norte de Cuba, 156, 157, 158

Unión de Morón, 158–60, 161–62

Unión Fraternal, 177

Union of Antillean Workers, 164–65, 185

United Fruit Company, 31, 63, 83–84, 132, 253n72; formation of and growth in Cuba, 27–28; and Garveyism, 267n25; immigration brokers used by, 60, 61; importation of braceros by, 29, 212, 224; in Jamaica, 236, 237, 238, 248n36; labor conflicts of, 142–43, 163; and repatriation of braceros, 225, 274n66; segregation on properties of, 86–87, 88, 89–90; shipping routes of, 58, 248n136; workers' housing for, 87, 103, 223–24

United States: bracero immigration to, 214–16; Cuba's neocolonial relationship to, 9, 11, 109, 131, 161, 208; Jim Crow in, 91, 130–31, 171, 234; military occupation of Cuba by, 1–2, 23–24; and Partido Independiente de Color protests, 40; Smoot-Hawley Tariff Act by, 219–20

Universal Negro Improvement Association (UNIA), 167, 169, 175, 187, 196; aims of, 168; black braceros and, 7, 113–14, 169, 182, 193–94, 195; and black women, 185, 188–89, 266n18; Costa Rica meetings of, 191–92; formation of, 171; leadership of Cuban branches, 184–85, 268n60; membership drives of, 187; mutual aid to braceros by, 189–90; racial and class solidarity actions of, 192–93; religious aspects of,

191–92, 269–70n84; in Santiago de Cuba, 183, 184–85, 268n54. *See also* Garveyism

U.S.-Cuban Reciprocity Treaty (1903), 242n9

Vacher de Lapouge, Georges, 91–92

Valentine, Richard, 214

vales, 1, 77, 78–79, 159, 203–4

Varona González, Enrique: assassination of, 166; and Garveyite narrative, 169, 182; leadership of labor struggles by, 159–61, 162, 163, 165, 194, 197, 228

Vaughn, Nathaniel, 44

Vertientes *central*, 163, 187

Vinton Davis, Herrieta, 196

violence against immigrants, 95, 98–100, 147–48, 255n113; and harassment, 6, 99; by rural guard, 41, 98, 193, 209–10, 254n96

Vodun (voodoo), 110–11, 112, 257n41

wages, 71, 75, 257n29, 263n66; of cane cutters, 72, 73, 136, 142, 153, 251n18; piece-rate, 110, 141–42, 144; workers' saving of, 108, 109

Wagley, Charles, 51

Walrond, H. N., 130–31

Warner, W. M., 187–88

War of Independence (1895–98), 2, 27

Washington, Booker T., 171

Watkins, Charles, 125

Watkins, J., 184

Weeks, Ernest, 215

Weeks, Mildred, 215

West Indian Star Society, 129–30, 131

West India Sugar Company (WISCO), 236, 237

Whitaker, Stanley, 119, 121, 124

Wilkins, Mira, 25

Williams, Alexander S., 57

Williams, Florence C., 187

Willis, Paul E., 265n104

Wilmot, A. E., 212–13

Wilson, Emilio, 38–39, 244n57

Wilson, Woodrow, 155–56

Wise, Edward, 139–40

women: in Garveyite movement, 185, 188–89, 266n18; Garvey on, 174, 266n18; Haitian, 58, 104–6; and immigration laws, 209; Jamaican, 49–50, 128; and prostitution, 58, 105–6, 211–12, 224, 248n133

Wood, Leonard, 29

The Workman, 130, 131, 249n149

World War I: black soldiers in, 173–74; and Cuban sugar, 25, 83, 85, 109; food shortages and speculation during, 141

xenophobia, 68, 90, 93, 178, 197, 207, 233, 235; and violence against immigrants, 147, 210

zafras: of 1911, 91; of 1913, 222; of 1917, 95, 251n18; of 1918, 90, 142; of 1919, 97, 145; of 1921, 152; of 1922, 153; of 1924, 166, 206; of 1926, 212; of 1930, 219; of 1932, 226

Zayas, Alfredo: and immigration question, 201, 206–8, 271n2; and sugarcane incendiarism, 141, 158

Zayas-Bazán, Rogelio, 162

Zubizarreta, Octavio, 225

9 780807 159521